Collins

White Rose Maths
Edexcel GCSE 9-1
Foundation
Student Book 2

Caroline Hamilton and Ian Davies

William Collins' dream of knowledge for all began with the publication of his first book in 1819. A self-educated mill worker, he not only enriched millions of lives, but also founded a flourishing publishing house. Today, staying true to this spirit, Collins books are packed with inspiration, innovation and practical expertise.

They place you at the centre of a world of possibility and give you exactly what you need to explore it.

Collins. Freedom to teach.

Published by Collins
An imprint of HarperCollins*Publishers*
The News Building
1 London Bridge Street
London
SE1 9GF

HarperCollins*Publishers*
Macken House
39/40 Mayor Street Upper
Dublin 1
D01 C9W8
Ireland

Browse the complete Collins catalogue at
collins.co.uk

10 9 8 7 6 5 4 3 2 1

ISBN: 978-0-00-866954-6

British Library Cataloguing-in-Publication Data
A catalogue record for this publication is available from the British Library.

Series editors: Caroline Hamilton and Ian Davies
Authors: Jennifer Clasper, Mary-Kate Connolly, Emily
  Fox and James Lansdale-Clegg
Publisher: Katie Sergeant
Product manager: Richard Toms
Development editor: Karl Warsi
Editorial: Richard Toms, Deborah Dobson
  and Amanda Dickson
Proofreading and answer checking: Steven Matchett,
  Eric Pradel, Trevor Senior and Anna Cox
Cover designer: Sarah Duxbury
Typesetter: Jouve India Private Limited
Production controller: Alhady Ali
Printed and bound in India

MIX
Paper | Supporting
responsible forestry
FSC™ C007454

This book contains FSC™ certified paper and other controlled sources to ensure responsible forest management.

For more information visit: www.harpercollins.co.uk/green

Text acknowledgements
The publishers gratefully acknowledge the permission granted to reproduce the copyright material in this book. Every effort has been made to trace copyright holders and to obtain their permission for the use of copyright material.

Contents

Geometry and measures   **Probability**   **Statistics**

Contents

Introduction

How to use this book

Welcome to the **Collins White Rose Maths Edexcel GCSE 9–1 Foundation tier** course.

There are two Student Books in the series:

- **Student Book 1** covers Number, Algebra, and Ratio, proportion and rates of change.
- **Student Book 2** covers Geometry and measures, Probability, and Statistics.

Sometimes you will need some knowledge of a different area of mathematics within the topic you are studying. For example, you may need to set up and solve an algebraic equation when solving a geometry problem. You will often be able to use your earlier knowledge and skills from Key Stage 3 to help you do this.

Here is a short guide to how to get the most out of this book. We hope you enjoy continuing your learning journey.

Caroline Hamilton and Ian Davies, series editors

Block overviews Each block of related chapters starts with a visual introduction to the key concepts and learning you will encounter.

Are you ready? Before you start each part of a chapter, remind yourself of the maths you should already know with these questions. If you need more practice, refer to the *Collins White Rose Maths Key Stage 3* course.

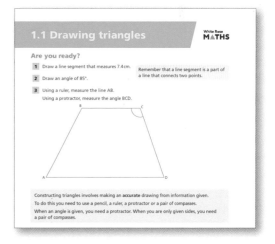

Explanatory text Key words and concepts are explained before moving on to worked examples.

Using your calculator Where appropriate, you are given advice on how to use the features of your calculator to find or check answers. Not all calculators work in the same way, so make sure you know how your model works.

Worked examples Learn how to approach different types of questions with worked examples that clearly walk you through the process of answering. Visual representations are provided to help when necessary.

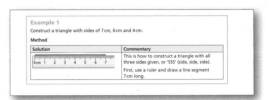

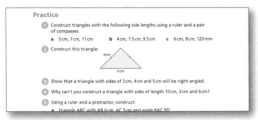

Practice Put what you have just learned into practice. Sometimes symbols are used in questions or whole sections to show when you should, or should not, use a calculator. If there is no symbol, the question or section can be approached in either way.

Many of the Practice sections conclude with a **What do you think?** exercise to encourage further exploration.

Consolidate Reinforce what you have learned in the chapter with additional practice questions.

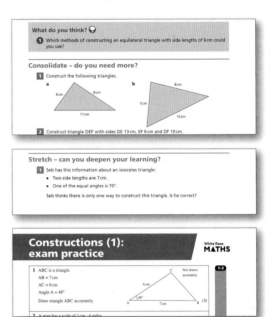

Stretch Take your learning further and challenge yourself to apply it in new ways or different areas of maths.

Exam practice At the end of each block, you will find exam-style questions to practise your learning. These are organised into grade bands of 1–3 and 3–5. There is extra practice at the end of the three main parts of the book.

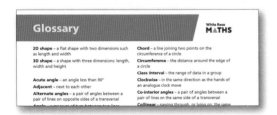

Glossary Look up the meanings of any key words and phrases you are not sure about.

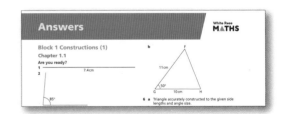

Answers Check your work using the answers provided at the back of the book.

1 Constructions (1)

In this block, we will cover...

1.1 Drawing triangles

Example 1

Construct a triangle with sides of 7 cm, 6 cm and

Method

Solution	Com
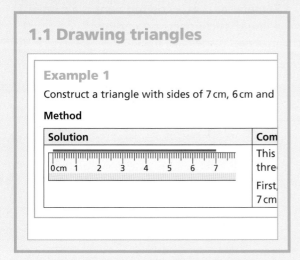	This three First, 7 cm

1.2 Scale diagrams

Practice (A)

1. A rectangle has dimensions of 14 cm and 6

   Each square on the grid represents 2 cm.

   What are the dimensions of the rectangle in squares?

1.3 Bearings

Consolidate – do you need more

1. Draw the bearings, when the bearing of B

   a 100°   **b** 120°   **c** 150

2. Draw diagrams for each statement.

   a B is on a bearing of 100° from A.

   The distance between A and B is 10 cm

   b B is on a bearing of 120° from A.

   The distance between A and B is 10 cm

   c B is on a bearing of 140° from A.

1.1 Drawing triangles

Are you ready?

1 Draw a line segment that measures 7.4 cm.

Remember that a line segment is a part of a line that connects two points.

2 Draw an angle of 85°.

3 Using a ruler, measure the line AB.

Using a protractor, measure the angle BCD.

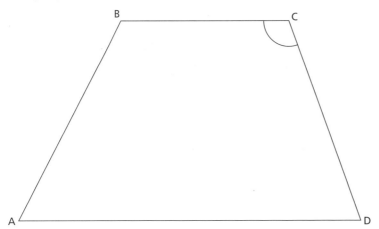

Constructing triangles involves making an **accurate** drawing from information given.

To do this you need to use a pencil, a ruler, a protractor or a pair of compasses.

When an angle is given, you need a protractor. When you are only given sides, you need a pair of compasses.

Example 1

Construct a triangle with sides of 7 cm, 6 cm and 4 cm.

Method

Solution	Commentary
![ruler 0cm to 7]	This is how to construct a triangle with all three sides given, or 'SSS' (side, side, side). First, use a ruler and draw a line segment 7 cm long.

	Then set your pair of compasses to 6 cm and draw an arc from one end of the line segment.
	Then set your pair of compasses to 4 cm and draw an arc from the other end of the line segment.
	Use a ruler and join where the arcs meet from each end of the line segment. Label your sides with the dimensions. Do not rub out your construction lines.

Example 2

Construct triangle ABC with AB 10 cm, AC 4 cm and angle BAC 45°.

Method

Solution	Commentary
	This is how to construct a triangle with two sides and the angle in-between given, or 'SAS' (side, angle, side). First, use a ruler to draw a horizontal line segment 10 cm long and label this AB.
	Using a protractor, measure and draw an angle of 45° from point A. Make sure you mark the point.

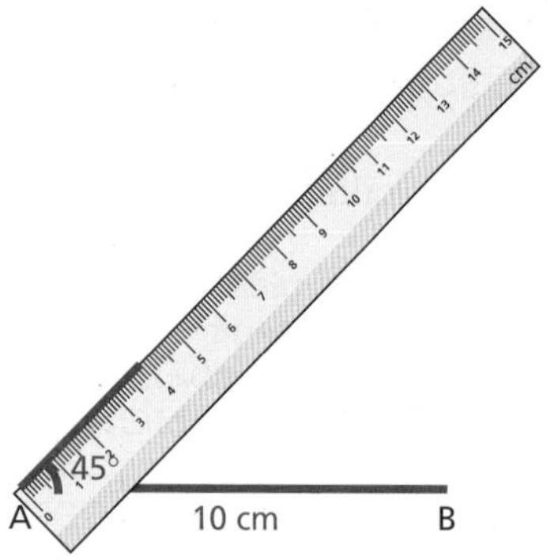	Using a ruler, line up the point A with the 45° point and measure 4 cm to find point C.
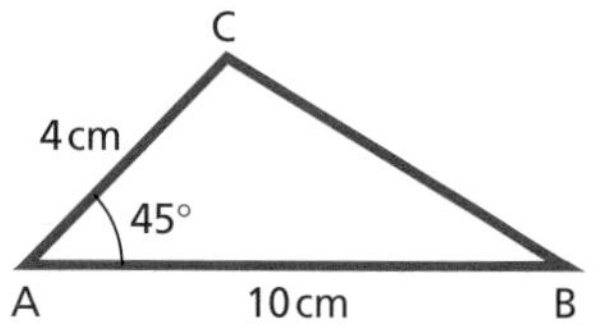	Draw line CB to complete the triangle. Don't forget to label the given information.

Example 3

Construct triangle ABC with AB 8 cm, BAC 55° and angle ABC 40°.

Method

Solution	Commentary
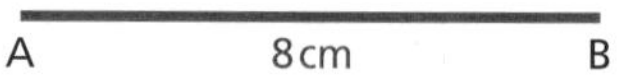	This is how to construct a triangle with two angles and the side in-between given, or 'ASA' (angle, side, angle). First, using a ruler draw a horizontal line segment 8 cm long. Label this line AB.
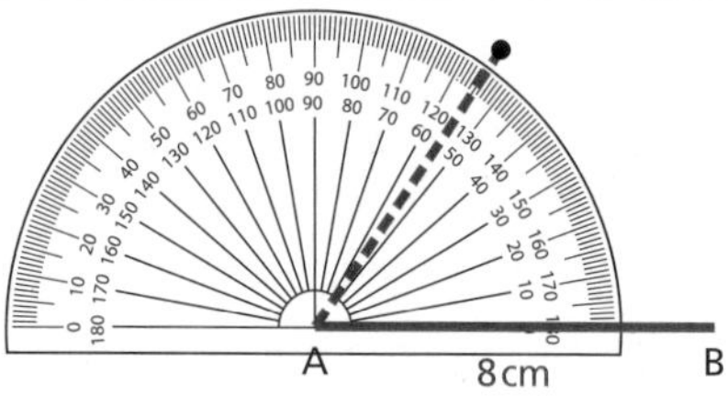	Using a protractor, measure and draw an angle of 55° from point A. Make sure you mark the point.
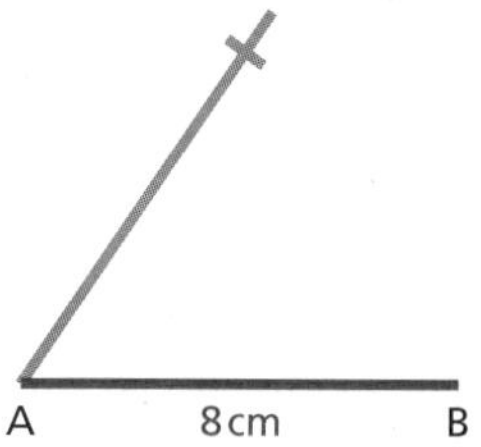	Using a ruler, draw a line from A through your mark.

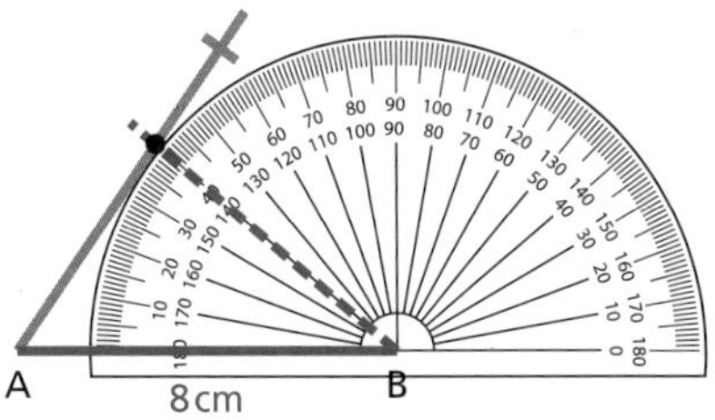 A 8 cm B	Now draw an angle of 40° from point B.
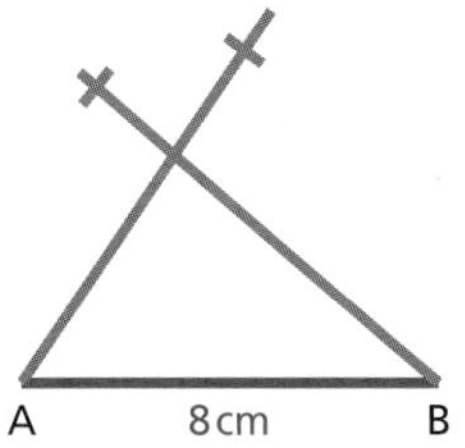 A 8 cm B	Using a ruler, draw a line from B through your mark. Where the two lines meet is point C.
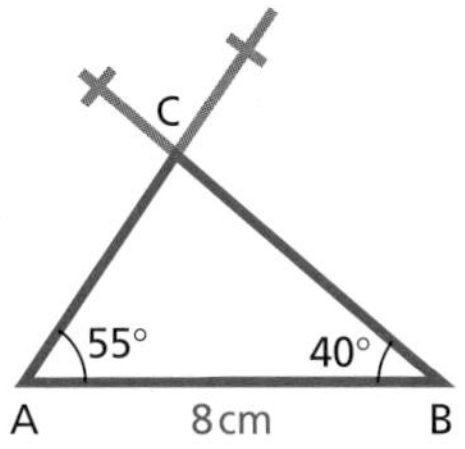 C 55° 40° A 8 cm B	Label your triangle.

Practice

1 Construct triangles with the following side lengths using a ruler and a pair of compasses.

    a   5 cm, 7 cm, 11 cm   **b**   4 cm, 7.5 cm, 9.5 cm   **c**   6 cm, 8 cm, 120 mm

2 Construct this triangle:

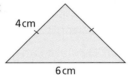

3 Show that a triangle with sides of 3 cm, 4 cm and 5 cm will be right-angled.

4 Why can't you construct a triangle with sides of length 10 cm, 3 cm and 6 cm?

5 Using a ruler and a protractor, construct:

    a   triangle ABC with AB 6 cm, AC 5 cm and angle BAC 95°

    b   triangle FGH with GH 10 cm, FG 11 cm and angle FGH 50°.

6 Construct the following triangles.

    a

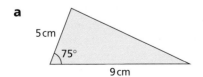

    b

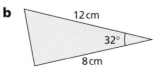

    c

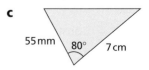

7 Using a ruler and a protractor, construct:

   a triangle ABC with AB 6 cm, angle CAB 50° and angle ABC 85°

   b triangle XYZ with YZ 12 cm, angle XYZ 35° and angle YZX 100°.

8 Construct the following triangles.

a
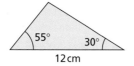

b
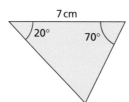

c
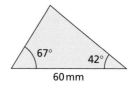

9 Which of these triangles can't be drawn? Why?

   A Triangle ABC with AB 10 cm, angle CAB 60° and angle ABC 95°

   B Triangle ABC with BC 10 cm, angle BAC 80° and angle ABC 80°

   C Triangle ABC with AB 10 cm, angle ABC 100° and angle CAB 100°

10 Construct the triangles. Which triangle has the greater perimeter?

A
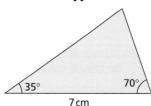

B
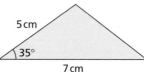

What do you think?

1 Which methods of constructing an equilateral triangle with side lengths of 6 cm could you use?

Consolidate – do you need more?

1 Construct the following triangles.

a
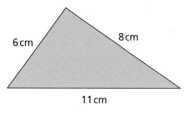

b
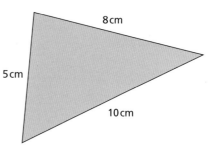

2 Construct triangle DEF with sides DE 13 cm, EF 6 cm and DF 10 cm.

3 Construct the following triangles.

a
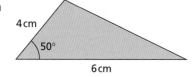

b
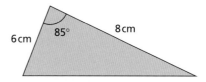

4 Construct triangle ABC with AB 66 mm, AC 4 cm and ∠BAC 75°.

5 Construct the following triangles.

a

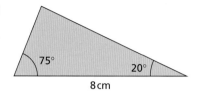

b

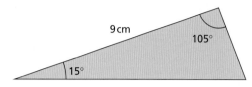

6 Construct triangle XYZ with XY 6 cm, ∠XYZ 53° and ∠YXZ 72°.

Stretch – can you deepen your learning?

1 Seb has this information about an isosceles triangle:

- Two side lengths are 7 cm.
- One of the equal angles is 70°.

Seb thinks there is only one way to construct this triangle. Is he correct?

1.2 Scale diagrams

Are you ready? (A)

1 How many centimetres are in 1 metre?

2 Convert each of the following into metres.

    a 200 cm   **b** 350 cm   **c** 472 cm

3 Convert each of the following into centimetres.

    a 4 m   **b** 5.6 m   **c** 1.236 m

Example

a Here is a scale drawing of a football pitch.

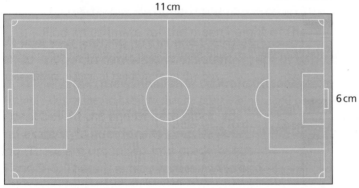

Scale 1 : 1000
11 cm
6 cm

    i Find the real length of the football pitch in metres.

    ii Find the real width of the football pitch in metres.

b A model bus is made with the scale 1 : 250

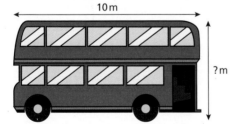

Actual bus
10 m
?m

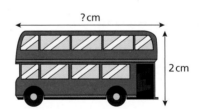

Model bus
?cm
2 cm

    i Work out the height of the actual bus in metres.

    ii Work out the length of the model in centimetres.

Method

Solution	Commentary
a **i** Length in the picture = 11 cm Length in real life = 11 × 1000 = 11 000 cm 11 000 cm = 110 m	The scale is 1 : 1000, meaning that 1 cm on the drawing is 1000 cm is real life.
ii Width in the picture = 6 cm Width in real life = 6 × 1000 = 6000 cm 6000 cm = 60 m	
b **i** Height of the model = 2 cm Height in real life = 2 × 250 = 500 cm 500 cm = 5 m	The scale is 1 : 250, meaning that 1 cm on the model is 250 cm in real life.
ii Length of the bus = 10 m 10 m = 1000 cm Length of the model = 1000 ÷ 250 = 4 cm	

Practice (A)

1 A rectangle has dimensions of 14 cm and 6 cm.

Each square on the grid represents 2 cm.

What are the dimensions of the rectangle in squares?

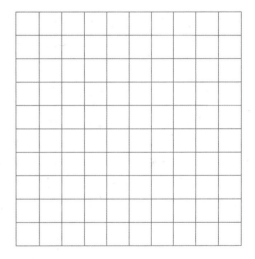

2 A rectangle has dimensions of 65 cm and 50 cm.

Each square on the grid represents 10 cm.

What are the dimensions of the rectangle in squares?

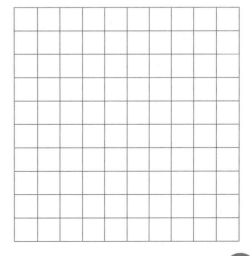

3 A rectangle has been sketched.

Draw an accurate diagram of the rectangle using the scale:

a 1 cm to 1 m **b** 1 : 200

8 m

6 m

4 This is a plan of a room using the scale 1 : 70

a What is the real length of the room in metres?

17 cm

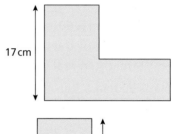

b An actual measurement of the same room is given.

What will be the two lengths on the scale drawing in centimetres?

7 m

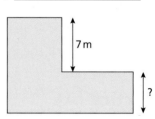

?

5 A model train is made using the scale 1 : 45

a What is the real height of the train in metres if the model is 9 cm high?

b What is the length of the model in centimetres if the real train is 13.5 m long?

What do you think? (A)

1 Two scales are given. 1 : 300 and 1 cm to 3 m

Are they the same or different? How do you know?

Are you ready? (B)

1 Which unit of measurement below would you use to measure the distance between two towns?

mm	cm	m	km

2 How many metres are in 1 kilometre?

3 How many centimetres are in 1 metre?

Example

a A map with a diagram of a lake uses the scale 1 : 4000

What is the real distance in metres from point A to point B?

b The scale of another map is 1 : 50 000

   i Two hotels are 8 cm apart on the map.

     What is the actual distance between them in kilometres?

   ii Two restaurants are 2.5 km apart in real life.

     How far apart are they on the map in centimetres?

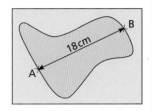

Method

Solution	Commentary
a Distance on the map = 18 cm Distance in real life = 18 × 4000 = 72 000 cm 72 000 cm = 720 m	The scale is 1 : 4000, meaning that 1 cm on the map is 4000 cm in real life.

b i Distance on the map = 8 cm
 	
    Distance in real life = 8 × 50 000 = 400 000 cm
 	
    400 000 cm = 4000 m = 4 km
	The scale is 1 : 50 000, meaning that 1 cm on the map is 50 000 cm in real life.

ii Distance in real life = 2.5 km
 	
    2.5 km = 2500 m = 250 000 cm
 	
    250 000 ÷ 50 000 = 5 cm	

Practice (B)

1 Copy and complete the table for a scale of 1 : 40 000

Map distance (cm)	Real distance (cm)	Real distance (m)	Real distance (km)
1		400	0.4
5	200 000		
		3000	
	1 000 000		10

2 A map has the scale 1 : 75 000

The distance between two points on the map is 11 cm.

Work out the real distance between the points. Give your answer in kilometres.

3 A map is drawn using a scale of 1 : 50 000

    a Find the real distance in kilometres from town A to town B.

    b Find the real distance in kilometres from town B to town C.

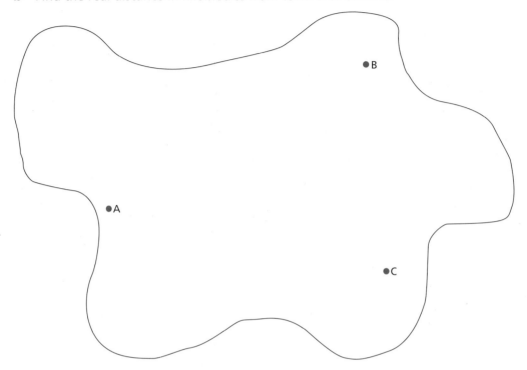

What do you think? (B)

1 Flo is going to drive from Chepstow to Bath.

To work out the distance, she uses a ruler to measure the straight line between Chepstow and Bath on a map. She then converts this measurement to kilometres using the scale.

Is her actual drive likely to be exactly the same distance or not? Explain your answer.

Consolidate – do you need more?

1 A triangle is drawn, as shown, using the scale 1 cm to 2 m.

    a What are the dimensions of the real triangle?

    b What is the area of the real triangle?

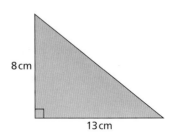

8 cm

13 cm

2 A rectangle is shown.

    a Draw an accurate diagram of the rectangle using a scale of 1 : 40

    b What is the perimeter of the scale diagram?

    c What is the area of the scale diagram?

1.2 m

90 cm

3 A model of a toy car is made using the scale 1 : 50

The length of the model is 14 cm.

What is the length of the car in real life? Give your answer in metres.

4 A scale of 1 : 25 000 is used to show the positions of three towns, A, B and C.

In real life, what distance would be travelled if you walked from A to B to C in straight lines? Give your answer in kilometres.

● B

● A

● C

Stretch – can you deepen your learning?

1 On a map with a scale of 1 : 50 000, two villages are 7.5 cm apart.

On a map with a scale of 1 : 100 000, how many centimetres apart are the same two villages?

2 On a map with a scale of 1 : 500 000, the distance between Edinburgh and Glasgow is 15 cm.

Marta is going to drive from Edinburgh to Glasgow at an average speed of 60 km/h.

How long will the drive take her? Give your answer in hours and minutes.

Are you ready? (A)

1 Copy and complete the missing compass points.

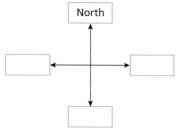

2 Work out the size of angle x.

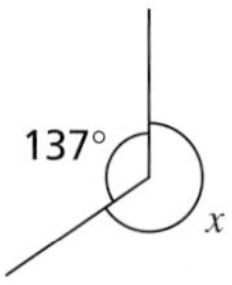

3 Draw the angles.

a 50°

b 120°

c 255°

4 Measure the marked angles.

a

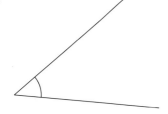

b

c

A **bearing** is an angle in degrees, measured clockwise from North. Bearings are written using three figures.

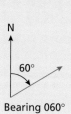

Bearing 060°

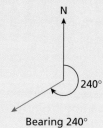

Bearing 240°

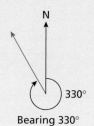

Bearing 330°

Example 1

a Find the bearing of B from A.

b Find the bearing of A from B.

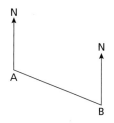

Method

Solution	Commentary
a 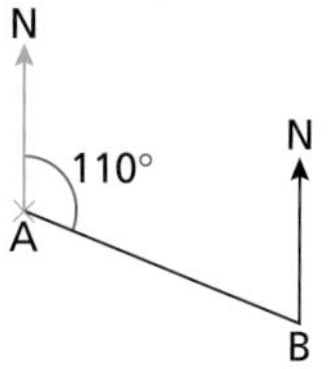 N 110° A N B The angle is 110°.	The bearing *from A* means you need to measure clockwise from the North line at A.
b N 110° A N 70° B 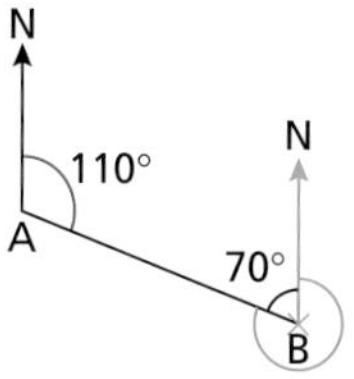 The angle is 360° − 70° = 290°	The bearing *from B* means you need to measure clockwise from the North line at B. Here, you need to use the fact that angles around a point sum to 360°.

Example 2

Point B is on a bearing of 060° from point A.

Draw a diagram to show this.

Method

Solution	Commentary
 N • A	Mark a point labelled A and draw a North line.

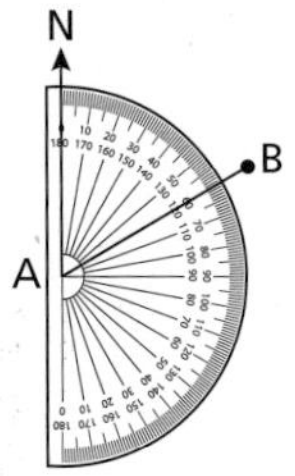 N •B A	Place a protractor, using the point A as the centre. Measure and mark a point at 60°. Label the point B.
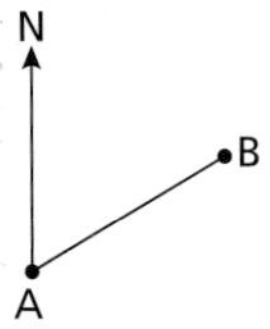 N •B A	Draw a line from A to the point B.

Practice (A)

1 Copy each diagram and mark the bearing of B from A.

a   **b** 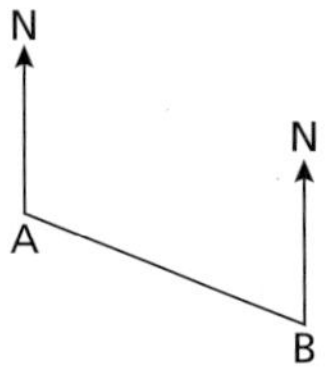   **c** 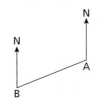 **d**

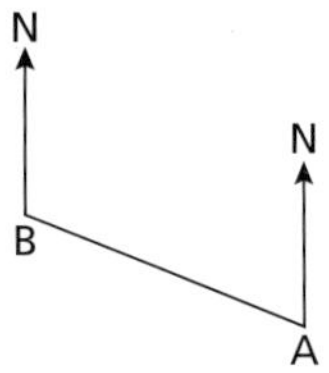

2 Find the bearings of B from A.

a 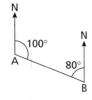 **b** 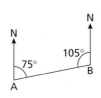 **c**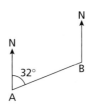

3 Find the bearings of A from B.

a 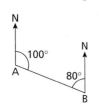 **b** 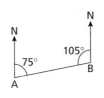 **c**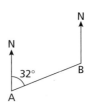

4 Use a protractor to measure the bearing of Q from P in each diagram.

a

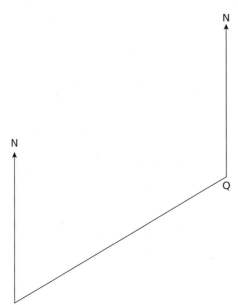

b

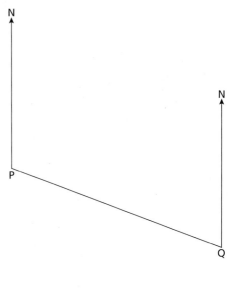

c

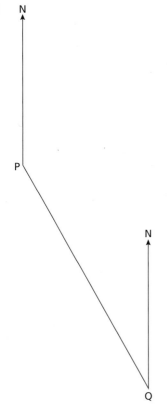

d

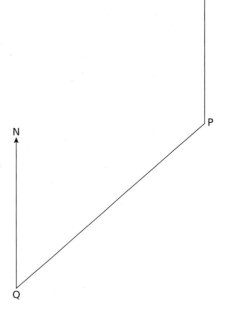

5 Draw diagrams for each statement.

  a The bearing of B from A is 070°.   **b** The bearing of D from C is 100°.

  c The bearing of Q from P is 200°.   **d** The bearing of M from L is 300°.

6 Without measuring, estimate the bearing of B from A in each diagram.

a

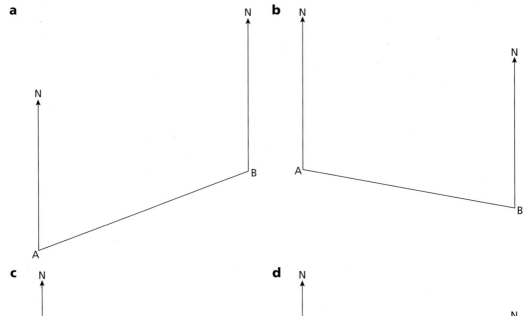

b

c

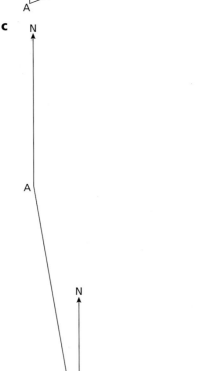

d

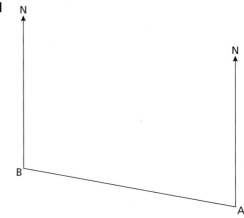

Check your answers by measuring.

What do you think? (A)

1 Here is a parallelogram:

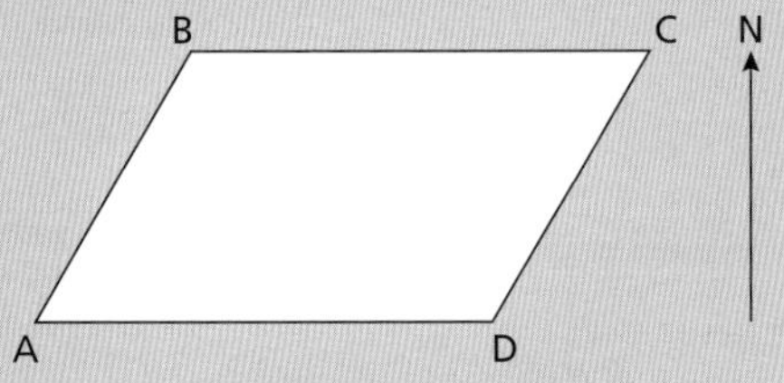

Which statements are **true**?

A	**B**	**C**
The bearing of B from A is the same as the bearing of C from D.	The bearing of C from B is the same as the bearing of D from A.	The bearing of C from A is the same as the bearing of D from B.

Are you ready? (B)

1 Accurately draw lines of each length.

   a 5 cm   **b** 8 cm   **c** 7.5 cm   **d** 10.3 cm

2 Draw each bearing.

   The bearing of B from A is:

   a 050°   **b** 100°   **c** 200°

3 The diagram shows two points on a map.

   Scale: 1 cm represents 2 km

Work out the actual distance between the two points.

Practice (B)

1. Draw diagrams for each statement.

   a B is on a bearing of 080° from A.

   The distance between A and B is 6 cm.

   b Q is on a bearing of 160° from P.

   The distance between P and Q is 10 cm.

   c M is on a bearing of 200° from L.

   The distance between L and M is 8 cm.

2. The map shows the locations of a church and a museum.

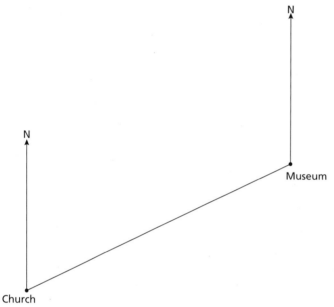

   a Measure the bearing of the museum from the church.

   b Measure the bearing of the church from the museum.

   On the map, 1 centimetre represents 5 metres.

   c What is the actual distance between the church and the museum in metres?

3. Mario cycles 16 miles on a bearing of 070° from his house.

   Draw a scale drawing of Mario's route, using 1 centimetre to represent 2 miles.

4. Denholme and Queensbury are 8 km apart.

   Queensbury is on a bearing of 150° from Denholme.

   Draw an accurate diagram of the location of Denholme and Queensbury using a scale of 1 cm to represent 0.5 km.

5. Kath travels from home on a bearing of 100° for 10 km.

   She then travels due East for 8 km.

   Draw an accurate diagram of Kath's journey using a scale of 1 cm to represent 2 km.

Consolidate – do you need more?

1 Draw the bearings, when the bearing of B from A is:

a 100° **b** 120° **c** 150° **d** 200° **e** 250°

2 Draw diagrams for each statement.

a B is on a bearing of 100° from A.

The distance between A and B is 10 cm.

b B is on a bearing of 120° from A.

The distance between A and B is 10 cm.

c B is on a bearing of 140° from A.

The distance between A and B is 6 cm.

d B is on a bearing of 170° from A.

The distance between A and B is 6 cm.

e B is on a bearing of 340° from A.

The distance between A and B is 12 cm.

Stretch – can you deepen your learning?

1 The point B is on a bearing of 080° from A.

The point C is on a bearing of 160° from B.

Draw a diagram to show the points A, B and C.

2 Jackson travels 10 km on a bearing of 100° from his house.

He then travels 8 km on a bearing of 040° to reach his office.

a Draw an accurate diagram of Jackson's journey, using a scale of 1 cm to represent 2 km.

b Measure the bearing of Jackson's office from his house.

3 The diagram shows that the bearing of B from A is 070°.

Work out the bearing of A from B. Draw a diagram to check your answer.

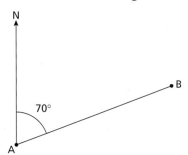

Constructions (1): exam practice

1 ABC is a triangle.

AB = 7 cm

AC = 6 cm

Angle A = 48°

Draw triangle ABC accurately.

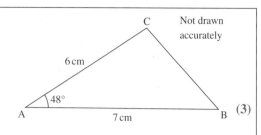

Not drawn accurately

(3)

2 A map has a scale of 1 cm : 4 miles.

On the map, the distance between two towns is 5 cm.

What is the actual distance between the two towns? **(2)**

3 Use a ruler and a pair of compasses to construct an equilateral triangle with sides 6 cm.

Show your construction lines. **(3)**

4 Work out the bearing of B from A. **(2)**

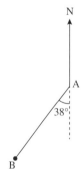

5 The diagram shows the positions of two towns, Bolton (B) and Whitefield (W).

Scale: 2 cm represents 5 miles

a) Work out the real distance, in miles, from Whitefield to Bolton. **(2)**

The town of Heywood (H) is on a bearing of 042° from Bolton.

On the diagram, H is 3 cm from B.

b) Construct and mark H with a cross (×) on an accurate copy of the diagram. **(2)**

2 Constructions (2)

In this block, we will cover...

2.1 Bisectors

Example

Draw an angle of 50° and construct its angle bise

Method

Solution

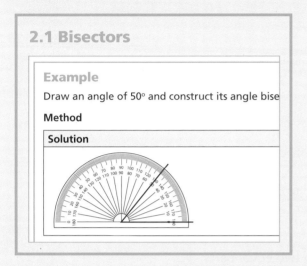

2.2 Perpendiculars to and from a line

Practice

For each question, copy the diagram as accurately

1. Construct the perpendicular to each line s

   a   ●A   b

   _____

   c   d

2.3 Loci

Consolidate – do you need more

1. Copy the lines using the dimensions given.
   Construct the locus of all points 2 cm from

   a _____
              7cm

Are you ready? (A)

1 Estimate the size of each angle.

a

b

2 Use a ruler, a protractor and a pair of compasses to construct accurate copies of the triangles.

a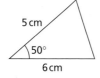

b

c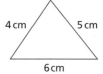

A **bisector** is a line that divides something into two equal parts. So an **angle bisector** will divide an angle into two equal parts.

An angle bisector shows the set of points which are **equidistant** from the two line segments that form the angle. 'Equidistant' means being the same or equal distance, so any point on the angle bisector is the same distance from each of the two line segments.

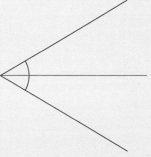

In geometry, there is an important difference between drawing angles and constructing angles. When drawing angles a protractor is used, and when constructing a pair of compasses is used. Constructing is usually regarded as being more accurate. Note the following example involves both drawing and constructing angles.

Example

Draw an angle of 50° and construct its angle bisector.

Method

Solution	Commentary
	Start by drawing an angle of 50°. Make the arms of the angle about 5 cm long.

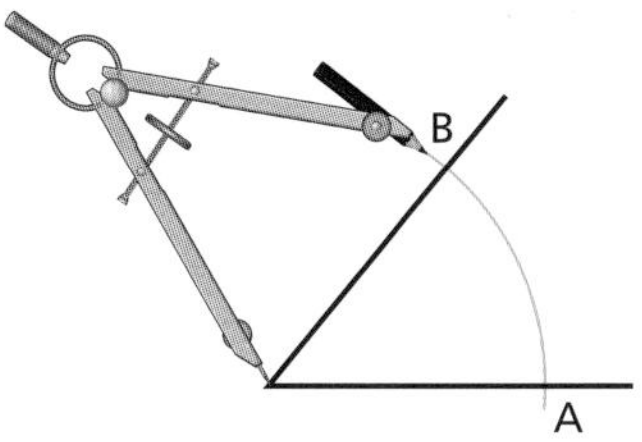	Use a pair of compasses to draw an arc of radius about 4 cm from the vertex of the angle that cuts both arms of the angle. Label these points of intersection A and B.
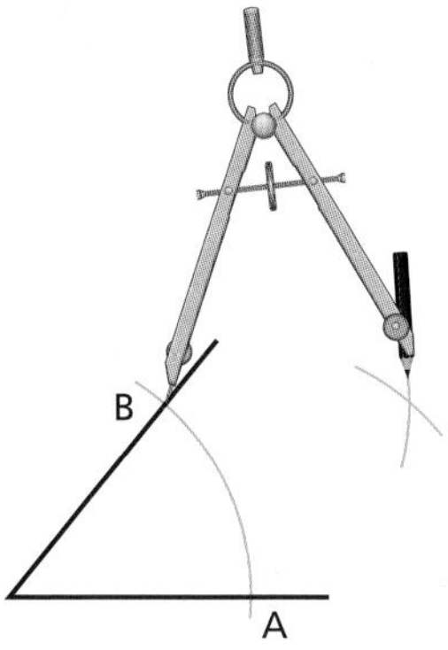	Next, draw arcs of the same length from A and B. Make sure you draw them long enough so that they meet.
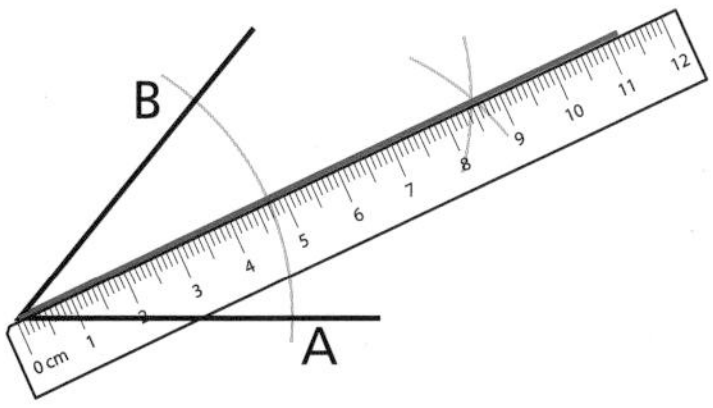	Draw a straight line from the vertex of the angle, through the point of intersection of the two arcs.
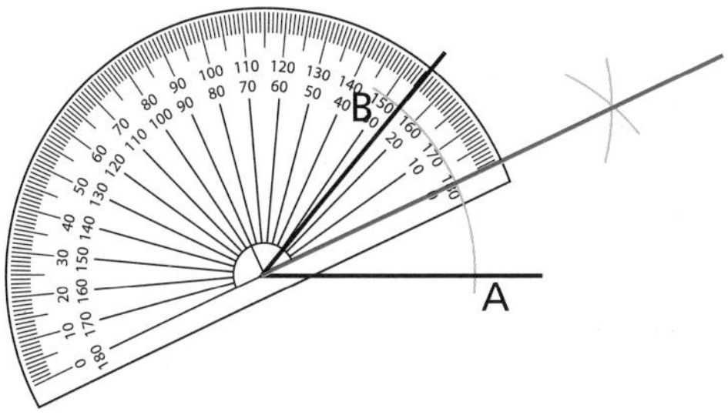	Verify that both angles formed are 25°. You have constructed the bisector of the 50° angle.

Practice (A)

For each question, show your construction lines.

1. Draw each angle and construct its angle bisector.

   a 60°   **b** 120°   **c** 146°

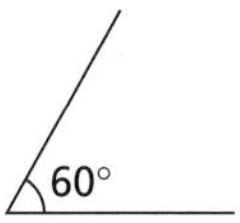

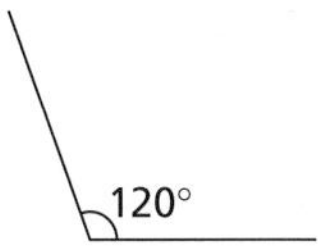

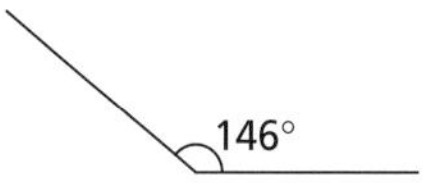

2. Draw each angle and construct its angle bisector.

   a 90°   **b** 160°   **c** 210°

3 Copy the diagram and construct a line to show all the points equidistant from AB and BC.

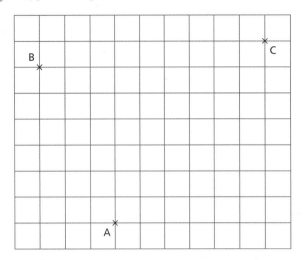

4 Emily says she has bisected this angle.

Is she correct? Give a reason for your answer.

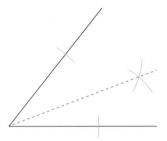

5 Here is a plan view of a garden.

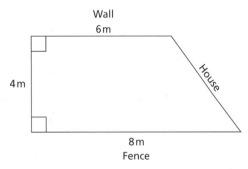

a Make a scale drawing of the garden using 1 cm to represent 1 m.

b Draw a line representing all points equidistant from the house and the fence.

What do you think? (A) 💡

1 Seb is looking at triangle ABC.

Seb thinks that the bisector of angle ABC will bisect the line AC.

Is he correct?

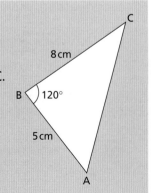

Are you ready? (B)

1 Diagrams A, B and C each show a pair of lines.

Which pairs of lines are perpendicular?

> Remember that perpendicular means 'at right angles to'.

A 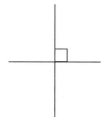   **B**    **C**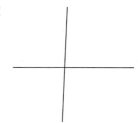

2 Copy each line, then draw another line perpendicular to each one.

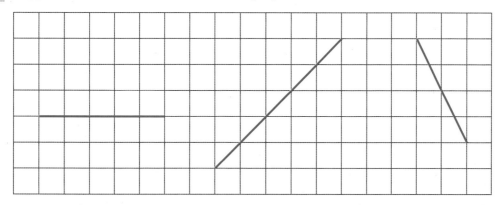

3 Draw a right-angled triangle with a base of 5 cm and a perpendicular height of 3 cm.

Constructions are accurate drawings made using a ruler and a pair of compasses. It is important that you do not rub out your construction lines once you have completed the construction.

A **bisector** is a line that divides something into two equal parts.

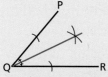

This construction shows the angle bisector of angle PQR.

An **angle bisector** is a line that divides an angle into two equal parts.

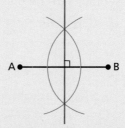

This construction shows the perpendicular bisector of line segment AB.

A **perpendicular bisector** is a line that divides a line segment into two equal parts and is perpendicular to the original line.

All the points on a perpendicular bisector are equidistant from the end points of the line segment it bisects.

Example

Draw a line segment about 6 cm long and construct its perpendicular bisector.

Solution	Commentary
 A ———————— B	Draw a 6 cm line segment and label it AB.
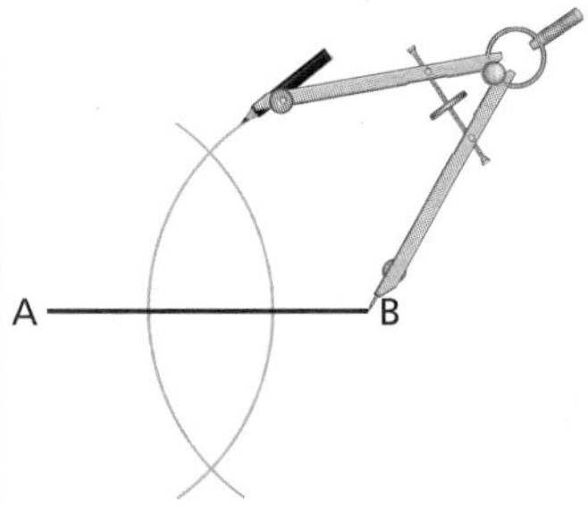	Draw arcs of length 4 cm from both end points of the line. This is to ensure the radius of the arcs is more than half the length of the line segment.
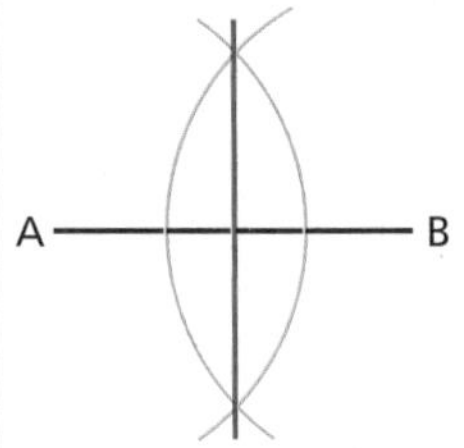	Join the points of intersection of the arcs with a straight line.
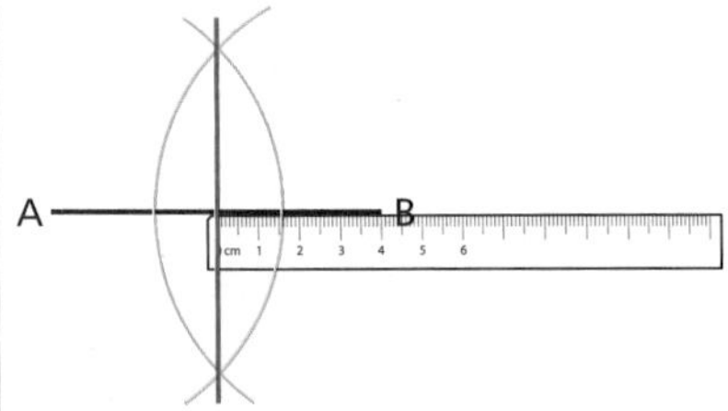	Use a ruler and a protractor to verify that this line bisects AB at right angles.

Practice (B)

For each question, show your construction lines.

1. Draw each line segment to the given length and construct its perpendicular bisector.

   a ———— 5 cm   **b** ———— 7 cm   **c** | 4 cm   **d** | 9 cm

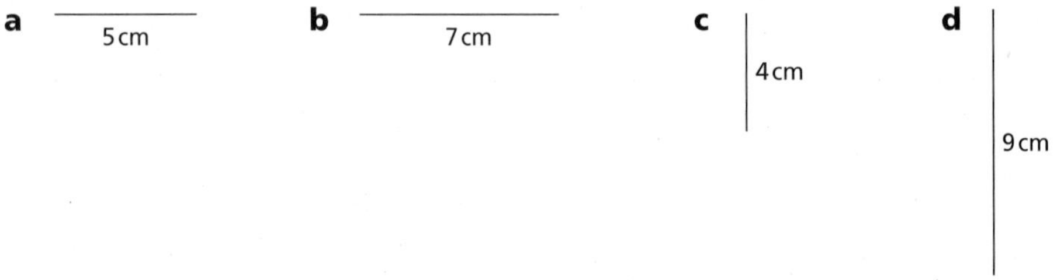

2. Draw each line segment to the given length and construct its perpendicular bisector.

   a 6 cm   **b** 9 cm   **c** 10.5 cm   **d** 7.5 cm

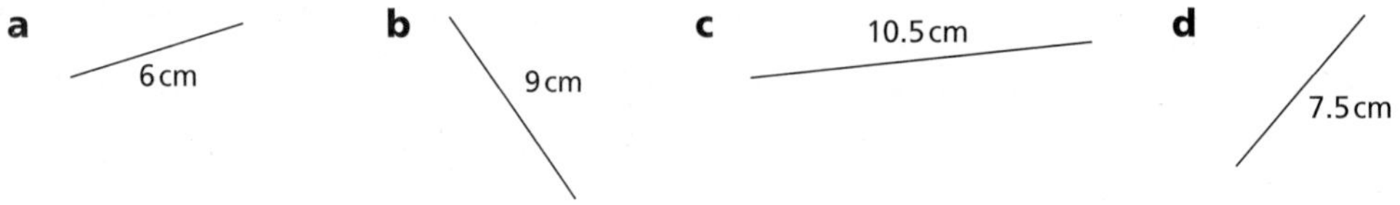

3 The map shows the location of a shop and a garage in a town.

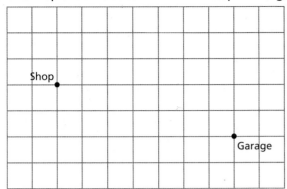

Copy the map and draw all the points equidistant from the shop and the garage.

4 Copy the triangle using the given dimensions and bisect the side QR.

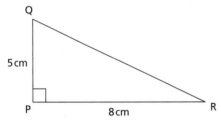

5 Here is the cross-section of the roof of a house.

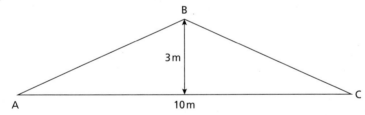

A support beam is to be added to make the roof safe.

The beam needs to be equidistant from B and C.

Where will the support beam be placed?

6 Explain what is wrong with this perpendicular bisector of CD.

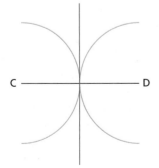

What do you think? (B)

1. Junaid says, "If you draw a square and bisect one of the angles, this will also bisect the opposite angle."

   Is Junaid correct?

Consolidate – do you need more?

For each question, show your construction lines.

1. Draw and bisect each angle.

   a 50° **b** 60° **c** 130° **d** 160°

2. Draw the line segments and construct a perpendicular bisector of each.

   a 6 cm **b** 8 cm **c** 10.5 cm **d** 15.5 cm

Stretch – can you deepen your learning?

For each question, show your construction lines.

1. Copy the rectangle using the given dimensions.

   Identify the point that is:

   • equidistant from A and C

   • and equidistant from AB and AD.

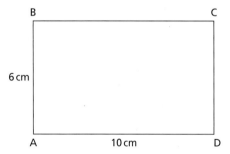

2. Draw a line segment.

   Investigate what angles you can construct without using a protractor.

3. Construct an equilateral triangle using the side-side-side construction method.

   Investigate what angles you can construct without using a protractor.

2.2 Perpendiculars to and from a line

Are you ready?

1 Draw the line segment to the given length and construct its perpendicular bisector.

_____
7 cm

2 Draw the two points and construct the perpendicular bisector between them.

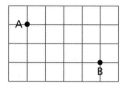

The method for constructing a perpendicular bisector of a line segment can be adapted to construct these two lines:

a perpendicular **from** a given point to a line segment…

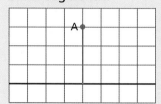

This is the shortest possible distance from the point to the line.

…and a perpendicular **to** a given point on a line segment

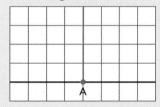

Here, the point is actually on the line segment.

Example 1

Use a ruler and a pair of compasses to construct the perpendicular to AB passing through C.

•C

A ——————— B

Method

Solution	Commentary
•C A ——⟍———⟋— B	Draw arcs using C as the centre. Ensure that the arcs intersect the line AB twice.

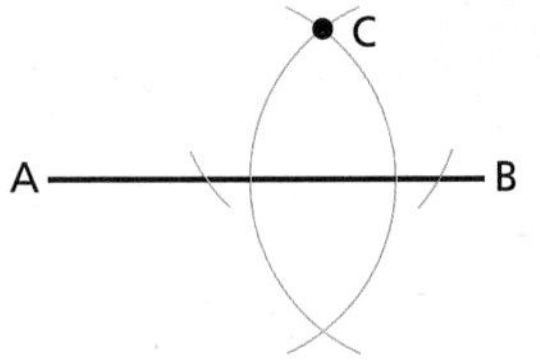	Using these two intersection points as centres, draw two further arcs with the same radius. Ensure the radius is big enough for the arcs to intersect.
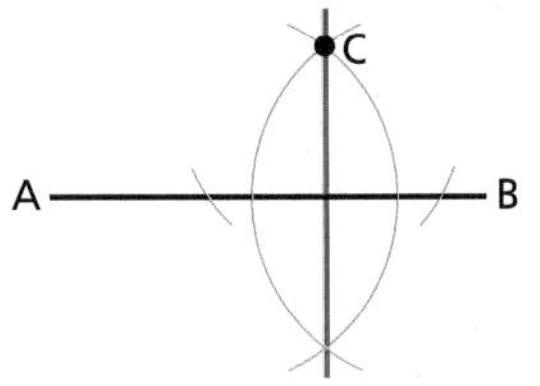	Join the intersection points of the arcs with a straight line. The line passes through C and is perpendicular to AB.

Example 2

Use a ruler and a pair of compasses to construct the perpendicular to AB passing through O.

Method

Solution	Commentary
	Draw arcs using O as the centre. Ensure that the arcs intersect the line AB twice.
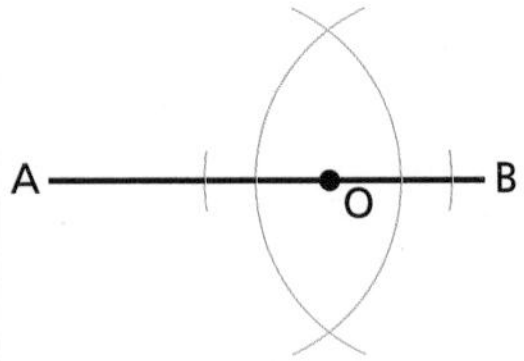	Using these two intersection points as centres, draw two further arcs with the same radius. Ensure the radius is big enough for the arcs to intersect.
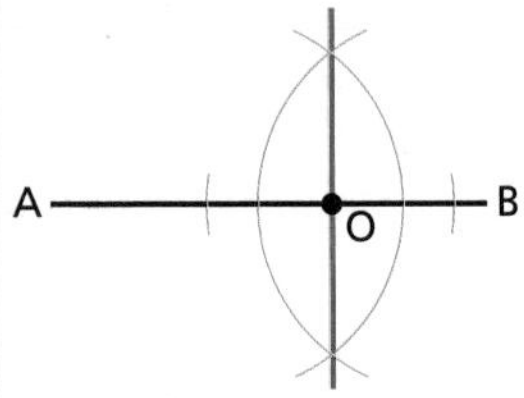	Join the intersection points of the arcs with a straight line. The line passes through O and is perpendicular to AB.

Practice

For each question, copy the diagram as accurately as you can and show your construction lines.

1 Construct the perpendicular to each line segment passing through A.

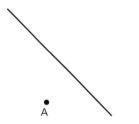

2 Construct the perpendicular to each line segment passing through A.

3 Construct the perpendicular to each line segment passing through A.

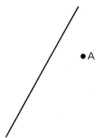

4 Draw the shortest line segment from point C to the line AB.

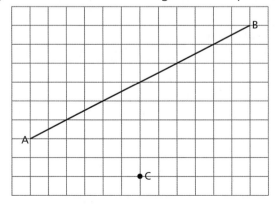

5 The scale diagram shows the location of a house (H), a barn (B) and a garage (G).

There is a straight path between the house and the barn.

Another straight path from the garage is perpendicular to the path between the house and the barn.

Copy the diagram and draw the two paths.

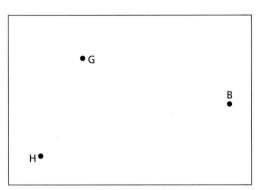

6 Construct the perpendicular to AB passing through O.

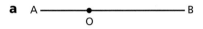

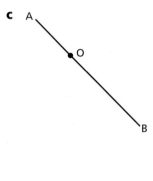

7 Here is the triangle PQR:

The point O is 4 cm from the point Q.

Copy the triangle using the dimensions given and construct the locus of all points perpendicular to QR passing through O.

> Locus (plural 'loci') is covered in Chapter 2.3

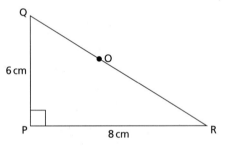

8 Here is a map showing the location of two power stations in a town. There is a power line connecting them, which passes through point C.

Two more power stations are going to be built.

They must be on a line perpendicular to the power line at C.

Mark two possible locations for the new power stations.

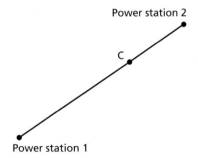

9 Copy the coordinate grid.

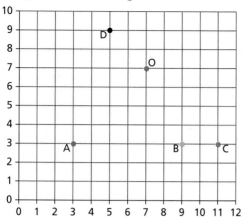

a Construct the line perpendicular to AB passing through the point O.

b Construct the perpendicular to CD passing through the point O.

c Write the coordinates of the point where your two lines intersect.

10 XY is 20 cm long.

Draw a perpendicular that divides XY in the ratio 2 : 3

What do you think?

1 Copy the diagram.

A•

•C

B

Is it possible to draw a line perpendicular to AB passing through the point C?

Consolidate – do you need more?

1 Copy the diagrams and construct the perpendicular from the point C to the line.

a  **b**  **c**

d 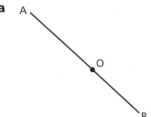 **e** 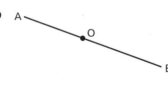 **f**

2 Copy the diagrams and construct the perpendicular to the line passing through O.

a 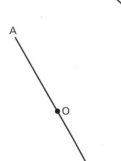 **b** 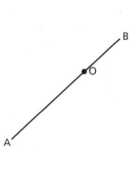 **c**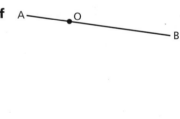

d 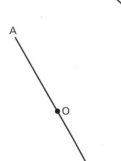 **e** 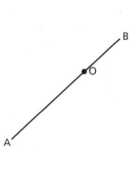 **f**

Stretch – can you deepen your learning?

1 Copy the diagram.

Construct the perpendicular from point C to AB.

Compare the gradients of the two lines.

What do you notice?

Will this always happen with two perpendicular lines?

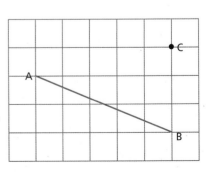

2.3 Loci

Are you ready? (A)

Use a pair of compasses for these questions.

1 Draw a circle with a radius of 5 cm.

2 Draw a semicircle with a radius of 4 cm.

3 Draw a quarter-circle with a radius of 6 cm.

A **locus** (plural **loci**) is a set of points that all have a particular property.

In the circle, OA = OB = OC = 4 cm. The circle is the locus of the points that are 4 cm from O.

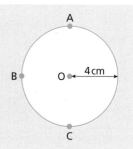

Example

ABCD is a square of side length 10 cm.

Draw the locus of all points inside the square that are 4 cm or less from A.

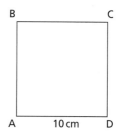

Method

Solution	Commentary
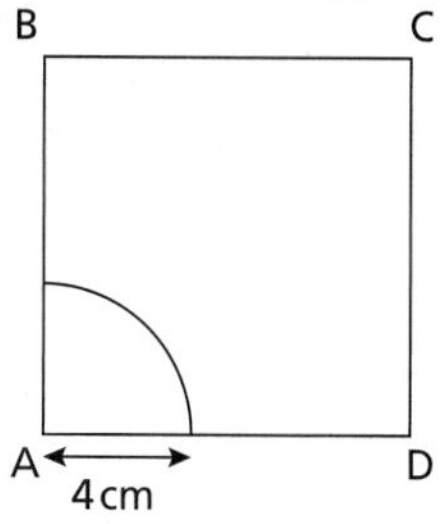 B _____ C A←→D 4 cm	Set a pair of compasses to 4 cm and draw an arc from the point A.
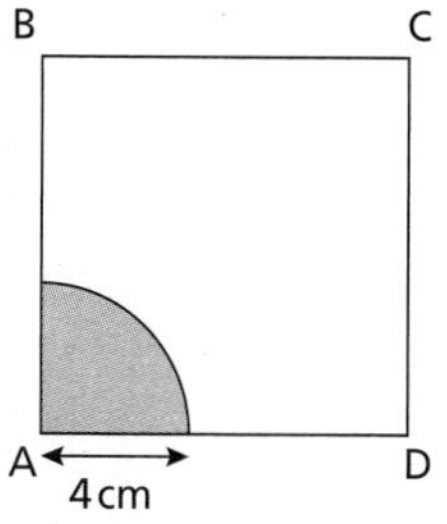 B _____ C A←→D 4 cm	The points inside the quarter-circle are less than 4 cm from A. Shade the region that is within the quarter-circle and within the square.

43

Practice (A)

1 Mark a point O on a page. Draw the locus of all points exactly 3 cm from O.

2 Mark a point A on a page.

   a Draw the locus of all points exactly 4 cm from A.

   b Draw the locus of all points exactly 3 cm from A.

   c Shade the region with points more than 3 cm but less than 4 cm from A.

3 Draw a line segment AB of length 10 cm.

   a Construct the locus of all points 7 cm from A.

   b Construct the locus of all points 5 cm from B.

   c Shade the region with points which are less than 7 cm from A and less than 5 cm from B.

4 Draw a line AB 10 cm long. P is a point exactly 6 cm from A and 8 cm from B.

   Show that there are exactly two possible locations for P.

5 Copy the rectangle ABCD using the dimensions given.

   a Draw the loci of the points that are exactly 4 cm from A and exactly 5 cm from C.

   b Shade the region with points that are less than 4 cm from A and less than 5 cm from C.

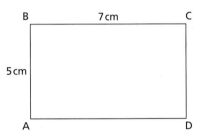

What do you think? (A)

1 Here is a straight line, 8 cm in length:

   A ————————————————— B

   Is it possible to identify points which are both less than 4 cm from A and less than 3 cm from B?

   Explain your answer.

Are you ready? (B)

1 Copy line AB. Draw the locus of points equidistant from A and B.

   A ————————————— B

   This is a perpendicular bisector.

2 Copy the rectangle ABCD to the given dimensions.

   Draw a line within the rectangle that represents the set of points that are 2 cm from AB.

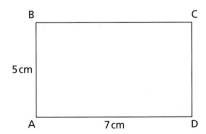

Example 1

Draw the locus of all points 2 cm from the line AB.

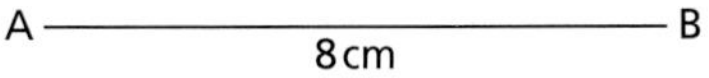

A ——————————— B
    8 cm

Method

Solution	Commentary
	Set a pair of compasses to 2 cm and draw an arc from the point A.
	This arc shows the locus of points 2 cm from A.
	Draw another arc from the point B.
	This arc shows the locus of points 2 cm from B.
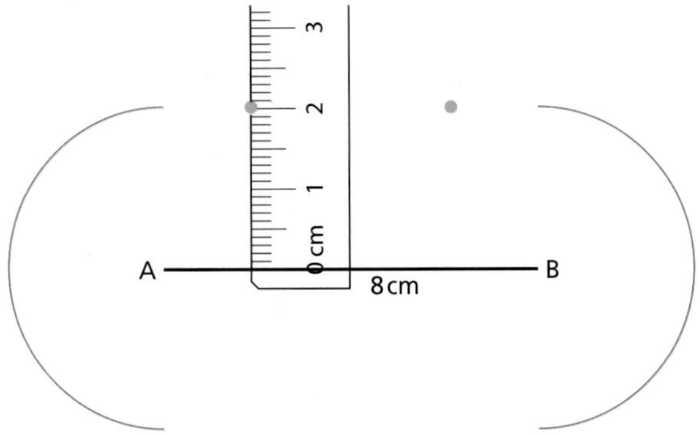	Use a ruler to mark two points 2 cm above the line AB.
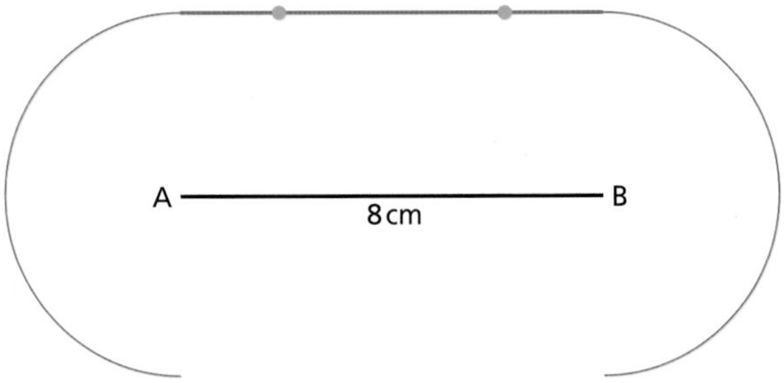	Draw a line through the points that intersects both arcs.
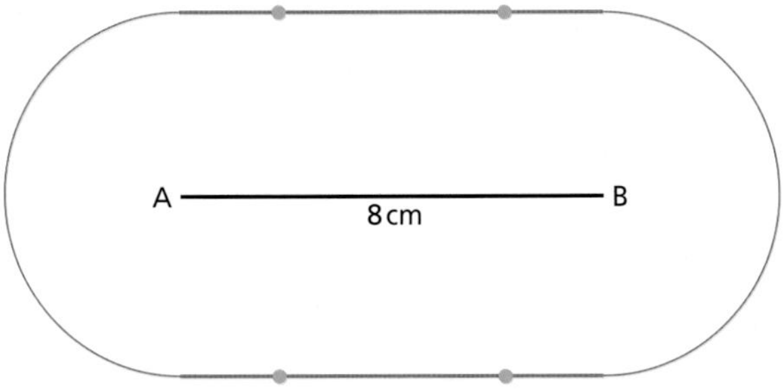	Mark two more points 2 cm below the line AB and draw a line through the points that intersects both arcs.

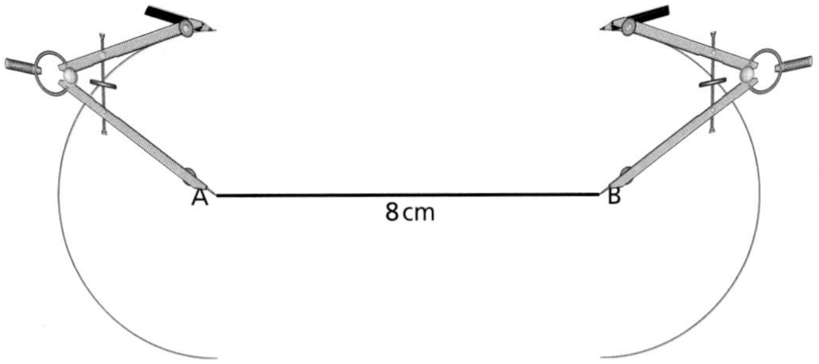

Example 2

ABCD is a square of side length 10 cm.

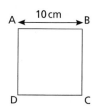

a   Draw the locus of all points inside the square and exactly 2 cm from AD.

b   Draw the locus of all points inside the square and 6 cm from D.

c   Shade the region of all points inside the square, less than 2 cm from AD and less than 6 cm from D.

Method

Solution	Commentary
a 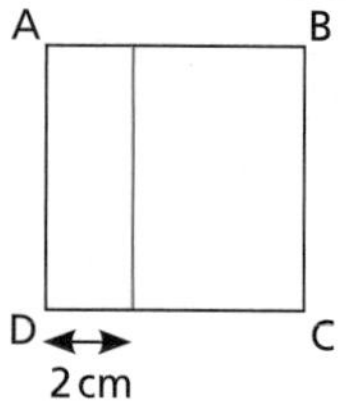	The locus is a line parallel to AD and 2 cm away from it. Every point on the line is 2 cm from AD.
b 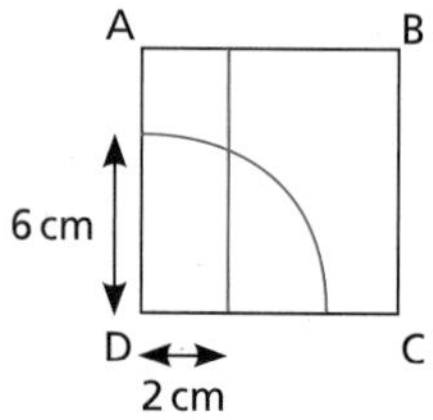	The locus of points exactly 6 cm from D would be a circle with centre D and radius 6 cm. You only need to draw the part of the circle inside the square.
c 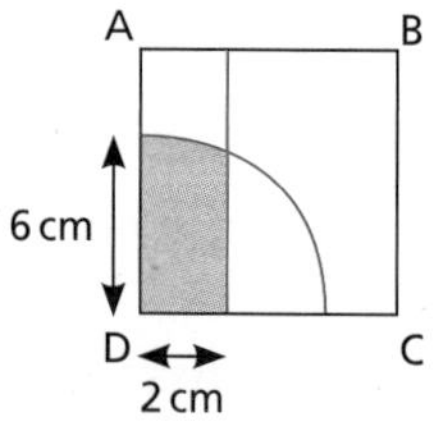	Less than 2 cm from AD means the region will be on the left-hand side of the locus drawn in part **a**. Less than 6 cm from D means the region will also need to be inside the circle drawn in part **b**. Shade the region that satisfies both these criteria.

Practice (B)

1   Copy the line AB, which is 5 cm in length.

A ————————————— B

Construct the locus of all points exactly 3 cm from the line.

2   Draw a square of side length 4 cm, as shown below.

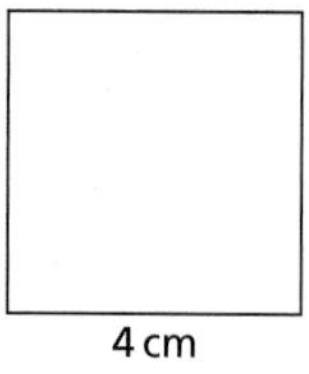

4 cm

Construct the locus of all points 2 cm outside the square.

3 Copy the rectangle ABCD using the dimensions given.

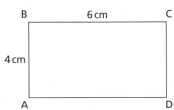

Draw the locus of points inside the rectangle that are 4 cm from AB and draw the locus of the points inside the rectangle that are 1 cm from BC.

4 The diagram shows the plan of a room.

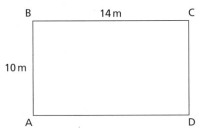

a Draw a scale diagram of the room using 1 cm to represent 2 m.

b Draw the locus of points inside the room that are 4 m from the wall BC and draw the locus of points inside the room that are 10 m from the wall AB.

c Shade the region with points less than 4 m from BC and more than 10 m from AB.

5 Draw the rectangle PQRS using the dimensions given.

a Draw the locus of points inside the rectangle that are 3 cm from QR and draw the locus of points inside the rectangle that are 4 cm from R.

b Shade the region with points more than 3 cm from QR and less than 4 cm from R.

6 The diagram shows Faith's garden.

Faith wants to plant a tree:

- more than 4 m from the house

- more than 5 m from the corner of the garden represented by B.

Draw a scale diagram of the garden using 1 cm to represent 2 m. Shade the region where Faith could plant the tree.

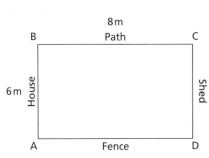

7 The rectangle ABCD is drawn on a centimetre grid.

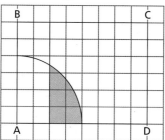

Describe the shaded region in terms of ABCD.

8 A goat is attached to the corner of a building in a field of grass with a 5 m rope.

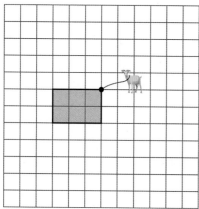

Using a scale of 1 cm = 1 m, draw the situation on a centimetre squared grid and shade the area of the grass that can be eaten by the goat.

What do you think? (B)

1 Why is this diagram incorrect for showing the locus of all points 2 cm from the red line?

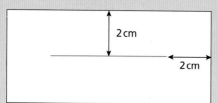

Consolidate – do you need more?

1 Copy the lines using the dimensions given.

Construct the locus of all points 2 cm from each line.

a ——— 7cm ———

b | 5 cm

c 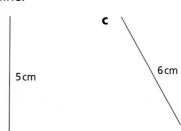 6 cm

2 Copy the shapes using the dimensions given.

Draw the locus of all points 3 cm from each shape.

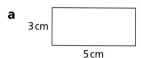

a   3 cm   5 cm

b   4 cm   6 cm

c   4 cm   4 cm

3 Make four copies of the rectangle using the dimensions given.

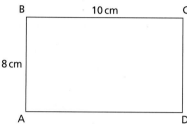

B   10 cm   C
8 cm
A   D

Shade the region with points:

a   less than 4 cm from AB and more than 5 cm from A

b   more than 4 cm from AB and more than 5 cm from A

c   more than 4 cm from BC and more than 4 cm from D

d   less than 4 cm from BC and more than 4 cm from D.

4 Copy the rectangle.

Shade the region with points that are:

- closer to PQ than RS
- closer to QR than PS
- further than 2 cm away from Q.

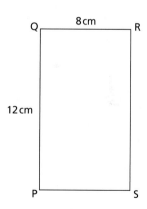

Q   8 cm   R
12 cm
P   S

Stretch – can you deepen your learning?

1 Line AB is 6 cm in length.

Work out the perimeter of the locus 3 cm from the line AB. Round your answer to 1 significant figure.

A———————————— B

2 ABCD is a square with sides of 5 cm.

Draw the locus of all points 2 cm outside the square.

Work out the area between the edge of the square and the locus of points. Round your answer to 1 decimal place.

Constructions (2): exam practice

1 Write down the letter of the pair of lines that are perpendicular. **(1)**

    A   **B**   **C**

 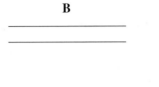 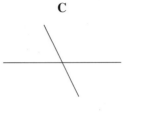

2 Copy the diagram.

Use a ruler and a pair of compasses to construct the perpendicular bisector of the line segment AB. **(2)**

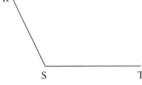

3 Copy the diagram.

Draw the locus of all points that are equidistant from lines RS and ST. **(2)**

R

S   T

4 Copy the diagram.

Draw the locus of points 3 cm from the line segment AB. **(2)**

A ——————————— B

5 Copy the diagram.

Use a ruler and a pair of compasses to construct the perpendicular to the line segment AB that passes through the point P. You must show all construction lines. **(3)**

3 Shapes and angles

In this block, we will cover...

3.1 Points, lines and triangles

Example 1

Work out the size of angle x.

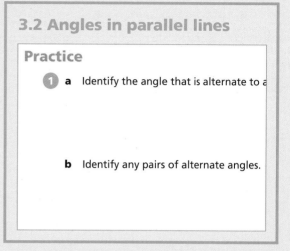

Method

3.2 Angles in parallel lines

Practice

1. **a** Identify the angle that is alternate to a

   b Identify any pairs of alternate angles.

3.3 Shape properties

Consolidate – do you need more

1. **a** Sketch a hexagon.   **b** Sketch a p

2. **a** Draw a parallelogram with angles of 7

   b Draw a kite with the equal angles bei

3. Work out the size of each lettered angle.

   a 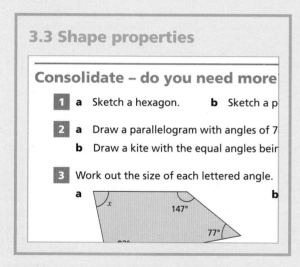   **b**

3.4 Angles in polygons

Stretch – can you deepen your le

1. The diagram shows part of a regular polyg

   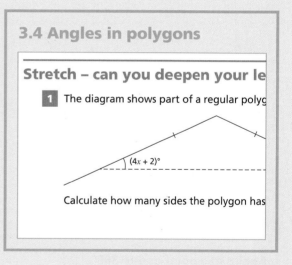

   Calculate how many sides the polygon has

3.1 Points, lines and triangles

White Rose MATHS

Are you ready? (A)

1 Name the type of each angle.

a

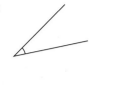

b

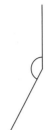

c

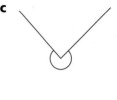

d

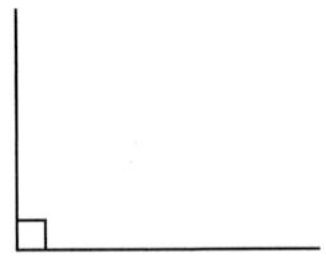

2 How many degrees are in a right angle?

A full turn is 360°.

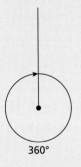

So half a turn is half of 360°, which is 180°.

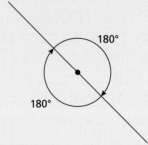

$360° \div 2 = 180°$

Half a turn is a straight line, so angles **adjacent** to each other on a straight line add up to 180°.

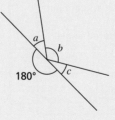

$a + b + c = 180°$

Angles at a point add to 360°.

Angles on a straight line add to 180°.

When two straight lines cross, they meet at a **vertex**. The two pairs of angles formed are called **vertically opposite angles**.

This is because they are opposite each other at a vertex – not because they are vertical.

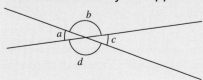

$a = c$ and $b = d$

Example 1

Work out the size of angle x.

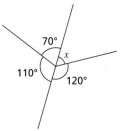

Method

Solution	Commentary
$x + 120° + 110° + 70° = 360°$	Angles at a point add up to 360°.
$x = 360° - (120° + 110° + 70°)$	
$x = 60°$	

Example 2

Work out the size of angle x.

Method

Solution	Commentary
$x + 40° = 180°$	Adjacent angles on a straight line add up to 180°.
$x = 180° - 40°$	
$x = 140°$	

Example 3

Work out the sizes of angles a and b.

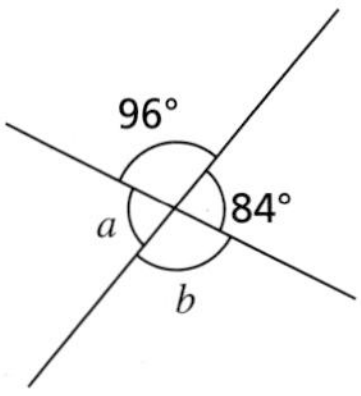

Method

Solution	Commentary
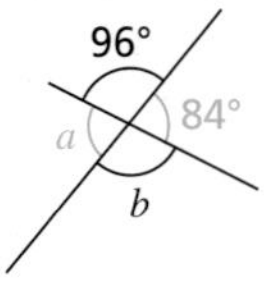 $a = 84°$	Vertically opposite angles are equal. Angle a and 84° are vertically opposite, so they are equal in size.
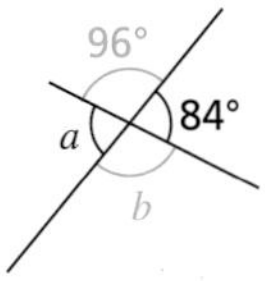 $b = 96°$	Angle b and 96° are vertically opposite, so they are equal in size.

Practice (A)

In each of these questions, use the given facts to calculate the angles. Do not use a protractor.

1 Find the size of angle x in each diagram.

a

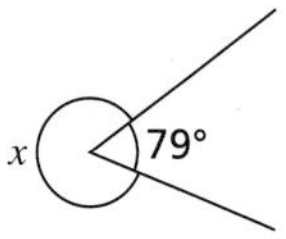

b

c

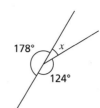

d

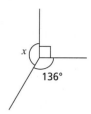

2 Work out the size of the lettered angles in each diagram.

a

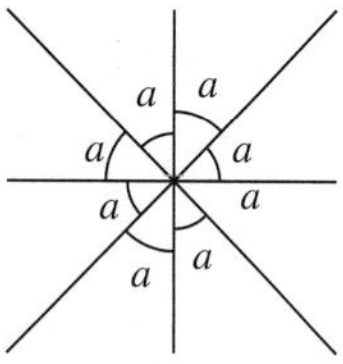

b

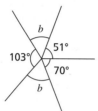

3 Which of the following diagrams show adjacent angles on a straight line?

A	**B**	**C**	**D**	**E**

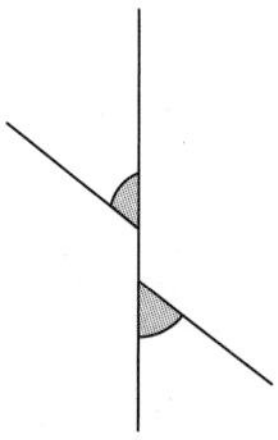

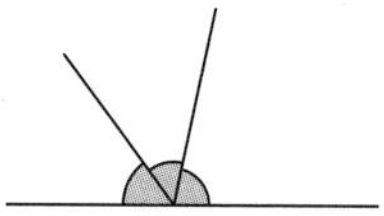

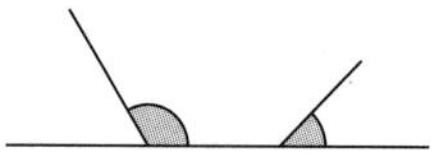

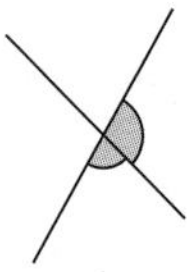

4 Find the size of angle y in each diagram.

a

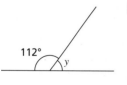

b

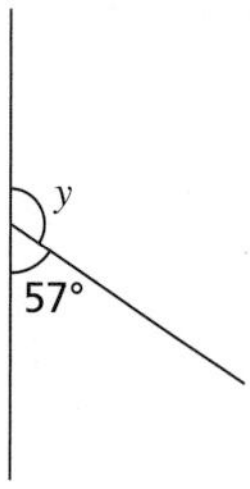

c

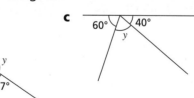

d

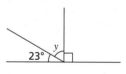

5 Is line ABC a straight line?

How do you know?

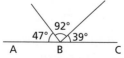

6 Work out the size of the labelled angles in each diagram.

a

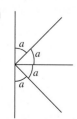

b

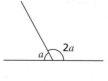

7 Which of the following diagrams show a pair of vertically opposite angles?

A   B 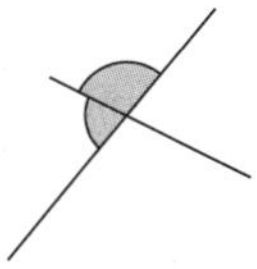   C D 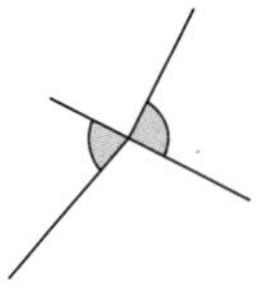 E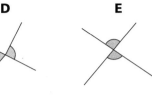

8 Find the size of angle z in each diagram.

a 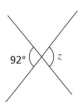 b 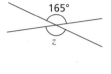 c 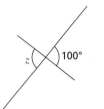 d

a 92° z

b 165° z

c z 100°

d 43° z

9 Work out the size of the unknown angles in each diagram.

a   b 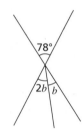 c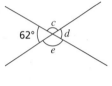

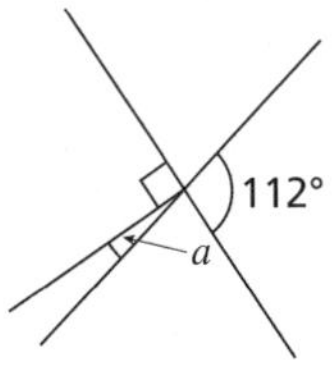

a 112° a

b 78° $2b$ b

c 62° c d e

What do you think? (A)

1 Work out the size of angle a.

How many different ways can you work out the size of angle a?

92° 88° 92° a

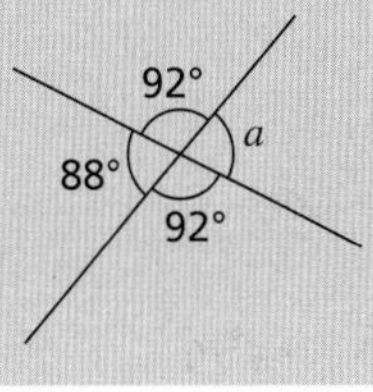

Are you ready? (B)

1 Name the type of each triangle.

a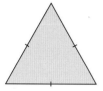

b

c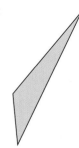

2 Which of these types of triangle could have a right angle in them?

Isosceles triangle   Equilateral triangle   Scalene triangle   Right-angled triangle

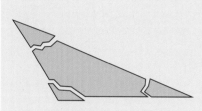 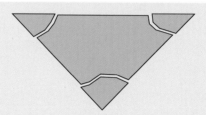

You can demonstrate that the angles in a triangle add up to 180° by tearing off the corners and arranging them to form a straight line. You already know the angles in a straight line add up to 180°.

Example 1

Find the size of angle y.

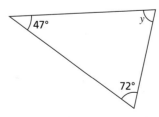

Method

Solution	Commentary
$y + 47° + 72° = 180°$	Angles in a triangle add up to 180°.
$y = 180° - (47° + 72°)$	
$y = 61°$	

Example 2

Find the size of the unknown angles.

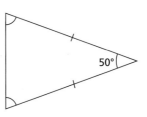

Method

Solution	Commentary
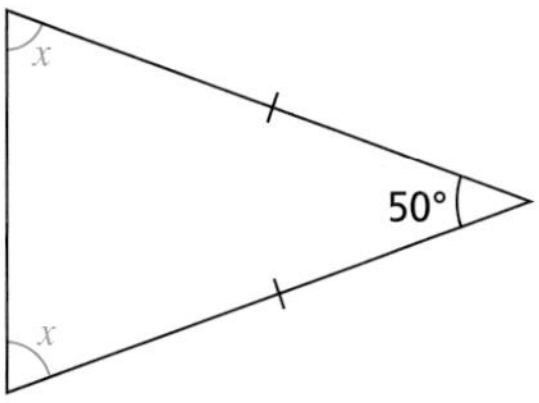 $50° + x + x = 180°$ $50° + 2x = 180°$ $2x = 180° - 50°$ $2x = 130°$ $x = 65°$	Angles in a triangle add up to 180°. The notation on the diagram indicates that the triangle is isosceles. The two unknown angles in this diagram will be equal. Note you can label equal angles similarly to how you label equal sides, but with arcs like this: 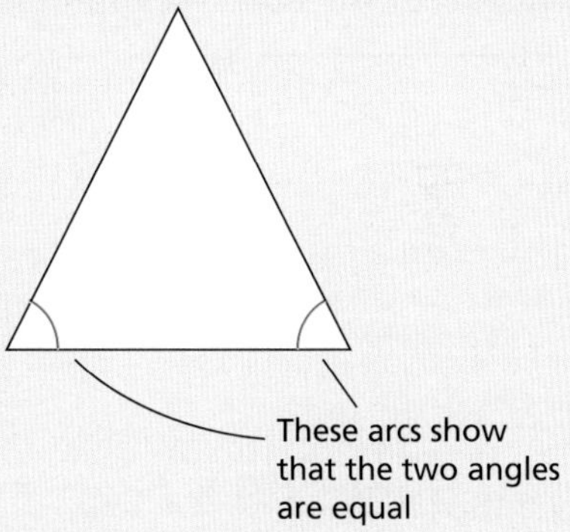 These arcs show that the two angles are equal

Practice (B)

1. Identify and label any equal angles in each triangle.

   a 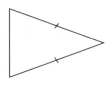   b 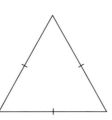   c

2. Find the size of each lettered angle.

   a 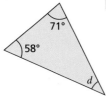   b 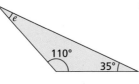   c   d

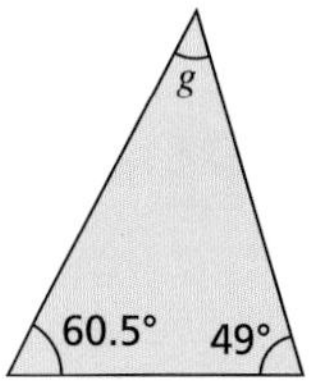

3 Find the size of each lettered angle.

a 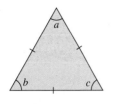 **b** 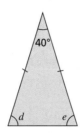 **c**  **d**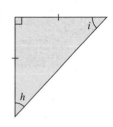

4 One angle in an isosceles triangle is 50°.

Marta says the other angles must each be 65°.

Ed says the other angles must be 80° and 50°.

Benji says both Marta and Ed could be correct. Why is Benji correct?

5 Find the size of the labelled angles in each diagram.

a 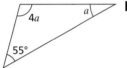 **b** 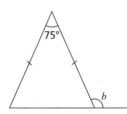 **c** 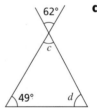 **d**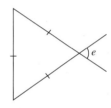

What do you think? (B)

1 One angle in a triangle is 60°.

Does this mean it is an equilateral triangle? How do you know?

Consolidate – do you need more?

Work out the size of the lettered angles in each diagram.

1 **a** 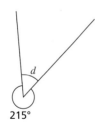 **b**

2 **a** 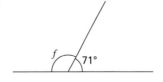 **b**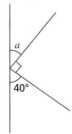

3 **a**

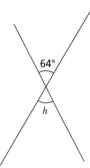

b

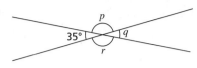

4 **a**

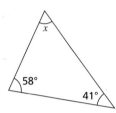

b

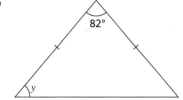

c

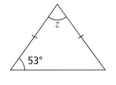

Stretch – can you deepen your learning?

1 Work out the sizes of angles a and b.

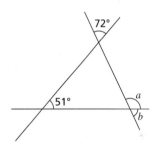

2 BCD is a straight line.

AB = AC

Is triangle ACD isosceles?
You must show your reasoning.

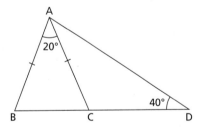

3 Work out the values of x, y and z.

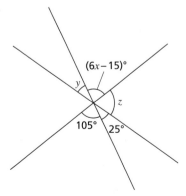

Are you ready?

1 Which pair of line segments are parallel?

A   **B**   **C**   **D**

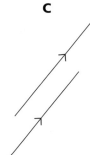

2 Work out the size of each lettered angle.

a   **b**   **c**   **d**

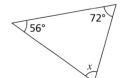

A line through a pair of parallel lines is called a **transversal**.

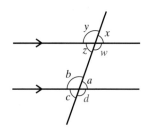

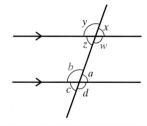

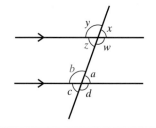

Angles w and d are called **corresponding** angles. They are to the right of the transversal and both below the parallel lines – they are in corresponding positions.	Angles w and b are called **alternate** angles. They are between the parallel lines but on alternate sides of the transversal.	Angles z and b are called **co-interior** angles. They are on the same side of the transversal and between the parallel lines.
Corresponding angles in parallel lines are equal, so $w = d$, $y = b$, $x = a$ and $z = c$	Alternate angles in parallel lines are equal, so $b = w$ and $z = a$	Co-interior angles add up to 180°, so $z + b = 180°$ and $a + w = 180°$

Example 1

Find the size of angle a.

Give reasons for your answer.

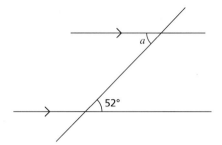

Method

Solution	Commentary
Alternate angles are equal, therefore $a = 52°$.	Angle a and 52° are alternate angles. They are both between the parallel lines and on opposite sides of the transversal.

Example 2

Find the size of angle b.

Give reasons for your answer.

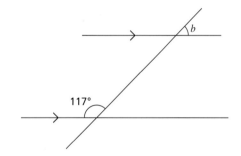

Method

Solution	Commentary
 The green angle is 117° because corresponding angles are equal. Angles on a straight line add up to 180°, therefore $b = 63°$.	For this question, there isn't one angle fact that will give you the size of angle b. Multiple angle facts will need to be used and there may be different ways to get to the answer. Make sure you write down your reasoning.

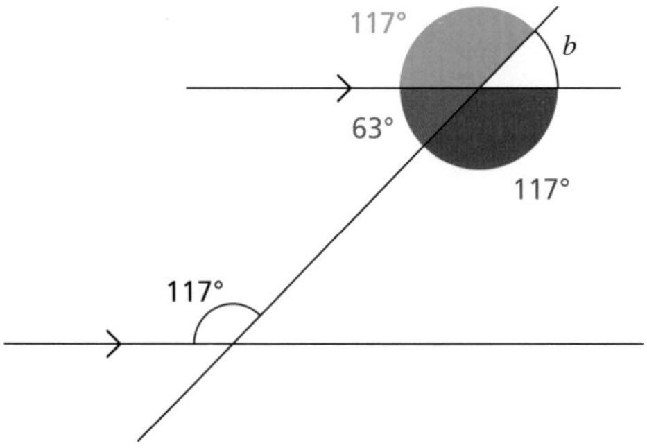

Practice

1 **a** Identify the angle that is alternate to angle *a*.

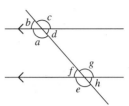

b Identify any pairs of alternate angles.

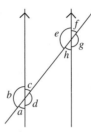

2 **a** Identify the angle that is corresponding to angle *d*.

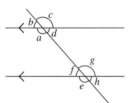

b Identify any pairs of corresponding angles.

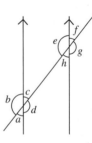

3 **a** Identify the angle that is co-interior to angle *f*.

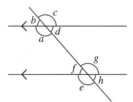

b Identify any pairs of co-interior angles.

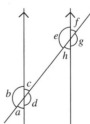

4 Work out the size of each lettered angle, giving reasons for your answers.

a  **b** 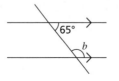 **c** 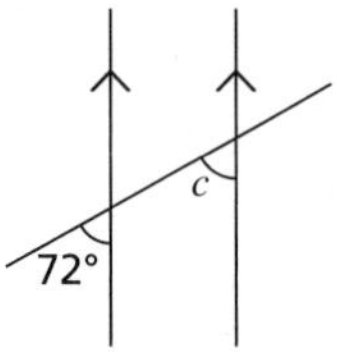   **d**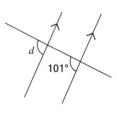

5 Work out the size of each lettered angle, giving reasons for your answers.

a   b   c   d

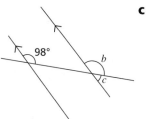
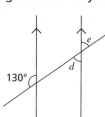
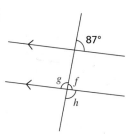

6 Work out the size of angle BCF.

Give a reason for your answer.

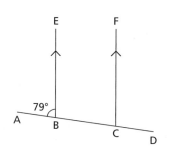

7 Flo says that the size of angle x is 110° because alternate angles are equal.

Do you agree? Explain your answer.

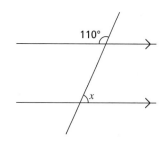

8 Work out the size of each lettered angle, giving reasons for your answers.

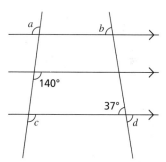

9 Work out the size of each lettered angle, giving reasons for your answers.

a   b   c

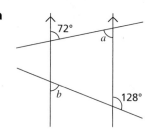
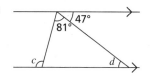
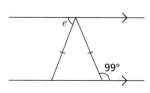

What do you think?

1 Are any of the horizontal pairs of lines parallel? How do you know?

a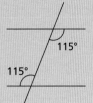

b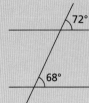

c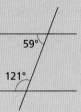

Consolidate – do you need more?

1 Use the diagram to copy and complete the statements.

a Angle ABD is corresponding to angle _____.

b Angle BFG is alternate to angle _____.

c Angle CBF is co-interior with angle _____.

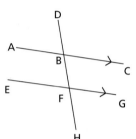

2 Work out the size of each lettered angle, giving reasons for your answers.

a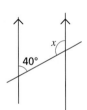

b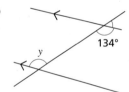

c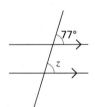

3 Work out the size of each lettered angle, giving reasons for your answers.

a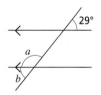

b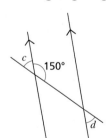

c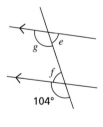

Stretch – can you deepen your learning?

1 The diagram shows two parallel line segments, AB and DE, connected by diagonals which intersect at C.

Angle ABC = 62° and angle CED = 85°

Work out the size of:

a angle BAC   **b** angle BCA

c angle ECD   **d** angle CDE.

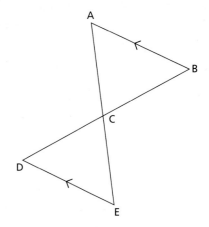

2 Work out the value of x.

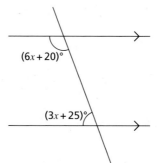

$(6x + 20)°$

$(3x + 25)°$

3 Work out the value of x.

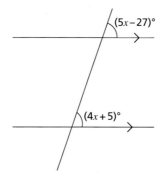

$(5x - 27)°$

$(4x + 5)°$

Are you ready?

1 How many sides does an octagon have?

2 Sketch a pair of parallel lines.

3 Sketch a pair of perpendicular lines.

4 Name the types of quadrilaterals.

a 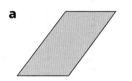 **b** 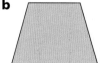 **c** 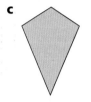 **d**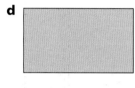

All shapes have their own properties, but there are special quadrilaterals with specific properties. The interior angles will always sum to 360°.

Because co-interior angles add up to 180°, two pairs of angles in a trapezium will add up to 180°.

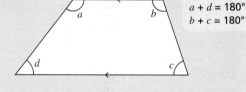

$a + d = 180°$
$b + c = 180°$

In an **isosceles** trapezium, there will also be two pairs of equal angles.

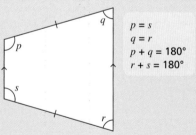

$p = s$
$q = r$
$p + q = 180°$
$r + s = 180°$

In both a parallelogram and a rhombus, **opposite angles** are equal, and **adjacent angles** add up to 180°.

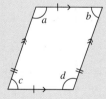

$a + b = 180°$
$b + d = 180°$, etc.
$a = d$
$b = c$

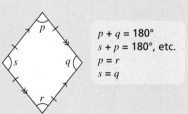

$p + q = 180°$
$s + p = 180°$, etc.
$p = r$
$s = q$

In a kite, one pair of opposite angles are equal.

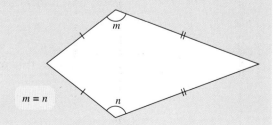

$m = n$

In both a rectangle and a square, opposite and adjacent angles are all equal to 90°.

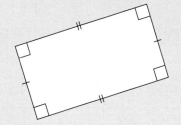 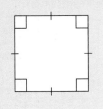

Example 1

Work out the size of angle x.

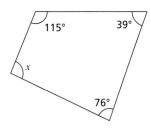

Method

Solution	Commentary
$x + 76° + 39° + 115° = 360°$ $x = 360° - (76° + 39° + 115°)$ $x = 130°$	Angles in any quadrilateral add up to 360°.

Example 2

Work out the size of each lettered angle.

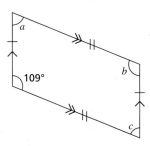

Method

Solution	Commentary
	Angles in any quadrilateral add up to 360°.
$a = 180° - 109°$ $a = 71°$	A parallelogram has two pairs of opposite equal angles and adjacent angles that add up to 180°. Angle a is adjacent to 109°.
$b = 109°$	Angle b is opposite to 109° so is equal in size.
$c = 71°$	Angle c is opposite to angle a so is equal in size.
	You can check the answers: $71° + 71° + 109° + 109° = 360°$

Practice

1. Write down the number of sides each shape has.

    a Triangle   **b** Hexagon   **c** Pentagon   **d** Quadrilateral   **e** Octagon

2. Match each shape to one of the names in the box.

    | Triangle   Octagon   Quadrilateral   Hexagon |

    a 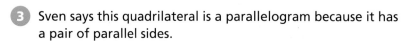   **b**   **c**   **d**

3. Sven says this quadrilateral is a parallelogram because it has a pair of parallel sides.

    Do you agree? Give a reason for your answer.

    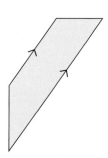

4. Which of the following shapes are pentagons? Give a reason for your answer.

    A   **B**   **C**   **D**   **E**

    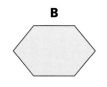 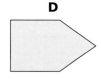

5. Work out the size of each lettered angle.

    a 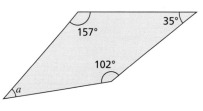   **b**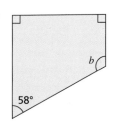

6. Work out the size of each lettered angle.

    a 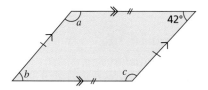   **b**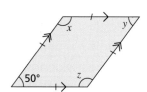

7 Work out the size of each lettered angle.

a

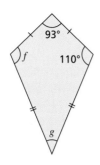

b

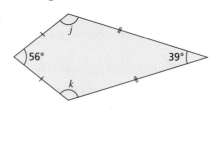

8 Work out the size of each lettered angle.

a

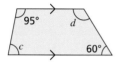

b

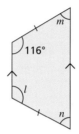

9 Work out the size of each lettered angle.

a

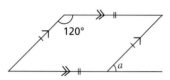

b

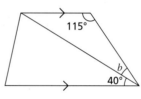

c

d

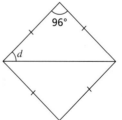

10 ABCD is a square.

Angle BEC = angle AED

Find three other pairs of angles that are equal.

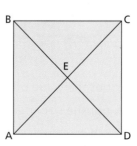

What do you think? 💡

1 Is a square a rectangle?

Consolidate – do you need more?

1 **a** Sketch a hexagon. **b** Sketch a pentagon.

2 **a** Draw a parallelogram with angles of 74° and 106°.

b Draw a kite with the equal angles being 82°.

3 Work out the size of each lettered angle.

a

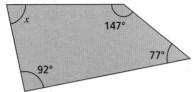

b

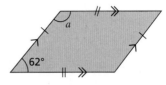

c

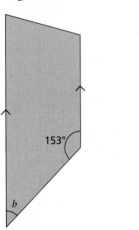

d

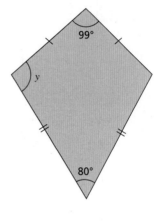

Stretch – can you deepen your learning?

1 Work out the value of a.

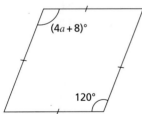

2 **a** Work out the value of y.

b Work out the size of angle PQR.

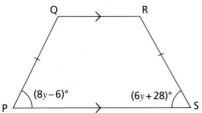

Are you ready? (A)

1 What is the sum of the angles in a triangle?

2 What is the sum of the angles in a quadrilateral?

3 State the number of sides of a:

   a pentagon   **b** octagon   **c** nonagon.

A **polygon** is a closed 2D shape with straight sides.

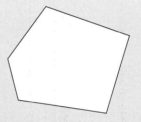

A **regular polygon** is a polygon whose sides are all equal in length and whose angles are all equal in size.

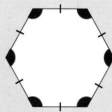

Interior angles are on the inside of the shape.

Exterior angles are between the side of a shape and a line extended from the adjacent side. They are formed by extending the sides of the polygon at each vertex.

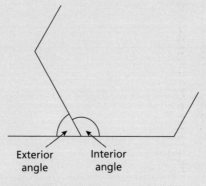

Exterior angle   Interior angle

Interior and exterior angles of a polygon are adjacent on a straight line, so they sum to 180°.

Example 1

Work out the size of one angle in a regular pentagon.

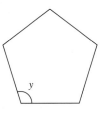

Method

Solution	Commentary
	You can work out the sum of the interior angles by splitting the shape into triangles. Start at one vertex and draw lines to all the other vertices.
	The number of triangles will always be two less than the number of sides.
	A pentagon has five sides so there will be three triangles.
Sum of the interior angles in a pentagon = $(5 - 2) \times 180°$	Sum of the interior angles = $(n - 2) \times 180°$
$= 540°$	
One interior angle in a regular pentagon = $\dfrac{540°}{5}$	'n' stands for the number of sides.
$= 108°$	In a regular polygon, all angles are equal. So, one interior angle in a regular polygon = $\dfrac{\text{sum of the interior angles}}{n}$

Example 2

Work out the size of angle x.

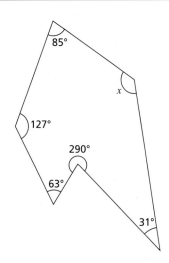

Method

Solution	Commentary
Sum of the interior angles in a hexagon = (6 – 2) × 180° = 720°	This is an irregular hexagon, so the angles won't be of equal size. You can use the formula to work out the sum of the interior angles. Sum of the interior angles = $(n - 2) \times 180°$
$x = 720° - (31° + 290° + 63° + 127° + 85°)$ $x = 124°$	

Practice (A)

1. Copy and complete the table.

Polygon	No. of sides	No. of triangles	Sum of the interior angles
Triangle	3	1	1 × 180 = 180°
Quadrilateral	4	2	2 × 180 = 360°
Pentagon	5	3	3 × 180 = 540°
Hexagon	6		
Heptagon	7		
Octagon	8		
Nonagon	9		
Decagon	10		
Hendecagon	11		
Dodecagon	12		
n-sided polygon	n		

2. If you are trying to work out the sum of its interior angles, which is the correct method for splitting the hexagon into triangles?

Method A

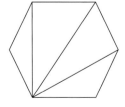

Method B

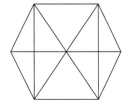

3 Work out the size of each lettered angle.

a 87° 84° 162° 130° *p*

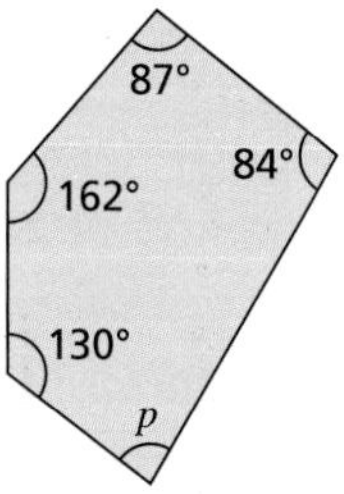

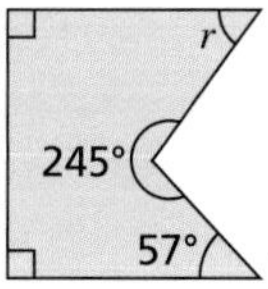

b 113° 104° 127° 78° *q* 100° 99°

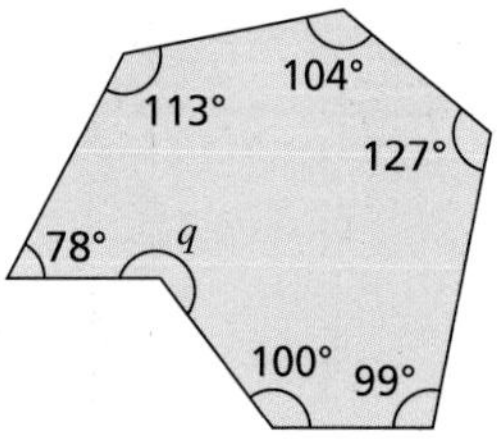

c *r* 245° 57°

d 167° 78° *s* 91° 137° 149°

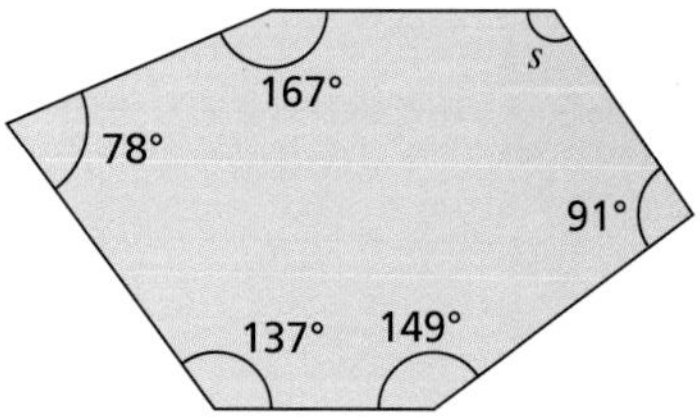

4 Work out the size of one interior angle in these regular polygons. Round your answer to 2 decimal places where appropriate.

a **b** 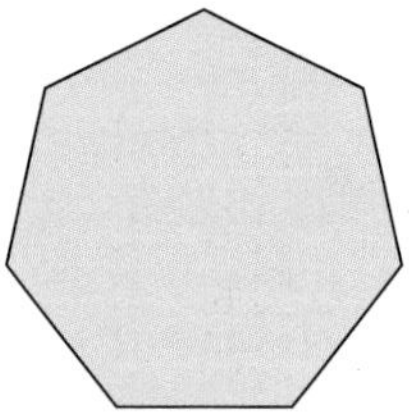 **c** 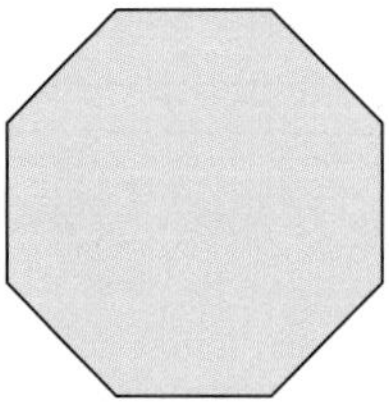 **d**

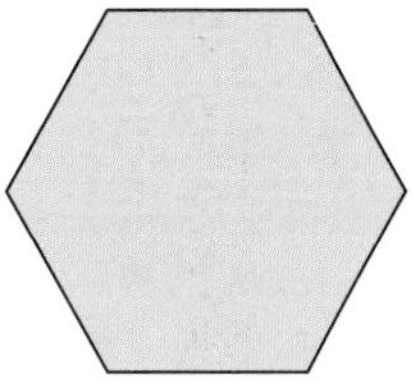

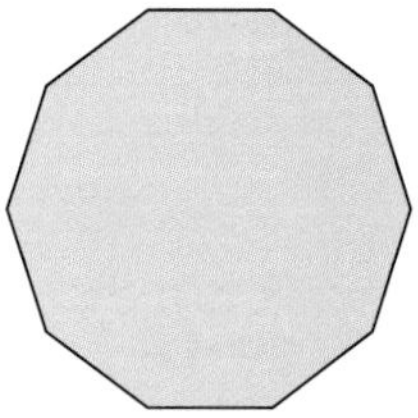

5 Jakub and Kath are trying to work out the sum of the interior angles in a nonagon.

Jakub

9 × 180° = 1620°

Kath

7 × 180° = 1260°

Who do you agree with? Give a reason for your answer.

6 The sum of the interior angles in a polygon is 2340°.

How many sides does it have?

7 The diagram shows a regular pentagon, a square and an equilateral triangle all joined together.

Work out the size of angle x.

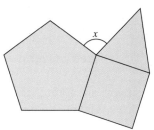

8 The diagram shows a square inside a regular octagon.

Work out the size of angle y.

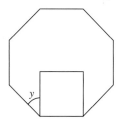

9 The diagram shows a regular pentagon.

Work out the size of angle z.

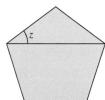

What do you think? (A) 💡

1 Is it possible for a regular polygon to have an interior angle of 100°?

Are you ready? (B)

1 What do angles on a straight line add up to?

2 What do angles at a point add up to?

3 Work out the size of angle y.

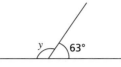

4 Work out the size of angle a.

Example 1

Work out the size of one exterior angle in a regular hexagon.

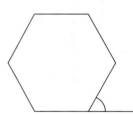

Method

Solution	Commentary
Method A	
Sum of the interior angles in a hexagon = (6 − 2) × 180° = 720°	Sum of the interior angles = $(n - 2) \times 180°$
One interior angle in a regular hexagon = $\dfrac{\text{Sum of the interior angles}}{n}$ = $\dfrac{720°}{6}$ = 120°	
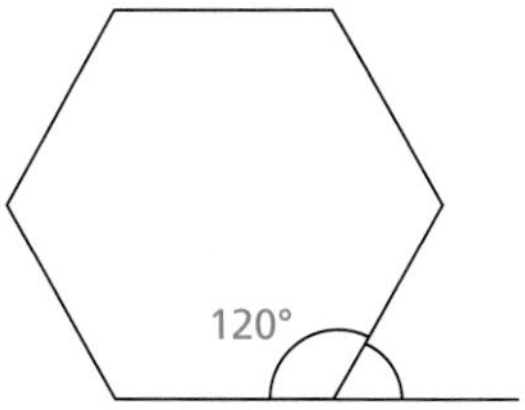 120° Exterior angle = 180° − 120° = 60°	The interior and exterior angles of a polygon are adjacent on a straight line so they sum to 180°. Interior angle + exterior angle = 180° Exterior angle = 180° − interior angle

Method B

One exterior angle in a regular hexagon $= \dfrac{360°}{6}$

$= 60°$

In a regular polygon, all angles are equal. The sum of exterior angles is always 360°.

One exterior angle in a regular polygon $= \dfrac{360°}{n}$

Example 2

Work out the size of angle x.

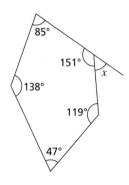

Method

Solution	Commentary
Exterior angle $x = 180° - 151°$	Interior angle + exterior angle = 180°
$x = 29°$	Exterior angle = 180° − interior angle

Practice (B)

1 Copy and complete the table for regular polygons.

Polygon	No. of sides	Sum of the exterior angles	One exterior angle
Triangle	3	360°	360° ÷ 3 = 120°
Quadrilateral	4	360°	
Pentagon	5	360°	
Hexagon	6	360°	
Heptagon	7	360°	
Octagon	8	360°	
Nonagon	9	360°	
Decagon	10	360°	
Hendecagon	11	360°	
Dodecagon	12	360°	
n-sided polygon	n	360°	

② Work out the size of each exterior angle in these regular shapes.

a

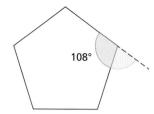

108°

b

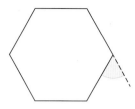

③ Work out the size of each lettered angle.

a

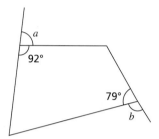

a

92°

79°

b

b

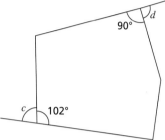

90°

d

c

102°

④ Draw a regular pentagon.

Show that the sum of the exterior angles is 360°.

⑤ Five of the exterior angles on a heptagon are 60°, 42°, 17°, 70° and 89°.

The remaining two exterior angles are equal. Calculate their size.

⑥ Three interior angles in a triangle are 80°, 65° and 35°.

Calculate the size of the exterior angles.

⑦ A regular polygon has an exterior angle of 22.5°.

How many sides does it have?

What do you think? (B) 💡

❶ Is it possible for a regular polygon to have an exterior angle of 85°?

Consolidate – do you need more?

1 Work out the sum of the interior angles in a:

    a hexagon   **b** nonagon   **c** decagon.

2 Work out the size of one interior angle in a:

    a regular quadrilateral   **b** regular octagon   **c** regular dodecagon.

3 Work out the size of one exterior angle in a:

    a regular triangle   **b** regular quadrilateral   **c** regular pentagon.

4 Work out the size of each lettered angle.

a
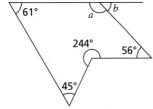

b
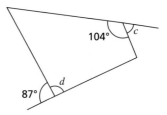

Stretch – can you deepen your learning?

1 The diagram shows part of a regular polygon.

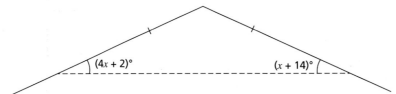

    Calculate how many sides the polygon has.

1 Use the correct word card to describe each angle. (2)

 Acute   Obtuse   Right angle   Reflex

a)    **b)** 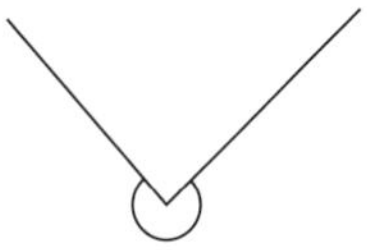   **c)** 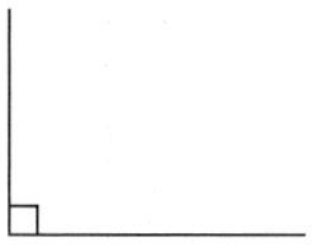   **d)**

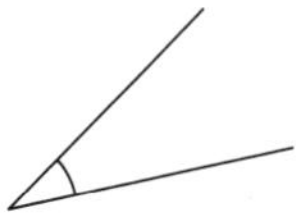

2 Write down the size of angle y. Give a reason for your answer. (2)

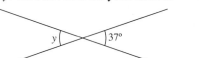

y 37°

3 Work out the size of angle x. Give reasons for your answer. (4)

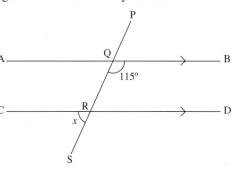

P

A ————— Q ————— B

115°

C ————— R ————— D

x

S

4 a) What type of angle is a? (1)

   b) Work out the size of angle a. (3)

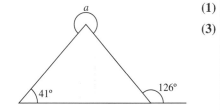

a

41°   126°

5 The diagram shows part of a regular 10-sided polygon.

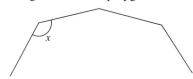

x

Work out the size of angle x. (3)

1–3

3–5

4 Congruence and similarity

In this block, we will cover...

4.1 Congruence

Example 1

Identify any shapes that are congruent to shape

> Congruent means exactly the same size and shape, but not necessarily the same orientation

Method

Solution	C
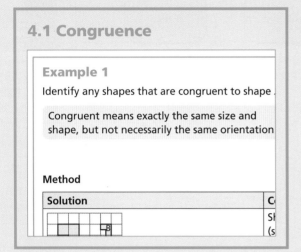	Sh (s

4.2 Similarity

Practice

1. Copy the grid and draw two shapes that a

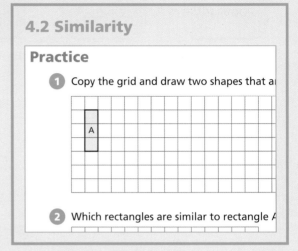

2. Which rectangles are similar to rectangle A

4.3 Congruent triangles

Consolidate – do you need more

1. State the condition which proves that each

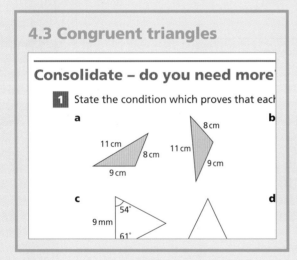

a

b

c

d

4.4 Similar triangles

Stretch – can you deepen your le

1. The ratio of AC : BC is 4 : 1
   a. Calculate the length of EC.
   b. Calculate the length of BD.

> You may need to refer to Pythagoras' theorem (Chapter 8.1).

2. Show that triangles ACE and BCD are simil

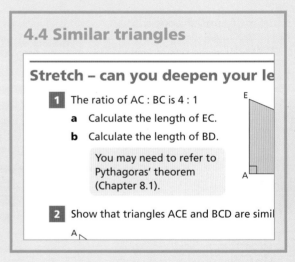

4.1 Congruence

Are you ready?

1 What is the same and what is different about squares A, B and C?

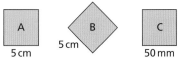

2 Are rectangles X and Y the same or different?

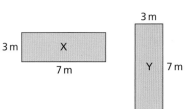

3 If two triangles both have angles of 87° and 64°, will their third angles be the same size? Give a reason for your answer.

Example 1

Identify any shapes that are congruent to shape A.

Congruent means exactly the same size and shape, but not necessarily the same orientation.

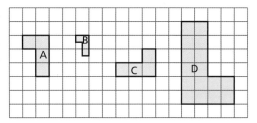

Method

Solution	Commentary
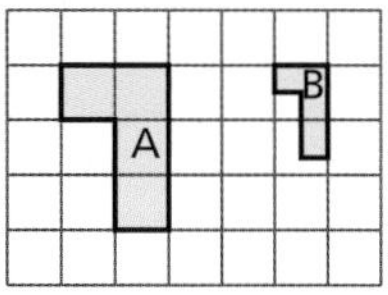	Shape B is a different size to shape A (smaller) so it is not congruent to shape A.
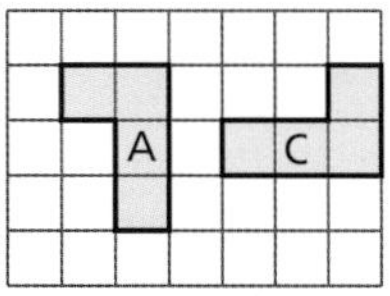	Shape C is exactly the same size as shape A. Even though it has a different orientation (it has been rotated), it is still congruent to shape A.
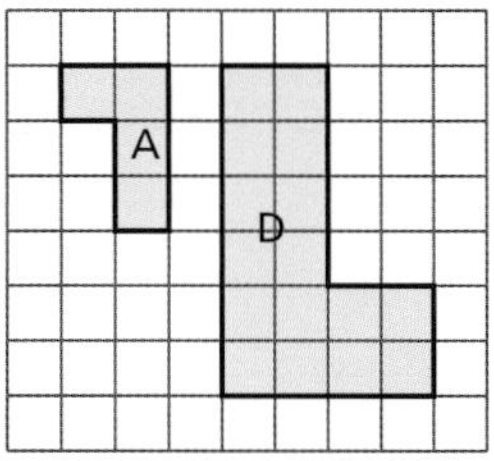	Shape D is larger than shape A so it is not congruent to shape A.
Only shape C is congruent to shape A.	

Example 2

Which shape, A, B or C, is congruent to the triangle shown here?
The side lengths are in arbitrary units.

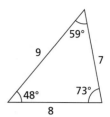

A 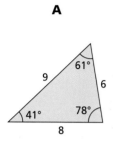   **B** 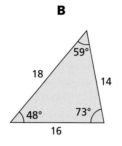   **C**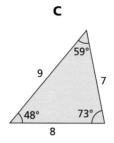

Method

Solution	Commentary
A 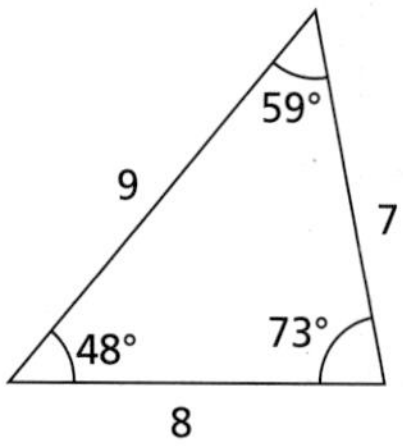 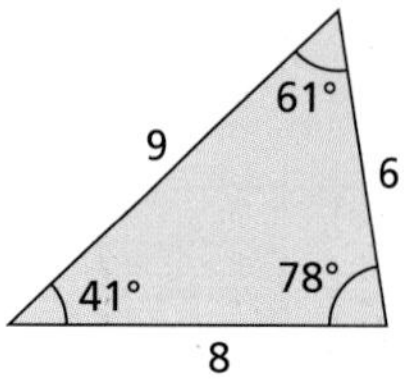 (triangles shown) Shape C is congruent to the original triangle.	Shape A has two sides of the same length but the third is different, so it is not congruent to the original triangle.
B 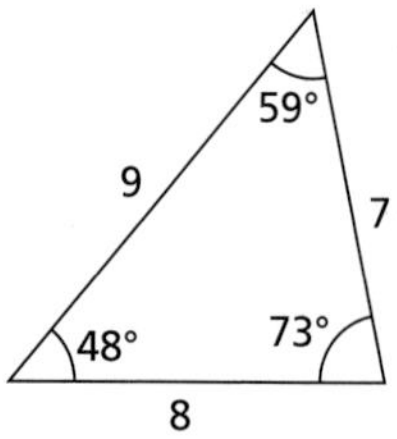 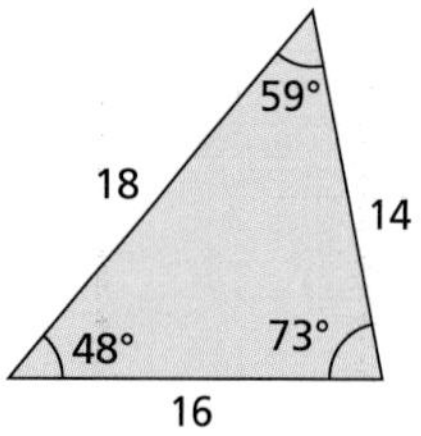 (triangles shown)	Shape B has the same angles but different side lengths, so it is not congruent to the original triangle. It is however **similar** to the original triangle. Two shapes are similar if they have the same angles.
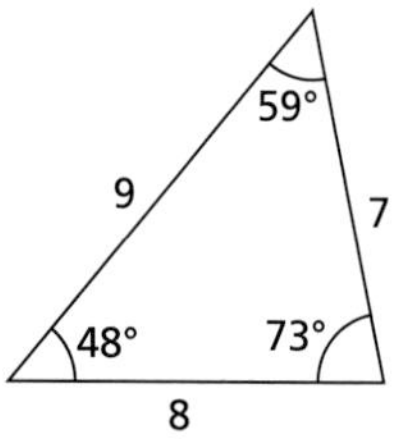 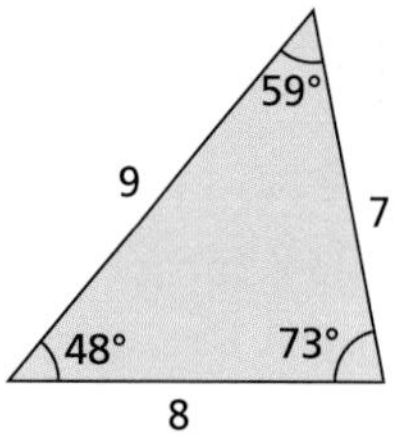 **C** (triangles shown)	Shape C has the same side lengths and same angles, therefore it is congruent to the original triangle. Note that the two triangles would still be congruent even if they were reflected or rotated into different positions.

Practice

1 For each pair of shapes, state whether they are congruent or not.

a

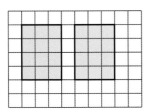

b

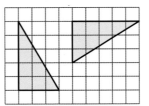

c

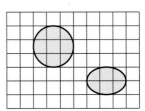

2 Identify any shapes that are congruent to shape A.

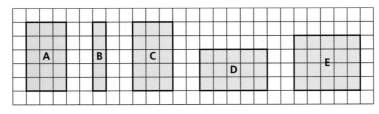

3 Draw a shape that is congruent to shape A.

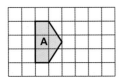

4 Lida says that these two triangles are congruent.

Zach disagrees and says that they might not be congruent.

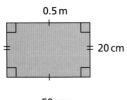

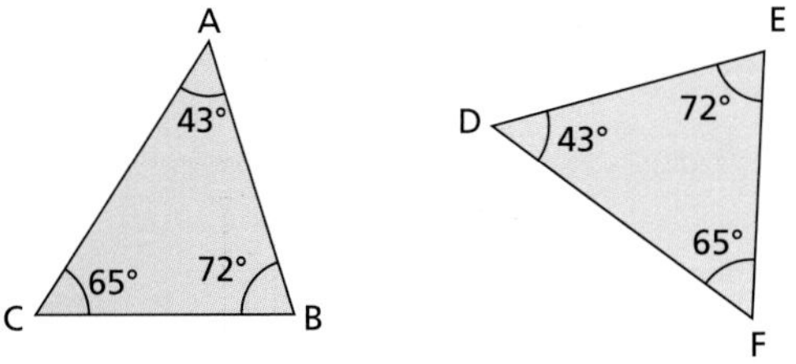

Who do you agree with? Give a reason for your answer.

5 For each pair of shapes, decide if they are congruent or not.

a

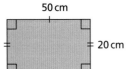

b

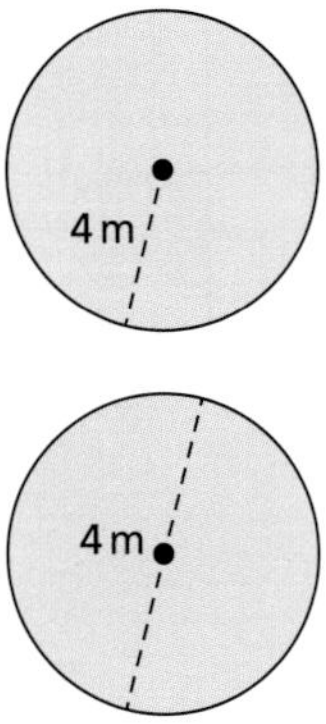

c

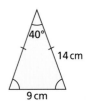

6 Triangles ABC and DEF are congruent.

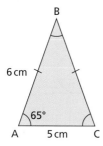 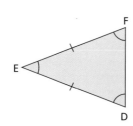

a Write down the size of angle EDF.

b Write down the length of line EF.

c Write down the size of angle DEF.

What do you think? 💭

1 Could these two rectangles be non-congruent?

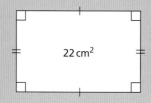 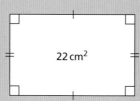

Consolidate – do you need more?

1 For each pair of shapes, state whether they are congruent or not.

a 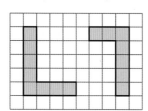   **b** 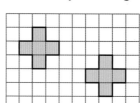   **c**

2 Which of these shapes are congruent?

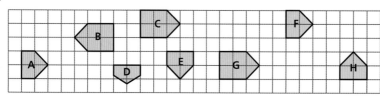

3 For each pair of shapes, state whether they are congruent, not congruent or if there is not enough information to tell.

a

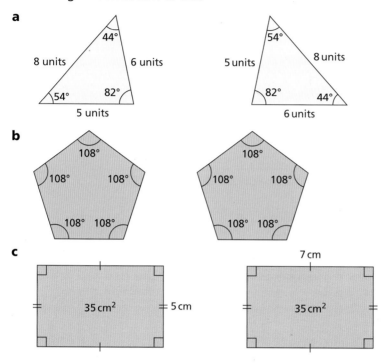

b

c

***

Stretch – can you deepen your learning?

1 Two rectangles, A and B, are congruent.

What is the ratio of the length of rectangle A to the length of rectangle B?

2 An octagon is drawn on isometric paper.

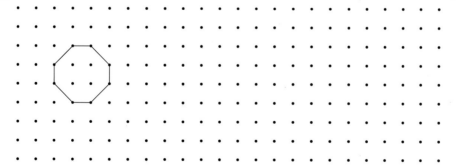

Using isometric paper, draw another three congruent octagons to show that they will not tessellate.

Are you ready?

1 Work out the following calculations.

   a $20 \div 4$ **b** $20 \times \frac{1}{4}$

2 Simplify the following ratios.

   a $10 : 5$ **b** $27 : 18$

3 Which length on rectangle WXYZ corresponds with length AB?

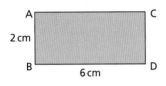 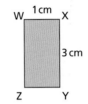

A **scale factor** tells you how much a shape has been enlarged by.

All angles in the rectangles below are 90°.

The angles in a shape don't change when it is enlarged.

The lengths of shape B are three times those of shape A.

You can describe this by saying, "Shape A has been **enlarged by scale factor 3** to give shape B."

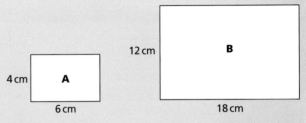

Or

"Shape B has been **enlarged by scale factor** $\frac{1}{3}$ to give shape A."

Notice that the ratio of any pair of corresponding sides in shape A and shape B is $1 : 3$

When two shapes are **similar**, their angles are the same and corresponding lengths are in the same ratio.

Example

Shapes A and B are similar.

a Calculate the lengths labelled x and y.

b Write down the size of angle t.

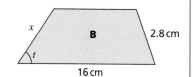

Method

Solution	Commentary
a	16 cm and 4 cm are corresponding sides. Use these to find the scale factor. $\frac{16}{4} = 4$ The scale factor is 4
$2.1 \times 4 = x$ $x = 8.4$ cm	To get from shape A to shape B, multiply by 4
$2.8 \div 4 = y$ $y = 0.7$ cm	To get from shape B to shape A, divide by 4
b $t = 59°$	Corresponding angles are the same size.

Practice

1 Copy the grid and draw two shapes that are similar to rectangle A.

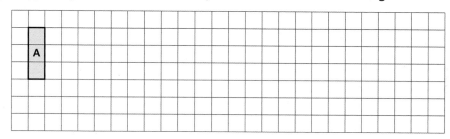

2 Which rectangles are similar to rectangle A?

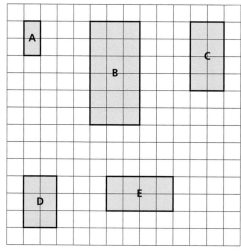

3 **a** These shapes are similar.

7 cm

21 cm

   i Find the ratio of the corresponding lengths.

   ii Find the scale factor used to enlarge the smaller shape to the larger shape.

b These shapes are similar.

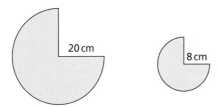

20 cm

8 cm

   i Find the ratio of the corresponding lengths.

   ii Find the scale factor used to enlarge the smaller shape to the larger shape.

4 A parallelogram has a length of 6 cm and a height of 4 cm.

Write down the dimensions of three parallelograms that are similar to this one.

5 State whether these pairs of shapes are similar or not.

For those that are similar:

   i write down the ratio of the corresponding lengths

   ii write down the scale factor used to enlarge the smaller shape to the larger shape.

a

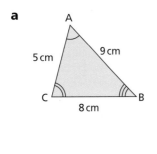

A
5 cm
9 cm
C
8 cm
B

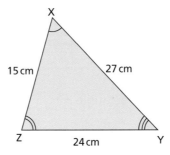

X
15 cm
27 cm
Z
24 cm
Y

b

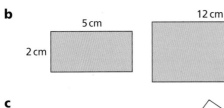

5 cm
2 cm

12 cm
6 cm

c

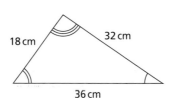

6 cm
9 cm
8 cm

18 cm
32 cm
36 cm

d

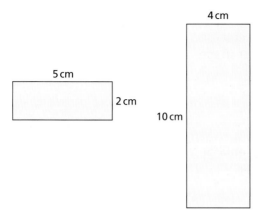

(6) Which triangles are similar to triangle A?

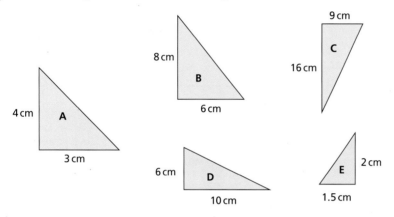

(7) Samira says that the two shapes cannot be similar because they are in different orientations.

Do you agree? Give a reason for your answer.

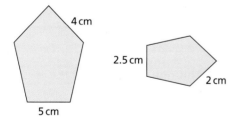

(8) **a** Here is a pair of similar shapes.

    i State the scale factor used to enlarge the smaller shape to the larger shape.

    ii Find the values of a and b.

    iii Find the size of angle x.

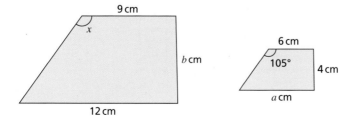

b Here is a pair of similar shapes.

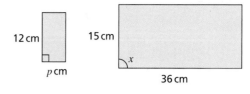

   i State the scale factor used to enlarge the smaller shape to the larger shape.

   ii Find the value of p.

   iii Find the size of angle x.

c Here is a pair of similar shapes.

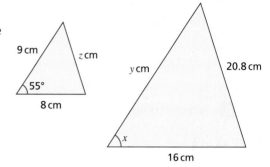

   i State the scale factor used to enlarge the smaller shape to the larger shape.

   ii Find the values of y and z.

   iii Find the size of angle x.

d Here is a pair of similar shapes.

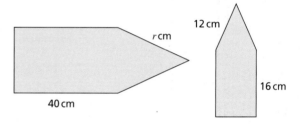

   i State the scale factor used to enlarge the smaller shape to the larger shape.

   ii Find the value of r.

What do you think? 💡

1 When enlarging a photograph, why is it important that the enlargement is similar to the original photograph?

Consolidate – do you need more?

1 Sketch three more rectangles that are similar to this one. State the scale factor you used.

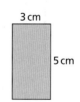

2 Which rectangles are similar to rectangle A?

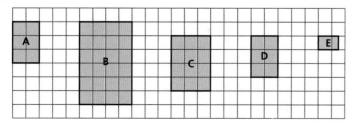

3 **a** Here is a pair of similar shapes.

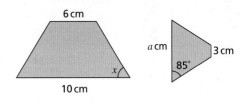

   i State the scale factor used to enlarge the smaller shape to the larger shape.

   ii Find the value of a.

   iii Find the size of angle x.

b Here is a pair of similar shapes.

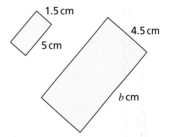

   i State the scale factor used to enlarge the smaller shape to the larger shape.

   ii Find the value of b.

c Here is a pair of similar shapes.

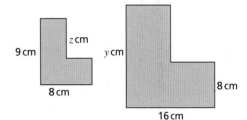

   i State the scale factor used to enlarge the smaller shape to the larger shape.

   ii Find the value of y.

   iii Find the value of z.

Stretch – can you deepen your learning?

1 Rob thinks that when you enlarge a rectangle by scale factor 2, the new shape will have double the perimeter and double the area of the original shape.

Do you agree? Show your answer with some similar rectangles and calculate their lengths, their perimeter and their area.

2 The ratio of the area of the triangle to the area of the rectangle is 1 : 4

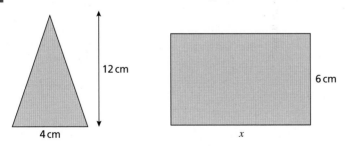

Work out the length, x, of the rectangle.

4.3 Congruent triangles

Are you ready?

1 Classify each triangle as **isosceles**, **equilateral** or **scalene**.

a   b   c   d 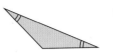   e

2 State whether each pair of triangles is **congruent**, **similar** or **neither**.

a 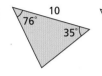   b 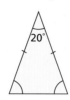   c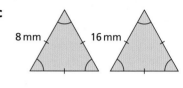

3 **a** Which side on triangle DEF corresponds with AC?

b Which angle in triangle ABC corresponds with angle EFD?

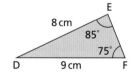

4 What information do you need to construct a triangle?

There are four sets of conditions which determine if two triangles are congruent.

Side, Side, Side (SSS)	Side, Angle, Side (SAS)
Three pairs of corresponding sides are equal.	Two sides and the angle between them in one triangle are equal to the corresponding sides and the angle between them in the other triangle.
Angle, Side, Angle (ASA) or Angle, Angle, Side (AAS)	**Right angle, Hypotenuse, Side (RHS)**
	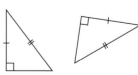
Two angles and one side of a triangle are equal to the corresponding angles and side of the other triangle.	One side and the hypotenuse in a right-angled triangle are equal to one side and the hypotenuse in the other right-angled triangle.

Example 1

Are triangles PQR and XYZ congruent?

Explain your answer.

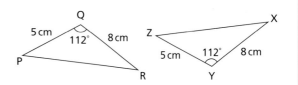

Method

Solution	Commentary
Side PQ corresponds with side YZ and is equal in length.	Given in both triangles are two sides and the angle between them (this is sometimes called the 'included angle').
Side QR corresponds with side XY and is equal in length.	You can use the SAS condition to check if they are congruent.
Angle PQR corresponds with angle XYZ and is equal in size.	
The two triangles are congruent (SAS).	

Example 2

Are triangles DEF and GHI congruent to triangle ABC?

Explain your answer.

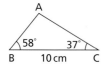 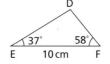 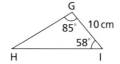

Method

Solution	Commentary
In triangle ABC, the 58° angle (angle ABC) corresponds with the 58° angle in triangle DEF (angle DFE). In triangle ABC, the 37° angle (angle ACB) corresponds with the 37° angle in triangle DEF (angle DEF). In triangle ABC, the 10 cm length (BC) corresponds with the 10 cm length in triangle DEF (EF). Triangles ABC and DEF are congruent (ASA).	Triangles ABC and DEF both have angles of 58° and 37° and a side length of 10 cm. You can use the ASA condition to check if they are congruent.

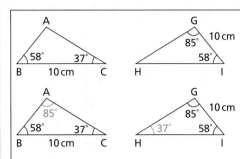

The angles are all equal in size and correspond with each other, but the side length BC does not correspond with side length GI. Therefore, triangles ABC and GHI are **not** congruent.

As shown previously, you can use your knowledge to work out the missing angle in each triangle.

Corresponding sides are opposite the same angle. Here the 10 cm sides are opposite different angles, so they are not corresponding.

Practice

1 Each pair of triangles are congruent.

State which condition for congruence can be used for each pair.

a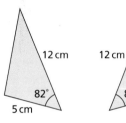

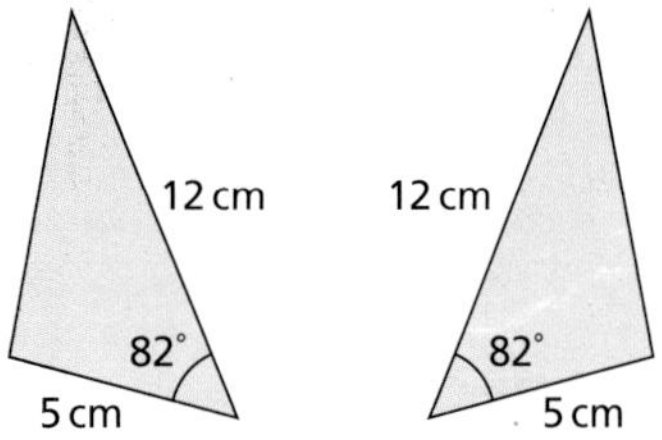

b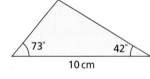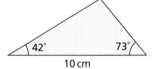

c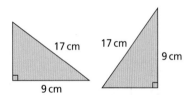

d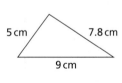

2 For each pair of triangles, state whether they are congruent or **not**. For any pair that are congruent, state the condition for congruence used.

a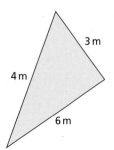

b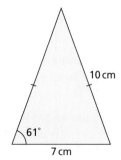

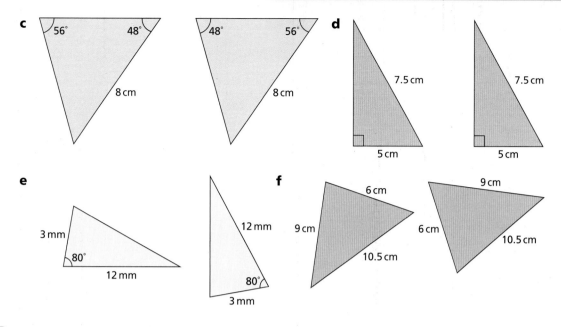

3 Here are triangles A, B and C.

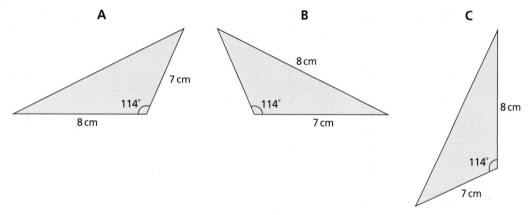

Which two triangles are congruent? State a reason for your answer.

4 Are these two triangles congruent? State a reason for your answer.

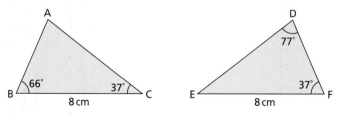

5 In triangle ABC, AB = 8 cm, angle BAC = 45° and angle ABC = 39°.

In triangle DEF, EF = 8 cm, angle DEF = 45° and angle DFE = 39°.

Are the two triangles congruent? If they are, state the condition.

6 ABCD is a rectangle.

Is triangle ADC congruent to triangle ABC?

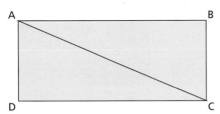

What do you think?

1 Here are two triangles.

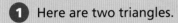

Chloe says, "I only need one more piece of information to prove the triangles are congruent."

Which rule of congruence is Chloe going to use?

Is there more than one rule she could use?

Consolidate – do you need more?

1 State the condition which proves that each pair of triangles are congruent.

a

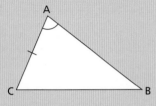

b

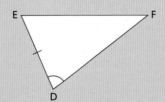

c

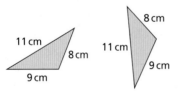

d

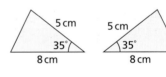

e

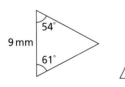

f

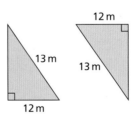

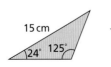

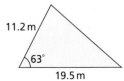

g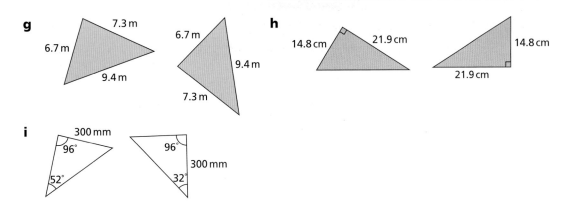

i

2 For each pair of triangles, state whether they are congruent or not. For any pair that are congruent, state the condition for congruence used.

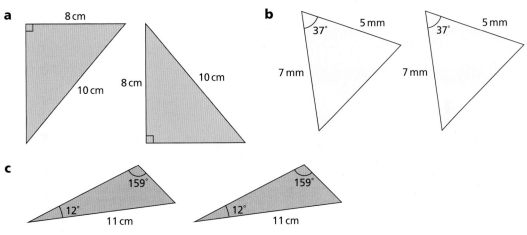

a

b

c

Stretch – can you deepen your learning?

1 The two triangles are congruent.

Work out the values of x and y.

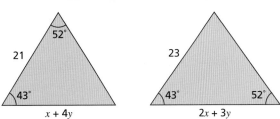

2 AE and CD are parallel.

Prove that the triangles ABE and BCD are congruent.

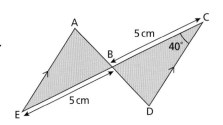

3 ABCD and EFGH are both squares.

Each vertex of EFGH touches the perimeter of ABCD.

Prove that the triangles formed are congruent.

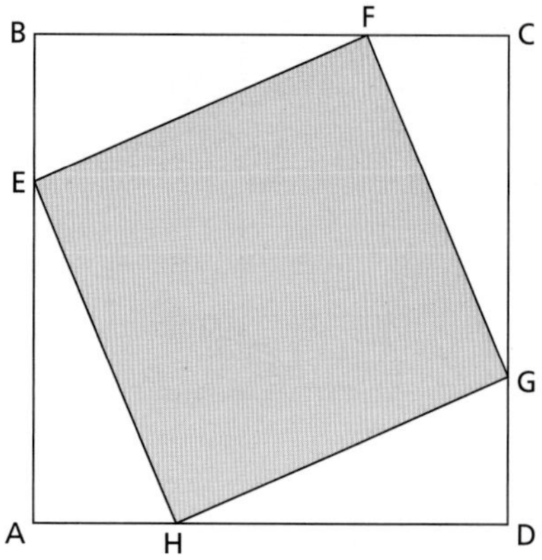

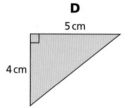

4 Which two of these triangles are congruent?

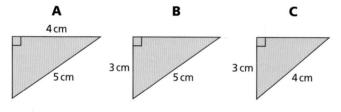

A
4 cm
5 cm

B
3 cm
5 cm

C
3 cm
4 cm

D
5 cm
4 cm

4.4 Similar triangles

Are you ready?

1 Are these two rectangles similar?

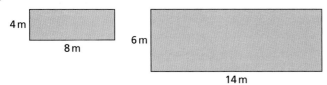

4 m

8 m

6 m

14 m

2 Work out the values of a and b in this pair of similar pentagons.

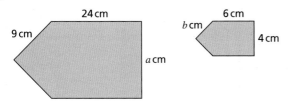

24 cm

9 cm

a cm

b cm

6 cm

4 cm

3 Triangle ABC is similar to triangle FGH.

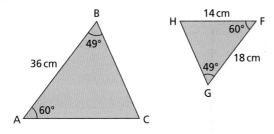

B

49°

36 cm

60°

A

C

H

14 cm

60°

F

49°

18 cm

G

a Which length in triangle FGH corresponds to AB?

b Which angle in triangle FGH corresponds to angle ABC?

c Calculate the scale factor of enlargement from triangle ABC to FGH.

Example 1

Triangles ADC and BCE are similar.

Work out the length AB.

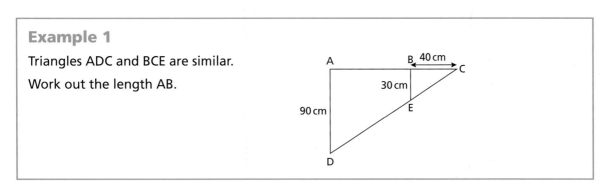

A

B

40 cm

C

30 cm

90 cm

E

D

Method

Solution	Commentary
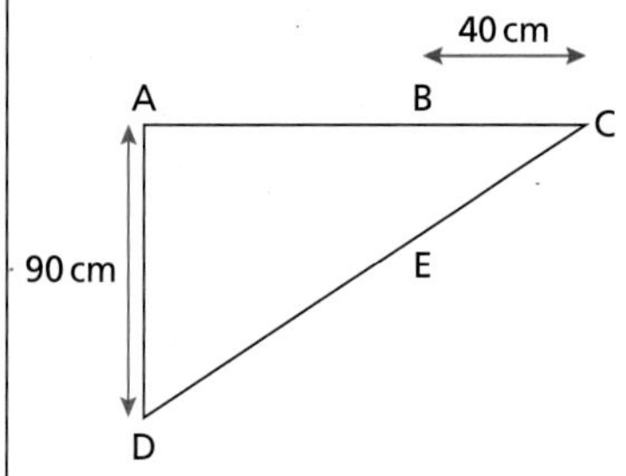 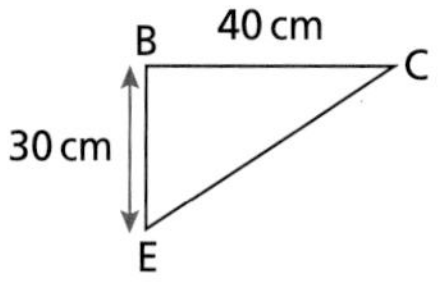 40 cm A B C 90 cm E D B 40 cm C 30 cm E	Splitting the shape into the two separate triangles makes it clearer to see where the dimensions for each side are.
Scale factor = $\dfrac{90}{30}$ = 3	Sides AD and BE are corresponding so you can calculate the scale factor used.
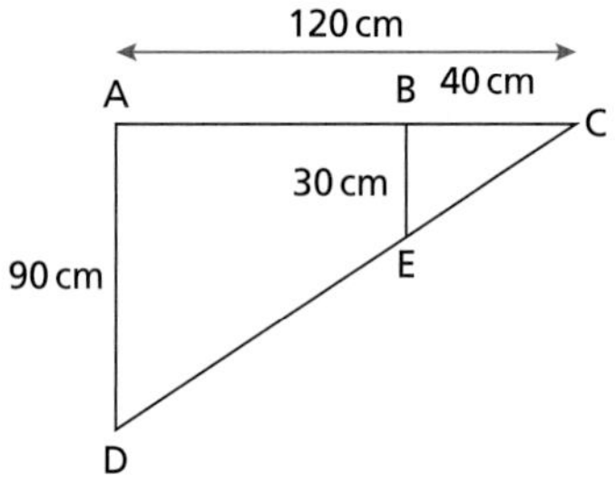 120 cm A B 40 cm C 30 cm E 90 cm D AC = BC × 3 AC = 40 × 3 = 120 cm AB = AC − BC AB = 120 cm − 40 cm AB = 80 cm	Sides AC and BC are corresponding.

Example 2

Calculate the value of x, giving reasons for your answer.

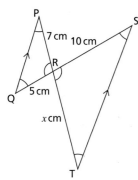

Method

Solution		Commentary
∠QPR = ∠RTS Alternate angles are equal. ∠PQR = ∠RST Alternate angles are equal. ∠PRQ = ∠TRS Vertically opposite angles are equal. Scale factor = $\dfrac{10}{5}$ = 2	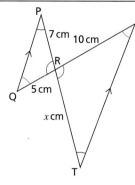	You can use your knowledge of angles in parallel lines to help determine which pairs of angles are equal. All the angles are equal, so the two triangles are similar. Sides RQ and RS are corresponding so you can calculate the scale factor used.
  RT = PR × 2 RT = 7 × 2 = 14 cm x = 14	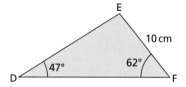	Sides PR and RT are corresponding.

Practice

1 Triangles ABC and DEF are similar.

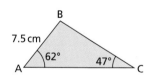

Copy and complete the table.

Side/angle in ABC	Corresponding side/angle in DEF
AB	
BC	
AC	
∠ABC	
∠ACB	
∠BAC	

2   These two triangles are similar.

Find the lengths of AC and QR.

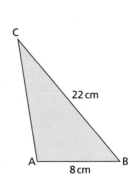 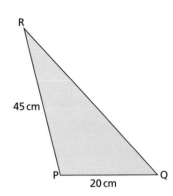

3   These two triangles are similar.

Find the values of a and b.

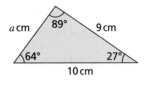 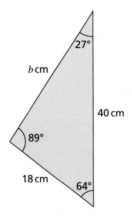

4   Triangles PQR and XYZ are similar.

Emily and Amir are working out
the length of PQ.

Emily says it is 12 cm.

Amir says it is 3 cm.

Who is correct? What mistake was made?

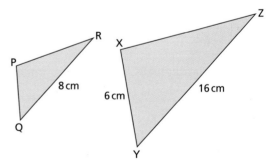

5   Calculate the value of y.

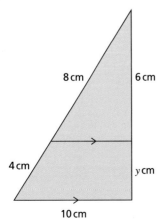

Are you ready? (A)

1 Which of these diagrams show a correct line of symmetry?

A 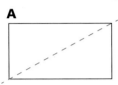 **B**   **C**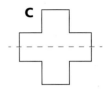

2 Which one of shapes A, B, C and D is congruent to the image shown on the right?

> Remember that 'congruent' means exactly the same size and shape.

A   **B** 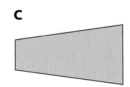 **C** **D**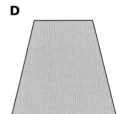

The diagram shows a **reflection**. You have already studied reflections in Key Stages 2 and 3.

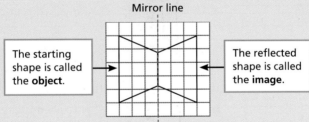

Mirror line

The starting shape is called the **object**.

The reflected shape is called the **image**.

Example

Reflect each shape in the given mirror line.

a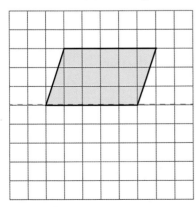

b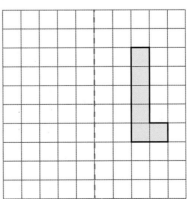

Method

Solution	Commentary
a (grid diagram with parallelogram reflected across horizontal mirror line, labelled 3, 3, 3, 3)	Count the squares vertically from each vertex to the mirror line and then count the same number of squares on the other side of the mirror line to find its image. Join the new vertices to draw the image of the shape. Two of the vertices of the parallelogram are on the mirror line. The other two are three squares away.
b (grid diagram with hexagon shapes and mirror line, labelled 2, 2, 4, 4)	The hexagon is positioned two squares away from the mirror line. Therefore, the reflected image must also be two squares away from the mirror line, on the other side. A reflected image is always congruent to the original object.

Practice (A)

1 Copy each shape onto squared paper and then draw the reflection.

   a 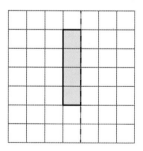   **b** 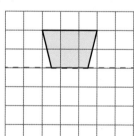   **c**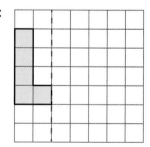

2 Copy each shape onto squared paper and then draw the reflection.

   a 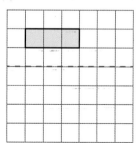   **b** 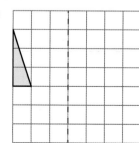   **c**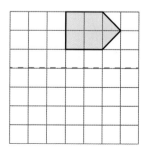

3 **a** Identify the correct reflection(s).

A 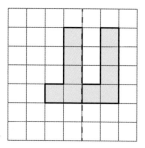   B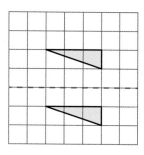

C 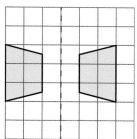   D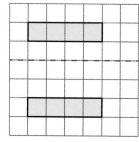

b What mistakes were made for the incorrect reflections?

4 Copy the diagrams onto squared paper and then draw the position of the mirror line for each of them.

a 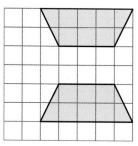   **b**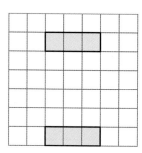

c 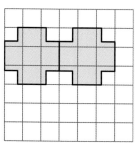   **d**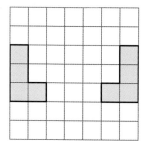

Are you ready? (B)

1 Write down the coordinates of A, B, C and D.

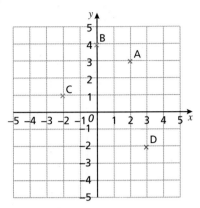

2 Some lines are drawn on the grid.

a Which lines are vertical?

b Which line has equation $y = 2$?

c Which line has equation $x = 2$?

d Write the equation of line D.

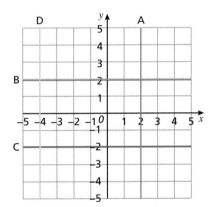

Example 1

a Reflect the shape in the line $y = -1$

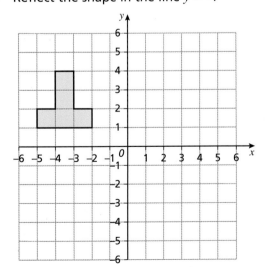

b Reflect the shape in the y-axis.

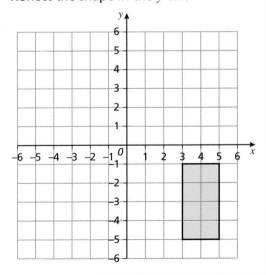

Method

Solution	Commentary
a 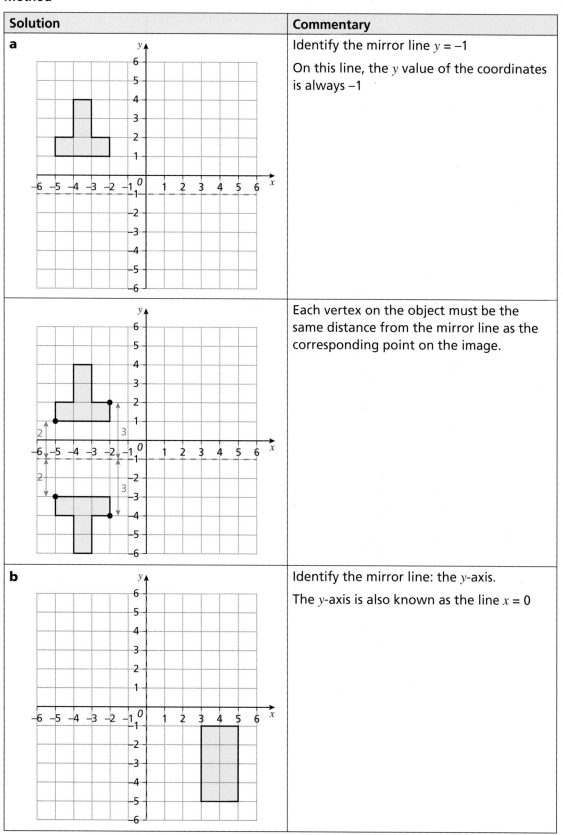	Identify the mirror line $y = -1$ On this line, the y value of the coordinates is always −1
	Each vertex on the object must be the same distance from the mirror line as the corresponding point on the image.
b	Identify the mirror line: the y-axis. The y-axis is also known as the line $x = 0$

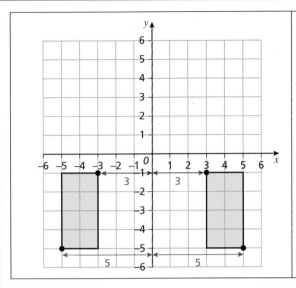

Each vertex on the object must be the same distance from the mirror line as the corresponding point on the image.

Practice (B)

1 Copy each shape onto squared paper and then draw the reflection.

a Reflect the shape in the line $x = -2$

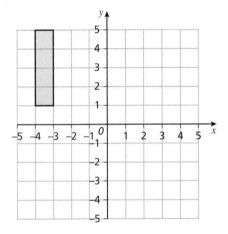

b Reflect the shape in the line $y = 1$

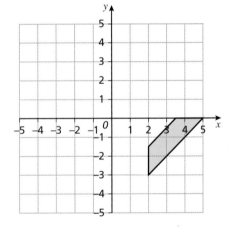

c Reflect the shape in the x-axis.

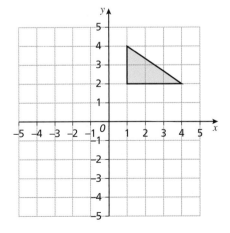

2 Which reflection, A, B or C, has been carried out correctly for the given instruction?

A: Reflect the shape in $x = -1$

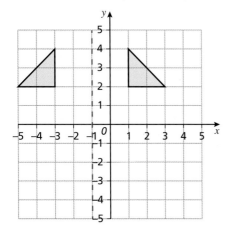

B: Reflect the shape in $y = 1$

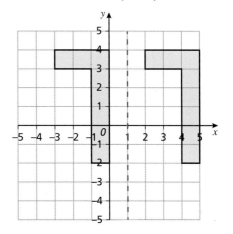

C: Reflect the shape in $x = 0$

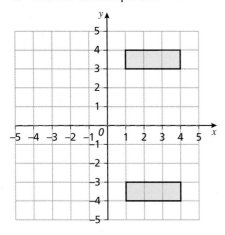

3 What mistakes were made for the incorrect reflections in question 2?

4 Identify the position of the mirror line.

a

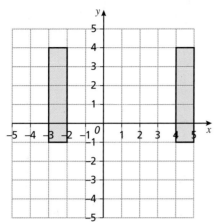

b

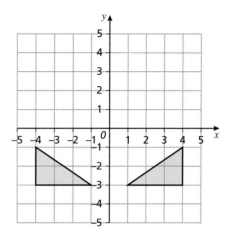

c

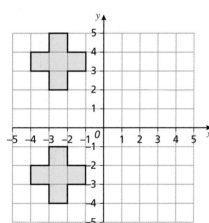

What do you think? (B) 🌑

1 Reflect the triangle in the mirror line.

Why is this reflection different to the others you have completed?

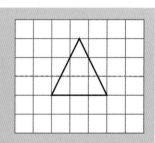

Are you ready? (C)

1 Copy and complete the table of values for the line $y = x$.

x	1	2	3	4	5
y					

2 Which of these points lie on the line $y = x$?

(3, 3)   (5, –5)   (–1, 1)   (3, 4)   (–6, –6)   (1.5, 1.5)

3 Which of these points lie on the line $y = -x$?

(2, 2)   (7, –7)   (1, –1)   (5, 0)   (4.5, –4.5)

Example

Reflect the shape in the line $y = x$.

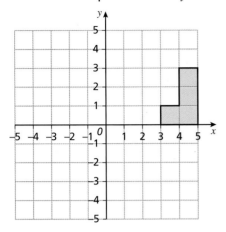

Method

Solution	Commentary
Method A 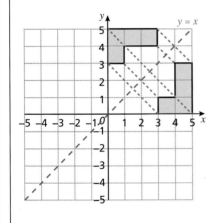	The line $y = x$ is a diagonal line that goes through (0, 0), (1, 1), (2, 2), and so on. To reflect the shape, count from each vertex to the mirror line and then count the same distance on the other side of the mirror line. Because the mirror line is diagonal, you should count diagonally through the squares. For example, from (3, 0) to the mirror line is one-and-a-half diagonals of the squares. The diagonal lines must be perpendicular to the mirror line.
Method B 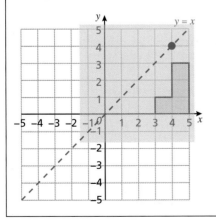	Draw a dot on the mirror line. Place tracing paper on your diagram and trace the mirror line, the dot and the shape.

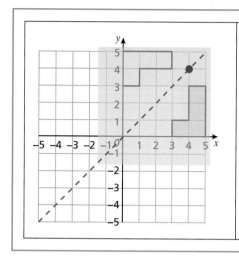

Flip the tracing paper over and line up the mirror line and the dot. The tracing paper will show you where to draw the reflection.

Practice (C)

1 Copy each shape onto squared paper and then draw the reflection.

a 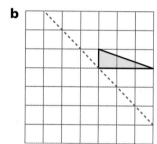   **b** 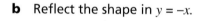   **c**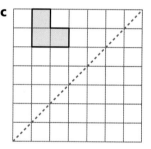

2 Copy each shape onto squared paper and then draw the reflection.

    a   Reflect the shape in $y = x$.   **b**   Reflect the shape in $y = -x$.

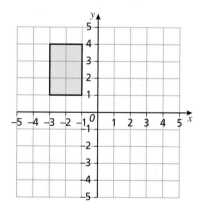   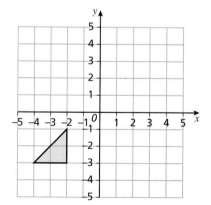

3 Zach has tried to reflect shape A in the given mirror line.

   a Explain the mistake Zach has made.

   b Draw the correct reflection.

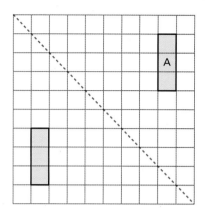

What do you think? (C)

1 Emily says, "If I reflect the square in the line, it won't move."

Do you agree with Emily? Explain your reasons.

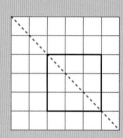

Consolidate – do you need more?

1 Copy each shape onto squared paper and then draw the reflection.

a

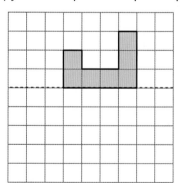

b

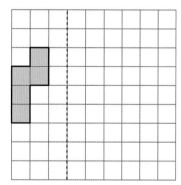

c

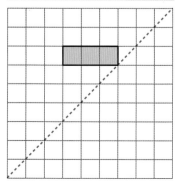

2 Copy each shape onto squared paper and then draw the reflection.

a Reflect the shape in $x = -1$

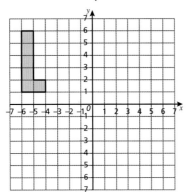

b Reflect the shape in $y = -2$

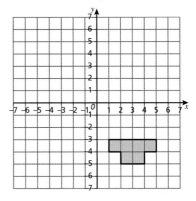

c Reflect the shape in $y = x$.

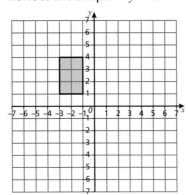

3 Identify the position of the mirror line.

a

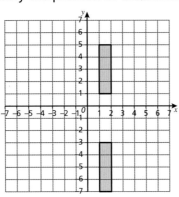

b

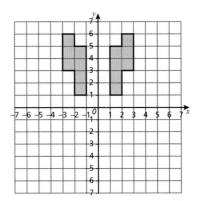

c

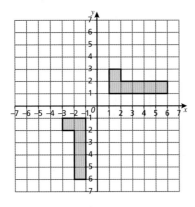

Stretch – can you deepen your learning?

1 Huda creates an isosceles trapezium on the grid.

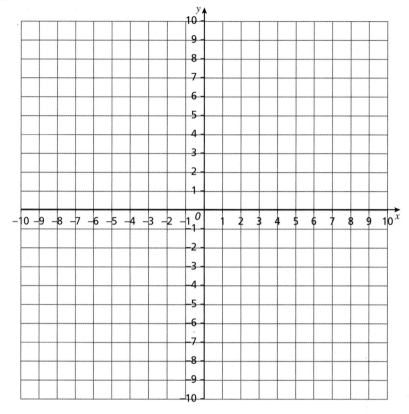

Three of the coordinates are (4, 10), (7, 10) and (8, 6).

a What is the fourth coordinate?

b If Huda reflects the shape in the line $y = 4$, what will the coordinates of the new shape be?

5.2 Rotation

White Rose MATHS

Are you ready?

1 Write down the coordinates of points A, B, C and D.

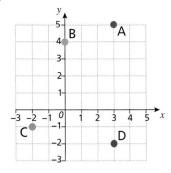

2 Draw a shape congruent to the rectangle shown.

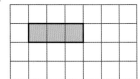

3 Write **anticlockwise** or **clockwise** to describe each turn.

a

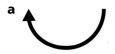

b

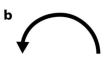

4 How many degrees are in a:

a quarter turn **b** half turn **c** full turn?

Rotation is the act of turning a shape around a fixed point called the **centre of rotation**.

Consider the hands on a clock. As time moves on, the hands rotate clockwise about the centre of the clock. Note that the opposite direction is called 'anticlockwise'.

The amount of rotation is usually specified by an angle.

Consider a compass. To move from North to East, the compass needle needs to rotate clockwise by 90°, or a right angle. A full turn would be a rotation through four right angles.

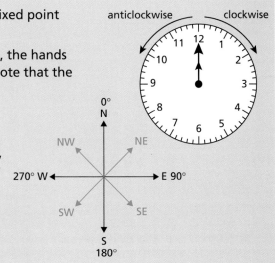

Example 1

Rotate the shape 270° clockwise about the centre of rotation marked.

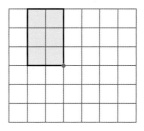

Method

Solution	Commentary
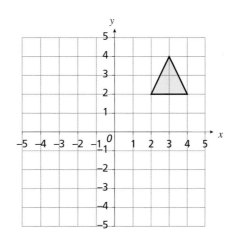	270° is equivalent to a three-quarter turn.
	The letters show how each vertex has been rotated. The vertices in black are for the original object, and the vertices in red are for the image.
	Note that the vertex labelled C does not move because this coincides with the centre of rotation.

Example 2

Rotate the shape 90° clockwise about the origin.

Method

Solution	Commentary
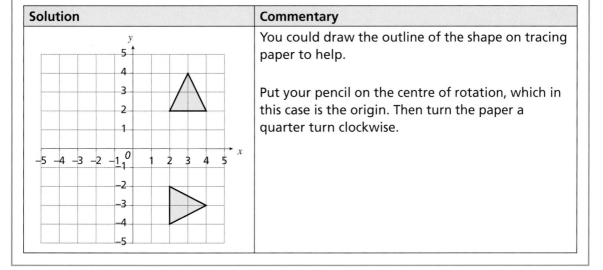	You could draw the outline of the shape on tracing paper to help.
	Put your pencil on the centre of rotation, which in this case is the origin. Then turn the paper a quarter turn clockwise.

Example 3

Describe fully the transformation from shape A to B.

A transformation of a shape is a geometrical change that is made to it.

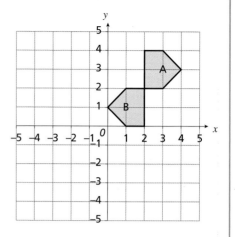

Method

Solution	Commentary
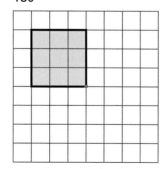 Rotation of 180° about the point (2, 2).	First, identify the centre of rotation. You may wish to use tracing paper to help you with this. Here it is (2, 2). Then identify how much the shape has been rotated by. Here it is 180°. The direction doesn't need to be stated as clockwise and anticlockwise would give the same answer for 180°.

Practice

1 Copy each grid and rotate each shape through the given angle using the marked point as the centre of rotation.

a 180°

b 90° clockwise

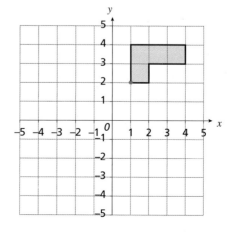

c 270° anticlockwise

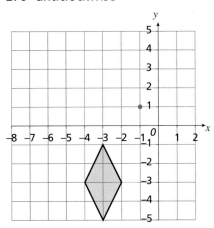

2 Copy each grid and rotate each shape through the given angle and the stated centre of rotation.

a 270° clockwise about the point (2, 0)   **b** 180° about the point (1, –1)

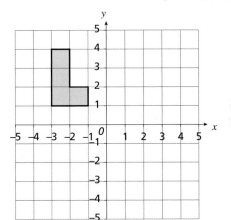   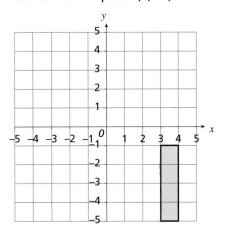

c 90° clockwise about the origin

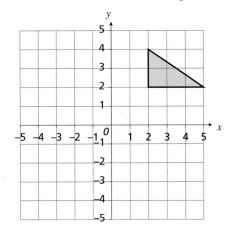

3 Which diagram, A, B or C, shows the correct rotation of rectangle A by 90° clockwise about the point P?

A   **B**   **C**

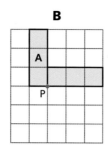
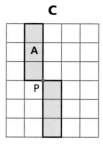

4 Describe fully the transformation that maps:

    a   shape A onto shape A′   **b**   shape B onto shape B′.

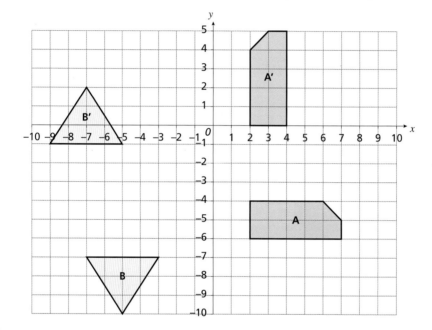

What do you think?

1 Which rotation is the same as 90° clockwise?

Consolidate – do you need more?

1 Rotate the shape 180° about the point given.

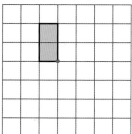

2 Rotate the shape 90° anticlockwise about the origin.

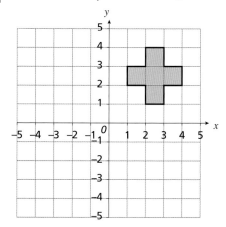

3 Rotate the shape 270° clockwise about the origin.

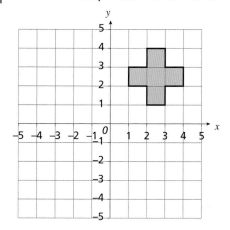

4 Compare your answers to questions 2 and 3.

5 Rotate the shape 180° about the point (−3, 1).

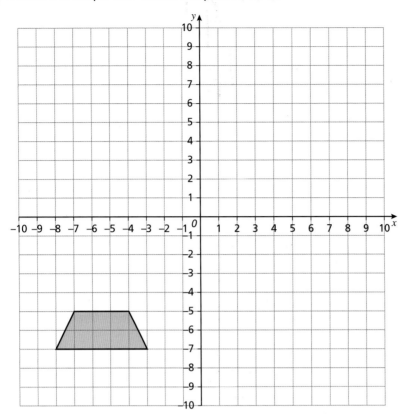

6 Describe fully the transformations from shape A to shape B.

a

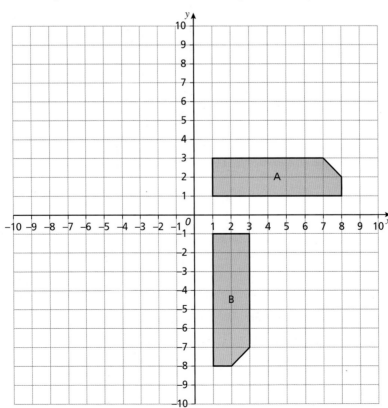

b

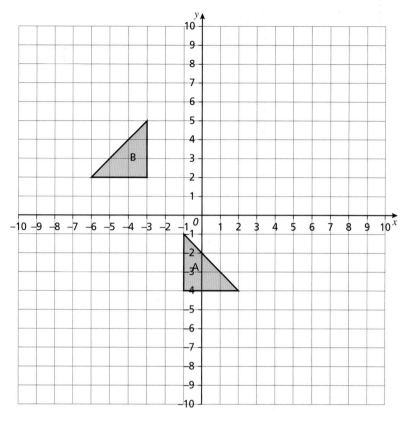

Stretch – can you deepen your learning?

1 Copy the grid.

a Rotate shape A 90° clockwise, using the origin as the centre of rotation.

Label this shape B.

b Rotate shape B half a turn, using the origin as the centre of rotation.

Label this shape C.

c Describe fully the single transformation that maps shape A onto shape C.

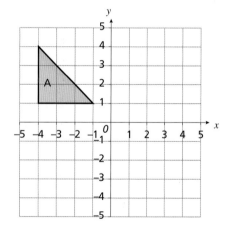

2 Rectangle A has vertices at (–8, –3), (–6, –3), (–8, –7) and (–6, –7). It is rotated 90° clockwise about (–2, –2) to give rectangle B.

a Find the coordinates of the vertices of shape B.

b Describe fully the single transformation that maps rectangle B onto rectangle A.

Are you ready?

1 Write down the coordinates of points A, B, C and D.

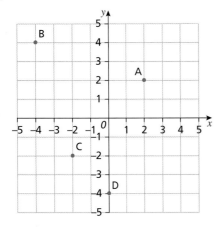

2 Look at the diagram in question 1.

What are the new coordinates of point D when moved 2 squares right and 1 square down?

3 Look again at the diagram in question 1.

Describe in words how to get from:

a point A to B **b** point B to A **c** point C to D.

A **translation** is the movement of a shape in a horizontal and/or vertical direction. The shape does not change in size.

A **column vector** is used for the notation.

$\begin{pmatrix} \text{horizontal} \\ \text{vertical} \end{pmatrix}$ $\begin{pmatrix} + \text{ right} / - \text{ left} \\ + \text{ up} / - \text{ down} \end{pmatrix}$

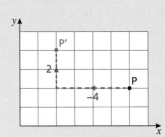

If a point has been moved 4 squares left and 2 squares up, you would write $\begin{pmatrix} -4 \\ 2 \end{pmatrix}$.

Example 1

Translate shape A by vector $\begin{pmatrix} -3 \\ -2 \end{pmatrix}$.

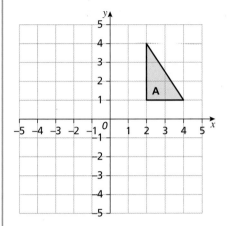

Method

Solution	Commentary
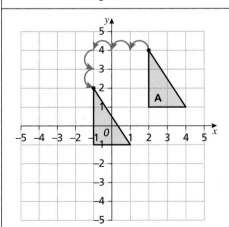	−3 in the vector $\begin{pmatrix} -3 \\ -2 \end{pmatrix}$ means 3 squares to the left.
	−2 in the vector $\begin{pmatrix} -3 \\ -2 \end{pmatrix}$ means 2 squares down.
	Start with one vertex and count 3 squares left to the new horizontal position, then 2 squares down to the new vertical position.
	Continue this method for the other vertices until the new shape is formed.
	Remember that the shape stays congruent – this means it is exactly the same size.
	The shape will also not change orientation.

Example 2

Describe fully the transformation from shape A to B.

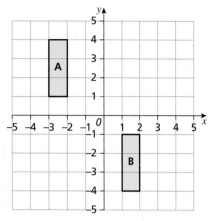

Method

Solution	Commentary
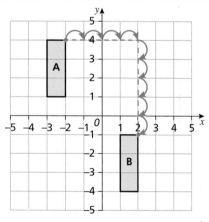	Start with one vertex on shape A and find the corresponding vertex on shape B.
Shape A has been translated by $\begin{pmatrix} 4 \\ -5 \end{pmatrix}$.	Count the squares for the horizontal movement. For this question, it is 4 squares to the right so the top number in the column vector will be 4 Then count the squares for the vertical movement. For this question, it is 5 squares downwards so the bottom number in the column vector will be −5

Practice

1 Which description is accurately represented by the column vector $\begin{pmatrix} -5 \\ 2 \end{pmatrix}$?

    A   5 squares left, 2 squares down

    B   5 squares left, 2 squares up

    C   5 squares right, 2 squares down

    D   5 squares right, 2 squares up

2 Copy the grids and translate each shape by the given column vector.

a $\begin{pmatrix} 3 \\ 2 \end{pmatrix}$

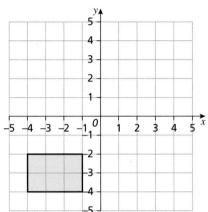

b $\begin{pmatrix} -4 \\ 1 \end{pmatrix}$

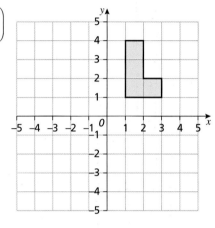

c $\begin{pmatrix} 0 \\ 5 \end{pmatrix}$

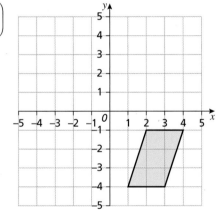

3 Describe fully the transformations from shape A to B.

a

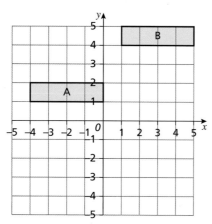

b

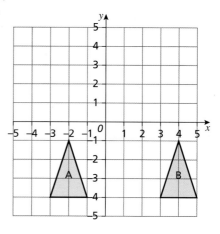

c

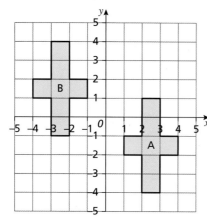

4 Shape A is translated by the vector $\begin{pmatrix} 4 \\ -3 \end{pmatrix}$ to shape B.

Shape B is translated by the vector $\begin{pmatrix} -2 \\ 1 \end{pmatrix}$ to shape C.

Describe the transformation from shape A to shape C.

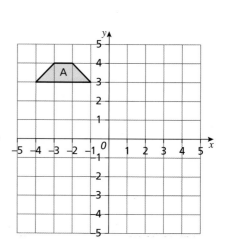

5 Junaid says that the translation from

shape A to B is $\begin{pmatrix} 5 \\ 5 \end{pmatrix}$.

Tiff says that the translation from

shape A to B is $\begin{pmatrix} -5 \\ 5 \end{pmatrix}$.

What mistakes have they made?

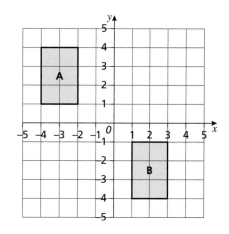

6 Which shapes are translations of each other?

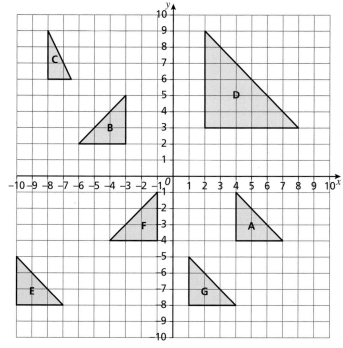

Can you spot any other transformations?

What do you think? 💭

1 Can you tell from the information given whether the transformation from shape A to shape B is a reflection, rotation or translation?

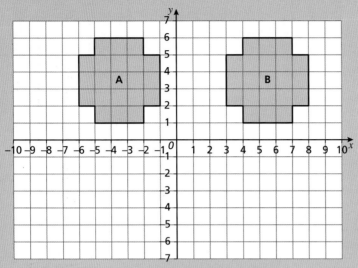

Consolidate – do you need more?

1 Copy the grids and translate each shape by the given column vector.

a $\begin{pmatrix} 6 \\ 1 \end{pmatrix}$

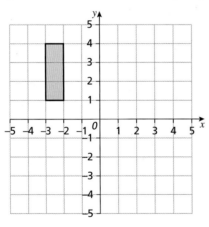

b $\begin{pmatrix} -2 \\ 0 \end{pmatrix}$

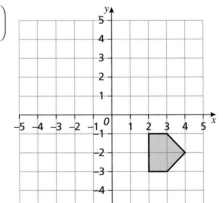

c $\begin{pmatrix} -4 \\ -5 \end{pmatrix}$

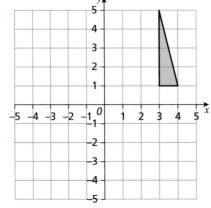

2 Describe fully the transformations from shape A to B.

a

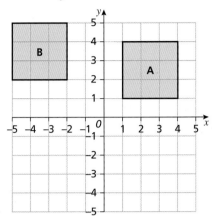

b

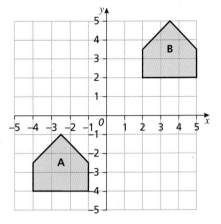

c

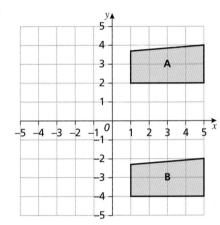

Stretch – can you deepen your learning?

1 The triangle has been translated by the column vector $\begin{pmatrix} 7 \\ 10 \end{pmatrix}$.

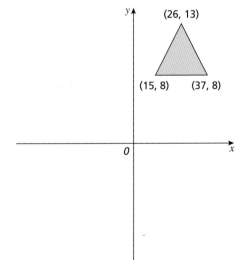

What were the coordinates of each vertex before the translation?

2 Chloe says that the transformation of A to B and C to D can be described with a translation using the column vector $\begin{pmatrix} 0 \\ -10 \end{pmatrix}$ or a reflection in the x-axis.

Do you agree on the reflection? State your reasons.

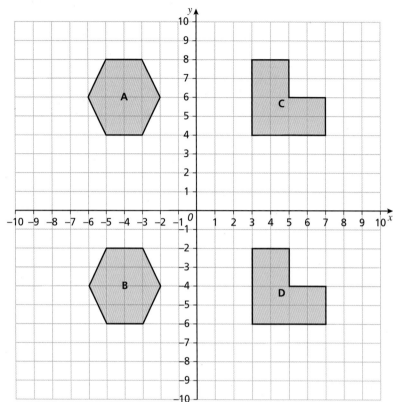

Are you ready? (A)

1 Work out:

    a 15 ÷ 5   **b** 4 × 3   **c** $8 \times \frac{1}{2}$

2 Are these two shapes similar?

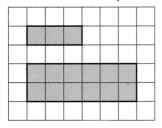

> Remember that for two shapes to be similar, their corresponding sides must be in the same ratio.

Enlargement is a transformation of a shape, where a **scale factor** is used to make a larger or smaller image. The two shapes will always be similar.

Example 1

a Enlarge the shape by scale factor 2

b Enlarge the shape by scale factor $\frac{1}{2}$

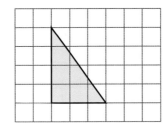

Method

Solution	Commentary
a ![shape with 4 and 3 labelled]	To enlarge the shape by a scale factor of 2, all dimensions need to be multiplied by 2 Diagonal lines are tricky to count, so stick to measuring the horizontal and vertical sides. Horizontal: 3 squares Multiply by scale factor 2: 3 × 2 = 6 The horizontal side on the enlarged shape will measure 6 squares.

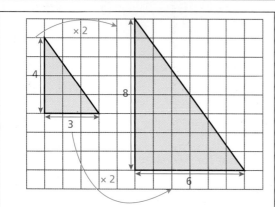

Vertical:

4 squares

Multiply by scale factor 2: $4 \times 2 = 8$

The vertical side on the enlarged shape will measure 8 squares.

Draw the new horizontal and vertical lines on the grid. The diagonal line can then be drawn.

b

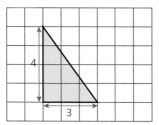

To enlarge by a scale factor of $\frac{1}{2}$, all dimensions should be multiplied by $\frac{1}{2}$

Measure the horizontal and vertical sides.

Horizontal:

3 squares

Multiply by scale factor $\frac{1}{2}$: $3 \times \frac{1}{2} = 1.5$

Vertical:

4 squares

Multiply by scale factor $\frac{1}{2}$: $4 \times \frac{1}{2} = 2$

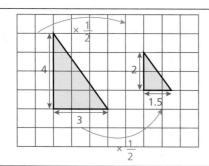

Draw the new horizontal and vertical lines, and then the diagonal line.

Example 2

Find the scale factor used to enlarge shape A to shape B.

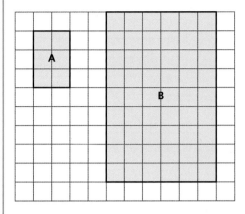

Method

Solution	Commentary
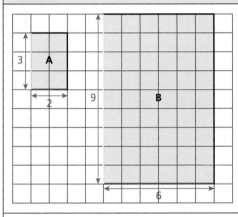	To find the scale factor, first find the pairs of corresponding sides. Because the two shapes are the same orientation, the horizontal lines correspond (2 and 6) and the vertical lines correspond (3 and 9).
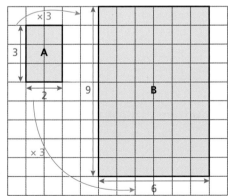 Shape A has been enlarged by a scale factor of 3	To calculate the scale factor, divide the enlarged side by the original side. $6 \div 2 = 3$ The answer 3 is the scale factor. You can check this answer by dividing another pair of corresponding sides. $9 \div 3 = 3$

Practice (A)

1 Using squared paper, enlarge each shape by the given scale factor.

a Scale factor 2

b Scale factor 3

c Scale factor $\frac{1}{3}$

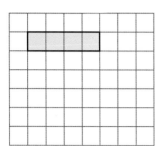 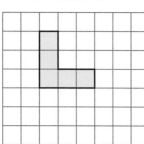 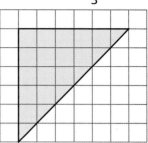

2 Find the scale factor of enlargement from shape A to shape B in each diagram.

a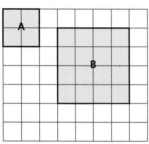

b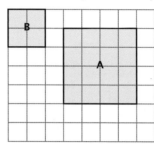

c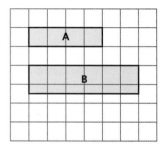

3 **a** Seb has enlarged shape A by scale factor 3 and drawn shape B.

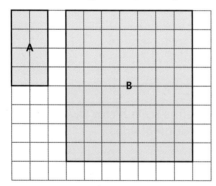

What mistakes has he made?

b Amina states that the scale factor of enlargement from shape A to shape B is 4

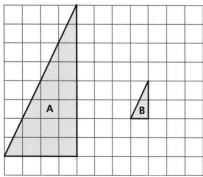

What mistake has she made?

c Kath states that the scale factor of enlargement from shape A to shape B is 3

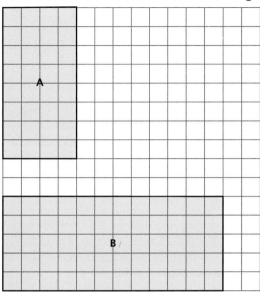

What mistake has she made?

What do you think? (A)

1 Is it possible to enlarge a shape by a scale factor of 1?

Are you ready? (B)

1 What are the coordinates of point A?

2 What are the coordinates of point B?

3 Copy the grid and plot the coordinates (3, 2). Label the point C.

4 What are the coordinates of the origin?

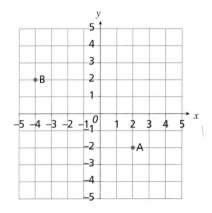

In the examples shown so far, the exact position of the image has not been specified.

To fully specify an enlargement, you need a **centre of enlargement**.

Example 1

Enlarge shape P by scale factor 3, centre (−7, −4).

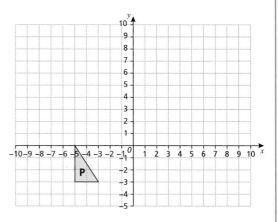

Method

Solution	Commentary
Method A 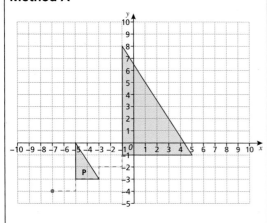	First plot the point (−7, −4) on the grid. This is the centre of enlargement. Count how far along and up it is from the centre of enlargement to one vertex of the given shape. In this case, it is two squares to the right and one square up. As you are enlarging the shape by scale factor 3, do this three times to find the corresponding vertex of the enlarged shape. Repeat this for the other vertices and draw the enlarged shape, ensuring that each side is three times the length of the corresponding side of the original shape.
Method B 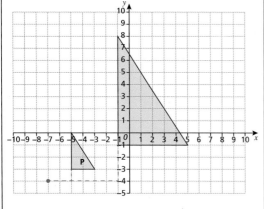	First plot the point (−7, −4) on the grid. This is the centre of enlargement. Count how far along and up it is from the centre of enlargement to one vertex of the shape. In this case it is two squares right and one square up. You can write this as the vector $\begin{pmatrix} 2 \\ 1 \end{pmatrix}$. You need to enlarge the shape by scale factor 3, so multiply this vector by 3: $\begin{pmatrix} 2 \\ 1 \end{pmatrix} \times 3 = \begin{pmatrix} 6 \\ 3 \end{pmatrix}$ Use the vector $\begin{pmatrix} 6 \\ 3 \end{pmatrix}$ from the centre of enlargement to decide where to draw the corresponding vertex of the new shape. Repeat for the other vertices and draw the enlarged shape, ensuring its sides are three times the length of the corresponding sides in the original shape.

Note that Method B relies on knowledge of vectors, which are covered in Block 9.

Example 2

Describe fully the single transformation that maps shape A onto shape B.

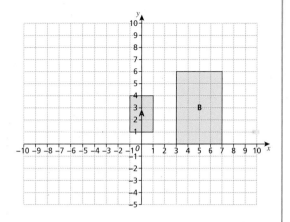

Method

Solution	Commentary
 Enlargement by scale factor 2, centre (–5, 2)	Each side of rectangle B is double the length of the corresponding side in rectangle A, so the scale factor for the enlargement is 2 Drawing ray lines through each vertex on the original shape and the corresponding vertex on the enlarged shape can help you to find the centre of enlargement. Extend the rays so that they meet at a point. This point is the centre of enlargement. In this case it is at (–5, 2).

Practice (B)

1   **a**   Using squared paper, enlarge each shape by the given scale factor and centre of enlargement.

i   Scale factor 2   **ii**   Scale factor 3   **iii**   Scale factor $\frac{1}{2}$

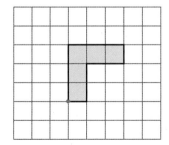 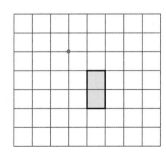 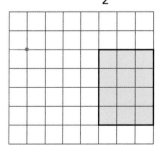

    b   Which of the enlargements in part **a** made the shape larger, and which ones smaller?

2 Enlarge each shape by the given scale factor and centre of enlargement.

a Scale factor 2, centre of enlargement (0, 0)

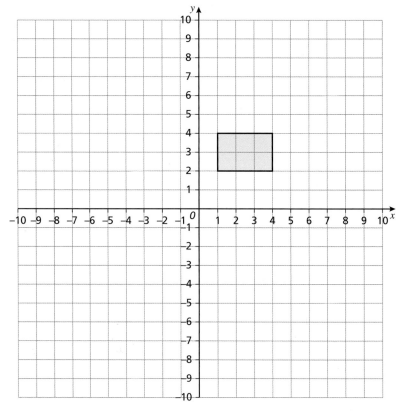

b Scale factor 3, centre of enlargement (–4, –5)

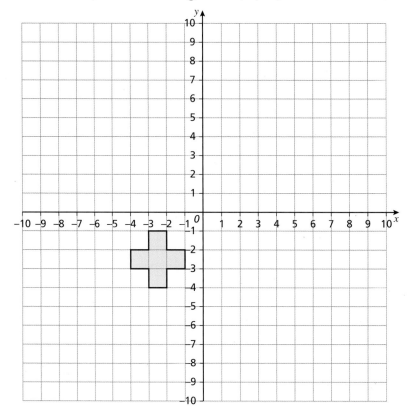

c Scale factor $\frac{1}{2}$, centre of enlargement (0, 1)

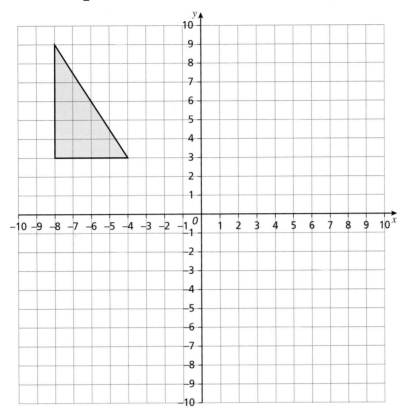

3 Describe fully the single transformation that maps shape A onto shape B.

a

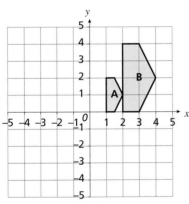

b

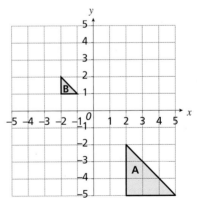

c

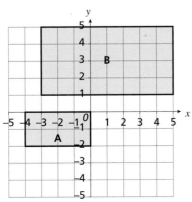

What do you think? (B) 💡

1 Chloe enlarges a shape by scale factor 3 and then enlarges her new shape by scale factor 4

She says, "I could have just enlarged the shape by scale factor 12"

Is Chloe correct? Draw an example to prove your answer.

Consolidate – do you need more?

1 Using squared paper, enlarge the shapes by the given scale factor.

a Scale factor 2

b Scale factor $\frac{1}{3}$

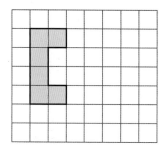
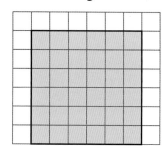

2 Find the scale factor of enlargement from shape A to shape B.

a

b

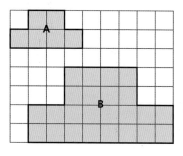
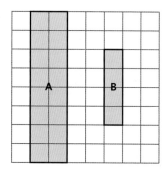

3 Enlarge each shape by the given scale factor and centre of enlargement.

a Scale factor 3

b Scale factor $\frac{1}{2}$

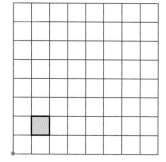
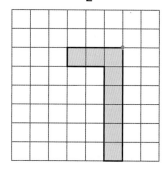

4 Enlarge each shape by the given scale factor and centre of enlargement.

a Scale factor $\frac{5}{2}$, centre of enlargement (0, 0)

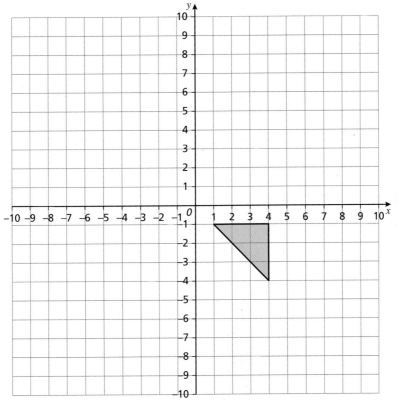

b Scale factor 2, centre of enlargement (0, −1)

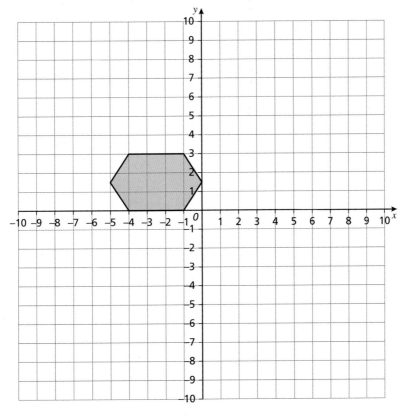

5   Describe fully the single transformation that maps shape A onto shape B.

a

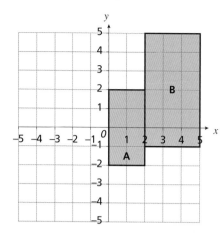

b

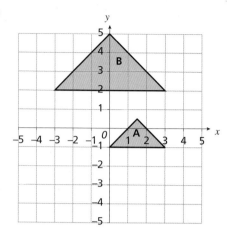

Stretch – can you deepen your learning?

1   A rectangle has vertices at the coordinates (2, 2), (7, 2), (2, 7) and (7, 7).

It is enlarged by scale factor 2

a   Show that the area of the new rectangle is **not** double the area of the original rectangle.

b   Write the ratio of the area of the original rectangle to the new rectangle in its simplest form.

2   A right-angled isosceles triangle has vertices at the coordinates (–7, –5), (–3, –5) and (–7, –1).

It is enlarged by scale factor 3, centre (–7, –5).

What are the coordinates of the enlarged shape?

How can the coordinates of the triangle and the coordinates of the centre of enlargement help you with this question?

Transformations: exam practice

For each question, copy the grid and draw the transformations as appropriate.

1-3

1 Enlarge the shape by scale factor 2   (2)

2 Reflect the shape in the given mirror line.   (2)

Mirror line

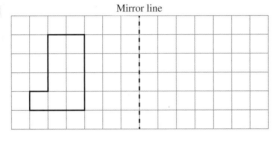

3-5

3

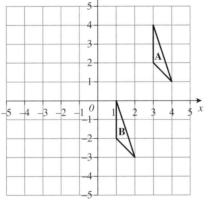

   a) Describe fully the single transformation that maps shape A to shape B.   (2)

   b) Reflect shape B in the line $x = -1$

       Label the new shape C.   (2)

   c) Rotate shape C by 180° about the point $(-3, 0)$.

       Label the new shape D.   (2)

6 Area and perimeter

In this block, we will cover...

6.1 Area and perimeter of polygons

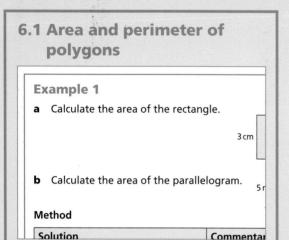

Example 1

a Calculate the area of the rectangle.

3 cm

b Calculate the area of the parallelogram.

5 r

Method

| Solution | Commentar |

6.2 Circles

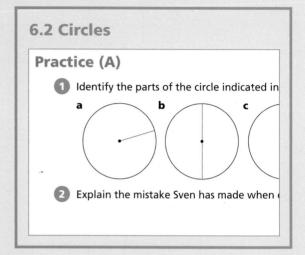

Practice (A)

1 Identify the parts of the circle indicated in

a   **b**   **c**

2 Explain the mistake Sven has made when

6.3 Parts of a circle

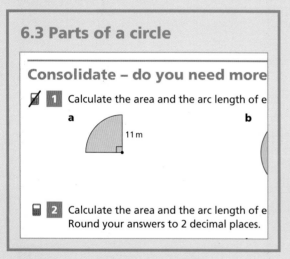

Consolidate – do you need more

1 Calculate the area and the arc length of e

a 11 m   **b**

2 Calculate the area and the arc length of e
Round your answers to 2 decimal places.

6.4 Compound shapes

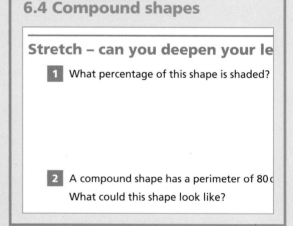

Stretch – can you deepen your le

1 What percentage of this shape is shaded?

2 A compound shape has a perimeter of 80
What could this shape look like?

Are you ready? (A)

1 Name each shape.

a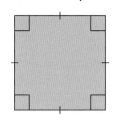

b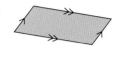

c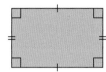

d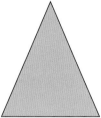

e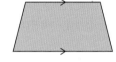

2 Work out:

a 4×2
b $\dfrac{3 \times 6}{2}$
c $\dfrac{1}{2} \times 5 \times 7$

3 Which pair of line segments are perpendicular?

A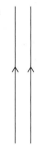

B

C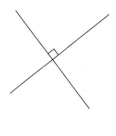

Area is the amount of space inside a 2D shape. Area is measured in square units, for example mm², cm², m², etc. You can find the area of a shape by counting the number of squares it covers on a grid or by using these formulae.

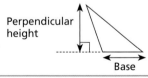	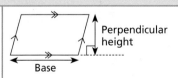		
Area of rectangle: length × width	**Area of triangle:** $\frac{1}{2}$ × base × perpendicular height	**Area of parallelogram:** base × perpendicular height	**Area of trapezium:** $\frac{1}{2} \times (a + b) \times h$

Remember that a square is a special type of rectangle where all the sides are the same length and a rhombus is a special type of parallelogram where all the sides are the same length.

Perimeter is the total distance around the outside of a shape.

Example 1

a Calculate the area of the rectangle.

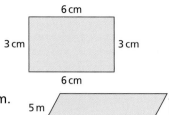

b Calculate the area of the parallelogram.

Method

Solution	Commentary
a 6 cm 3 cm 3 cm 6 cm Area = $l \times w$ Area = 6×3 Area = $18\,cm^2$	The formula for the area of a rectangle is length × width. This is equivalent to base × perpendicular height. The unit of area here is cm^2. Identify one length and one width. On a rectangle, these sides always meet at a right angle.
b 5 m 4 m 8 m Area = $b \times h$ Area = 8×4 Area = $32\,m^2$	The formula for the area of a parallelogram is base × perpendicular height. The unit of area here is m^2. Identify one base and one perpendicular height. On a parallelogram, remember to not use diagonal lengths.

Example 2

Calculate the area of the triangle.

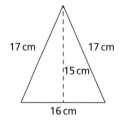

Method

Solution	Commentary
17 cm 17 cm 15 cm 16 cm Area = $\frac{1}{2} \times b \times h$ Area = $\frac{1}{2} \times 16 \times 15$ Area = $120\,cm^2$	The formula for the area of a triangle is $\frac{1}{2} \times$ base × perpendicular height. This can also be written as $\dfrac{\text{base} \times \text{perpendicular height}}{2}$ The unit of area here is cm^2. Identify one base and one perpendicular height. On a triangle, remember to not use diagonal lengths.

Example 3

Calculate the area of the trapezium.

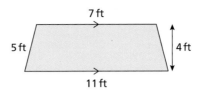

Method

Solution	Commentary
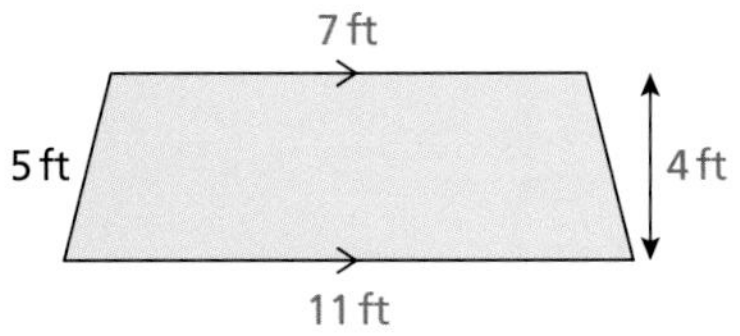 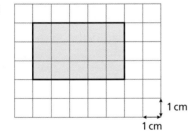 Area = $\frac{1}{2}$ × (a + b) × h Area = $\frac{1}{2}$ × (7 + 11) × 4 Area = 36 ft²	The formula for the area of a trapezium is $\frac{1}{2}$ × (a + b) × perpendicular height. This can also be written as $\frac{(a+b)}{2}$ h a and b refer to the pair of parallel sides on the trapezium. Remember to identify the perpendicular height, not the diagonal height. The unit of area here is ft².

Practice (A)

1 Calculate the area of each rectangle.

a

b

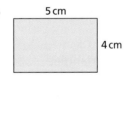

5 cm

4 cm

c

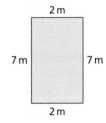

2 m

7 m   7 m

2 m

d

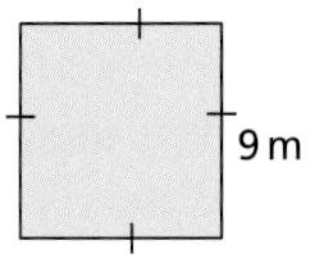

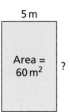

9 m

e

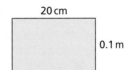

20 cm

0.1 m

2 Calculate the length of the side marked ? in each shape.

a

5 m

Area = 60 m²

?

b

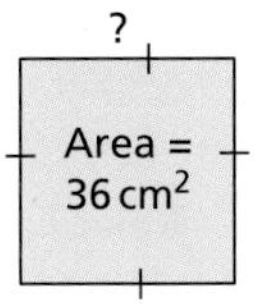

?

Area = 36 cm²

3 Calculate the area of each parallelogram.

a
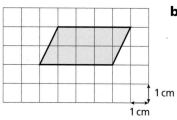

b
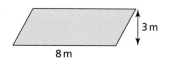

3 m
8 m

c
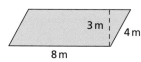

3 m
4 m
8 m

d
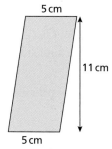

5 cm
11 cm
5 cm

e
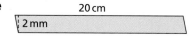

20 cm
2 mm

4 Calculate the length marked ? in each shape.

a
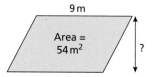

9 m
Area = 54 m²
?

b
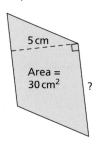

5 cm
Area = 30 cm²
?

5 Calculate the area of each triangle.

a
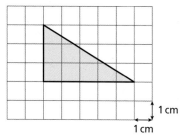

1 cm
1 cm

b
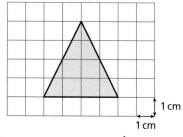

1 cm
1 cm

c
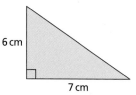

6 cm
7 cm

d
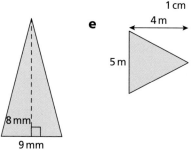

8 mm
9 mm

e
4 m
5 m

f
3 cm
4 cm
5 cm

g
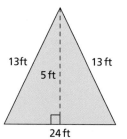

13 ft   13 ft
5 ft
24 ft

h
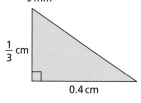

$\frac{1}{3}$ cm
0.4 cm

i
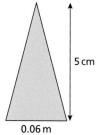

5 cm
0.06 m

6 Calculate the length marked ? in each diagram.

a

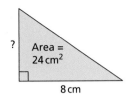

Area = 24 cm²

?

8 cm

b

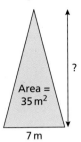

Area = 35 m²

?

7 m

7 Calculate the area of each trapezium.

a

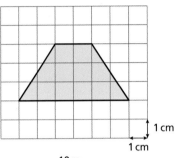

1 cm

1 cm

b

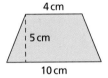

4 cm

5 cm

10 cm

c

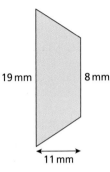

19 mm

8 mm

11 mm

d

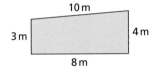

10 m

3 m

4 m

8 m

e

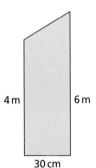

4 m

6 m

30 cm

8 Calculate the length of the side marked ? in each shape.

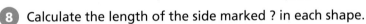

a

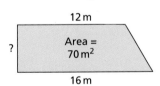

12 m

Area = 70 m²

?

16 m

b

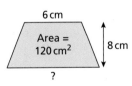

6 cm

Area = 120 cm²

8 cm

?

9 Suggest the mistake that has been made in working out each area.

a Area = 576 cm²

b Area = 24 cm²

c Area = 60 cm²

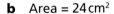

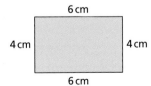

6 cm

4 cm

4 cm

6 cm

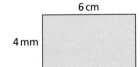

6 cm

4 mm

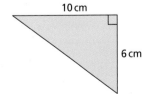

10 cm

6 cm

10 Junaid states that the sides of the rhombus must be 8 cm.

Do you agree? Explain your answer.

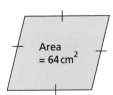

Area = 64 cm²

11 Flo wants to paint a wall in her living room.

The wall is shown in the diagram.

Each tin of paint costs £8.99 and covers 6 square metres.

What is the total cost of paint for the wall?

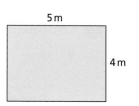

5 m

4 m

12 A farmer wants to put some cows in the triangular field shown.

Each cow needs 50 square metres.

How many cows can he put in the field?

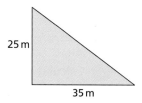

25 m

35 m

What do you think? (A)

1 What is the difference between calculating area and calculating perimeter?

Are you ready? (B)

1 Work out:

a 4 + 5 + 3 + 7 **b** 1.2 + 2.7 + 0.86

2 Are any of these shapes regular polygons? Why?

A 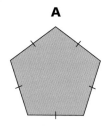 **B** 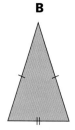 **C** 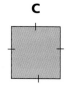 **D**

3 What types of triangles can you name and sketch?

Example 1

Calculate the perimeter of the shape.

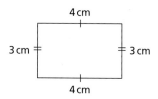

4 cm

3 cm   3 cm

4 cm

Method

Solution	Commentary
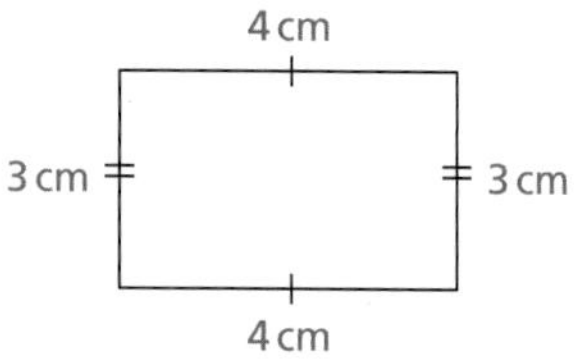 4 cm 3 cm ⊨ ⊨ 3 cm 4 cm Perimeter = 4 + 3 + 4 + 3 = 14 cm	To calculate the perimeter, you must add up the lengths of every side on the shape. The unit for this question is cm.

Example 2

Calculate the perimeter of the shape.

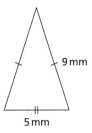

9 mm

5 mm

Method

Solution	Commentary
 9 mm 9 mm 5 mm Perimeter = 9 + 9 + 5 = 23 mm	To calculate the perimeter, you must add up the lengths of every side on the shape. The shape is an isosceles triangle, therefore it has two sides with the same length. The unit for this question is mm. The notation indicates that the missing side will be 9 mm.

Example 3

Calculate the perimeter of the shape.

2 m

Method

Solution	Commentary
2 m 2 m 2 m 2 m 2 m 2 m Perimeter = 2 + 2 + 2 + 2 + 2 + 2 = 12 m	To calculate the perimeter, you must add up the lengths of every side on the shape. The unit for this question is m. The notation on this shape indicates that it is a regular hexagon, therefore all the sides are 2 m.

Practice (B)

1 Calculate the perimeter of each shape.

a

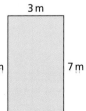

3 m

7 m   7 m

3 m

b

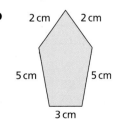

2 cm   2 cm

5 cm   5 cm

3 cm

c

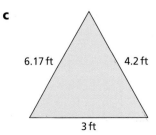

6.17 ft   4.2 ft

3 ft

2 Calculate the perimeter of each regular polygon.

a

5 cm

b
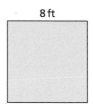
8 ft

c
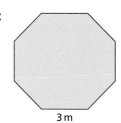
3 m

3 Calculate the perimeter of each shape.

a
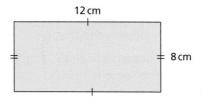
12 cm
8 cm

b
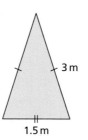
3 m
1.5 m

c
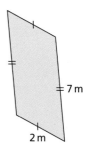
7 m
2 m

4 Which answer is correct for the perimeter of this rectangle?

   A 21 m   **B** 20 m   **C** 10 m

   What mistakes have been made with the other two options?

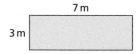
7 m
3 m

5 Abdullah wants to put a fence around the garden shown in the diagram.

   It will cost Abdullah £21.99 for every 1 m of fencing.

   He has £550

   Does he have enough money?

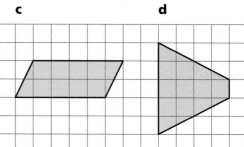
2.5 m
11 m

What do you think? (B) 🗨

1 What are the main points to look out for when deciding if the question is asking for the perimeter of the shape or the area?

Consolidate – do you need more?

1 Calculate the area of each shape drawn on the centimetre grid.

   a   **b**   **c**   **d**

1 cm
1 cm

2 Calculate the area of each shape.

a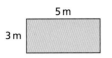
5 m
3 m

b
2.5 ft

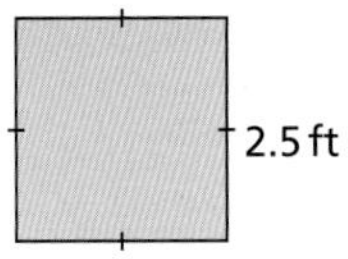

c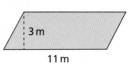
3 m
11 m

d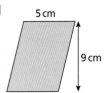
5 cm
9 cm

e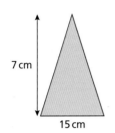
7 cm
15 cm

f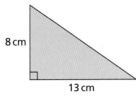
8 cm
13 cm

g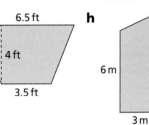
6.5 ft
4 ft
3.5 ft

h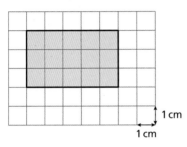
6 m
7 m
3 m

3 Calculate the perimeter of each shape.

a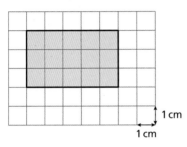
1 cm
1 cm

b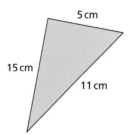
5 cm
15 cm
11 cm

c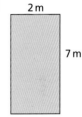
2 m
7 m

d
8 mm

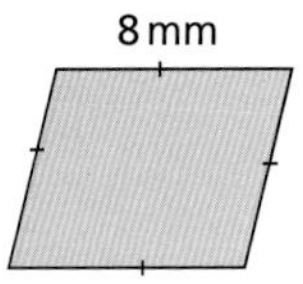

e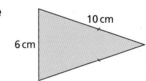
10 cm
6 cm

Stretch – can you deepen your learning?

1 Jackson wants to tile his bathroom wall.

The diagrams show the bathroom wall and one tile.

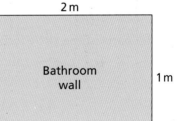
2 m
Bathroom wall
1 m

10 cm
Tile   10 cm

How many tiles will Jackson need?

2 The diagram shows an isosceles triangle. Its perimeter is 31 cm.

Calculate the value of x.

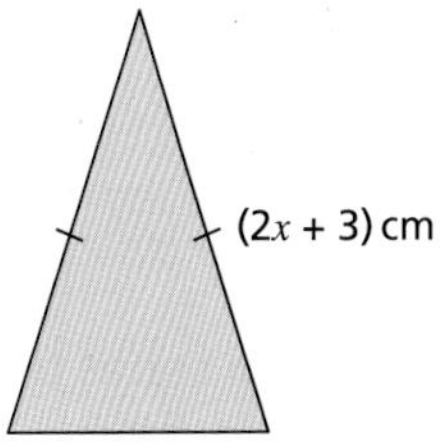

$(2x + 3)$ cm

x cm

Are you ready? (A)

1 Read the descriptions in the shaded box below and use them to label the parts of a circle given in parts **a** and **b**. It will help if you copy the two circle diagrams first.

The **centre** of the circle is indicated by the dot.

a 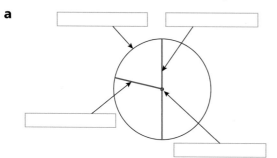 **b**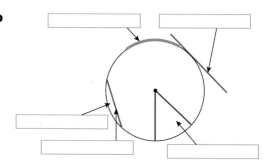

The **circumference** is the outside of the circle.

The **diameter** is a straight line that runs from one part of the circumference to another, passing through the centre.

The **radius** is a straight line that runs from one part of the circumference to the centre.

An **arc** is a section of the circumference.

A **tangent** is a straight line that touches the circumference.

A **sector** is a section of the circle that is bounded by an arc and two radii. It is like a 'slice' of the circle.

A **chord** is a straight line that runs from one part of the circumference to another, and doesn't have to pass through the centre.

A **segment** is bounded by an arc and a chord.

Practice (A)

1 Identify the parts of the circle indicated in red.

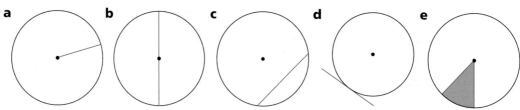

2 Explain the mistake Sven has made when drawing a diameter.

3 Kath states that a segment and a sector are the same circle part.

Do you agree? Give a reason for your answer.

What do you think?

1 Is the diameter a chord?

Are you ready? (B)

1 Which diagram correctly shows a radius? Give a reason for your answer.

A	B	C
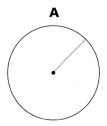	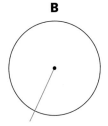	

2 Which diagram correctly shows a diameter? Give a reason for your answer.

A	B	C
	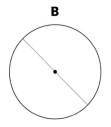	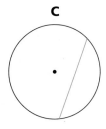

3 Round 3.141 59 to:

   a 2 decimal places   **b** 1 significant figure.

Here are two useful formulae that you need to know.

Area of a circle = πr^2

r represents the radius.

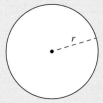

π is a Greek letter pronounced 'pie', and in maths it has the decimal value 3.141 592 654.... It is used mainly in connection with circles.

Circumference of a circle = πd

d represents the diameter.

The radius is exactly half the diameter, and the diameter is exactly double the radius.

Using your calculator

Throughout this chapter, you will need to use the π button on your scientific calculator.

On some models, you need to press

Example 1

a Calculate the area of the circle.

Leave your answer in terms of π.

b Calculate the area of the circle.

Round your answer to 3 significant figures.

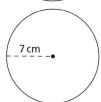

Method

Solution	Commentary
a Area = πr^2	The formula for the area of a circle is πr^2.
Area = $\pi \times 5^2$	The unit of area for this question is m².
Area = 25π m²	For area, you need the radius. In this question, it has been given.
	No rounding is needed as the question says to leave your answer in terms of π.
b Area = πr^2	The formula for the area of a circle is πr^2.
Area = $\pi \times 7^2$	The unit of area for this question is cm².
Area = 49π	For area, you need the radius. In this question, it has been given.
Area = 153.938 04...	
Area = 154 cm² (to 3 s.f.)	For this question, you need to round the answer to 3 significant figures.

Example 2

a Calculate the circumference of the circle.

Leave your answer in terms of π.

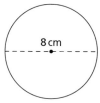

b Calculate the circumference of the circle.

Round your answer to 3 significant figures.

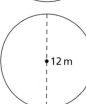

Method

Solution	Commentary
a Circumference = πd Circumference = $\pi \times 8$ Circumference = 8π cm	The formula for the circumference of a circle is πd. The unit for this question is cm. For circumference, you need the diameter. In this question, it has been given. There is no rounding needed as the question states to leave your answer in terms of π.
b Circumference = πd Circumference = $\pi \times 12$ Circumference = 12π Circumference = 37.699 111 84... Circumference = 37.7 m (to 3 s.f.)	The formula for the circumference of a circle is πd. The unit for this question is m. For circumference, you need the diameter. In this question, it has been given. For this question, the answer should be rounded to 3 significant figures.

Practice (B)

1 Calculate the area of each circle. Leave your answers in terms of π.

a 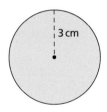 3 cm   **b** 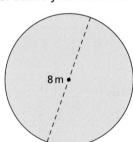 8 m   **c** 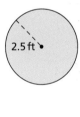 2.5 ft

2 Calculate the area of each circle. Round your answers to 2 decimal places.

a 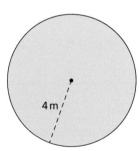 4 m   **b** 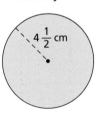 $4\frac{1}{2}$ cm   **c** 7 cm

3 Calculate the circumference of each circle. Leave your answers in terms of π.

a 3 mm   **b** 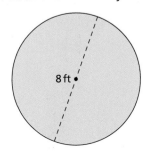 8 ft   **c** 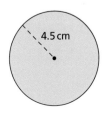 4.5 cm

4 Calculate the circumference of each circle. Round your answers to 2 decimal places.

a
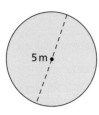
5 m

b

$5\frac{1}{2}$ cm

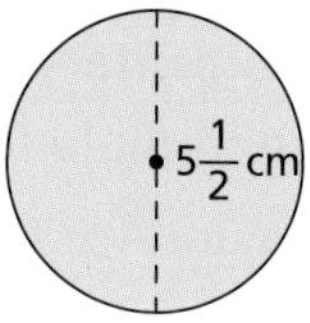

c
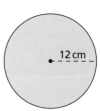
12 cm

5 Calculate the length of the radius and the diameter of each circle.

a Area = 49π cm²
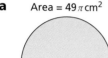

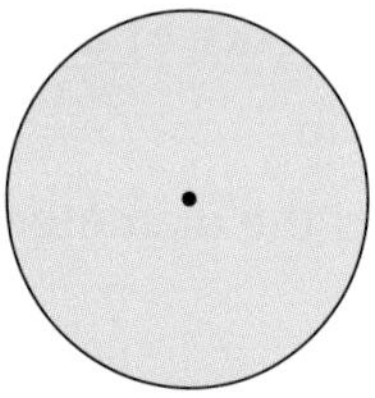

b Circumference = 20π cm

6 Calculate the length of the radius of each circle.
Round your answers to 3 significant figures.

a Area = 150 m²

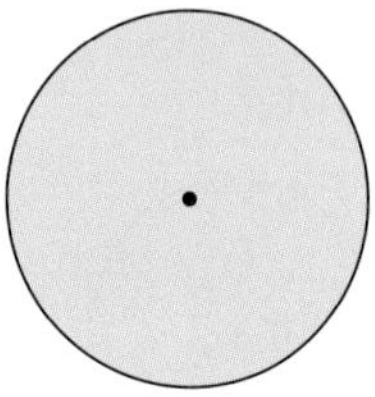

b Circumference = 275 cm

7 Tiff states that the area of this circle is 81π cm².

What mistake has she made?

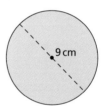
9 cm

8 The area of a circle is 75 cm².

What is its circumference? Round your answer to 2 decimal places.

Consolidate – do you need more?

1 Calculate the area and the circumference of each circle. Leave your answers in terms of π.

a
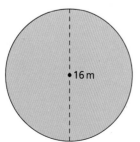
16 m

b
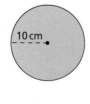
10 cm

2 Calculate the area and the circumference of each circle.
Round your answers to 3 significant figures.

a

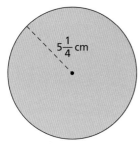

$5\frac{1}{4}$ cm

b

1.5 mm

3 Calculate the length of the radius and the diameter of each circle.

a   Area = 64π cm^2

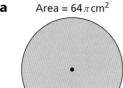

b   Circumference = 37π cm

4 Calculate the length of the radius and the diameter of each circle.
Round your answers to 2 decimal places.

a   Area = 61 ft^2

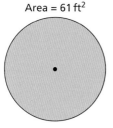

b   Circumference = 122 m

Stretch – can you deepen your learning?

1 The circle and the square have the same area.

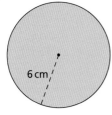

6 cm

Calculate the length of one side of the square. Round your answer to 1 decimal place.

2 A circle is placed inside a square, as shown.

What percentage of the square does the area of the
circle cover? Round your answer to the nearest integer.

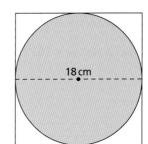

18 cm

3 A wheel has a diameter of 2 m. It travels 2 km.

How many revolutions does it complete?

6.3 Parts of a circle

Are you ready? (A)

1 Label the parts of the circle shown on the diagram.

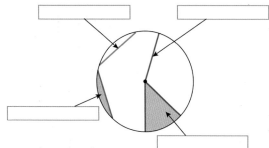

2 What fraction of each circle is shaded?

a 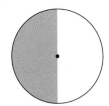 **b** 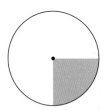 **c** 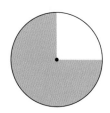 **d**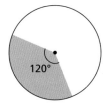

3 What is the formula for finding the area of a circle?

Example 1

a Calculate the area of the sector.

Leave your answer in terms of π.

8 cm

b Calculate the area of the sector.

Round your answer to 1 significant figure.

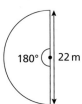

180° 22 m

Method

Solution	Commentary
a Area of sector = $\frac{1}{4}\pi r^2$ Area of sector = $\frac{1}{4} \times \pi \times 8^2$ Area of sector = 16π cm²	The formula for the area of a circle is πr^2. In this question, the radius has been given.
	The sector represents a quarter of a circle, so you need to multiply the area of a circle by $\frac{1}{4}$
	The unit of area in this question is cm².
	There is no rounding needed as the question states to leave your answer in terms of π.

b Area of sector = $\frac{1}{2}\pi r^2$ Area of sector = $\frac{1}{2} \times \pi \times 11^2$ Area of sector = 60.5π Area of sector = 190.066 3555... Area of sector = 200 m² (to 1 s.f.)	The formula for the area of a circle is πr^2. For area, you need the radius. In this question, you have the diameter. To calculate the radius, you need to divide 22 by 2 The sector represents half of a circle, so you need to multiply the area of a circle by $\frac{1}{2}$ The unit of area in this question is m². For this question, you need to round the answer to 1 significant figure.

Example 2

Calculate the area of the sector.

Round your answer to 3 significant figures.

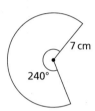

Method

Solution	Commentary
Area of sector = $\frac{2}{3}\pi r^2$	The formula for the area of a circle is πr^2. For area, you need the radius. In this question, it has been given.
Area of sector = $\frac{2}{3} \times \pi \times 7^2$	The sector represents $\frac{240}{360}$ of the full circle.
Area of sector = $\frac{98}{3}\pi$	You can multiply by this fraction or simplify it to $\frac{2}{3}$
Area of sector = 102.625 36... Area of sector ≈ 103 cm² (to 3 s.f.)	The unit of area in this question is cm². For this question, you need to round the answer to 3 significant figures.

Practice (A)

1 Calculate the area of each sector. Leave your answers in terms of π.

a 4 m

b 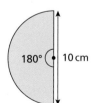 180° 10 cm

c 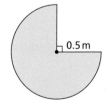 0.5 m

2 Calculate the area of each sector. Round your answers to 1 decimal place.

a 3.2 ft

b 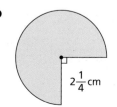 $2\frac{1}{4}$ cm

c 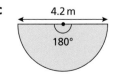 4.2 m   180°

3 Calculate the area of each sector. Round your answers to 3 significant figures.

a

300°

2 cm

b

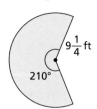

36° 21 mm

c

$9\frac{1}{4}$ ft

210°

4 Calculate the length of the radius.

Sector area = 25π cm²

5 Calculate the length of the radius.
Round your answer to 1 decimal place.

Sector area = 50 cm²

200°

6 Calculate the size of the angle.
Round your answer to 1 decimal place.

Sector area = 120 cm²

10 cm

Are you ready? (B)

1 Label the parts of the circle on the diagram.

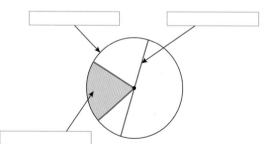

2 What fraction of each circle is shaded?

a

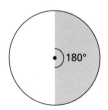

180°

b

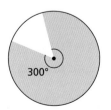

300°

c

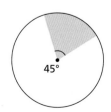

45°

3 What is the formula for the circumference of a circle?

Example 1

a   Calculate the length of the arc.

   Leave your answer in terms of π.

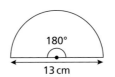

b   Calculate the length of the arc.

   Round your answer to 1 decimal place.

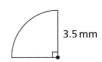

Method

Solution	Commentary
a Arc length $= \frac{1}{2}\pi d$ Arc length $= \frac{1}{2} \times \pi \times 13$ Arc length $= 6.5\pi$ cm	The formula for the circumference of a circle is πd. For circumference, you need the diameter. Here, it is given. The sector represents half a circle, so multiply the circumference by $\frac{1}{2}$ The unit for this question is cm. There is no rounding needed as the question states to leave your answer in terms of π.
b $\qquad$ 3.5 mm $\qquad$ $d = 7$ mm 3.5 mm Arc length $= \frac{1}{4}\pi d$ Arc length $= \frac{1}{4} \times \pi \times 7$ Arc length $= 1.75\pi$ Arc length $= 5.497\,787\,144...$ Arc length $= 5.5$ mm (to 1 d.p.)	The formula for the circumference of a circle is πd. For circumference, you need the diameter. You have the radius so multiply 3.5 by 2 The sector represents a quarter of a circle, so multiply the circumference by $\frac{1}{4}$ The unit for this question is mm. For this question, round the answer to 1 decimal place.

Example 2

Calculate the length of the arc.

Round your answer to 3 significant figures.

Method

Solution	Commentary
5 cm 110° 5 cm Arc length $= \dfrac{11}{36}\pi d$ Arc length $= \dfrac{11}{36} \times \pi \times 10$ Arc length $= \dfrac{55}{18}\pi$ Arc length $= 9.599310\ldots$ Arc length $= 9.60\,$cm (to 3 s.f.)	The formula for the circumference of a circle is πd. The sector represents $\dfrac{110}{360}$ of the full circle. Multiply the circumference by $\dfrac{110}{360}$ or simplify to $\dfrac{11}{36}$ For the circumference, you need the diameter. You have the radius so multiply 5 by 2 The unit for this question is cm. For this question, round your answer to 3 significant figures.

Practice (B)

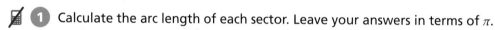

1 Calculate the arc length of each sector. Leave your answers in terms of π.

a
4 m

b
180° 10 cm

c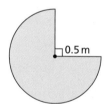
0.5 m

2 Calculate the arc length of each sector. Round your answers to 1 decimal place.

a 3.2 ft

b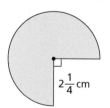
$2\frac{1}{4}$ cm

c 4.2 m
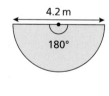
180°

3 Calculate the arc length of each sector. Round your answers to 3 significant figures.

a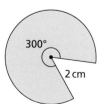
300°
2 cm

b
36° 21 mm

c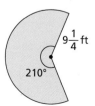
$9\frac{1}{4}$ ft
210°

4 Calculate the length of the diameter of this semicircle.

Arc length = 20π cm

5 Calculate the length of the diameter.
Round your answer to 1 decimal place.

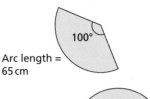

100°

Arc length = 65 cm

6 Calculate the angle size of the sector.
Round your answer to 1 decimal place.

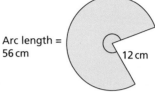

Arc length = 56 cm

12 cm

Consolidate – do you need more?

1 Calculate the area and the arc length of each sector. Leave your answers in terms of π.

a

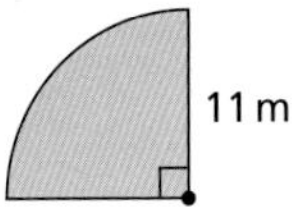

11 m

b

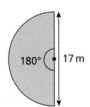

180° 17 m

2 Calculate the area and the arc length of each sector.
Round your answers to 2 decimal places.

a

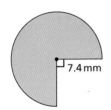

7.4 mm

b

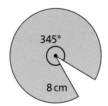

345°

8 cm

3 Calculate the radius of each sector and the diameter of the whole circle.
Round your answers to 1 decimal place where appropriate.

a   Sector area = 64π cm²

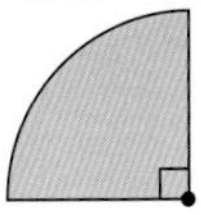

b   Arc length = 80 cm

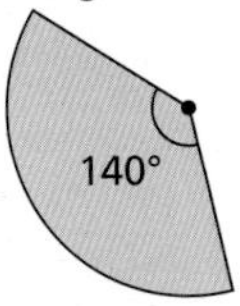

140°

4 Calculate the angle size of each sector. Round your answers to 1 decimal place.

a   Sector area = 250 cm²

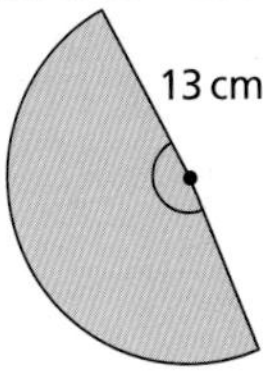

13 cm

b   Arc length = 45 cm

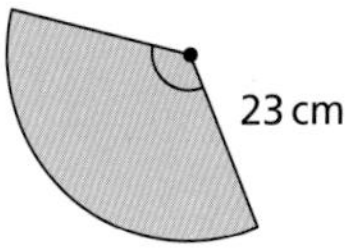

23 cm

Stretch – can you deepen your learning?

1 Calculate the perimeter of the sector. Round your answer to 2 decimal places.

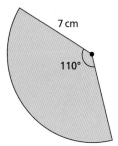

7 cm

110°

2 Work out the area of the region shaded orange. Leave your answer in terms of π.

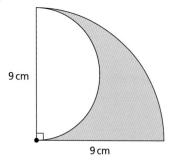

9 cm

9 cm

3 The area of a semicircle is 120 cm².

Calculate its perimeter. Round your answer to 3 significant figures.

Are you ready? (A)

1 Calculate the area of each shape.

a
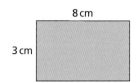
8 cm
3 cm

b
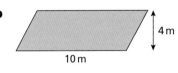
4 m
10 m

c
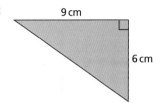
9 cm
6 cm

2 Calculate the perimeter of each shape.

a
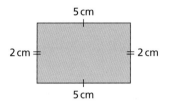
5 cm
2 cm
2 cm
5 cm

b
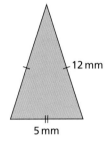
12 mm
5 mm

3 What is the length of the vertical side of this shape?

4 m
11 m

A **compound shape** is made up of two or more shapes, either connected together or subtracted.

Example

Work out the area of this compound shape.

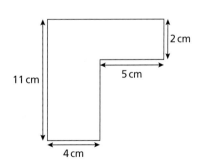
2 cm
5 cm
11 cm
4 cm

Method

Solution	Commentary
Method A 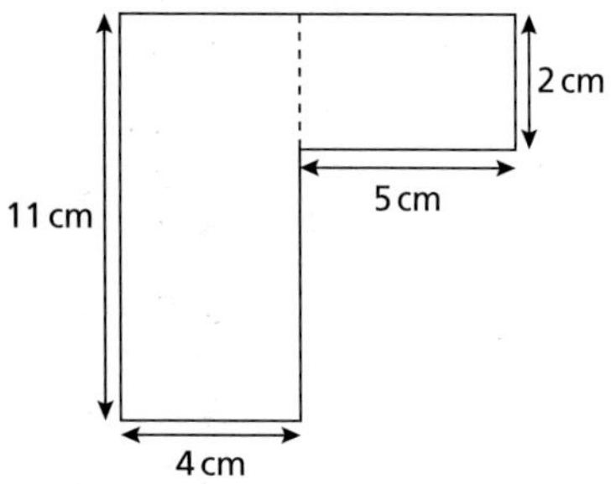 	Split the shape into two rectangles.
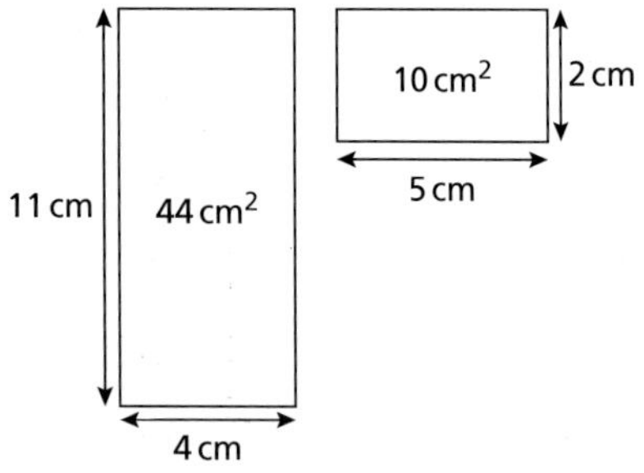 44 + 10 = 54 Area = 54 cm²	It is useful to sketch the two rectangles and label the side lengths. Work out the area of each rectangle. Add the areas together. Do not forget to write the units.
Method B 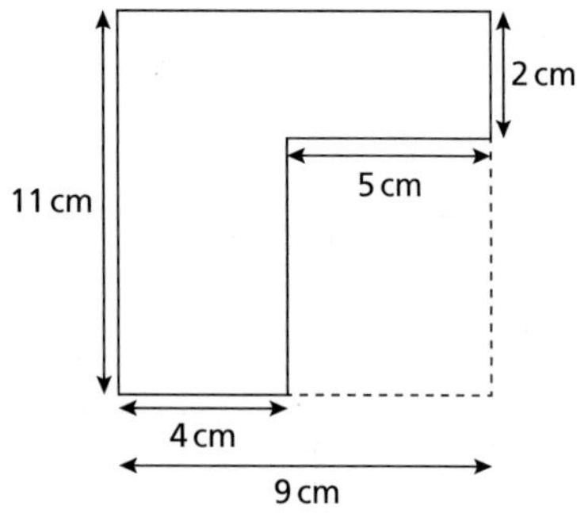 	You could think of the compound shape as a complete rectangle and then subtract the area of the blank space. If it were complete, it would measure 11 cm by 9 cm, giving an area of 99 cm².
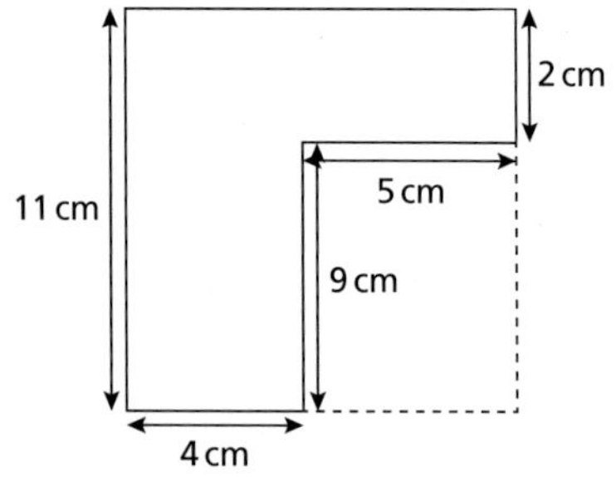 99 − 45 = 54 Area = 54 cm²	The blank space has an area of 9 × 5 = 45 cm² Subtract the blank space from the total area to give the area of the compound shape.

Practice (A)

1 Calculate the area of each compound shape.

a
6 cm
7 cm
2 cm
10 cm

b
12 m
7 m
8 m
4 m

c
11 mm
5 mm
12 mm
4 mm

d
3 cm   2 cm   3 cm
6 cm
15 cm

2 Calculate the perimeter of each compound shape from question 1.

3 Work out the area of each compound shape.

a
14 cm
9 cm
8 cm

b
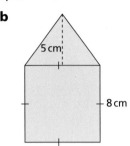
5 cm
8 cm

4 Work out the shaded area in each diagram.

a
7 m
3 m   8 m
12 m

b
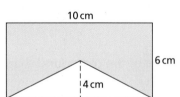
10 cm
6 cm
4 cm

5 Tiff wants to put fencing around her garden, shown in this diagram.

How many metres of fencing will she need?

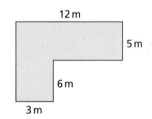
12 m
5 m
6 m
3 m

6 Rhys does the following calculation for the area of this compound shape.

$48 + 96 = 154 \text{ cm}^2$

What mistake has he made?

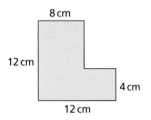
8 cm
12 cm
4 cm
12 cm

What do you think? (A) 💭

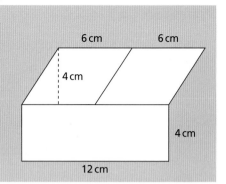

1 Will the total area of the two parallelograms be the same as the area of the rectangle?

Explain your answer.

Are you ready? (B)

1 Calculate the area of each shape. Give your answers in terms of π where necessary.

a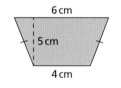

b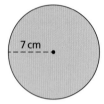

c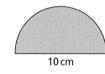

2 Work out the perimeter of each shape in question 1.

Example

Calculate the area of the compound shape.

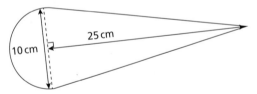

Method

Solution	Commentary
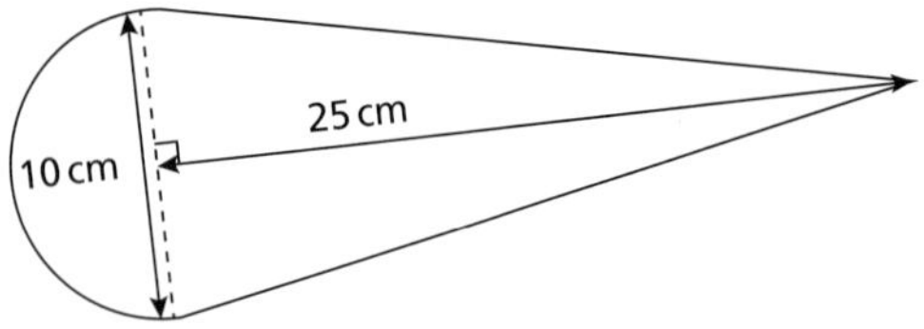 25 cm 10 cm	This compound shape is made up of a semicircle and a triangle. Work out the area of each shape individually and then add them together.
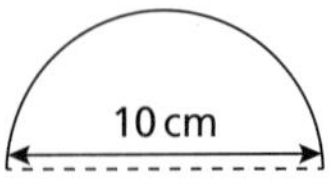 10 cm Area of semicircle $= \dfrac{\pi r^2}{2}$ $\qquad = \dfrac{\pi \times 5^2}{2}$ $\qquad = 39.269\,908\,17\ldots$	You have been given the diameter so you need to halve it to find the radius: $10 \div 2 = 5$ Do not round your answer here as you are ɔ at the end of the question yet.

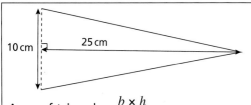

	Find the area of the triangle.
Area of triangle = $\dfrac{b \times h}{2}$ $= \dfrac{10 \times 25}{2}$ $= 125\,\text{cm}^2$	
Total area = 39.269 908 17... + 125 $\quad\quad$ = 164.269 9082... $\quad\quad$ = 164 cm² (to 3 s.f.)	Round the final answer to a reasonable degree of accuracy. This is usually to 3 significant figures.

Practice (B) 🖩

1 Calculate the area of each compound shape.

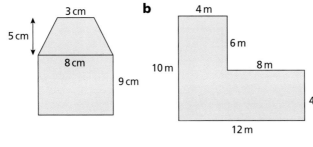

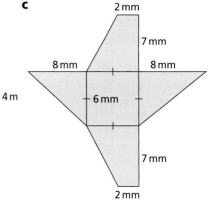

2 Calculate the area of each compound shape. Round your answers to 2 decimal places.

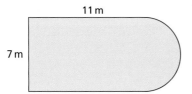

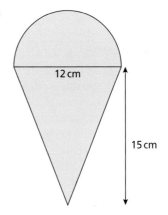

3 A quarter circle is placed in a square with sides of 20 cm, as shown.

Calculate the area of the shaded region. Round your answer to 1 decimal place.

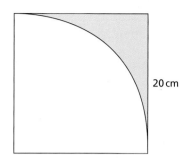

20 cm

4 A compound shape is made by placing two semicircles against the heights of a rectangle, as shown.

Lida says, "You only need to calculate the area of one circle as the semicircles will be congruent."

Rhys says, "You have to work out the area of each semicircle."

Who do you agree with?

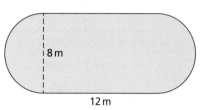

8 m

12 m

5 Mario wants to lay some new grass on the lawn of his garden.

The garden is shown in this diagram.

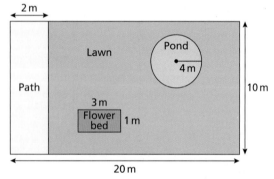

One roll of grass covers 20 m².

Each roll costs £8.99

How much will Mario need to pay?

What do you think? (B) 💡

1 How many ways can you find to split up this compound shape?

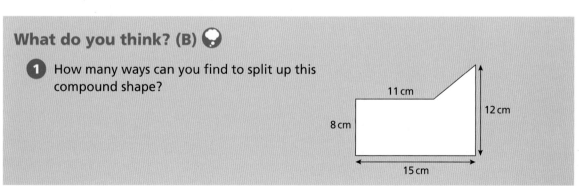

11 cm

12 cm

8 cm

15 cm

Consolidate – do you need more? 🖩

1 Calculate the area of each shape. Round your answers to 2 decimal places where necessary.

a
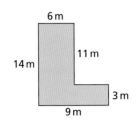

b
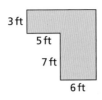

c
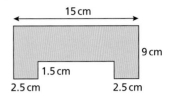

d
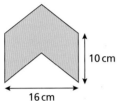

e
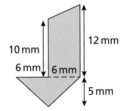

f
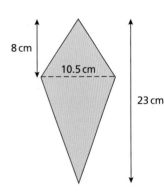

g

h
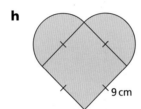

2 Where possible, calculate the perimeter of each shape in question 1.

Stretch – can you deepen your learning?

1 What percentage of this shape is shaded?

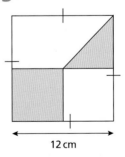

2 A compound shape has a perimeter of 80 cm.

What could this shape look like?

3 **a** Work out an algebraic expression for the perimeter of this shape.

b The perimeter of the shape is 56 cm.

Work out the value of y.

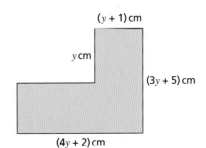

1 The shape is drawn on a centimetre squared grid.

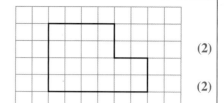

1–3

   a) What is the area of the shape?
Give units with your answer. (2)

   b) What is the perimeter of the shape?
Give units with your answer. (2)

2 Work out the area of the triangle.

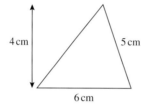

4 cm   5 cm   6 cm

(2)

3 A square has sides of length 11 mm.

   What is the perimeter of the square? (2)

4 A circle has a diameter of 7 ft.

3–5

   a) What is the circumference of the circle? Give your answer to 2 decimal places. (2)

   b) What is the area of the circle? Give your answer to 2 decimal places. (3)

5 The diagram shows the plan of a field.

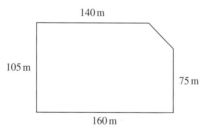

140 m   105 m   75 m   160 m

   A farmer rents out the field to organisers of a festival for £6 per square metre.

   Work out the total amount of money the farmer should receive. (5)

6 Work out the area of the sector. Give your answer to 2 decimal places. (3)

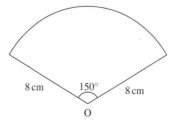

8 cm   150°   8 cm

O

In this block, we will cover...

7.1 Volume of prisms

Example 1

Work out the volume of the cuboid.

Method

Solution	Commenta
Area = $l \times w$	A cuboid is
Area = 5×3	cross-secti
Area = 15 cm²	Fi

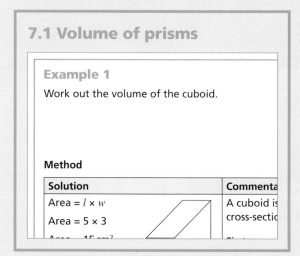

7.2 Cylinders, cones and spheres

Practice

1. The table gives information about some c
   Copy and complete the table. Round your

Radius (cm)	Diameter (cm)	Height (
3		12
	10	18
7		
		20
	17	
		25

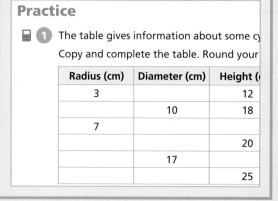

7.3 Surface area

Consolidate – do you need more

1. Calculate the surface area of each shape.

   a 6.5 cm
   3 cm
   4 cm

   b
   3 cm
   8

2. Which shape has the greatest surface area

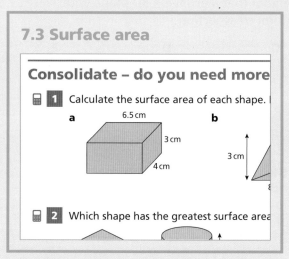

7.4 Plans and elevations

Stretch – can you deepen your le

1. The diagram shows a square-based right p

   Using the scale 2 cm: 1 m, draw the plan vi
   elevation and the side elevation on a cent

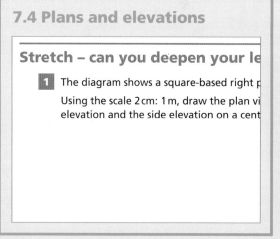

7.1 Volume of prisms

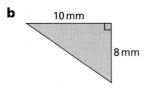

Are you ready?

1 Work out the area of each shape.

a

7 cm
3 cm   3 cm
7 cm

b

10 mm
8 mm

2 Name these 3D shapes.

a   **b**   **c**
 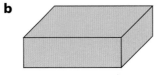 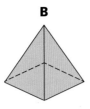

3 Which of these shapes are prisms?

> Remember that a prism is a 3D shape with a uniform cross-section.

A   **B**   **C**   **D**   **E**

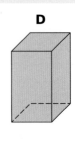
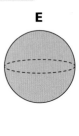

Volume of a prism = area of cross-section × length

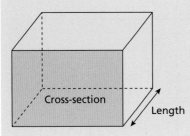
Cross-section
Length

Example 1

Work out the volume of the cuboid.

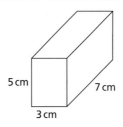

Method

Solution	Commentary
Area = $l \times w$ Area = 5×3 Area = $15\,cm^2$	A cuboid is a type of prism with a rectangle as its cross-section. First, you need to work out the area of the rectangle, which is length × width. This is equivalent to base × perpendicular height. The unit of area in this example is cm^2.
Volume = area of the cross-section × length Volume = 15×7 Volume = $105\,cm^3$	You then need to multiply the area of the cross-section by the length. The unit of volume in this example is cm^3.

Example 2

Work out the volume of the triangular prism.

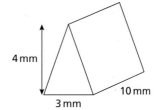

Method

Solution	Commentary
Area = $\frac{1}{2} \times b \times h$ Area = $\frac{1}{2} \times 3 \times 4$ Area = $6\,mm^2$	A triangular prism has a triangle as its cross-section. First, work out the area of the triangle. The formula for the area of a triangle is $\frac{1}{2}$ × base × perpendicular height. This can also be written as $\dfrac{base \times perpendicular\ height}{2}$ The unit of area in this example is mm^2.
Volume = area of the cross-section × length Volume = 6×10 Volume = $60\,mm^3$	Now multiply the area of the cross-section by the length. The unit of volume in this example is mm^3.

Practice

1. Work out the volume of each prism. Each small cube has volume 1 cm³.

   a 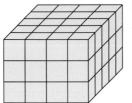   **b** 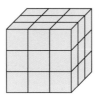   **c**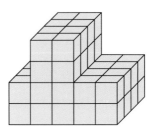

2. Work out the volume of each shape.

   a 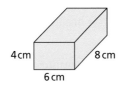   **b** 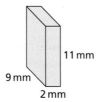   **c** 5 cm   **d**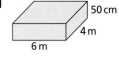

3. Work out the volume of each shape.

   a 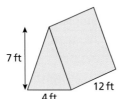   **b** 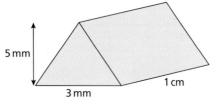   **c**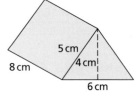

4. Work out the volume of each prism.

   a 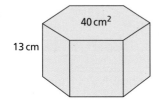   **b** 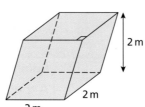   **c**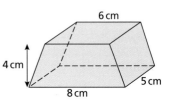

5. Work out the volume of each shape.

   a 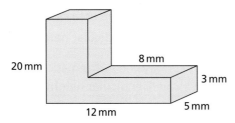   **b**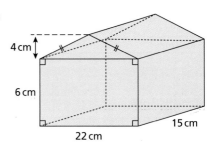

6 Work out the value of x in each diagram.

a Cuboid
Volume = 60 m³

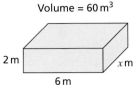

2 m
x m
6 m

b Cube
Volume = 729 cm³

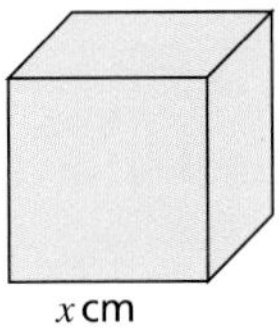

x cm

c Triangular prism
Volume = 37.5 ft³

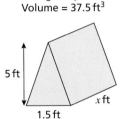

5 ft
x ft
1.5 ft

d Triangular prism
Volume = 135 cm³

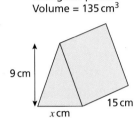

9 cm
15 cm
x cm

7 Rhys uses his van to deliver boxes.

To carry the boxes, his van has space in the shape of a cuboid with:

length 3 m   width 2 m   depth 5 m

Each box is a cuboid measuring 60 cm × 30 cm × 50 cm.

How many boxes can he fit in at one time?

8 A container measures 20 cm × 65 cm × 1 m.

1 litre = 1000 cm³

A tap can fill the container at a rate of 13 litres per minute.

How long will it take to fill the container?

What do you think? 💭

1 A cuboid is shown.

Which of these calculations will find the correct
answer for the volume of the cuboid?
Give a reason for your answer.

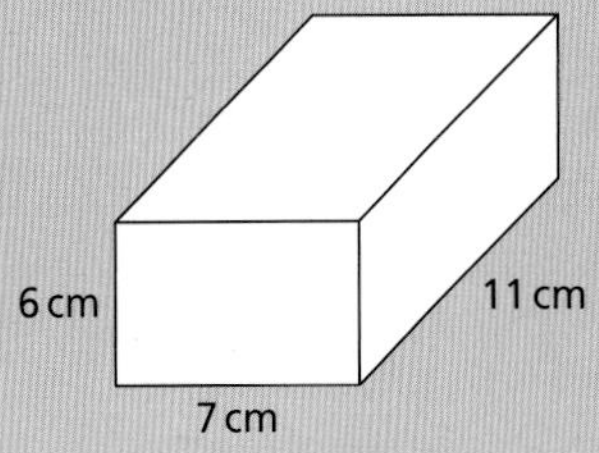

6 cm
11 cm
7 cm

┌─────────────┐   ┌─────────────┐   ┌─────────────┐
│ 6 × 7 × 11 │   │ 11 × 6 × 7 │   │ 7 × 11 × 6 │
└─────────────┘   └─────────────┘   └─────────────┘

Consolidate – do you need more?

1 Work out the volume of each prism.

a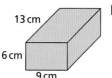
13 cm
6 cm
9 cm

b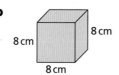
8 cm
8 cm
8 cm

c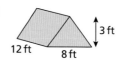
3 ft
12 ft
8 ft

d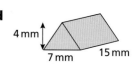
4 mm
7 mm
15 mm

2 Work out the volume of each prism.

a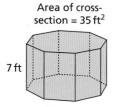
Area of cross-section = 35 ft²
7 ft

b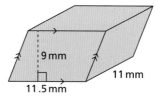
9 mm
11 mm
11.5 mm

c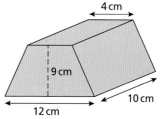
4 cm
9 cm
12 cm
10 cm

3 Calculate the volume of this shape.

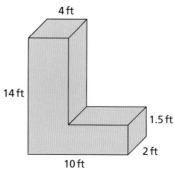
4 ft
14 ft
1.5 ft
2 ft
10 ft

4 Work out the value of x in each diagram.

a Cuboid
Volume = 132 mm³

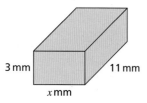
3 mm
11 mm
x mm

b Triangular prism
Volume = 234 cm³

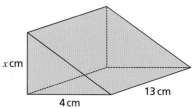
x cm
4 cm
13 cm

Stretch – can you deepen your learning?

1 This shape has volume 300 cm³.

Calculate the value of x.

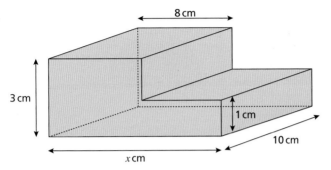

2 A water tank in the shape of a rectangular cuboid measures 5 m × 90 cm × 2 m.

1 litre = 1000 cm³

It is currently filled to $\frac{4}{9}$ of its capacity.

How many complete 250 ml cups can be filled using the water?

3 The diagram shows the shape of Emily's pond.

She wants to empty the water with a pump.

The water will decrease at a constant rate.

The volume of water goes down by 1000 litres in the first hour.

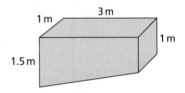

How long will it take for the pond to be emptied of water?
Give your answer in hours and minutes.

4 A carton of juice measures 20 cm × 10 cm × 5 cm.

The juice has a depth of 5 cm when the carton is standing upright, as shown.

When the carton is put on its side, as shown below, what is the new depth of the juice?

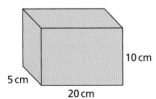

Are you ready?

1 Work out the area of each shape. Round your answers to 3 significant figures.

a

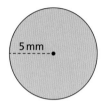

5 mm

b

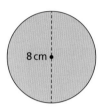

8 cm

c

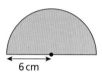

6 cm

2 Both shapes have an area of 15 cm².

Work out the length of each lettered side.

a

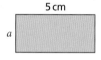

5 cm

a

b

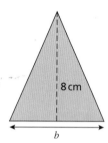

8 cm

b

3 $r = 4$

Work out the value of each term.

a $3r$ **b** r^2 **c** $5r^2$ **d** $\frac{1}{4}r^2$

In the following formulae, V stands for volume, r stands for radius and h stands for the perpendicular height.

Cylinder

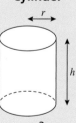

$V = \pi r^2 h$

Cone

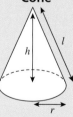

$V = \frac{1}{3}\pi r^2 h$

Sphere

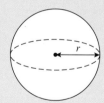

$V = \frac{4}{3}\pi r^3$

Example 1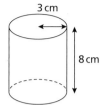

Work out the volume of the cylinder.

Leave your answer in terms of π.

Method

Solution	Commentary
Volume = $\pi r^2 h$	Use the formula for the volume of a cylinder.
$= \pi \times 3^2 \times 8$	The unit of volume here is cm³. There is no rounding needed as the
$= 72\pi$ cm³	question states to leave your answer in terms of π.

Example 2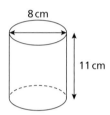

Calculate the volume of the cylinder.

Round your answer to 3 significant figures.

Method

Solution		Commentary
Volume = $\pi r^2 h$	4 cm	Use the formula for the volume of a cylinder.
$= \pi \times 4^2 \times 11$		The unit of volume here is cm³. For this
$= 176\pi$ cm³	11 cm	cylinder, you are given the diameter.
$= 552.92...$ cm³		Divide it by 2 to get the value of the radius.
$= 553$ cm³ (to 3 s.f.)		Round the answer to 3 significant figures.

Example 3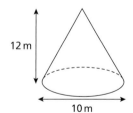

Calculate the volume of the cone.

Round your answer to 2 decimal places.

Method

Solution		Commentary
Volume = $\frac{1}{3}\pi r^2 h$		Use the formula for the volume of a cone.
$= \frac{1}{3} \times \pi \times 5^2 \times 12$	12 m	Divide the diameter by 2 to get the value of the radius.
$= 314.1592...$ m³		
$= 314.16$ m³ (to 2 d.p.)	5 m	Round the answer to 2 decimal places.

Example 4 🖩

Calculate the volume of the sphere.

Leave your answer in terms of π.

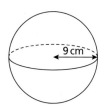

9 cm

Method

Solution	Commentary
Volume = $\frac{4}{3}\pi r^3$	Use the formula for the volume of a sphere.
Volume = $\frac{4}{3} \times \pi \times 9^3$	The unit of volume here is cm³.
Volume = 972π cm³	There is no rounding needed as the question states to leave your answer in terms of π.

Practice

🖩 **1** The table gives information about some cylinders.

Copy and complete the table. Round your answers to 1 decimal place if necessary.

Radius (cm)	Diameter (cm)	Height (cm)	Volume (cm³)
3		12	
	10	18	
7			360
		20	400
	17		750
		25	1000

2 Calculate the volume of each shape, giving your answer:

i in terms of π **ii** to 2 decimal places.

a
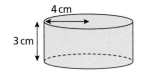
4 cm
3 cm

b
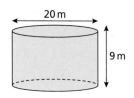
20 m
9 m

c
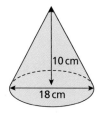
10 cm
18 cm

d
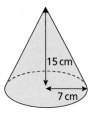
15 cm
7 cm

e
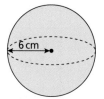
6 cm

f
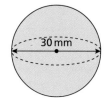
30 mm

3 Calculate the lettered lengths. Round your answer to the nearest integer where appropriate.

a   Volume = 360π cm³

6 cm

h

b   Volume = 942 cm³

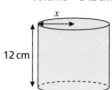

x

12 cm

c   Volume = 392π cm³

x

7 cm

d   Volume = 524 cm³

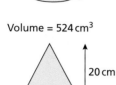

20 cm

x

e   Volume = 288π m³

x

f   Volume = 34 m³

y

4 Calculate the volume of each shape. Round your answers to 1 decimal place.

a

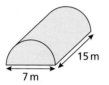

15 m

7 m

b

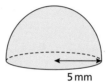

5 mm

5 Calculate the volume of each shape. Round your answers to 3 significant figures.

a

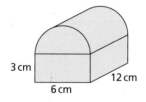

3 cm

6 cm

12 cm

b

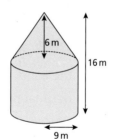

6 m

16 m

9 m

6 Spot the mistake in the workings below.

12 cm

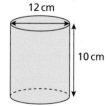

10 cm

Volume = $\pi \times 12^2 \times 10$
Volume = 1440π cm³

7 A solid sphere has a volume of 50 900 cm³.

Do you think the sphere is likely to be the size of a golf ball, a football or a giant beach ball? Explain your reasoning.

What do you think?

1 Why is a cylinder not a prism?

Consolidate – do you need more?

1 Calculate the volume of each shape in terms of π.

a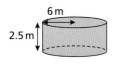
6 m
2.5 m

b
80 cm
3 m

c
7 cm
12 cm

d
11 mm
17 mm

e
3 cm

f
18 mm

2 Calculate the volume of each shape. Round your answers to 2 significant figures.

a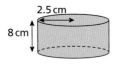
2.5 cm
8 cm

b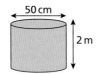
50 cm
2 m

c
7 cm
9 cm

d
11 mm
10 mm

e
7 cm

f
8 m

Stretch – can you deepen your learning?

1 Calculate the volume of the cone.

Round your answer to 1 decimal place.

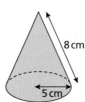
8 cm
5 cm

2 A sphere and a cube have the same volume.

The cube has a side length of 8 cm.

Work out the radius of the sphere, giving your answer to 3 significant figures.

3 The sphere and the cone have the same volume.

Find the height of the cone.

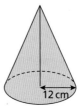
12 cm

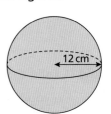
12 cm

4 A sphere has a radius of 15 cm.

It is placed inside a box, touching all six faces when closed.

Find the volume of the space left inside the box.

Round your answer to 1 decimal place.

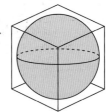

Are you ready?

1 List the number of faces, edges and vertices of a cuboid and a triangular prism.

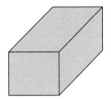 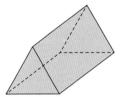

2 Give the name of each of the 3D shapes that can be made from these nets.

a 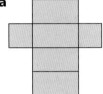 **b** 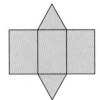 **c** **d**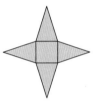

3 Calculate the area of each 2D shape. Round your answer to 2 decimal places where necessary.

a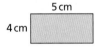
5 cm
4 cm

b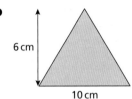
6 cm
10 cm

c
2.5 cm
10 cm

d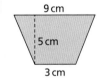
9 cm
5 cm
3 cm

e
7 cm

f
10 cm

Surface area is the total area of all the faces of a 3D shape. To work out the surface area, find the area of all the faces individually and add them together.

Drawing a **net** may help you calculate the dimensions of the faces. A net is a 2D shape that can be folded to make a 3D shape.

This is a net for making a cube. It is made up of six squares.

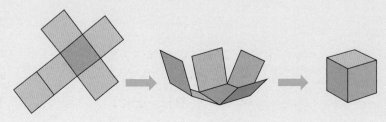

This is a net for a sqaure-based pyramid. It is made up of one square (the base) and four triangles.

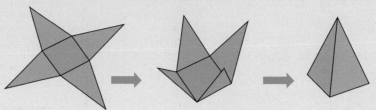

Example 1

Calculate the surface area of the cuboid.

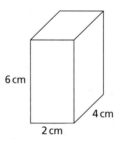

Method

Solution	Commentary
2 cm **A** 2 cm 4 cm 4 cm 6 cm **B** **C** **D** **E** 6 cm 4 cm **F** 2 cm	The net of a cuboid is made from six rectangles. The faces come in pairs: top and base, front and back, and the two sides.
Top and base: A = 4 × 2 = 8 cm² F = 4 × 2 = 8 cm²	
Front and back: B = 6 × 2 = 12 cm² D = 6 × 2 = 12 cm²	
Sides: C = 4 × 6 = 24 cm² E = 4 × 6 = 24 cm²	
Total area = 88 cm²	You could alternatively find the area of one face from each pair and then double your answer. 2(8 + 12 + 24) = 88 cm²

Example 2

Calculate the surface area of the triangular prism.

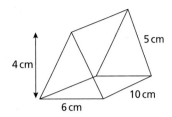

Method

Solution	Commentary
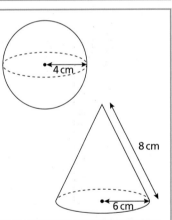	The net of a triangular prism is made from: • two matching triangles (front and back) • two matching rectangles (two sides) • a rectangular base.
Base: D = 10 × 6 = 60 cm²	
Front and back: A = 0.5 × 6 × 4 = 12 cm² B = 0.5 × 6 × 4 = 12 cm²	
Sides: C = 10 × 5 = 50 cm² E = 10 × 5 = 50 cm²	
Total area = 184 cm²	

Example 3 📱

a The formula for the surface area of a sphere is $A = 4\pi r^2$

Use the formula to work out the surface area of the sphere.

Write your answer to 2 decimal places.

b The formula for the surface area of a cone is $A = \pi r^2 + \pi r l$, where r is the radius and l is the slant height.

Use the formula to work out the surface area of the cone.

Write your answer to 1 decimal place.

Method

Solution	Commentary
a $A = 4\pi r^2$	
$A = 4 \times \pi \times 4^2$	Substitute the radius into the formula.
$A = 4 \times \pi \times 16$	
$A = 201.061\,929\ldots$	
$A = 201.06$ cm² (to 2 d.p.)	Remember to include units in your answer.
b $A = \pi r^2 + \pi r l$	Substitute the radius and the slant height into the formula.
$A = \pi \times 6^2 + \pi \times 6 \times 8$	
$A = \pi \times 36 + \pi \times 48$	You could write $\pi \times 36 + \pi \times 48$ more simply as 84π.
$A = 263.9$ cm² (to 1 d.p.)	Remember to include units in your answer.

Example 4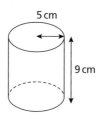

Calculate the surface area of the cylinder.

Round your answer to 2 significant figures.

5 cm

9 cm

Method

Solution	Commentary
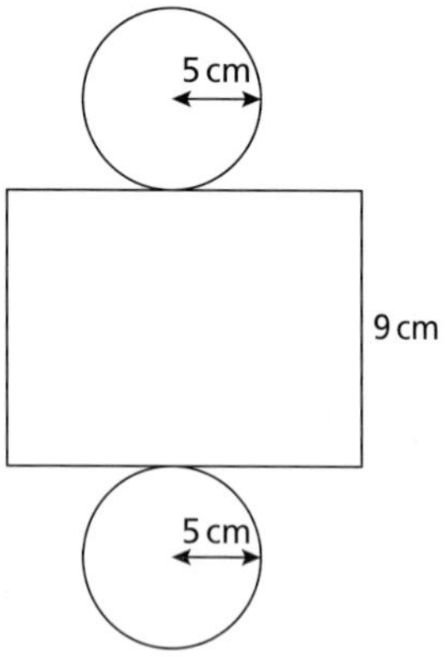 5 cm 9 cm 5 cm	The net of a cylinder is made from: • two matching circles • one rectangle (the circumference of the circle creates one side of the rectangle).
Circles: Area = 2 × πr^2 Area = 2 × π × 5^2 Area = 157.0796… cm^2	
Rectangle/curved surface: Area = πd × h Area = π × 10 × 9 Area = 282.7433… cm^2	
Total area = 439.8229… cm^2 Total area = 440 cm^2 (to 2 s.f.)	Add together your unrounded values for the area of the circles and the rectangle/curved surface. Round the total to 2 significant figures as required.

Practice

1️⃣ Calculate the surface area of each cuboid.

a

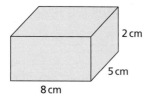

2 cm

5 cm

8 cm

b

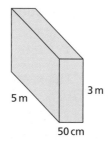

5 m

3 m

50 cm

2 Calculate the surface area of each triangular prism.

a

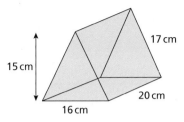

17 cm
15 cm
20 cm
16 cm

b

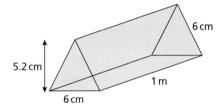

6 cm
5.2 cm
1 m
6 cm

3 Calculate the surface area of each cylinder. **a**
Round your answers to 1 decimal place.

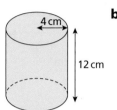

4 cm
12 cm

b

10 cm
14 cm

4 Calculate the surface area of each shape.

a

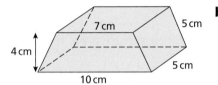

7 cm
5 cm
4 cm
5 cm
10 cm

b

8 m
6 m
10 m
4 m
5 m
10 m

5 The formula for the surface area of a sphere is $A = 4\pi r^2$
Use the formula to work out the surface area of the sphere.
Give your answer to 2 decimal places.

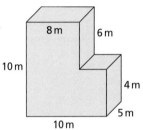

7 cm

6 The formula for the surface area of a cone is $A = \pi r^2 + \pi r l$,
where r is the radius and l is the slant height.

Use the formula to work out the surface area of the cone.

Give your answer to 1 decimal place.

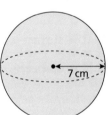

9.1 cm
6.8 cm

7 The surface area of a cube is 486 m².
Find the length of a side of the cube.

8 The volume of a cube is 216 cm³.
Work out the surface area of the cube.

9 A gift box is to be wrapped in paper.
It is in the shape of a cuboid, as shown.

Wrapping paper costs £1.20 per sheet and
can only be bought in whole sheets.

Each sheet covers 1 m².

Find the minimum cost of wrapping the gift box.

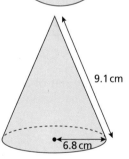

20 cm
50 cm
80 cm

What do you think? 🌐

1. How many possible nets can you make for a cube?

Consolidate – do you need more?

🔲 **1** Calculate the surface area of each shape. Round your answers to 1 significant figure.

a
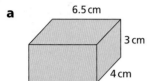
6.5 cm
3 cm
4 cm

b
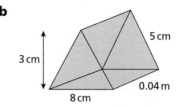
5 cm
3 cm
8 cm
0.04 m

c
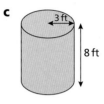
3 ft
8 ft

🔲 **2** Which shape has the greatest surface area, the cube or the cylinder?

8 cm

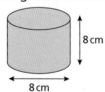
8 cm
8 cm

3 The surface area of the cuboid is 146 cm².

Calculate the value of a.

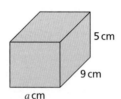
5 cm
9 cm
a cm

Stretch – can you deepen your learning?

🔲 **1** The net of a triangular prism is placed on the rectangle.

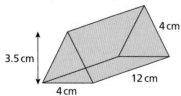
4 cm
3.5 cm
12 cm
4 cm

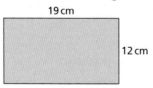
19 cm
12 cm

What percentage of the rectangle is **not** covered by the net of the triangular prism? Give your answer to the nearest integer.

2 A cuboid has two square faces with side length y cm.

The length of the cuboid is 8 cm longer than the height.

Write an expression for the surface area of the cuboid.

Are you ready?

1 State the number of faces, edges and vertices of each 3D shape.

   a 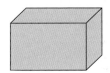   **b**   **c**   **d**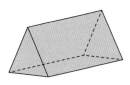

2 How many faces does each 3D shape have, and what shape are these faces?

   a 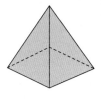   **b** 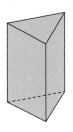   **c** 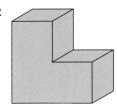   **d**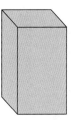

Plans and **elevations** show an object from three different persectives.

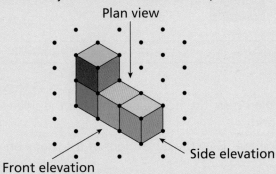

The **plan view** is the view when looking down on the object.

The **side elevation** is the view from one side.

The **front elevation** is the view from the front.

Example 1

The diagram shows a shape made with centimetre cubes.

On a centimetre grid, draw:

a the front elevation

b the side elevation

c the plan view.

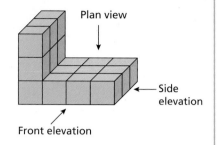

Plan view

Side elevation

Front elevation

Method

Solution	Commentary
a 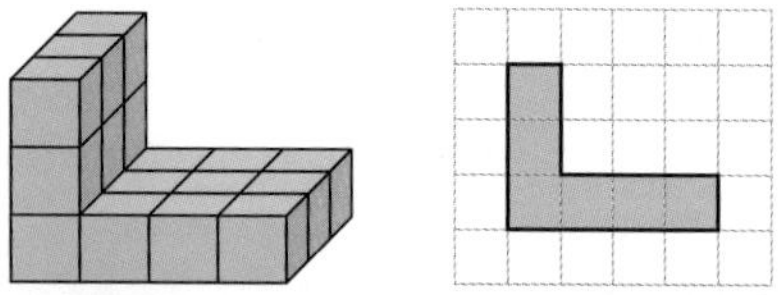	The front elevation is determined by the four cubes at the base and the cubes on the left-hand side.
b 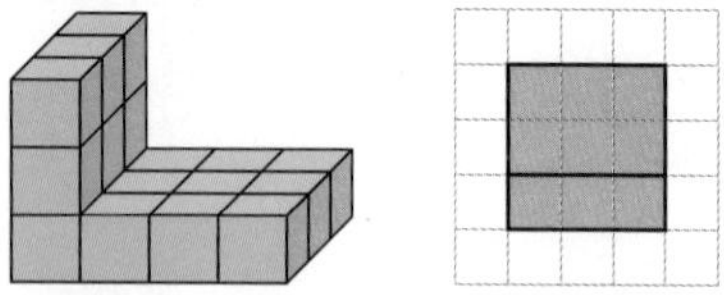	For the side elevation, show the internal line that connects the two parts of the view.
c 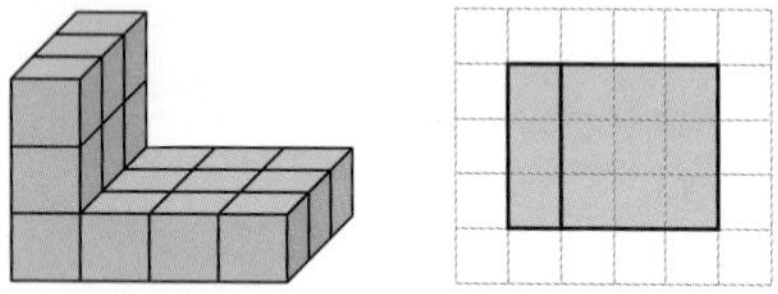	Likewise for the plan view.

Example 2

The diagram shows the plan view, the front elevation and the side elevation of a 3D shape drawn on a centimetre grid.

Draw a sketch of the 3D shape. Give the dimensions of the shape on your sketch.

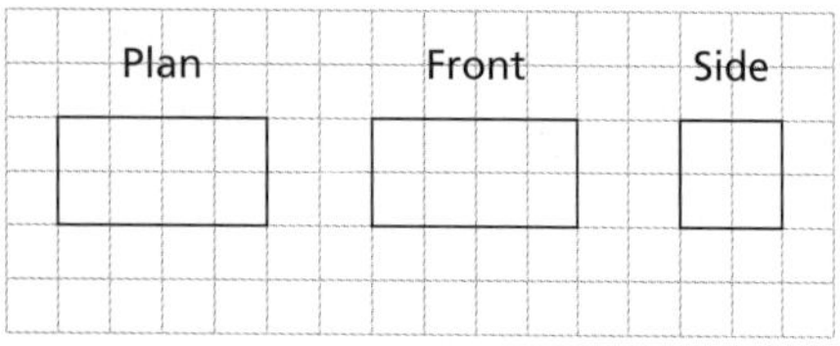

Plan   Front   Side

Method

Solution	Commentary
	From the top and front, you can see two identical rectangles.
	From the side, you can see a square.
	This shape will be a cuboid, so sketch the cuboid.
2 cm 4 cm 2 cm	From the grid, you can see that the length is 4 cm, the height 2 cm and the depth is 2 cm.
	Show this on your sketch.

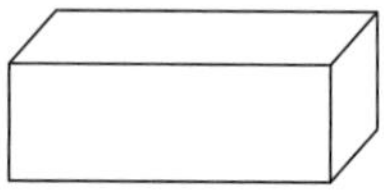

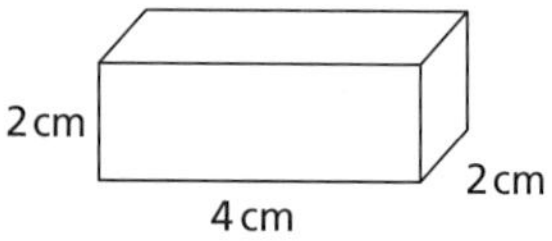

Practice

1 The diagrams show three different shapes made with centimetre cubes.

For each shape, draw the plan view, the front elevation and the side elevation on a centimetre grid.

a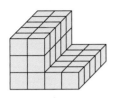

b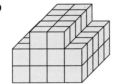

c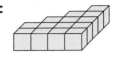

2 For each shape, draw the plan view, the front elevation and the side elevation on a centimetre grid.

a

b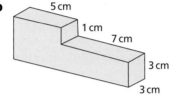

c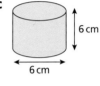

3 Write down the name of each 3D shape based on the information given.

a Front elevation = rectangle

Side elevation = rectangle

Plan view = rectangle

b Front elevation = rectangle

Side elevation = rectangle

Plan view = circle

c Front elevation = triangle

Side elevation = triangle

Plan view = square

4 The diagrams show the plan view, the front elevation and the side elevation of a 3D shape drawn on a centimetre grid.

Draw a sketch of the 3D shape.

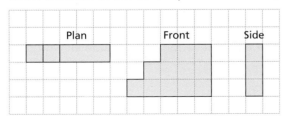

5 Each diagram shows the plan view, the front elevation and the side elevation of a 3D shape drawn on a centimetre grid.

Draw a sketch of each 3D shape. Give the dimensions of the shape on your sketch.

a

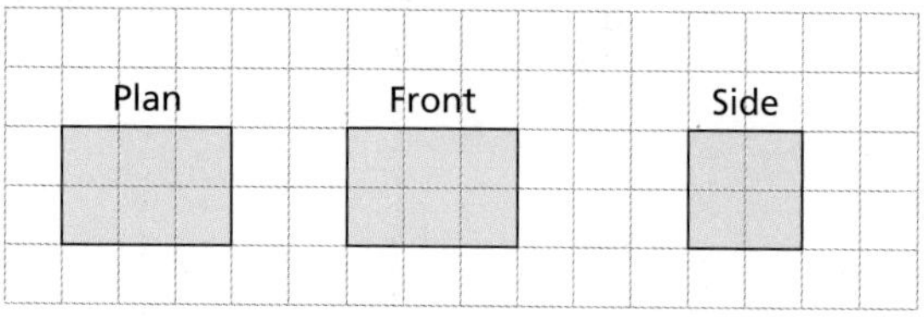

Plan   Front   Side

b

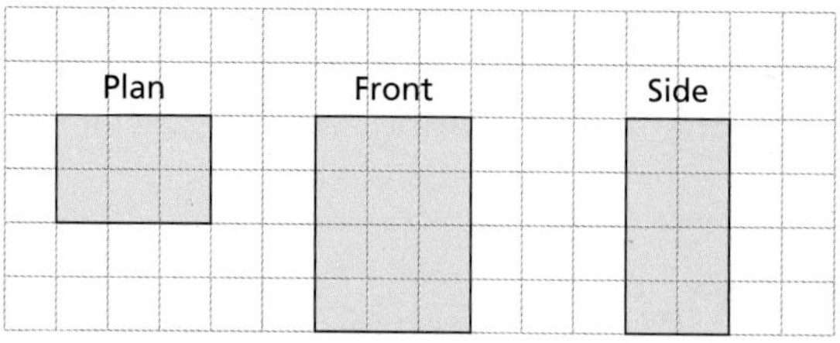

Plan   Front   Side

6 The diagrams show the plan view, the front elevation and the side elevation of a 3D shape.

Draw a sketch of each 3D shape.

a   Plan   Front   Side   b   Plan   Front   Side

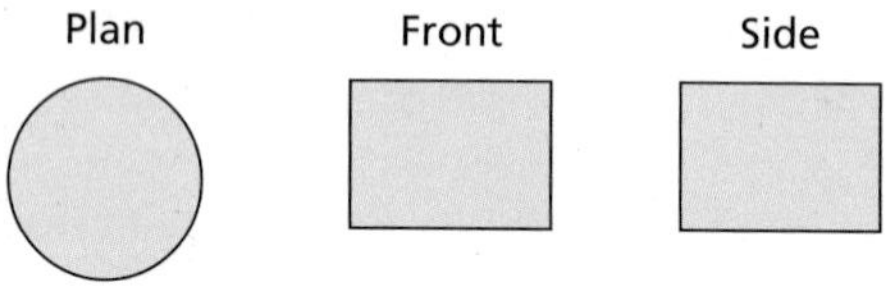

What do you think?

1 The front and side elevations of a 3D shape are given.

They are both rectangles measuring 5 cm by 3 cm.

Rhys says the shape must be a cuboid.

Do you agree? Explain your reasoning.

Consolidate – do you need more?

1 The diagram shows the plan view, the front elevation and the side elevation of a 3D shape drawn on a centimetre grid.

Sketch the 3D shape.

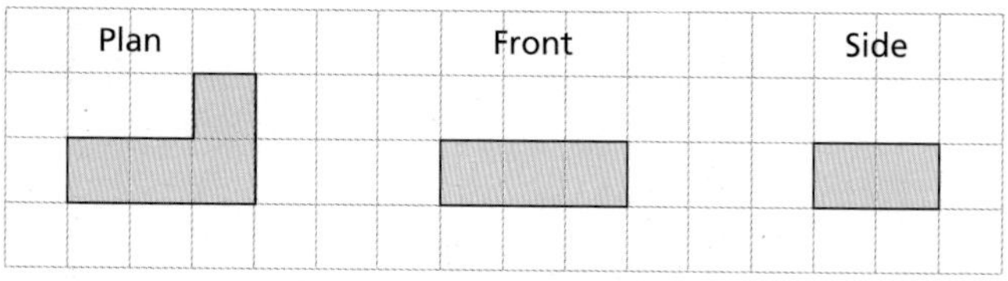

Plan   Front   Side

2 The diagrams show the plan view, the front elevation and the side elevation of a 3D shape.

Sketch the 3D shape.

Plan   Front   Side

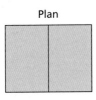 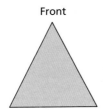 

3 The diagram shows the plan view, the front elevation and the side elevation of a 3D shape drawn on a centimetre grid.

Sketch the 3D shape. Give the dimensions of the shape on your sketch.

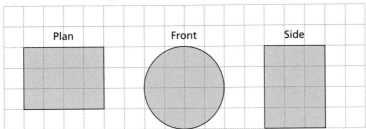

4 For each shape, draw the plan view, the front elevation and the side elevation on a centimetre grid.

a 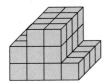   **b**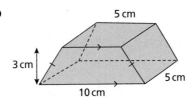

Stretch – can you deepen your learning?

1 The diagram shows a square-based right pyramid.

Using the scale 2 cm : 1 m, draw the plan view, the front elevation and the side elevation on a centimetre grid.

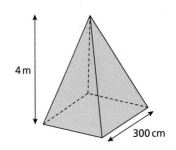

1 Write down the mathematical name of each of these 3D shapes. (2)

a)   **b)**

2 Here is a cube.

Write down the number of:

a) faces (1)

b) edges (1)

c) vertices. (1)

3 This solid object is made from five 1 cm cubes.

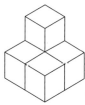

Draw the plan of the solid object on a copy of this square centimetre grid. (2)

4 Work out the volume of a cube with side lengths of 20 m. Give units with your answer. (3)

5 Here is a triangular prism.

a) Work out the volume of the prism.
Give units with your answer. (3)

b) Work out the surface area of the prism.
Give units with your answer. (4)

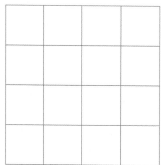
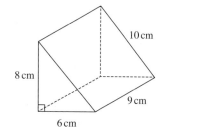

10 cm

8 cm

9 cm

6 cm

1–3

3–5

In this block, we will cover...

8.1 Pythagoras' theorem

Example 1

a Identify the longest side in each of these righ[...]

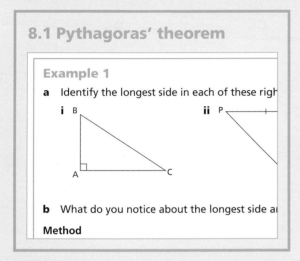

i B

ii P

b What do you notice about the longest side a[...]

Method

8.2 Trigonometry

Practice (A)

1. Label the opposite, adjacent and hypoten[...]

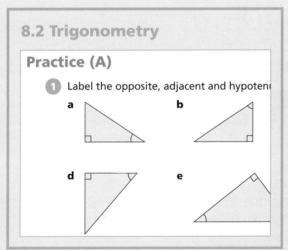

a   **b**

d   **e**

8.3 Exact values

Consolidate – do you need more

1. Work out the length of each lettered side.

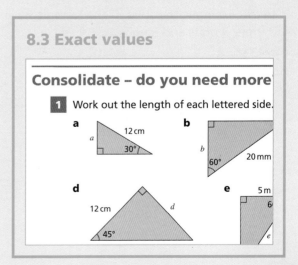

a 12 cm, a, 30°   **b** b, 60°, 20 mm

d 12 cm, d, 45°   **e** 5 m, 6[...], e

Are you ready? (A)

1 Which is a right angle?

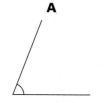  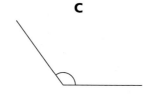 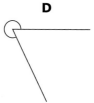

A   **B**   **C**   **D**

2 Work out $5^2 + 4^2$

3 What is $\sqrt{144}$?

4 $\boxed{}^2 = 225$

What is the missing number?

Using your calculator 🖩

Make sure you know how to use these buttons.

You can use this button (x^2) to square a number.

You can use this button ($\sqrt{\square}$) to square root a number.

Use a calculator to double check any answers that you work out mentally or using a written method.

Pythagoras' theorem states that 'in a right-angled triangle, the square on the **hypotenuse** is equal to the sum of the squares on the other two sides'.

In this example, the sides of the triangle have lengths 3 units, 4 units and 5 units.

$3^2 + 4^2 = 5^2$

$9 + 16 = 25$

This can be generalised by labelling the sides of the triangle as a, b and c, where c is the hypotenuse.

Then $a^2 + b^2 = c^2$

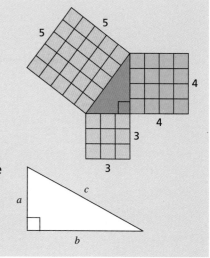

Example 1

a Identify the longest side in each of these right-angled triangles.

i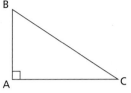

ii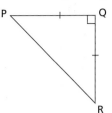

iii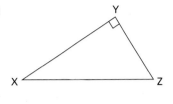

b What do you notice about the longest side and the angles?

Method

Solution	Commentary
a i BC	You could measure the sides with a ruler to check.
ii PR	
iii XZ	
b The longest side in a right-angled triangle is always opposite the right angle.	The longest side of a right-angled triangle is the hypotenuse.

Example 2

Write the length of the hypotenuse in each of these right-angled triangles.

a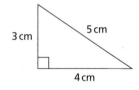

b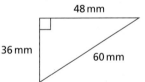

c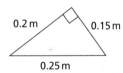

Method

Solution	Commentary
a 5 cm	The hypotenuse is the longest side and is always opposite the right angle.
b 60 mm	
c 0.25 m	

Practice (A)

1 Write the length of the hypotenuse of each right-angled triangle.

a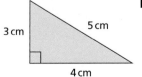

b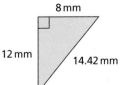

c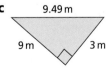

d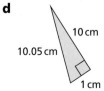

2 Use letter notation to identify the hypotenuse of each right-angled triangle.

The first one is done for you.

a hypotenuse = AB

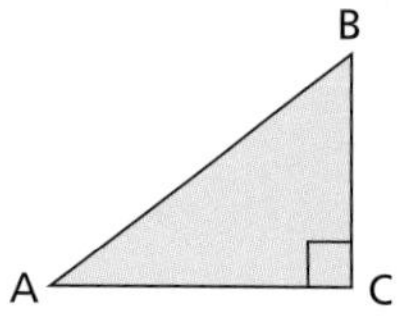

b

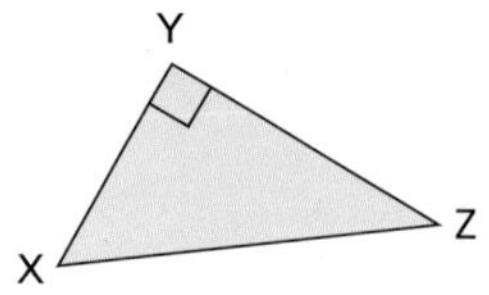

c

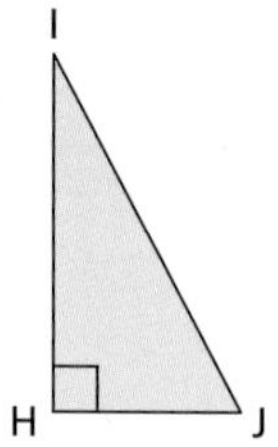

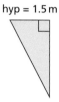

d

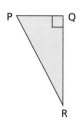

3 The length of the hypotenuse of each right-angled triangle is given.

Label it on a copy of each triangle.

a hyp = 12 cm

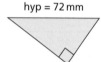

b hyp = 18 m

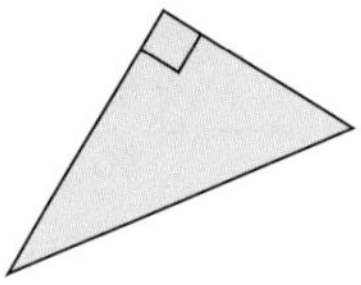

c hyp = 1.5 m

d hyp = 72 mm

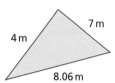

e hyp = 9.6 cm

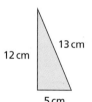

f hyp = 10 cm

4 Each of the triangles are right-angled.

Draw the right angles in the correct position.

a

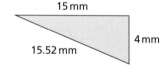

4 m 7 m 8.06 m

b

12 cm 13 cm 5 cm

c

15 mm 4 mm 15.52 mm

What do you think?

1 The lengths of the two shorter sides of a right-angled triangle are 54 cm and 72 cm.

Which of these **could** be the length of the hypotenuse?

A	B	C	D
72 cm	90 cm	67 cm	29 cm

How do you know?

Are you ready? (B)

1 What is 8^2?

2 Work out $6^2 + 7^2$

3 What is $\sqrt{121}$?

4 $\boxed{}^2 = 169$

What is the missing number?

Example 🖩

Work out the length of the hypotenuse in each right-angled triangle. Round your answer to 1 decimal place where necessary.

a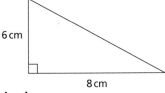

b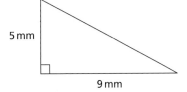

Method

Solution	Commentary
a 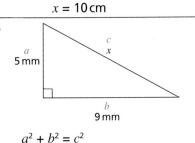 $a^2 + b^2 = c^2$ $6^2 + 8^2 = x^2$ $36 + 64 = x^2$ $100 = x^2$ $x = \sqrt{100}$ $x = 10\,\text{cm}$	Label the sides a, b and c. Make sure that c is the hypotenuse. Substitute the values you know into the formula for Pythagoras' theorem and solve for x.
b $a^2 + b^2 = c^2$ $5^2 + 9^2 = x^2$ $25 + 81 = x^2$ $106 = x^2$ $x = \sqrt{106}$ $x = 10.3\,\text{mm}$ (to 1 d.p.)	Label the sides a, b and c. Make sure that c is the hypotenuse. Substitute the values you know into the formula for Pythagoras' theorem and solve for x.

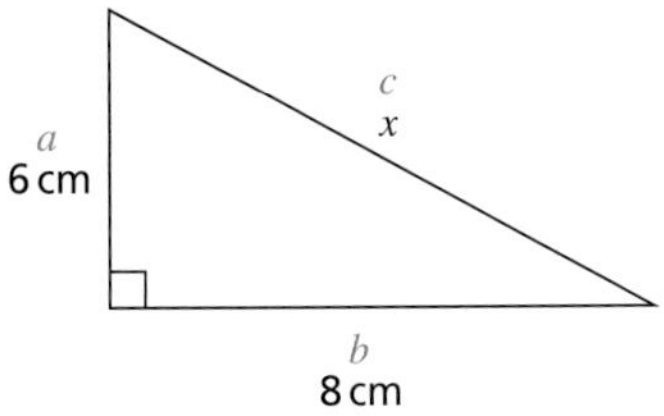

Practice (B) 🖩

Round answers to 1 decimal place where appropriate.

1 Work out the length of the hypotenuse in each right-angled triangle.

a
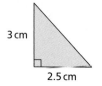
5 cm
12 cm

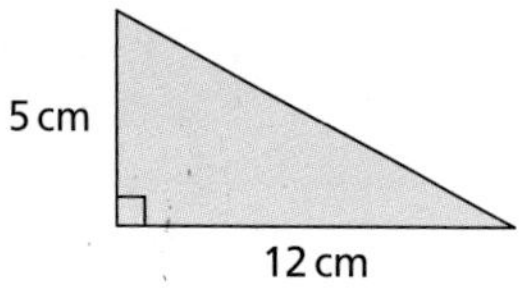

b
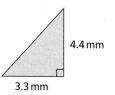
4 mm
3 mm

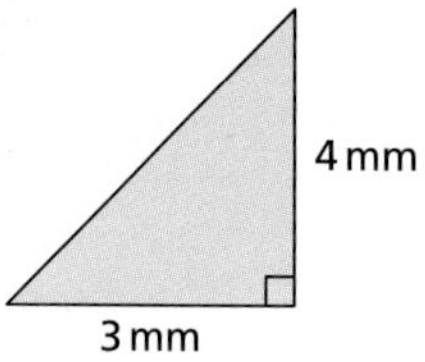

c
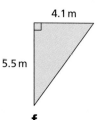
7 m
24 m

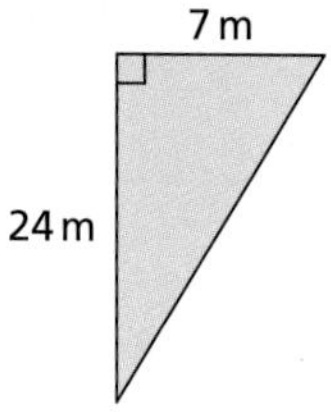

d
35 cm
12 cm

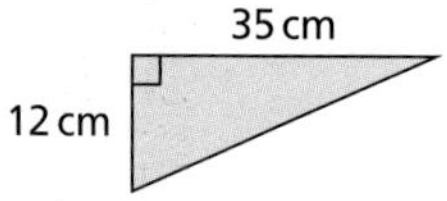

e
27 mm
36 mm

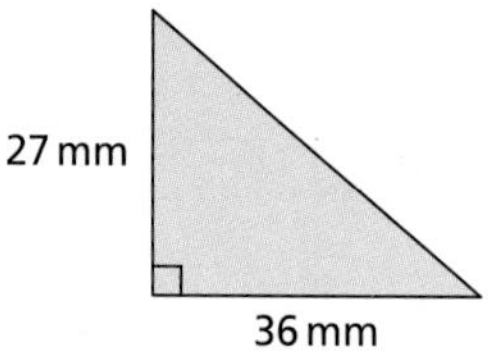

f
84 cm
13 cm

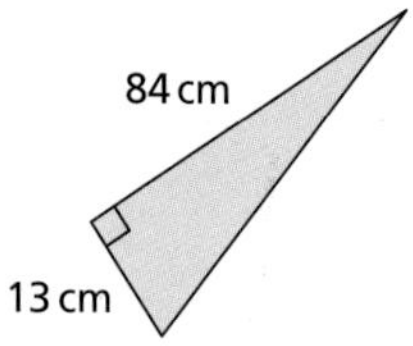

2 Calculate the length of the hypotenuse in each triangle.

a
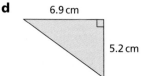
3 cm
2.5 cm

b
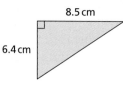
4.4 mm
3.3 mm

c
4.1 m
5.5 m

d
6.9 cm
5.2 cm

e
8.5 cm
6.4 cm

f

9.7 m
7.3 m

3 Work out the length of the side AB.

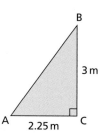
B
3 m
A
2.25 m
C

4 Calculate the length of GH.

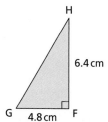
H
6.4 cm
G
4.8 cm
F

5 Decide whether each of these triangles is right-angled. Show your working.

a

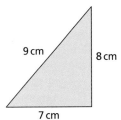

9 cm   8 cm

7 cm

b

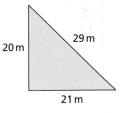

20 m   29 m

21 m

c

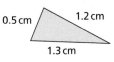

0.5 cm   1.2 cm

1.3 cm

Are you ready? (C)

1 What is the length of the hypotenuse?

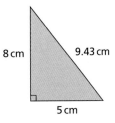

8 cm   9.43 cm

5 cm

2 Work out the length of the hypotenuse.

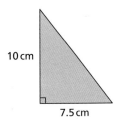

10 cm

7.5 cm

3 Calculate $5^2 - 1^2$

Example

Calculate the length of the unknown side in the triangle.

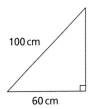

100 cm

60 cm

Method

Solution	Commentary
100 cm / 60 cm / ? $60^2 + ?^2 = 100^2$ $3600 + ?^2 = 10\,000$ $?^2 = 6400$ $? = \sqrt{6400}$ $? = 80\,cm$	The hypotenuse is given. You need to work out the length of one of the shorter sides. Substitute in the values you know, and then solve to find the other side length.

Practice (C) 🖩

Round answers to 3 significant figures where appropriate.

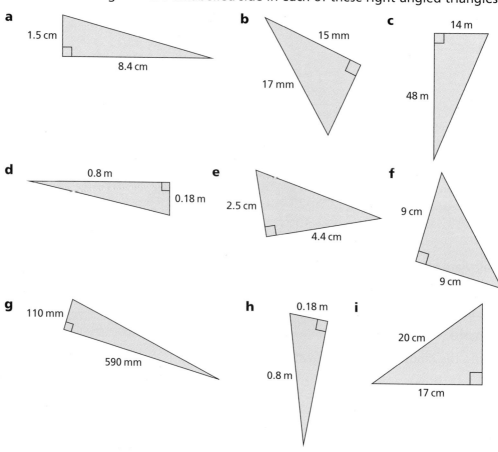

1 Work out the length of the unlabelled side in each triangle.

a 30 cm, 38 cm

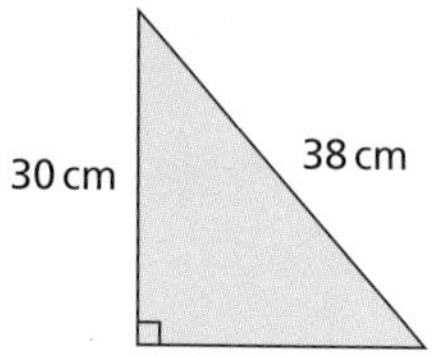

b 2.9 m, 4 m

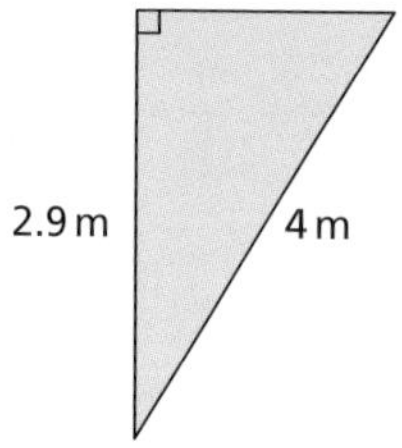

c 5.3 mm, 13 mm

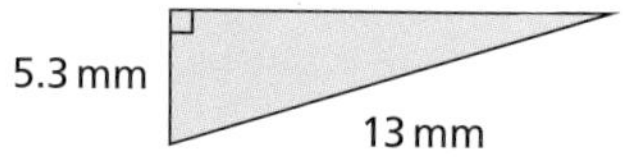

2 Work out the length of the unlabelled side in each of these right-angled triangles.

a 1.5 cm, 8.4 cm

b 15 mm, 17 mm

c 14 m, 48 m

d 0.8 m, 0.18 m

e 2.5 cm, 4.4 cm

f 9 cm, 9 cm

g 110 mm, 590 mm

h 0.18 m, 0.8 m

i 20 cm, 17 cm

3 Calculate the perpendicular height of the trapezium.

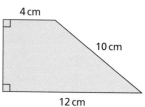

4 cm

10 cm

12 cm

4 Town A is 181 km due East of Town B.

Town C is 165 km due North of Town B.

Calculate the distance between Town A and Town C. Give your answer correct to the nearest kilometre.

Consolidate – do you need more?

1 Write the length of the hypotenuse in each right-angled triangle.

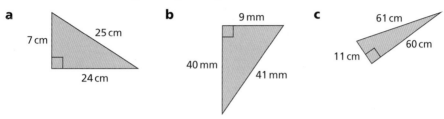

a 4.9 cm 4.4 cm 2.1 cm

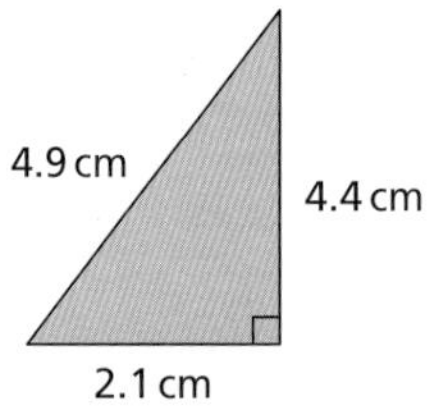

b 3.6 mm 4.7 mm 3 mm

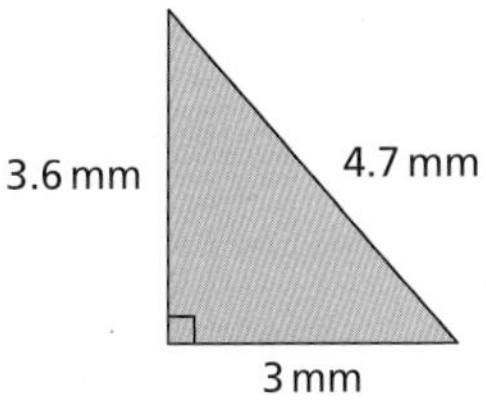

c 9 m 5.4 m 7.2 m

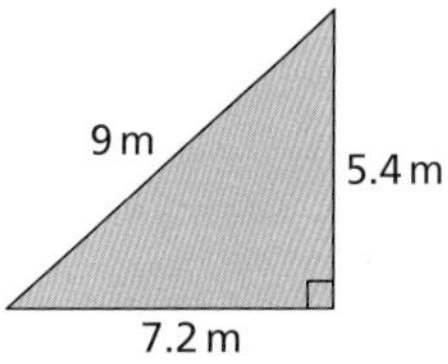

d 10.7 cm 8.8 cm 6.1 cm

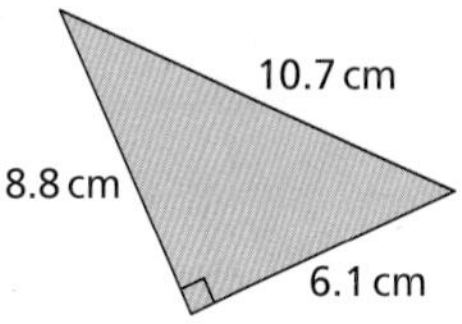

2 Show that each triangle is right-angled.

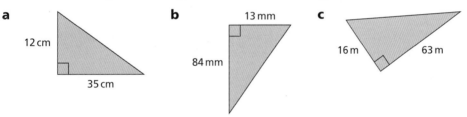

a 7 cm 25 cm 24 cm

b 9 mm 40 mm 41 mm

c 61 cm 60 cm 11 cm

3 Work out the length of the hypotenuse in each triangle.

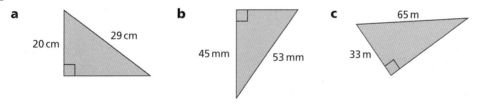

a 12 cm 35 cm

b 13 mm 84 mm

c 16 m 63 m

4 Work out the length of the unknown side in each right-angled triangle.

a 20 cm 29 cm

b 45 mm 53 mm

c 65 m 33 m

Stretch – can you deepen your learning?

1 The lengths of a right-angled triangle are 22.4 cm, 168 mm and 28 cm.
What is the length of the hypotenuse?

2 The two shorter sides of a right-angled triangle have lengths 17 cm and 15 cm.
Work out the length of the longest side.

3 A triangle has sides of length 2.4 cm, 32 mm and 0.04 m.
Show that the triangle is right-angled.

Are you ready? (A)

1 Which side of this triangle is the hypotenuse?

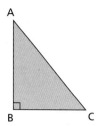

2 What is the missing angle?

3 $a = \dfrac{b}{c}$

Work out the value of a when $b = 400$ and $c = 50$

Trigonometry is a branch of maths that relates the angles and sides of a right-angled triangle. It is very helpful in fields like engineering, physics and architecture to calculate distances, heights or angles in various practical situations.

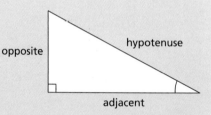

In a right-angled triangle, there is a 90° angle. There is also often another angle that is either given or to be found.

The sides of the triangle are labelled in relation to this other angle:

- hypotenuse (the longest side, opposite the right angle)

- adjacent (next to the angle being considered)

- opposite (opposite the angle being considered)

To remember these ratios, you can use the acronym SOH-CAH-TOA:

SOH: **S**ine = **O**pposite ÷ **H**ypotenuse

CAH: **C**osine = **A**djacent ÷ **H**ypotenuse

TOA: **T**angent = **O**pposite ÷ **A**djacent

For any right-angled triangle, three **trigonometric ratios** can be defined. These ratios help to find unknown sides or angles.

Ratio	How it is calculated
sine (abbreviated 'sin')	Divide the opposite by the hypotenuse: $$\sin(\text{angle}) = \frac{\text{opposite}}{\text{hypotenuse}}$$
cosine (abbreviated 'cos')	Divide the adjacent by the hypotenuse: $$\cos(\text{angle}) = \frac{\text{adjacent}}{\text{hypotenuse}}$$
tangent (abbreviated 'tan')	Divide the opposite by the adjacent: $$\tan(\text{angle}) = \frac{\text{opposite}}{\text{adjacent}}$$

Using your calculator 🖩

You should become familiar with the trigonometry keys on your calculator. They will be labelled **sin**, **cos** and **tan**.

Above these keys will be the inverse of each function, which are 'sin⁻¹', 'cos⁻¹' and 'tan⁻¹'. To access these inverse keys, you may need to press 'SHIFT' or '2ⁿᵈ' depending on your make of calculator.

Example

Label the opposite, adjacent and hypotenuse on each right-angled triangle.

a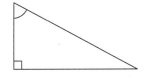

b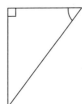

Method

Solution	Commentary
a 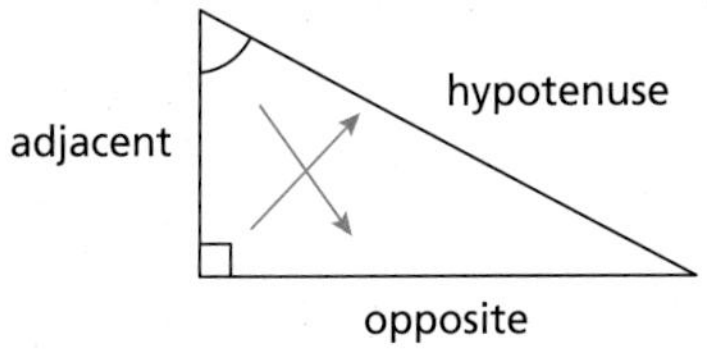 adjacent / hypotenuse / opposite	The 'hypotenuse' is always opposite the right angle. The 'opposite' is always opposite the angle you are interested in. The 'adjacent' is always next to the angle you are interested in.
b adjacent / opposite / hypotenuse	

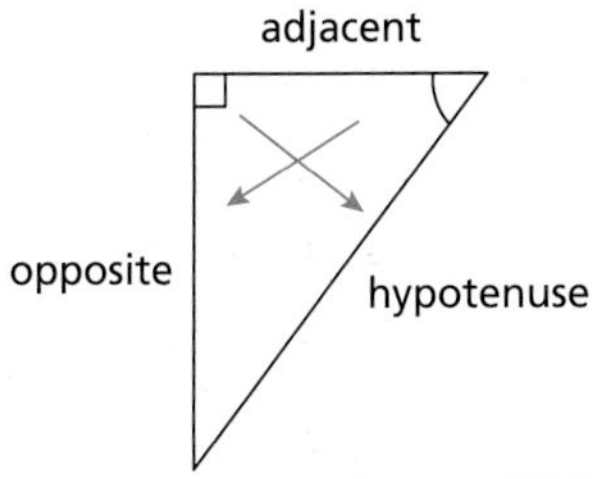

Practice (A)

1 Label the opposite, adjacent and hypotenuse on each triangle.

a

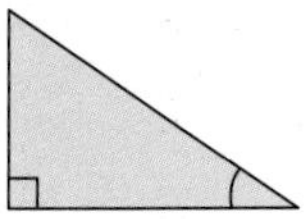

b

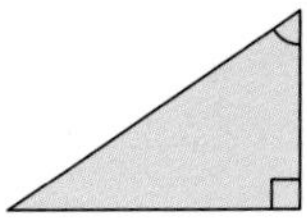

c

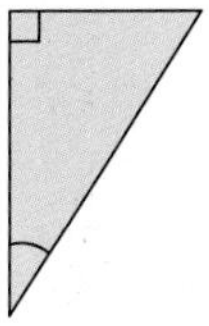

d

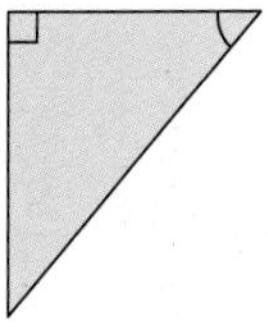

e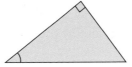

f

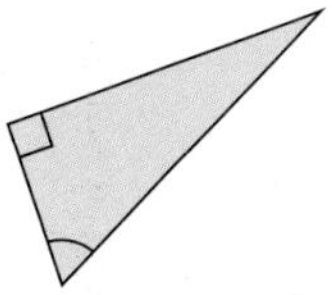

2 Use letter notation to identify the adjacent side in each right-angled triangle.

a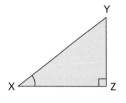

b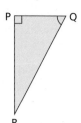

c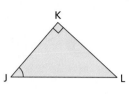

3 Use letter notation to identify the opposite side in each right-angled triangle.

a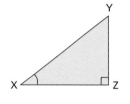

b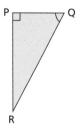

c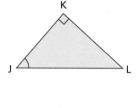

4 Label the side lengths on copies of these diagrams.

a
opp = 6.71 cm
adj = 9.95 cm
hyp = 12 cm

b
opp = 35.67 mm
adj = 32.12 mm
hyp = 48 mm

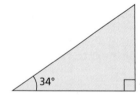

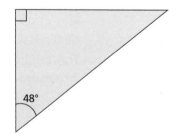

What do you think? 💭

1 The length of the adjacent is 100 m.

Label it on the diagram.

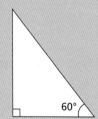

Are you ready? (B)

1 Label the opposite, adjacent and hypotenuse on each right-angled triangle.

a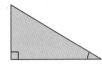
b
c

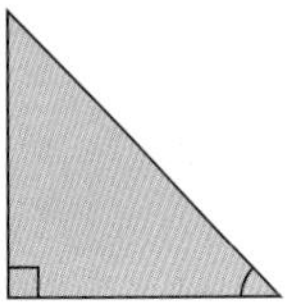

Example 1

Which ratio is needed to work out the side length labelled with a question mark in each triangle?

a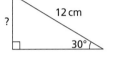

b

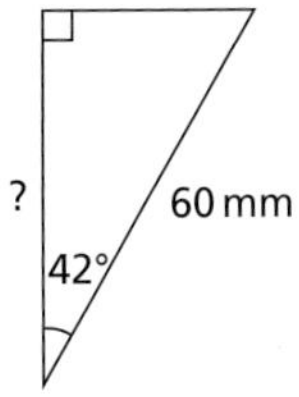

> Start by labelling the opposite, adjacent and hypotenuse.
>
> Then circle the length you know and the length you want to find out.

Method

Solution	Commentary
a 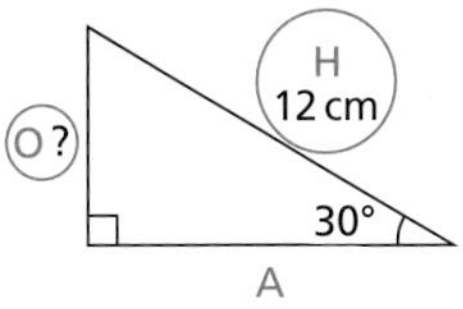 sine	You know the hypotenuse (H) and you want to find the opposite (O), so use the sine ratio $\left(= \dfrac{O}{H} \right)$.
b 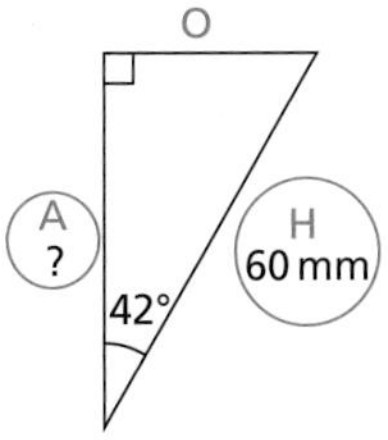 cosine	You know the hypotenuse (H) and you want to find the adjacent (A), so use the cosine ratio $\left(= \dfrac{A}{H} \right)$.

Example 2

Which ratio is needed to work out the marked angle in each triangle?

a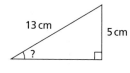

b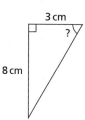

> Start by labelling the opposite, adjacent and hypotenuse.
>
> Then circle the lengths you know.

Method

Solution	Commentary
a H 13 cm, O 5 cm, ? A sine	You know the hypotenuse (H) and the opposite (O) so use the sine ratio $\left(= \dfrac{O}{H} \right)$.
b A 3 cm, ?, O 8 cm, H tangent	You know the opposite (O) and the adjacent (A) so use the tangent ratio $\left(= \dfrac{O}{A} \right)$.

Practice (B)

1 Which ratio do you need to use to work out the length of each lettered side?

a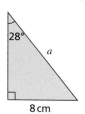

b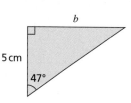

c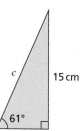

d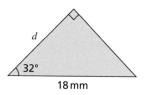

e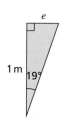

f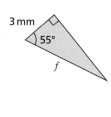

2 Which ratio do you need to use to work out the size of each lettered angle?

a
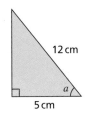
12 cm
5 cm
a

b
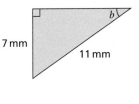
7 mm
11 mm
b

c
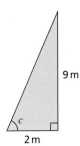
9 m
2 m
c

d
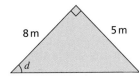
8 m
5 m
d

e
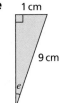
1 cm
9 cm
e

f
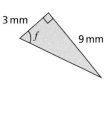
3 mm
9 mm
f

3 Sketch three right-angled triangles in which you would need to use the sine ratio to work out either a missing side or angle.

4 Sketch three right-angled triangles in which you would need to use the cosine ratio to work out either a missing side or angle.

5 Sketch three right-angled triangles in which you would need to use the tangent ratio to work out either a missing side or angle.

Are you ready? (C)

1 Which ratio do you need to use to work out the length of each lettered side?

a
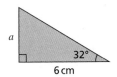
a
32°
6 cm

b
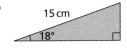
15 cm
18°
b

c

10 cm
47°
c

2 Which ratio do you need to use to work out the size of each lettered angle?

a

5 cm
x
4 cm

b
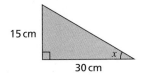
15 cm
30 cm
x

c
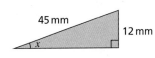
45 mm
12 mm
x

Example 1 🖩

Work out the length of each lettered side. Give your answer to 1 decimal place where appropriate.

a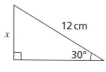

b

Method

Solution	Commentary
a $\times 12 \left(\sin 30° = \dfrac{x}{12} \right) \times 12$ $12 \times \sin 30° = x$ $x = 6\,\text{cm}$ 	Remember it is the angle that goes next to sin, cos or tan. So you use sin 30° and you know it is equal to the opposite divided by the hypotenuse.
b $\times 60 \left(\cos 42° = \dfrac{y}{60} \right) \times 60$ $60 \times \cos 42° = y$ $y = 44.588...$ $y = 44.6\,\text{mm}$ (to 1 d.p.)	Here you use cos 42° and you know it is equal to the adjacent divided by the hypotenuse. The answer comes out as 44.588..., which rounds to 44.6 to 1 decimal place.

Example 2 🖩

Work out the size of each lettered angle.

a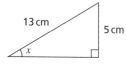

b 3 cm
y
8 cm

Method

Solution	Commentary
a 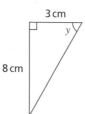 SOH $\sin x = \dfrac{5}{13}$ $x = \sin^{-1}\left(\dfrac{5}{13}\right)$ $= 22.6°$ (to 1 d.p.)	When you want to work out an angle, you need to use inverse functions. The inverse of sin is $\sin^{-1}$, the inverse of cos is $\cos^{-1}$ and the inverse of tan is $\tan^{-1}$. You can find these buttons on your calculator, usually by pressing 'shift' and then 'sin', 'cos' or 'tan'.

b

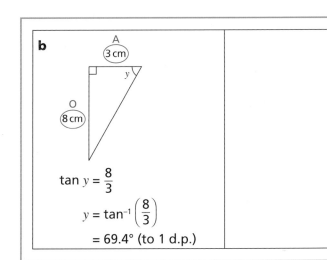

$\tan y = \dfrac{8}{3}$

$y = \tan^{-1}\left(\dfrac{8}{3}\right)$

$= 69.4°$ (to 1 d.p.)

Practice (C)

1 Use the sine ratio to work out the length of each lettered side.

Give your answers to 1 decimal place.

a

12 cm

46°

b

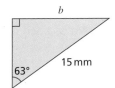

b

63°

15 mm

c

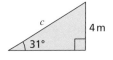

c

31°

4 m

2 Use the cosine ratio to work out the length of each lettered side.

Give your answers to 1 decimal place.

a

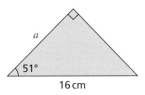

a

51°

16 cm

b

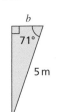

b

71°

5 m

c

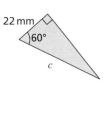

22 mm

60°

c

3 Use the tangent ratio to work out the length of each lettered side.

Give your answers to 1 decimal place.

a

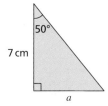

50°

7 cm

a

b

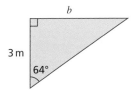

b

3 m

64°

c

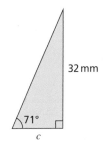

32 mm

71°

c

④ Use the sine ratio to work out the size of each lettered angle.

Give your answers to 1 decimal place.

a
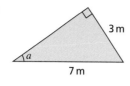
3 m
7 m

b
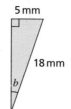
5 mm
18 mm

c
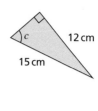
c
12 cm
15 cm

⑤ Use the cosine ratio to work out the size of each lettered angle.

Give your answers to 1 decimal place.

a
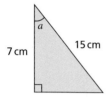
a
7 cm
15 cm

b
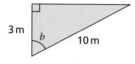
3 m
b
10 m

c
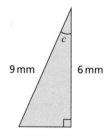
c
9 mm
6 mm

⑥ Use the tangent ratio to work out the size of each lettered angle.

Give your answers to 1 decimal place.

a
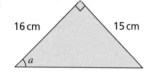
16 cm
15 cm
a

b
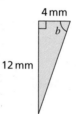
4 mm
b
12 mm

c
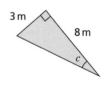
3 m
8 m
c

⑦ Work out the length of each lettered side.

Give your answers to 1 decimal place.

a
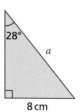
28°
a
8 cm

b
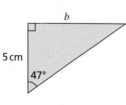
b
5 cm
47°

c
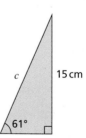
c
15 cm
61°

d
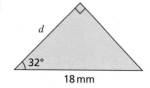
d
32°
18 mm

e
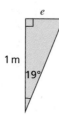
e
1 m
19°

f
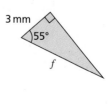
3 mm
55°
f

8 Work out the size of each lettered angle.

Give your answers to 1 decimal place.

a

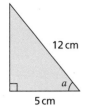
12 cm
5 cm
a

b

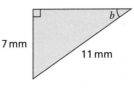
7 mm
11 mm
b

c

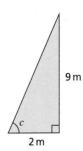
9 m
2 m
c

d

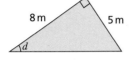
8 m
5 m
d

e

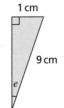
1 cm
9 cm
e

f

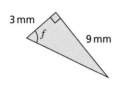
3 mm
9 mm
f

Consolidate – do you need more? 🖩

1 Use trigonometry to work out the length of each side labelled *x*. Give your answers to 1 decimal place where appropriate.

a

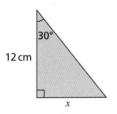
30°
12 cm
x

b

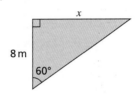
x
8 m
60°

c

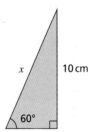
x
10 cm
60°

d

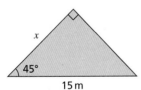
x
45°
15 m

e

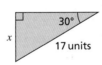
30°
x
17 units

f

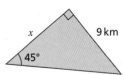
x
9 km
45°

g

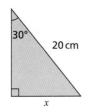
30°
20 cm
x

h

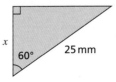
x
60°
25 mm

i

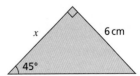
x
6 cm
45°

2 Use trigonometry to work out the size of each angle labelled x. Give your answers to 1 decimal place.

a

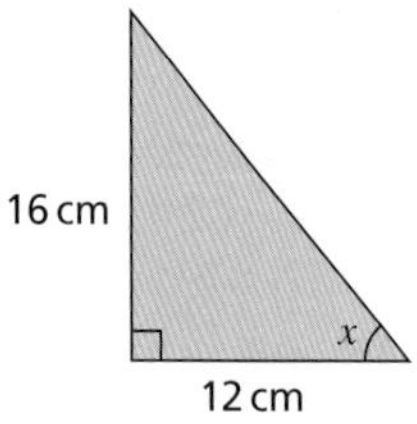

16 cm
12 cm
x

b

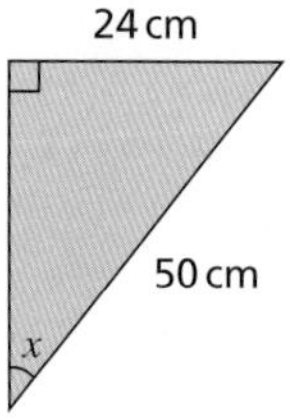

24 cm
50 cm
x

c

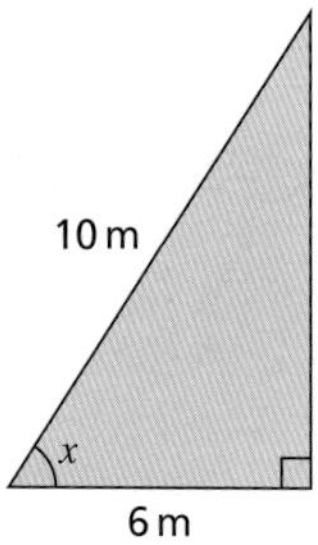

10 m
6 m
x

d

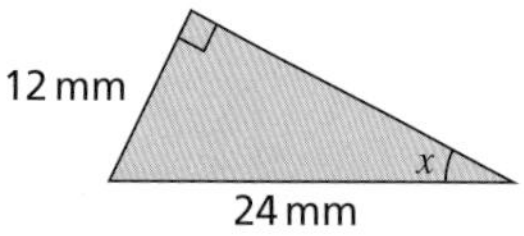

12 mm
24 mm
x

e

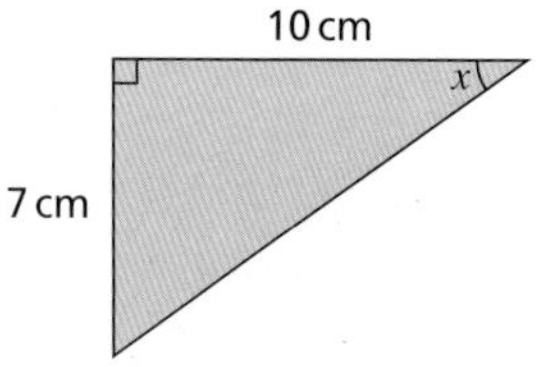

10 cm
7 cm
x

f

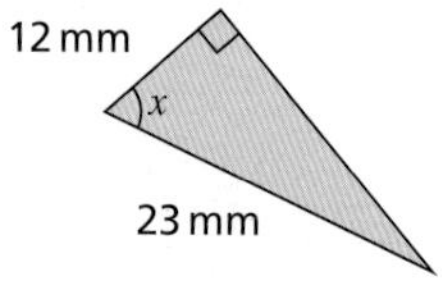

12 mm
23 mm
x

g

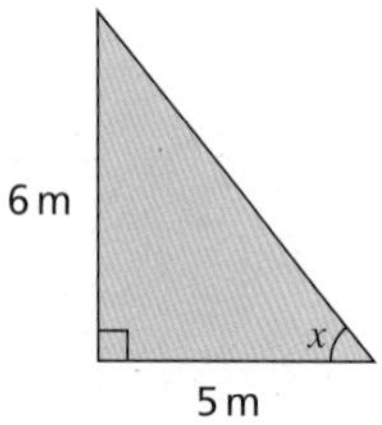

6 m
5 m
x

h

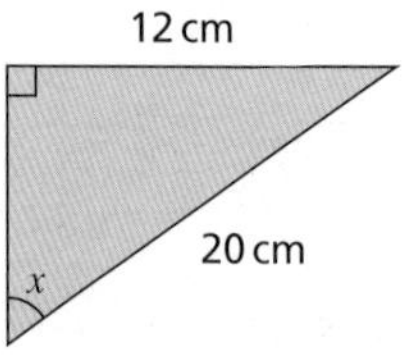

12 cm
20 cm
x

i

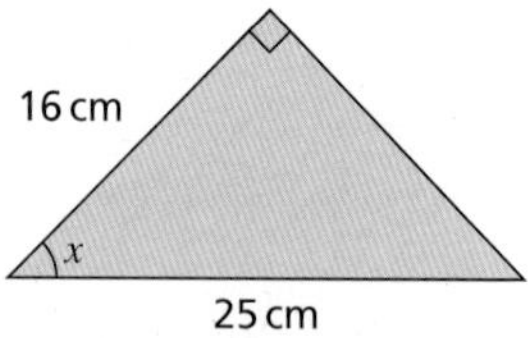

16 cm
25 cm
x

Stretch – can you deepen your learning? 🖩

1 In a right-angled triangle, the hypotenuse measures 20 cm.

The adjacent side to an unknown angle is 12 cm.

Calculate the sizes of the two acute angles in the triangle.

2 In a right-angled triangle, the hypotenuse is 25 cm.

The opposite side to an unknown angle is 15 cm.

Calculate the sizes of the two acute angles in the triangle.

3 An isosceles triangle has two sides of length 8 cm.

Calculate the length of the hypotenuse using trigonometry.

Now calculate the length of the hypotenuse using Pythagoras' theorem.

Which was easier?

Are you ready? (A)

1 Work out the length of AB.

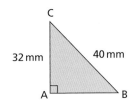

2 Work out the length of RP.

3 Work out: **a** $\frac{2}{3} + \frac{2}{3}$ **b** $1 - \frac{2}{3}$

The previous chapter described using trigonometry to work out lengths and angles in right-angled triangles. This involved using a calculator. However, there are some values, known as **exact values**, which can be worked out without a calculator.

Exact values for sine, cosine and tangent of angles measuring 30°, 60° and 90° can all be worked out from an equilateral triangle where each side length is 1 unit, also known as a unit triangle.

Example

Use the unit triangle to work out the value of tan 30°.

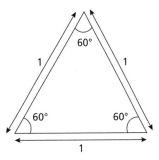

Method

Solution	Commentary
	Start by splitting the triangle into two right-angled triangles, and then labelling the lengths and angles you know.

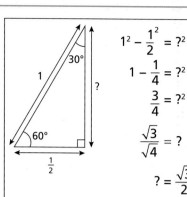

$$1^2 - \frac{1^2}{2} = ?^2$$

$$1 - \frac{1}{4} = ?^2$$

$$\frac{3}{4} = ?^2$$

$$\frac{\sqrt{3}}{\sqrt{4}} = ?$$

$$? = \frac{\sqrt{3}}{2}$$

Now consider one of these right-angled triangles.

You can use Pythagoras' theorem to work out the missing length. You might need a calculator to help find the square root of $\frac{3}{4}$

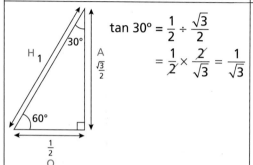

$$\tan 30° = \frac{1}{2} \div \frac{\sqrt{3}}{2}$$

$$= \frac{1}{2} \times \frac{2}{\sqrt{3}} = \frac{1}{\sqrt{3}}$$

Next, if you focus on the 30° angle, you can label the opposite, adjacent and hypotenuse and then work out the value of tan 30°.

If you put tan 30° in your calculator, it will give $\frac{\sqrt{3}}{3}$. The fractions $\frac{1}{\sqrt{3}}$ and $\frac{\sqrt{3}}{3}$ are equivalent.

Practice (A)

1 Use the right-angled triangle to work out the exact values of sin 30°, cos 30° and tan 30°.

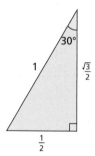

2 Use the right-angled triangle to work out the exact values of sin 60°, cos 60° and tan 60°.

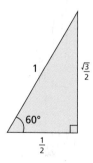

3 Copy and complete the table to show the exact values.

First fill in the values you worked out in questions 1 and 2. Then use your calculator to fill in the others.

	0°	30°	45°	60°	90°
sin					
cos					
tan					Undefined

Do you notice any patterns?

Try to work out the value of tan 90° on your calculator. Why do you think it is undefined?

4 Work out the calculations.

a sin 30° + cos 60° **b** sin 90° + cos 90° **c** tan 45° − cos 0°

d sin 45° + cos 90° **e** sin 90° − cos 60° **f** tan 0° × cos 45°

g 7 × sin 30° **h** cos 0° + tan 45°+ sin 90°

Are you ready? (B)

1 Without looking back in your book, copy and complete as much of the table as you can.

	0°	30°	45°	60°	90°
sin					
cos					
tan					Undefined

Now look back to check your answers.

Example 1

Work out the length of the side labelled y.

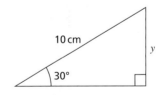

Method

Solution	Commentary
$\times 10 \left(\begin{array}{c} \sin 30° = \dfrac{y}{10} \\ 10 \times \sin 30° = y \end{array} \right) \times 10$ $10 \times \dfrac{1}{2} = y$ $y = 5\,\text{cm}$	

Example 2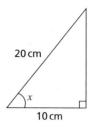

Work out the size of angle x.

Method

Solution	Commentary
$$\cos x = \frac{10}{20}$$ $$\frac{10}{20} = \frac{1}{2}$$ and $\cos 60° = \frac{1}{2}$ so $x = 60°$	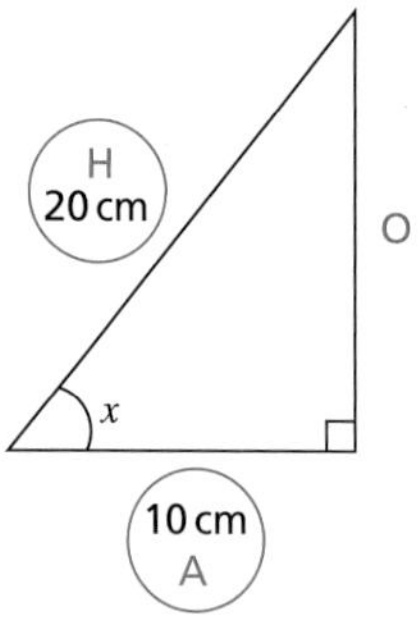

Practice (B)

1 Work out the length of each lettered side.

a

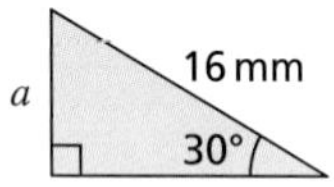

b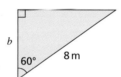

c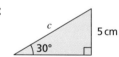

d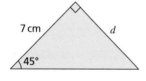

e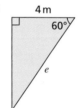

f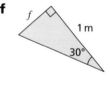

2 Work out the size of each lettered angle.

a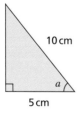

b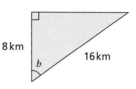

c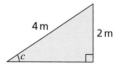

d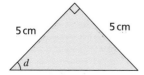

e

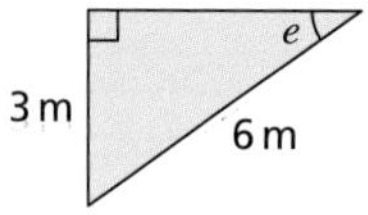

f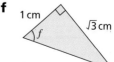

Consolidate – do you need more?

1 Work out the length of each lettered side.

a
12 cm
a
30°

b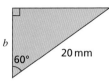
b
60°
20 mm

c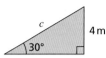
c
4 m
30°

d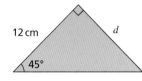
12 cm
d
45°

e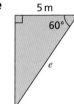
5 m
60°
e

f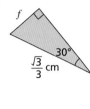
f
30°
$\frac{\sqrt{3}}{3}$ cm

2 Work out the size of each lettered angle.

a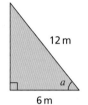
12 m
a
6 m

b
4 cm
8 cm
b

c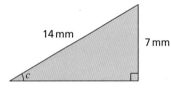
14 mm
7 mm
c

d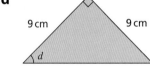
9 cm
9 cm
d

e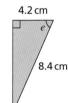
4.2 cm
e
8.4 cm

f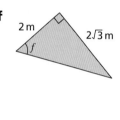
2 m
$2\sqrt{3}$ m
f

Stretch – can you deepen your learning?

1 Use the triangle to work out the exact values of sin 45°, cos 45° and tan 45°.

You will need to use Pythagoras' theorem.

> The memory aid SOH-CAH-TOA may help.

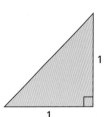
1
1

Right-angled triangles: exam practice

1 Draw a right-angled triangle on a copy of the grid. **(1)**

1–3

2 The diagram shows three towns.

Duffield is 68 km due East of Crompton.

Nordon is 57 km due North of Crompton.

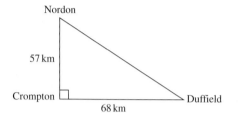

Calculate the shortest distance between Duffield and Nordon. Give your answer correct to the nearest kilometre. **(3)**

3–5

3 The diagram shows a plan of Mario's garden.

Mario needs to replace the fence between the two gates.

Each fence panel is 3 metres wide.

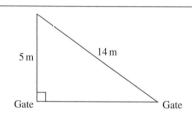

How many fence panels does Mario need? **(3)**

4 Write down the exact value of cos 60°. **(1)**

5 ABC is a right-angled triangle.

Angle B = 90°

Angle A = 36°

AB = 9.7 cm

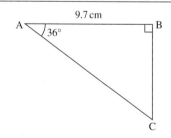

Work out the length of BC. Give your answer in centimetres correct to 3 significant figures. **(3)**

9 Vectors

MATHS

In this block, we will cover...

9.1 Drawing vectors

Example 1

Describe the vector $\begin{pmatrix} 5 \\ -1 \end{pmatrix}$ in words.

Method

Solution	Commer
The top number is positive 5 This means 5 units to the right.	The top bottom
The bottom number is negative 1 This means 1 unit down.	Positive
The vector means 5 units to the right and 1 unit down.	

9.2 Vector arithmetic

Practice (A)

1. Work out the vector calculations. Give you

   a $\begin{pmatrix} 4 \\ 6 \end{pmatrix} + \begin{pmatrix} 3 \\ 1 \end{pmatrix}$ **b** $\begin{pmatrix} 5 \\ 2 \end{pmatrix} + \begin{pmatrix} 0 \\ 9 \end{pmatrix}$

   d $\begin{pmatrix} 0 \\ 5 \end{pmatrix} + \begin{pmatrix} 6 \\ -2 \end{pmatrix}$ **e** $\begin{pmatrix} 3 \\ 11 \end{pmatrix} + \begin{pmatrix} -9 \\ -1 \end{pmatrix}$

   g $\begin{pmatrix} -1 \\ 4 \end{pmatrix} + \begin{pmatrix} -3 \\ 6 \end{pmatrix}$ **h** $\begin{pmatrix} -11 \\ 7 \end{pmatrix} + \begin{pmatrix} 2 \\ - \end{pmatrix}$

2. Work out the vector calculations. Give you

231

Are you ready? (A)

1 Write directions to get from point A to point B in each diagram.

a

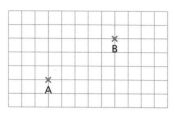

b

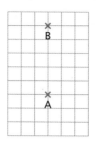

c

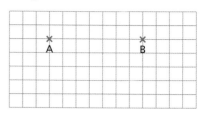

Imagine you are giving someone directions. A **vector** acts like clear instructions on how far and which way they need to move to get from one point to another.

A vector has two parts:

1. **Magnitude**: This is the distance, which could be the number of steps you need to take.

2. **Direction**: This shows which way to move – left, right, up, down, or at an angle.

A vector can be represented by an arrow. The length of the arrow represents how far you need to move, and the arrow's direction shows which way to go. The vector in the diagram shown here says, "Move three units right and two units up." It can be written mathematically as a **column vector** $\begin{pmatrix} 3 \\ 2 \end{pmatrix}$

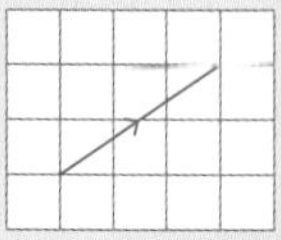

- The top number represents the horizontal movement. If it is positive, you move right. If it is negative, you move left.

- The bottom number represents the vertical movement. If it is positive, you move up. If it is negative, you move down.

> Vectors are used to describe the translation of shapes. Translations were covered in Chapter 5.3

Example 1

Describe the vector $\begin{pmatrix} 5 \\ -1 \end{pmatrix}$ in words.

Method

Solution	Commentary
The top number is positive 5 This means 5 units to the right.	The top number tells you how far across and the bottom number tells you how far up or down.
The bottom number is negative 1 This means 1 unit down.	Positive 1 would mean 1 up; negative 1 is 1 d⊙
The vector means 5 units to the right and 1 unit down.	

Example 2

Write the vector that represents 4 units to the left and 7 units up.

Method

Solution	Commentary
The vector is $\begin{pmatrix} -4 \\ 7 \end{pmatrix}$	First think about the top number, which is how far across. You are told 4 to the left so the number on the top is either positive or negative 4. Since it is to the left, it will be negative 4
	The bottom number is how far up or down. So 7 up means the bottom number is positive 7

Practice (A)

1 Describe each of these vectors in words.

a $\begin{pmatrix} 6 \\ 2 \end{pmatrix}$ **b** $\begin{pmatrix} 6 \\ -2 \end{pmatrix}$ **c** $\begin{pmatrix} -6 \\ 2 \end{pmatrix}$ **d** $\begin{pmatrix} -6 \\ -2 \end{pmatrix}$

What do you notice?

2 Write these instructions as column vectors.

a 9 left and 5 up   **b** 9 right and 5 up

c 9 right and 5 down   **d** 9 left and 5 down

What do you notice?

3 Describe each of these vectors in words.

a $\begin{pmatrix} 7 \\ 3 \end{pmatrix}$ **b** $\begin{pmatrix} 12 \\ -5 \end{pmatrix}$ **c** $\begin{pmatrix} -16 \\ 1 \end{pmatrix}$ **d** $\begin{pmatrix} 19 \\ -19 \end{pmatrix}$

e $\begin{pmatrix} -6 \\ -3 \end{pmatrix}$ **f** $\begin{pmatrix} 1 \\ 2 \end{pmatrix}$ **g** $\begin{pmatrix} -8 \\ 4 \end{pmatrix}$ **h** $\begin{pmatrix} -15 \\ -19 \end{pmatrix}$

i $\begin{pmatrix} 5 \\ 0 \end{pmatrix}$ **j** $\begin{pmatrix} -3 \\ 0 \end{pmatrix}$ **k** $\begin{pmatrix} 0 \\ 12 \end{pmatrix}$ **l** $\begin{pmatrix} 0 \\ -1 \end{pmatrix}$

4 Write these instructions as column vectors.

a 5 right and 1 down   **b** 6 left and 3 down   **c** 12 right and 14 up

d 16 left and 4 up   **e** 1 left and 5 up   **f** 9 right and 11 down

g 12 right   **h** 8 left   **i** 3 down

5 Here is the map of a town.

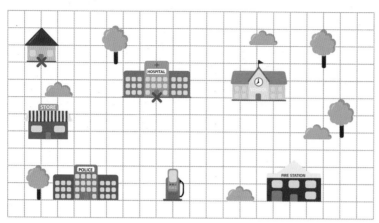

a In words, describe the journey that gives the shortest distance from the house to the hospital.

b Write the column vector that represents the journey in part **a**.

6 Two points are plotted on the coordinate grid.

a **i** Describe in words the journey from point A to point B.

ii Write the vector that shows the journey from point A to point B.

b **i** Describe in words the journey from point B to point A.

ii Write the vector that shows the journey from point B to point A.

What do you notice?

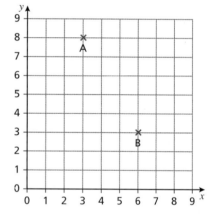

7 Two points are plotted on the coordinate grid.

a **i** Describe in words the journey from point A to point B.

ii Write the vector that shows the journey from point A to point B.

b **i** Describe in words the journey from point B to point A.

ii Write the vector that shows the journey from point B to point A.

What do you notice?

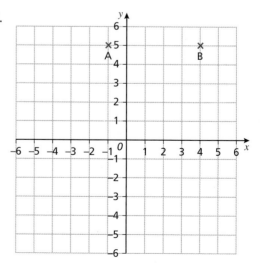

Are you ready? (B)

1 Sketch to show the position of point D for each instruction.

a D is 3 to the right and 1 up from C.

b D is 6 to the right and 3 up from C.

Example 1

What column vector is shown?

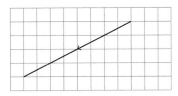

Method

Solution	Commentary
(graph showing vector with −8 horizontal and −4 vertical) $\begin{pmatrix} -8 \\ -4 \end{pmatrix}$	Notice how the arrow is going left and down, meaning that both numbers are negative. Count the number of squares to work out what the numbers are.

Example 2

Draw the column vector $\begin{pmatrix} 9 \\ 2 \end{pmatrix}$

Method

Solution	Commentary
(grid with a point marked ×)	First draw a point to start from.
(grid with × and 9 to the right)	Then count nine squares to the right.
(grid showing 9 across and 2 up to new point)	Now count two up and mark with a point where you land.
(grid showing vector connecting points, 9 across and 2 up)	Then connect your points to draw the vector. Don't forget to include the arrow showing direction.

Practice (B)

1 Write these as column vectors.

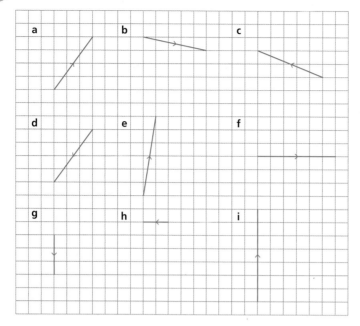

2 Draw each of the column vectors on squared paper.

a $\begin{pmatrix} 4 \\ 3 \end{pmatrix}$ **b** $\begin{pmatrix} 1 \\ -5 \end{pmatrix}$ **c** $\begin{pmatrix} -6 \\ 1 \end{pmatrix}$ **d** $\begin{pmatrix} 9 \\ -9 \end{pmatrix}$

e $\begin{pmatrix} -1 \\ -3 \end{pmatrix}$ **f** $\begin{pmatrix} 1 \\ 5 \end{pmatrix}$ **g** $\begin{pmatrix} -7 \\ 4 \end{pmatrix}$ **h** $\begin{pmatrix} -5 \\ -1 \end{pmatrix}$

i $\begin{pmatrix} 6 \\ 0 \end{pmatrix}$ **j** $\begin{pmatrix} -2 \\ 0 \end{pmatrix}$ **k** $\begin{pmatrix} 0 \\ 1 \end{pmatrix}$ **l** $\begin{pmatrix} 0 \\ -4 \end{pmatrix}$

Consolidate – do you need more?

1 Describe each of these vectors in words.

a $\begin{pmatrix} 1 \\ 8 \end{pmatrix}$ **b** $\begin{pmatrix} 2 \\ -4 \end{pmatrix}$ **c** $\begin{pmatrix} -10 \\ 10 \end{pmatrix}$ **d** $\begin{pmatrix} 11 \\ -9 \end{pmatrix}$

e $\begin{pmatrix} -1 \\ -6 \end{pmatrix}$ **f** $\begin{pmatrix} 3 \\ 12 \end{pmatrix}$ **g** $\begin{pmatrix} -15 \\ 7 \end{pmatrix}$ **h** $\begin{pmatrix} -5 \\ -9 \end{pmatrix}$

i $\begin{pmatrix} 8 \\ 0 \end{pmatrix}$ **j** $\begin{pmatrix} -16 \\ 0 \end{pmatrix}$ **k** $\begin{pmatrix} 0 \\ 14 \end{pmatrix}$ **l** $\begin{pmatrix} 0 \\ -10 \end{pmatrix}$

2 Write each of these as column vectors.

     a 8 right and 4 down   **b** 9 left and 1 down   **c** 2 right and 5 up

     d 6 left and 1 up   **e** 5 left and 9 up   **f** 2 right and 1 down

     g 5 right   **h** 7 left   **i** 6 up

3 Write these as column vectors.

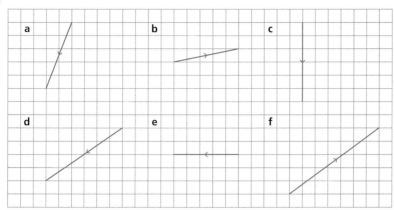

4 Draw each of these column vectors on squared paper.

a $\begin{pmatrix} 5 \\ 2 \end{pmatrix}$
b $\begin{pmatrix} 2 \\ -3 \end{pmatrix}$
c $\begin{pmatrix} -8 \\ 3 \end{pmatrix}$
d $\begin{pmatrix} 6 \\ -2 \end{pmatrix}$

Stretch – can you deepen your learning?

1 The directions from A to C are given by the column vector $\begin{pmatrix} 5 \\ 1 \end{pmatrix}$

The direction from A to B is 3 to the right and 2 up.

Write the directions from B to C both in words and as a column vector.

2 The column vector from X to Y is $\begin{pmatrix} 3 \\ -1 \end{pmatrix}$

The column vector from Y to Z is $\begin{pmatrix} -1 \\ 5 \end{pmatrix}$

a Write the column vector from X to Z.

b Describe the shape XYZ.

3 Shape A has been translated by a vector to give shape B.

a Describe the translation from A to B.

b Describe the translation from B to A.

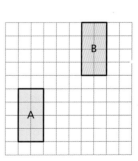

Are you ready? (A)

1 Draw each of these vectors.

a $\begin{pmatrix} 3 \\ 5 \end{pmatrix}$ **b** $\begin{pmatrix} -2 \\ 1 \end{pmatrix}$ **c** $\begin{pmatrix} -6 \\ -5 \end{pmatrix}$ **d** $\begin{pmatrix} 7 \\ -2 \end{pmatrix}$

2 Write the vectors shown below as column vectors.

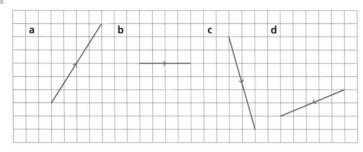

A vector tells you how far and which way you need to move from one point to another.

Vectors can be added or multiplied, and rules of arithmetic apply to them.

Adding vectors means following one set of instructions after another.

Here, the first set of instructions is 'move 2 to the right and 3 up'. The second set is 'move 5 to the right and 1 up'.

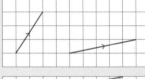

Combining the two sets of instructions can be shown by placing the second vector at the end of the first one. The resultant vector is the straight line from the start point to the end point. It is 7 to the right and 4 up.

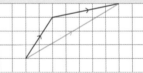

Subtracting vectors is like reversing instructions.

Shown right are vectors **a** and **b**.

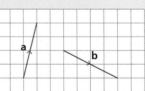

To represent vector **a** – **b**:

Reverse the direction of **b** to give –**b**. Then move it to the end of **a**.

The resultant vector **a** – **b** is shown.

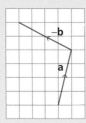

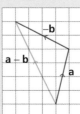

Scaling (or multiplying) a vector means changing the distance you move without changing the direction.

If a vector **a** says, 'move 3 units to the right and 1 up', scaling it by 2 would be 'move 6 units to the right and 2 up'. This would be vector **2a** and would be twice as long.

Example 1

Work out $\begin{pmatrix} 3 \\ 5 \end{pmatrix} + \begin{pmatrix} 2 \\ -1 \end{pmatrix}$

Method

Solution	Commentary
$\begin{pmatrix} 3 \\ 5 \end{pmatrix} + \begin{pmatrix} 2 \\ -1 \end{pmatrix} = \begin{pmatrix} 3 + 2 \\ 5 + -1 \end{pmatrix} = \begin{pmatrix} 5 \\ 4 \end{pmatrix}$ 	To add vectors, you simply add the horizontal instructions and add the vertical instructions. You can draw it to help you, especially when working with negative numbers. If drawing, start with the first vector, then draw the second one from where the first one ends. The resultant vector is the vector that describes the start point to the end point.

Example 2

Work out $\begin{pmatrix} -6 \\ 9 \end{pmatrix} - \begin{pmatrix} 2 \\ -3 \end{pmatrix}$

Method

Solution	Commentary
$\begin{pmatrix} -6 \\ 9 \end{pmatrix} - \begin{pmatrix} 2 \\ -3 \end{pmatrix} = \begin{pmatrix} -6 - 2 \\ 9 - -3 \end{pmatrix} = \begin{pmatrix} -8 \\ 12 \end{pmatrix}$ 	When subtracting, you just subtract the numbers. If drawing, subtracting $\begin{pmatrix} 2 \\ -3 \end{pmatrix}$ means you do the opposite so, rather than 2 right and 3 down, you do 2 left and 3 up. Be careful when subtracting with negatives.

Practice (A)

1 Work out the vector calculations. Give your answers as column vectors.

a $\begin{pmatrix} 4 \\ 6 \end{pmatrix} + \begin{pmatrix} 3 \\ 1 \end{pmatrix}$
b $\begin{pmatrix} 5 \\ 2 \end{pmatrix} + \begin{pmatrix} 0 \\ 9 \end{pmatrix}$
c $\begin{pmatrix} -2 \\ 3 \end{pmatrix} + \begin{pmatrix} 7 \\ 4 \end{pmatrix}$

d $\begin{pmatrix} 0 \\ 5 \end{pmatrix} + \begin{pmatrix} 6 \\ -2 \end{pmatrix}$
e $\begin{pmatrix} 3 \\ 11 \end{pmatrix} + \begin{pmatrix} -9 \\ -1 \end{pmatrix}$
f $\begin{pmatrix} -8 \\ 0 \end{pmatrix} + \begin{pmatrix} 2 \\ 7 \end{pmatrix}$

g $\begin{pmatrix} -1 \\ 4 \end{pmatrix} + \begin{pmatrix} -3 \\ 6 \end{pmatrix}$
h $\begin{pmatrix} -11 \\ 7 \end{pmatrix} + \begin{pmatrix} 20 \\ -10 \end{pmatrix}$
i $\begin{pmatrix} 168 \\ -15 \end{pmatrix} + \begin{pmatrix} 47 \\ 200 \end{pmatrix}$

2 Work out the vector calculations. Give your answers as column vectors.

a $\begin{pmatrix} 10 \\ 5 \end{pmatrix} - \begin{pmatrix} 6 \\ 3 \end{pmatrix}$
b $\begin{pmatrix} 20 \\ 0 \end{pmatrix} - \begin{pmatrix} 12 \\ 5 \end{pmatrix}$
c $\begin{pmatrix} 13 \\ -1 \end{pmatrix} - \begin{pmatrix} 5 \\ 4 \end{pmatrix}$

d $\begin{pmatrix} -2 \\ 6 \end{pmatrix} - \begin{pmatrix} -5 \\ 6 \end{pmatrix}$
e $\begin{pmatrix} 3 \\ 7 \end{pmatrix} - \begin{pmatrix} 12 \\ 15 \end{pmatrix}$
f $\begin{pmatrix} 6 \\ -7 \end{pmatrix} - \begin{pmatrix} -5 \\ -2 \end{pmatrix}$

g $\begin{pmatrix} 100 \\ 50 \end{pmatrix} - \begin{pmatrix} 50 \\ 100 \end{pmatrix}$
h $\begin{pmatrix} -17 \\ 83 \end{pmatrix} - \begin{pmatrix} -20 \\ 42 \end{pmatrix}$
i $\begin{pmatrix} 260 \\ -100 \end{pmatrix} - \begin{pmatrix} -40 \\ -55 \end{pmatrix}$

3 Use the values of **a**, **b** and **c** to work out the calculations. Give your answers as column vectors.

$a = \begin{pmatrix} 7 \\ 2 \end{pmatrix}$
$b = \begin{pmatrix} -5 \\ 0 \end{pmatrix}$
$c = \begin{pmatrix} 0 \\ 8 \end{pmatrix}$
$d = \begin{pmatrix} 10 \\ -3 \end{pmatrix}$

a a + b
b b + c
c c + d
d d – a

e c – b
f b – d
g a + b + c + d
h b + c – d

Are you ready? (B)

1 $p = 2$ and $q = -3$

Evaluate:

a $2p + q$
b $-p + 3q$
c $3p - 2q$

2 The vector **a** is shown.

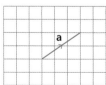

Write the letter of the diagram that shows the vector 2**a**.

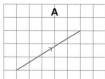 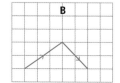 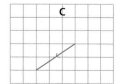 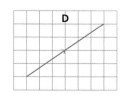

Example 1

$\mathbf{a} = \begin{pmatrix} 3 \\ -1 \end{pmatrix}$

Write 5**a** as a column vector.

Method

Solution	Commentary
$\begin{pmatrix} 15 \\ -5 \end{pmatrix}$	As explained on page 239, multiplying a vector is called 'scaling'. The number you are multiplying by is a **scalar quantity**. In this case, the journey is going to be five times as far in both directions. You can draw it to help you.

Example 2

$\mathbf{p} = \begin{pmatrix} 2 \\ 3 \end{pmatrix}$ and $\mathbf{q} = \begin{pmatrix} -5 \\ 4 \end{pmatrix}$

Work out 2**p** + **q**. Give your answer as a column vector.

Method

Solution	Commentary
$2\mathbf{p} = 2 \times \begin{pmatrix} 2 \\ 3 \end{pmatrix} = \begin{pmatrix} 4 \\ 6 \end{pmatrix}$	First work out 2**p**.
$2\mathbf{p} + \mathbf{q} = \begin{pmatrix} 4 \\ 6 \end{pmatrix} + \begin{pmatrix} -5 \\ 4 \end{pmatrix} = \begin{pmatrix} 4 + -5 \\ 6 + 4 \end{pmatrix} = \begin{pmatrix} -1 \\ 10 \end{pmatrix}$	Then you can add on **q**.

Practice (B)

1 $\mathbf{a} = \begin{pmatrix} 5 \\ -1 \end{pmatrix}$

Write each of these as column vectors.

a 2a **b** 5a **c** 7a **d** 10a

2 The vector **p** is shown.

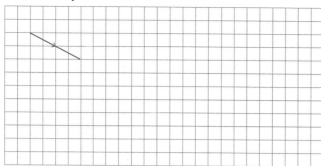

Draw the resultant vectors.

a 2**p**   b 3**p**   c 5**p**   d 10**p**

3 Use the values of **a**, **b** and **c** to work out the calculations. Give your answers as column vectors.

$$\mathbf{a} = \begin{pmatrix} 7 \\ 2 \end{pmatrix} \qquad \mathbf{b} = \begin{pmatrix} -5 \\ 0 \end{pmatrix} \qquad \mathbf{c} = \begin{pmatrix} 0 \\ 8 \end{pmatrix} \qquad \mathbf{d} = \begin{pmatrix} 10 \\ -3 \end{pmatrix}$$

a 2**a** + **b**   b **b** + 3**c**   c 5**c** + **d**   d 6**d** − **a**

e **c** − 2**b**   f 3**b** − **d**   g 3**a** + **b** + **c** + **d**   h **b** + **c** − 2**d**

4 Use the values of **q**, **r** and **s** to work out the calculations. Give your answers as column vectors.

$$\mathbf{q} = \begin{pmatrix} 3 \\ -2 \end{pmatrix} \qquad \mathbf{r} = \begin{pmatrix} -4 \\ 1 \end{pmatrix} \qquad \mathbf{s} = \begin{pmatrix} 0 \\ 8 \end{pmatrix}$$

a 2**q** + 3**r**   b 5**s** + 2**r**   c 3**s** − 2**q**   d 10**q** − 2**r**

e 5**r** + 2**q** + 3**s**   f 2**s** + 8**q**   g 3**r** − 2**s**   h 2**q** + 10**r** − 5**s**

Consolidate – do you need more?

1 Work out the vector calculations. Give your answers as column vectors.

a $\begin{pmatrix} 5 \\ 12 \end{pmatrix} + \begin{pmatrix} 6 \\ 4 \end{pmatrix}$ b $\begin{pmatrix} 10 \\ 2 \end{pmatrix} + \begin{pmatrix} 7 \\ 0 \end{pmatrix}$ c $\begin{pmatrix} 7 \\ -4 \end{pmatrix} + \begin{pmatrix} -2 \\ 4 \end{pmatrix}$ d $\begin{pmatrix} -8 \\ 6 \end{pmatrix} + \begin{pmatrix} -5 \\ 2 \end{pmatrix}$

2 Work out the vector calculations. Give your answers as column vectors.

a $\begin{pmatrix} 10 \\ 3 \end{pmatrix} - \begin{pmatrix} 5 \\ 1 \end{pmatrix}$ b $\begin{pmatrix} 0 \\ 9 \end{pmatrix} - \begin{pmatrix} 6 \\ 3 \end{pmatrix}$ c $\begin{pmatrix} -2 \\ 5 \end{pmatrix} - \begin{pmatrix} 4 \\ 6 \end{pmatrix}$ d $\begin{pmatrix} -3 \\ -1 \end{pmatrix} - \begin{pmatrix} -2 \\ 4 \end{pmatrix}$

3 Use the values of **a**, **b** and **c** to work out the calculations. Give your answers as column vectors.

$$\mathbf{a} = \begin{pmatrix} 3 \\ 0 \end{pmatrix} \qquad \mathbf{b} = \begin{pmatrix} 0 \\ 1 \end{pmatrix} \qquad \mathbf{c} = \begin{pmatrix} 5 \\ 4 \end{pmatrix}$$

a a + b   **b** a + c   **c** b + c

d a – b   **e** c – b   **f** a + b – c

4 Use the values of **p** and **q** to work out the calculations. Give your answers as column vectors.

$$\mathbf{p} = \begin{pmatrix} 4 \\ 1 \end{pmatrix} \qquad \mathbf{q} = \begin{pmatrix} 3 \\ 0 \end{pmatrix}$$

a 2p   **b** 3q   **c** 5q   **d** 6p

e 10p   **f** 12q   **g** 2p + q   **h** 3q – p

i 5p – q   **j** 2p + 3q   **k** 5q + 6p   **l** 10p – 5q

Stretch – can you deepen your learning?

1 Work out the value of x.

$$\begin{pmatrix} 5 \\ 2 \end{pmatrix} + \begin{pmatrix} x \\ -3 \end{pmatrix} = \begin{pmatrix} 12 \\ -1 \end{pmatrix}$$

2 Work out the values of p and q.

$$\begin{pmatrix} p \\ 8 \end{pmatrix} - \begin{pmatrix} 5 \\ q \end{pmatrix} = \begin{pmatrix} 4 \\ 10 \end{pmatrix}$$

3 Work out the values of r and s.

$$2\begin{pmatrix} r \\ 1 \end{pmatrix} + \begin{pmatrix} 3 \\ s \end{pmatrix} = \begin{pmatrix} 17 \\ 0 \end{pmatrix}$$

4 $\mathbf{a} = \begin{pmatrix} 12 \\ 0 \end{pmatrix}$ and $\mathbf{b} = \begin{pmatrix} 9 \\ 7 \end{pmatrix}$

What is AB as a column vector?

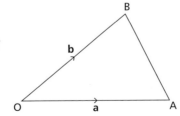

Vectors: exam practice

1 Vectors **b** and **c** are shown below.

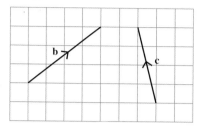

    a) Write the column vector that represents **b**.   (1)

    b) Write the column vector that represents **c**.   (1)

2 Draw and label the vector $\begin{pmatrix} -2 \\ -5 \end{pmatrix}$ on a copy of the grid.   (1)

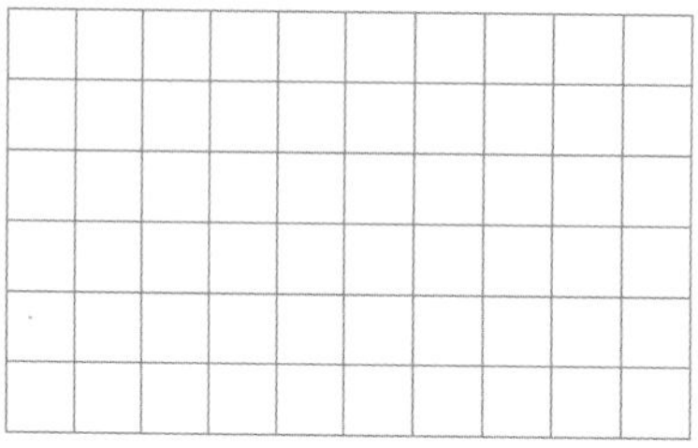

3 The vector **y** is shown on the grid.

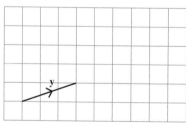

    Draw and label the vector 2**y** on a copy of grid.   (1)

4 $\mathbf{x} = \begin{pmatrix} -1 \\ -6 \end{pmatrix}$ and $\mathbf{y} = \begin{pmatrix} 3 \\ -2 \end{pmatrix}$

    a) Work out **x** − **y** as a column vector.   (1)

    b) Work out 2**y** + **x** as a column vector.   (2)

3–5

Geometry and measures: exam practice

White Rose
M▲THS

1 Work out the area of the triangle. Give units with your answer. **(2)**

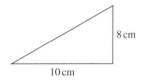

8 cm

10 cm

1–3

2 Draw a circle with a radius of 5 cm. **(1)**

3 Reflect the shape in the given mirror line on a copy of this diagram. **(2)**

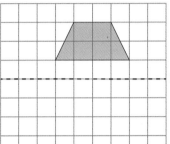

Mirror line

4 ABCD is a quadrilateral.

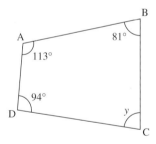

A
113°
94°
D
B
81°
y
C

Find the size of angle y. **(2)**

5 Chloe has measured the angle below with her protractor.

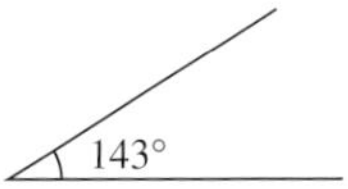

143°

Explain why she must have measured incorrectly. **(1)**

6 Write the column vector that maps point P to point Q. **(2)**

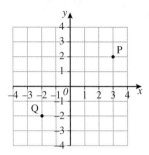

7 WXY is an isosceles triangle.

WYZ is a straight line.

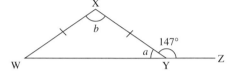

a) Work out the size of angle *a*. **(1)**

b) Work out the size of angle *b*. **(2)**

8 The perimeter of this rectangle is 44 cm.

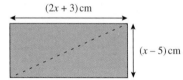

Find the length of the diagonal. Write your answer to 2 decimal places. **(5)**

9 ABCD is a square that has sides of length 3 cm.

E and F are the midpoints of two of the sides.

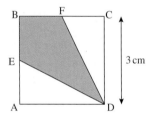

Find the area of the shaded region. **(3)**

10 Four congruent triangles are shown.

The coordinates of three points are given: A (5, 2), B (18, 2) and C (5, 7).

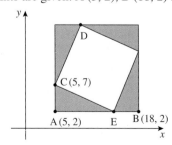

a) Find the coordinates of D. **(2)**

b) Find the length of CE. Write your answer to 2 decimal places. **(3)**

10 Single event probability

White Rose MATHS

In this block, we will cover...

10.1 The probability scale

Example

A spinner is shown.

It is spun and the colour that it lands on is noted

10.2 Basic probability

Practice

1 **a** A bag contains some coloured counter

5 counters are green and the remainin

A counter is selected at random.

Find the probability that the counter i

b A box of chocolates contains 4 fudge,

Zak selects a chocolate from the box a

Find the probability that the chocolate

i fudge **ii** fudge or toff

c A box contains whiteboard pens

Are you ready?

1 Which phrase best describes the probability of each event happening?

| Certain | Impossible | Likely | Unlikely | Even chance |

a A coin landing on a head

b Snow in London in April

c Rolling a 0 on a six-sided dice numbered 1 to 6

d There will be either 30 or 31 days in a randomly chosen month

2 This spinner is spun.

Copy and complete the sentences.

a There is an equal chance of landing on _____ and _____ .

b It is most likely to land on _____ .

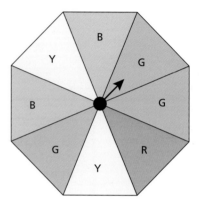

3 Copy and complete the number lines.

a

b

Probability is a measure of how likely something is to happen. The lower the probability, the less chance of that event happening. The higher the probability, the more chance of that event happening.

You can represent probabilities using fractions, decimals or percentages. The probability of something happening will lie between 0 and 1, or 0% and 100%.

The probability scale is a number line from 0 to 1 where you can place the probability of events occurring. Events can range from 'impossible' to 'certain'. If something has a probability of 0 then it is impossible. If something has a probability of 1 then it is certain.

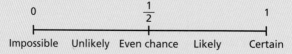

The notation **P(event)** is used to represent the probability of an event happening. For example, if you wanted to write the probability of getting a head when flipping a coin, you could write P(head).

Example

A spinner is shown.

It is spun and the colour that it lands on is noted.

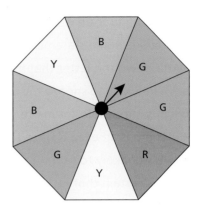

On this number line, draw an arrow to show each probability.

a P(red)　　　**b** P(green or blue)　　　**c** P(red or green or yellow or blue)

Method

Solution	Commentary
a ⊢――↑――――――――――――――⊣ 0　　　　　　　　　　　　　　1 P(red) = $\frac{1}{8}$	One out of the eight sections on the spinner is red, therefore the probability of it landing on red is $\frac{1}{8}$ The number line goes up in eighths so the arrow is pointing to $\frac{1}{8}$
b ⊢―――――――――――↑―――――⊣ 0　　　　　　　　　　　　　　1 P(green or blue) = $\frac{5}{8}$	Five out of eight sections are green or blue, therefore the probability of the spinner landing on green or blue is $\frac{5}{8}$ The number line goes up in eighths so the arrow is pointing to $\frac{5}{8}$
c ⊢―――――――――――――――――↑⊣ 0　　　　　　　　　　　　　　1 P(red or green or yellow or blue) = 1	Eight out of eight sections are red, green, yellow or blue, therefore the spinner is certain to land on one of these colours. The arrow is pointing to $\frac{8}{8}$ or 1 whole.

Practice

1 A probability scale is shown.

Anil makes some statements.

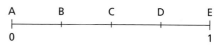

Write down the letter that matches each of Anil's statements.

a I am likely to snooze my alarm in the morning.

b It is impossible for me to grow to be 8 feet tall.

c There is an even chance that I will win my chess match.

d It is unlikely to rain tomorrow.

e It is certain that I will do some maths tomorrow.

2 Seb rolls a fair, six-sided dice numbered 1 to 6.

Copy the probability scale below and mark with a cross the probability of rolling:

> In probability, **fair** means there is an equal chance of each outcome.

a an even number   **b** 7   **c** 1, 2, 3, 4, 5 or 6

3 Ron, Sophie and Iqra are discussing the probability of flipping a head on a fair coin.

Ron says, "The probability is 50%"

Sophie says, "The probability is $\frac{1}{2}$"

Iqra says, "The probability is 0.5"

Who is correct? Explain your answer.

4 There are 3 red counters and 2 yellow counters in a bag.

Max and Kim have each marked on the scale the probability of choosing a red counter at random.

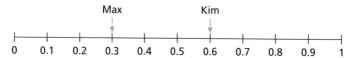

Who is correct?

5 Here is a probability scale:

A box contains 8 pens. One pen is red and the other 7 pens are blue.

On a copy of the scale, mark the probability of choosing one of the following at random.

a A red pen   **b** A blue pen   **c** A green pen

6 A spinner is shown.

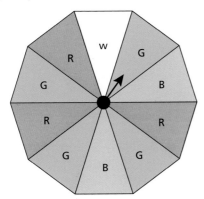

On a copy of the number line, mark the probability of the spinner landing on each colour.

7 A shape is picked from this bag at random.

Draw and label a probability scale to show:

a P(a black square)

b P(a triangle)

c P(a triangle or a square).

What do you think?

1 There are 12 counters in a bag. The counters are coloured red, white or blue.

The scale shows the probability that a counter taken at random is red or white.

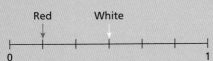

a What is the probability that the counter taken is red?

b What is the probability that the counter taken is white?

c How many blue counters are in the bag?

Consolidate – do you need more?

1 Here is a probability scale:

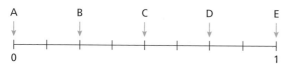

Write down the letter that shows each likelihood.

a Likely   **b** Impossible   **c** Certain   **d** Unlikely   **e** Even chance

2 Which letter shows the probability of each event happening?

a Next week, Tuesday will be the day after Monday.

b There will be 33 days in February next year.

c It will be warm and sunny in London in December.

d It will snow in Scotland in January.

e A randomly chosen integer will be even.

3 A box contains some red counters and some blue counters as shown below.

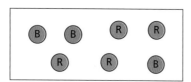

a Copy and complete the sentences.

i _____ out of _____ counters are red.

ii _____ out of _____ counters are blue.

b A counter is chosen at random.

i Work out the probability that the counter is red.

ii Work out the probability that the counter is blue.

c Copy and complete the number line. Mark the probability of choosing each colour of counter.

Stretch – can you deepen your learning?

1 A spinner is shown.

Max says there is an equal chance of landing on each colour because there are only two options, blue or yellow.

Do you agree? Explain your answer.

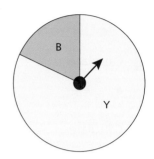

2 The probability that a bus is late is 0.1

Which of the following statements is the most reasonable?

A The bus is unlikely to be late.

B The bus is certain to be late.

C The bus is likely to be late.

Explain why you have chosen your answer.

3 A machine sells sweets in five different flavours: strawberry, lime, orange, lemon or blueberry.

There are the same number of each flavour in the machine.

The machine dispenses flavours at random.

Anil does **not** like orange sweets or lemon sweets. Zak likes them all.

a Copy the scale and draw an arrow to show the probability that Anil will get a sweet that he likes.

b On your scale, draw an arrow to show the probability that Zak will get a sweet that he likes.

c Iqra buys one sweet. The arrow on the scale below shows the probability that Iqra gets a sweet that she likes.

How many flavours does Iqra like?

Are you ready?

1 Calculate:

  a $\frac{3}{5} + \frac{1}{5}$ **b** 0.3 + 0.2   **c** 0.27 + 0.5

2 Calculate:

  a $1 - \frac{3}{10}$ **b** 1 − 0.6   **c** 1 − 0.84

3 What is the probability of flipping a head on a fair coin?

4 What is the probability of rolling a 4 on a fair, six-sided dice?

There are some important things you need to know when working with probability.

An **experiment** is the act of doing something random, such as rolling a dice or selecting a random digit from 0 to 9

An **outcome** is a possible result of an experiment, like rolling a 5 on a dice or selecting the digit 9

An **event** is a collection of outcomes, like rolling an even number on a dice or selecting a digit that is a multiple of 3

The probability of an event A can be calculated using the formula:

$$P(A) = \frac{\text{number of outcomes leading to event A}}{\text{total number of outcomes}}$$

If all the outcomes have an equal chance of occurring, the probabilities will all be the same. For example, a fair, six-sided dice is rolled. The outcomes are 1, 2, 3, 4, 5 and 6 and because the dice is **fair**, each of these outcomes are equally likely. The probability of each of these outcomes is $\frac{1}{6}$. If the outcomes do not have an equal chance of occurring, then the experiment is **biased**.

The sum of probabilities for all possible outcomes is 1. You can calculate unknown probabilities using this fact. You will also be able to calculate the probability of an event not happening. For example, the probability of rolling a 6 on a fair dice is $\frac{1}{6}$, therefore the probability of **not** rolling a 6 is $1 - \frac{1}{6} = \frac{5}{6}$

Example 1

The table shows the probability of a spinner landing on a particular colour.

Red	Yellow	Blue	Green
$\frac{3}{10}$	$\frac{1}{10}$		$\frac{5}{10}$

What is the probability that the spinner lands on blue?

Method

Solution	Commentary
$\frac{3}{10} + \frac{1}{10} + \frac{5}{10} = \frac{9}{10}$	The probabilities for red, yellow and green sum to $\frac{9}{10}$
$1 - \frac{9}{10} = \frac{1}{10}$ Therefore P(blue) = $\frac{1}{10}$	Probabilities must sum to 1, therefore the probability of landing on blue is $\frac{1}{10}$

Example 2

A game has outcomes A, B, C or D. The table shows the probability of outcome A and the probability of outcome B.

Outcome	A	B	C	D
Probability	0.4	0.34		

The probability of outcome C is the same as outcome D.

What is the probability of outcome D?

Method

Solution	Commentary
0.4 + 0.34 = 0.74	First add up the probabilities of outcomes A and B to get 0.74
1 − 0.74 = 0.26	Then subtract from 1 to get 0.26
0.26 ÷ 2 = 0.13 Therefore P(D) = 0.13	The probabilities of outcomes C and D are the same so divide 0.26 by 2 to get 0.13

Example 3

The probability that it will rain tomorrow is 0.47

What is the probability that it will **not** rain tomorrow?

Method

Solution	Commentary
1 − 0.47 = 0.53 Therefore, P(no rain) = 0.53	An event can either happen or not happen. Therefore, the probability of something happening and the probability of it not happening must sum to 1

Practice

1 **a** A bag contains some coloured counters.

5 counters are green and the remaining 4 are white.

A counter is selected at random.

Find the probability that the counter is green.

b A box of chocolates contains 4 fudge, 3 toffee and 2 strawberry.

Zak selects a chocolate from the box at random.

Find the probability that the chocolate selected is:

i fudge **ii** fudge or toffee **iii** **not** toffee.

c A box contains whiteboard pens.

4 of the pens are black, 3 are green, 2 are blue and 1 is red.

A pen is selected at random.

Find the probability that the pen chosen is:

i red **ii** green or blue **iii** **not** green.

2 A spinner has four coloured sections: red, green, orange and blue.

The table shows the probability of spinning the colours red, green and orange.

Colour	Red	Green	Orange	Blue
Probability	0.3	0.4	0.2	

a What is the probability of spinning red or green?

b What is the probability of spinning blue?

c What is the probability of **not** spinning red?

3 The probability that Bobbie will go on holiday this year is 0.55

What is the probability that she will **not** go on holiday this year?

4 The probability that a biased coin will show tails when flipped is $\frac{2}{5}$

What is the probability that the coin will show heads?

5 The table shows the probability that a shop sells a particular colour of shoe to a customer.

Colour	Probability
White	
Black	0.33
Brown	0.29
Other	0.16

Find the probability that the next pair of shoes sold is:

a white **b** black or brown **c** **not** brown.

6 There are three exits from a roundabout: Exit 1, Exit 2 and Exit 3, as shown.

The probability that a vehicle takes Exit 1 or Exit 2 is shown in the table.

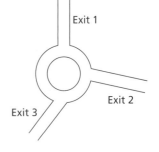

Exit	Exit 1	Exit 2	Exit 3
Probability	0.54	0.27	

Find the probability that a vehicle takes:

a either Exit 1 or Exit 2   **b** Exit 3

7 a A spinner has some numbered sections.

The probability of spinning a particular number is shown in the table.

Number	1	2	3	4	5
Probability	0.17		0.51	0.02	0.1

The spinner is spun once.

Find the probability of spinning:

i the number 2   **ii** an odd number   **iii** a number greater than 2

b Another spinner has lettered sections A, B and C.

The probability of spinning each letter is shown in the table.

Letter	A	B	C
Probability	$\frac{1}{5}$	$\frac{3}{10}$	

Find the probability of spinning the letter C.

8 A game has four outcomes: A, B, C and D.

The probability of outcomes A and B are shown in the table.

Outcome	A	B	C	D
Probability	0.3	0.4		

The probability of outcome C is the same as the probability of outcome D.

Find the probability of outcome C.

9 A bag contains five different coloured sweets.

The table shows the probability of getting each colour.

Purple	Yellow	Red	Green	Blue
0.1	0.3	0.2	0.08	

A sweet is selected at random.

Find the following probabilities.

a P(blue)   **b** P(yellow or red)   **c** P(not green)

Consolidate – do you need more?

1 A fair, six-sided dice is rolled.

What is the probability of:

a rolling a 3   **b** rolling an 8   **c** rolling an odd number

d **not** rolling a 3   **e** rolling a multiple of 2   **f** rolling a square number

g rolling a number greater than 1   **h** rolling a number less than 10?

2 A drawer contains some socks.

There are 8 white socks in the drawer.

There are 6 black socks in the drawer.

A sock is taken out of the drawer at random.

a What is the probability that the sock is white?

b What is the probability that the sock is **not** white?

3 A jar contains some sweets. There are 50 mints, 25 chocolates and 15 jelly sweets.

A sweet is chosen at random.

a What is the probability of choosing a jelly sweet?

b What is the probability of choosing a mint or a jelly sweet?

4 The probability that Chloe will win a game of darts against Iqra is 0.27

What is the probability that Iqra will win?

5 A spinner has three different coloured sections. The table shows the probability of spinning red and the probability of spinning green.

Colour	Red	Green	Blue
Probability	$\frac{5}{11}$	$\frac{2}{11}$	

The spinner is spun.

What is the probability of spinning blue?

6 The table shows the probabilities of students being picked at random from particular year groups.

Year 7	Year 8	Year 9	Year 10	Year 11
0.2	0.24	0.3		0.06

A student is selected at random.

Find the following probabilities.

a P(Year 10)   **b** P(Year 7 or Year 8)   **c** P(not Year 9)

Stretch – can you deepen your learning?

1 The table below shows the number of students in each year at a school.

Year group	Year 7	Year 8	Year 9	Year 10	Year 11
Number	120	150	175	165	120

A student is selected at random.

Find the probability that the student will:

a be from Year 7   **b** be from Year 10 or Year 11   **c** **not** be from Year 8

2 Sophie has a box of coloured pencils.

The probability that Sophie takes a brown pencil is $\frac{3}{8}$

The probability that Sophie takes a green pencil is $\frac{7}{12}$

Find the probability that Sophie takes a brown or green pencil.

3 A charity is running a raffle.

The charity sells 250 red tickets numbered 1 to 250

The charity sells 170 green tickets numbered 1 to 170

A ticket is chosen at random to win a holiday.

Find the probability that the ticket selected will be:

a green   **b** numbered 100   **c** numbered 201

Single event probability: exam practice

White Rose
M▲THS

1 Choose the correct card to complete each sentence.

1–3

(certain)   (likely)   (even chance)   (unlikely)   (impossible)

a) It is _____ that each day will have 24 hours. **(1)**

b) It is _____ that, if a sweet is chosen randomly from a bag of 7 pink sweets and 2 yellow sweets, it will be pink. **(1)**

2 Mark each probability described below with a cross (×) on copies of the probability scales.

a) Mark the probability that you will get an odd or even number when rolling an ordinary, six-sided dice. **(1)**

b) Mark the probability that you will get a 0 when rolling an ordinary, six-sided dice. **(1)**

c) Mark the probability that you will get a head when you throw an unbiased coin. **(1)**

3 The diagram shows a spinner. It can land on A or B or C.

Ron spins the spinner.

Write down the probability that the spinner will land on C. **(1)**

4 Alex has a bag of 20 pieces of fruit.

7 of the pieces of fruit are strawberries.

11 are grapes.

2 are raspberries.

Alex takes a piece of fruit from the bag at random.

Write down the probability that Alex:

a) takes a strawberry **(1)**

b) does **not** take a grape. **(1)**

5 A bag contains some beads that are purple, orange, gold or silver.

The table shows the probability of choosing each colour of bead from the bag.

Colour	Purple	Orange	Gold	Silver
Probability	0.2	0.1		0.4

a) What is the probability of choosing a gold bead? **(2)**

b) There are 10 beads in total. How many beads are silver? **(1)**

In this block, we will cover...

11.1 Systematic listing

Example 1

Here are the starter and main options on a menu

Starter	Main
Soup	Chicken
Mushrooms	Lasagne
Bread	Burger
	Salad

List all the possible combinations of starter and m

Method

11.2 Frequency trees

Practice

1 Copy and complete the frequency trees.

a

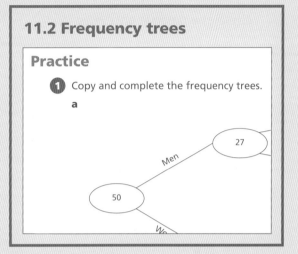

11.3 Sample space diagrams

Consolidate – do you need more

1 A spinner has four equal sections labelled

		First spin			
		A	B	B	C
	A	AA	BA	BA	
Second spin	B				
	B				
	C				

a Copy and complete the sample space d

11.4 Venn diagrams

Stretch – can you deepen your le

1 ξ = {Letters in the word UNCOPYRIGHTABL

A = {vowels}

B = {consonants}

a Explain why the intersection will be bl

b Explain why there will be no letters on

c Draw and complete a Venn diagram to

2 200 people were surveyed about their ph

• 176 sent a text message

Are you ready?

1 A standard six-sided dice is rolled.

List all the possible outcomes.

2 A coin is flipped.

List all the possible outcomes.

3 A bag contains 5 red counters, 4 blue counters and 1 yellow counter.

A counter is selected at random.

What are the possible outcomes?

4 What do probabilities sum to?

In maths, **systematic listing** is a method used to organise information in a methodical way, especially when dealing with counting or finding possible outcomes. It is like making a structured list to ensure that no options are missed or counted twice.

For example, let's say you want to list all the possible combinations of numbers when rolling two dice. Instead of randomly writing down numbers, you can systematically go through each possibility. This would result in (1, 1), (1, 2), (1, 3), and so on, as demonstrated below:

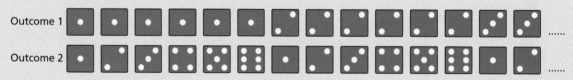

In total there are 36 outcomes for rolling two dice (6 × 6 = 36).

Example 1

Here are the starter and main options on a menu:

Starter	Main
Soup	Chicken
Mushrooms	Lasagne
Bread	Burger
	Salad

List all the possible combinations of starter and main.

Method

Solution	Commentary
Soup, Chicken (SC) Soup, Lasagne (SL) Soup, Burger (SB) Soup, Salad (SS)	Choose an appropriate abbreviation for each word. In this case it makes sense to use the first letter.
Mushrooms, Chicken (MC) Mushrooms, Lasagne (ML) Mushrooms, Burger (MB) Mushrooms, Salad (MS)	Start with the first starter, and then list all the mains it could have with it. Then do the second starter, and so on. By working systematically, you ensure that nothing is missed.
Bread, Chicken (BC) Bread, Lasagne (BL) Bread, Burger (BB) Bread, Salad (BS)	Notice there are 12 possible combinations in total. This is because there are three starters and four mains, and $3 \times 4 = 12$

Example 2

List all the different three-digit numbers that can be made using these digits.

Method

Solution	Commentary
257 275 527 572 725 752	Start by putting one digit first, and then there are two ways the other two digits can be arranged. Then repeat by putting each other digit first.

Practice

1 Seb has three choices of tops: long-sleeved, plain and striped.

He has four choices of bottoms: shorts, joggers, jeans and cargo.

List all the combinations of tops and bottoms that Seb could choose.

2 Kim rolls a fair, six-sided dice twice.

List all the possible outcomes.

3 A fair, six-sided dice is rolled and a fair coin is flipped.

List all the possible outcomes.

4 A fair coin is flipped three times.

List all the possible outcomes.

5 In a meal deal you get to choose one sandwich, one snack and one drink.

Sandwich	Snack	Drink
Cheese	Cake	Water
Turkey	Biscuit	Juice
Beef	Fruit	Fizzy

List all the possible combinations.

6 List all the possible three-digit numbers that can be formed using these digit cards.

7 List all the possible three-letter combinations that can be formed using these letter cards.

8 A bag contains red balls, blue balls and green balls. There is more than one of each colour in the bag.

List all the possible combinations of two balls that can be drawn.

9 Find all the possible two-digit numbers that can be formed using the digits 4, 5, and 6 without repetition.

10 A bag contains four different coloured socks: red, blue, green, and yellow.

List all the possible pairs of socks that can be formed. Each pair must have two different colours.

11 Using the letters X, Y, Z, and W, list all the possible four-letter combinations that can be formed without repetition.

12 A two-digit number is formed using the digits 1, 2, 3, and 4

List all the possible two-number combinations that can be formed without repetition.

Consolidate – do you need more?

1 Max has five different hats (A, B, C, D and E) and four different scarves (1, 2, 3 and 4).

List all the different combinations of hat and scarf that Max could choose. The first two have been done for you.

A1, A2, …

2 A spinner is split into five equal sections numbered 1 to 5

It is spun twice.

List all the different possible outcomes. The first two have been done for you.

1 1, 1 2,

3 Jack has a bag of blue counters, yellow counters and green counters.

There is more than one of each colour in the bag.

He chooses two counters at random.

List all the possible outcomes. The first two have been done for you.

BB, BY, …

4 The table shows the starter, main and dessert options at a restaurant.

Starter	Main	Dessert
Soup	Sandwich	Cake
Prawn cocktail	Chicken	Ice-cream
	Lasagne	

List all the possible combinations of starter, main and dessert.

5 List all the three-digit numbers that can be made using each digit card only once.

6 List all the different three-letter combinations that can be made using these letters.

265

Stretch – can you deepen your learning?

1 Here is a list of possible toppings on a pizza:

Two different toppings can be chosen.

List all the different possible combinations.

2 Here are some letter cards:

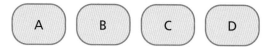

Here are some number cards:

Ron chooses a letter card and a number card at random.

a List all the possible outcomes Ron could choose.

b What is the probability that he picks A and 5?

c What is the probability that he picks B and an even number?

3 Kim makes a three-digit number using these digit cards.

List all the three-digit numbers that Kim could make.

4 Mo makes a three-digit number using these digit-cards.

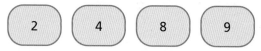

The tens digit in Mo's number is less than 5

a List all the possible numbers that Mo can make.

b What is the probability his number is even?

11.2 Frequency trees

Are you ready?

1 A bag contains 100 counters.

54 of the counters are red. The rest are yellow.

How many yellow counters are there?

2 A group of 52 men and women answered a survey.

27 of the people were women.

How many were men?

3 Work out $\frac{3}{5}$ of 120

4 Calculate 30% of 350

A **frequency tree** organises data by categories, counting how many times each category occurs. You start with the total number of items and then break this down into two or more groups. Then each of those groups is split into groups.

For example, people were surveyed on a busy high street. Data was captured on their gender, and whether they were wearing a hat or not. The frequency tree represents the results of the survey:

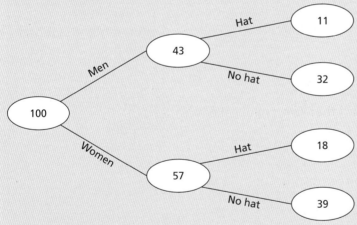

This frequency tree shows that:

- 100 people were surveyed in total
- 43 of them were men and the other 57 were women
- of the 43 men, 11 were wearing a hat and 32 were not
- of the 57 women, 18 were wearing a hat and the other 39 were not.

You can use this diagram to work out other facts, such as 29 people in total were wearing a hat.

You can also work out probabilities. The probability of choosing a person at random and them being a woman wearing a hat is $\frac{18}{100}$ or 0.18, because there are 18 women wearing hats and 100 people in total.

Example 1

A group of 100 men and women were asked whether they had pets.

Of the 45 men asked, 22 of them had pets.

35 of the women did **not** have pets.

a Draw a frequency tree to represent this information.

b How many people had pets altogether?

c If a person is selected at random, what is the probability they are a woman with a pet?

d If a woman is selected at random, what is the probability they do **not** have a pet?

Method

Solution	Commentary
a 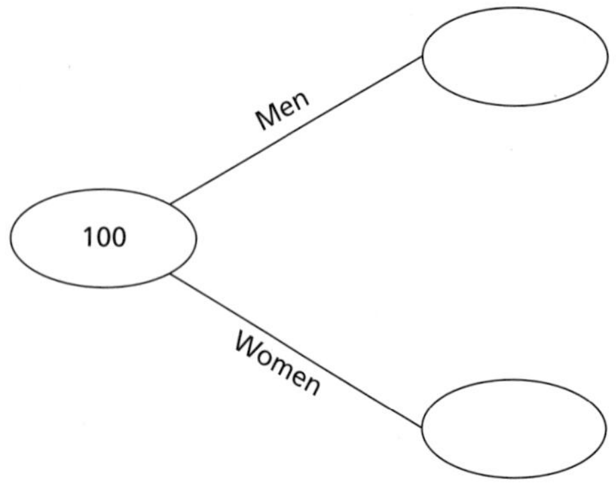 Men 100 Women	First draw a frequency tree. You know that there were 100 people, and they were either men or women.
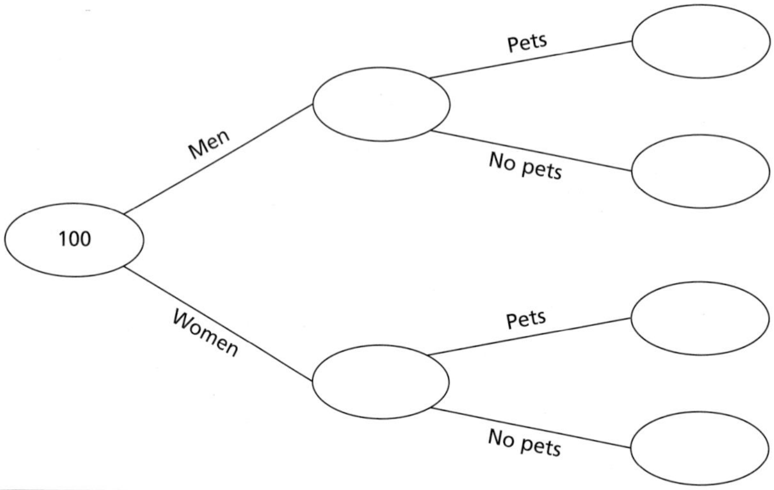 Men — Pets / No pets 100 Women — Pets / No pets	Then you have information about pets or no pets. Once you have drawn your frequency tree, start to fill in the numbers.

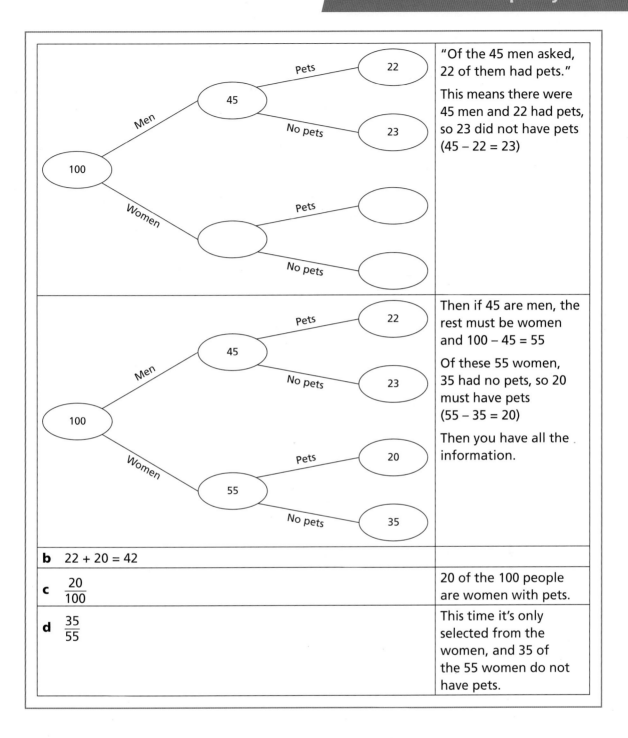

"Of the 45 men asked, 22 of them had pets."

This means there were 45 men and 22 had pets, so 23 did not have pets (45 − 22 = 23)

Then if 45 are men, the rest must be women and 100 − 45 = 55

Of these 55 women, 35 had no pets, so 20 must have pets (55 − 35 = 20)

Then you have all the information.

b 22 + 20 = 42

c $\dfrac{20}{100}$

20 of the 100 people are women with pets.

d $\dfrac{35}{55}$

This time it's only selected from the women, and 35 of the 55 women do not have pets.

Practice

1 Copy and complete the frequency trees.

a

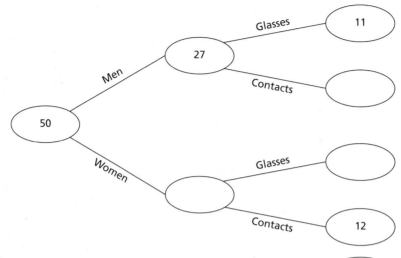

b

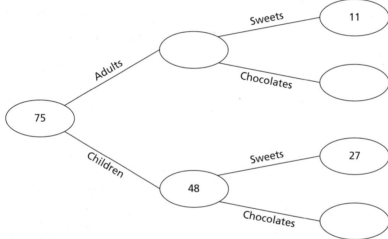

c

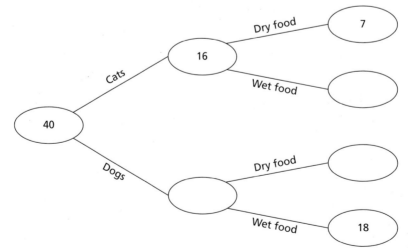

d

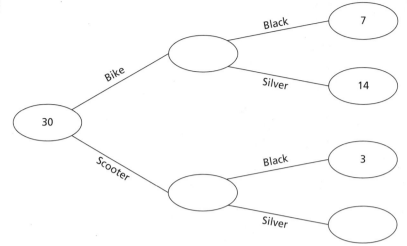

2 Whitney recorded whether it rained or not over a period of 30 days, and whether her bus was late or not.

It rained on 18 of the days.

On the days when it rained, her bus was late six times.

On the days when it did not rain, her bus was late five times.

a Copy and complete the frequency tree to show this information.

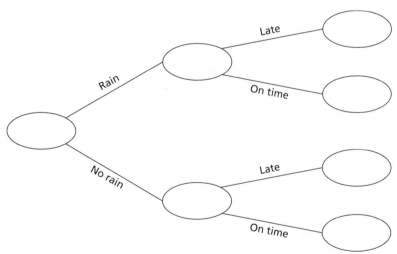

b On how many days was Whitney's bus on time altogether?

3 A group of 80 boys and girls are asked whether they prefer football or rugby.

50 are boys and the rest are girls.

30 of the boys prefer football.

48 of the children in total prefer football.

a Copy and complete the frequency tree to show this information.

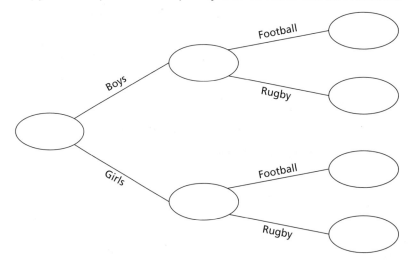

b If a child is selected at random, what is the probability that they are a girl who prefers rugby?

4 A group of 200 males and females are asked whether they prefer tea or coffee.

Of the 89 males asked, 53 of them prefer coffee.

61 women prefer tea.

a Copy and complete the frequency tree to show this information.

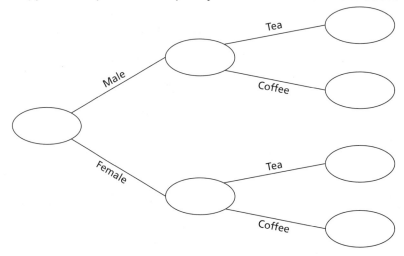

b A person is selected at random.

What is the probability they are a man?

c A man is selected at random.

What is the probability they prefer tea?

5 A hotel has 250 guest rooms.

120 of the hotel rooms are deluxe rooms, and the rest are standard.

86 of the deluxe rooms have showers, and the rest have baths.

18 of the standard rooms have baths, and the rest have showers.

a Draw a frequency tree to show this information.

b If a room is selected at random, what is the probability that it is a deluxe room with a bath?

c If a standard room is selected at random, what is the probability that it has a shower?

6 In a school, there are 480 students in total in years 10 and 11

Of the 280 students in Year 10, 56 of them did not do their homework.

98 students in total did not do their homework.

a Draw a frequency tree to show this information.

b A Year 11 student is selected at random.

What is the probability that they did their homework?

Consolidate – do you need more?

1 A group of 2000 first- and second-year university students are asked if they live in halls of residence.

1200 first-year students are asked and 860 of them live in halls.

543 second-year students do not live in halls.

a Copy and complete the frequency tree to show this information.

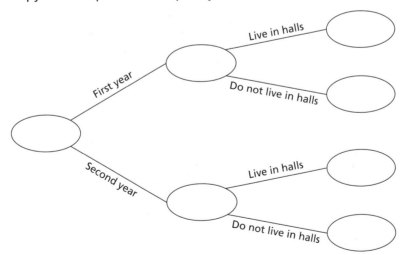

b A student is selected at random.

What is the probability that they are in their second year and live in halls?

2 A group of 45 people who walked or took the bus to work are asked if they ate breakfast.

19 of the people walked and 7 of them skipped breakfast.

18 people skipped breakfast in total.

a Copy and complete the frequency tree to show this information.

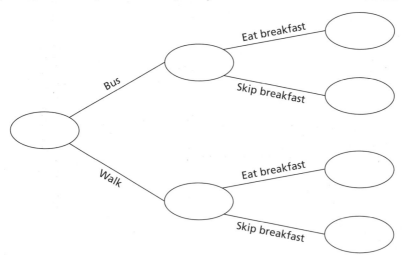

b A person who walked is selected at random.

What is the probability they ate breakfast?

3 110 rooms in a hotel have either a sea view or a pool view.

Of the 38 sea-view rooms, 11 are twin rooms and the rest are double.

Of the pool-view rooms, 25 are twin rooms and the rest are double.

a Copy and complete the frequency tree to show this information.

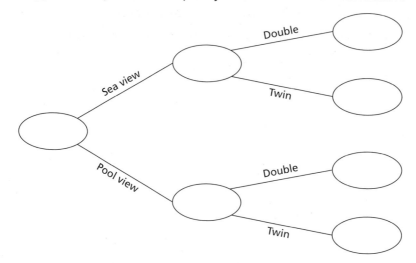

b A pool-view room is selected at random.

What is the probability that it is a double room?

Stretch – can you deepen your learning?

1 In an office there are 180 men and women.

60% of the people are men.

$\frac{1}{3}$ of the men wear glasses.

79 people in total wear glasses.

a Draw a frequency tree to show this information.

b A person who wears glasses is selected at random.

What is the probability that they are a man?

2 Ron surveys the cars and vans that are driving along a road.

Of the 300 vehicles he sees, 85% of them are cars.

Of the cars, $\frac{1}{5}$ are red.

There are 10 more white cars than red cars.

The rest of the cars are black.

There are no red vans.

$\frac{7}{9}$ of the vans are white and the rest are black.

a Draw a frequency tree to show this information.

b A van is selected at random.

What is the probability that it is black?

3 In a school, 480 students in years 7 and 8 study either French, Spanish or German.

There are the same number of students in each year group.

In Year 7, half of the students study Spanish, and twice as many students study French as study German.

In Year 8, 45% of the students study French. The same number of students study German as Spanish.

a Draw a frequency tree to represent this information.

b A student who studies German is selected at random.

What is the probability they are in Year 8?

Are you ready?

1 A spinner is split into five equal sections labelled 1 to 5

The spinner is spun twice.

List all the possible outcomes.

A **sample space diagram** is used to display all possible outcomes of an experiment. This could be as a list or a table of values.

For example, if a coin is flipped twice then you need to consider the first flip and the second flip, and the possible outcomes of each. These will form the rows and columns of your sample space diagram.

		Second flip	
		Heads (H)	Tails (T)
First flip	Heads (H)		
	Tails (T)		

Once you have set up your table, you can fill in the possible outcomes as shown.

		Second flip	
		Heads (H)	Tails (T)
First flip	Heads (H)	HH	HT
	Tails (T)	TH	TT

Then, assuming the coin is fair, you can find probabilities. For example, the probability of the coin landing on tails twice is $\frac{1}{4}$. This is because there are four possible outcomes, and only one of them is tails twice.

Example 1

A fair spinner is split into five equal sections numbered 1 to 5

The spinner is spun and a fair coin is flipped.

a Construct a sample space diagram to show the possible outcomes.

b Find the probability that the spinner lands on an even number and the coin lands on heads.

Method

Solution	Commentary
a <table><tr><td></td><td></td><td colspan="2">Coin</td></tr><tr><td></td><td></td><td>Heads (H)</td><td>Tails (T)</td></tr><tr><td rowspan="5">Spinner</td><td>1</td><td>1H</td><td>1T</td></tr><tr><td>2</td><td>2H</td><td>2T</td></tr><tr><td>3</td><td>3H</td><td>3T</td></tr><tr><td>4</td><td>4H</td><td>4T</td></tr><tr><td>5</td><td>5H</td><td>5T</td></tr></table>	There are two things happening here: the spin of the spinner and the flip of the coin. The spinner can land on 1, 2, 3, 4 or 5 so these form your rows (or columns – it doesn't matter which way around you do it) and the coin can land on heads or tails so these form your columns (or rows). Once you have set up your sample space diagram, you can fill in the possible outcomes.
b <table><tr><td></td><td></td><td colspan="2">Coin</td></tr><tr><td></td><td></td><td>Heads (H)</td><td>Tails (T)</td></tr><tr><td rowspan="5">Spinner</td><td>1</td><td>1H</td><td>1T</td></tr><tr><td>2</td><td>2H</td><td>2T</td></tr><tr><td>3</td><td>3H</td><td>3T</td></tr><tr><td>4</td><td>4H</td><td>4T</td></tr><tr><td>5</td><td>5H</td><td>5T</td></tr></table> $\dfrac{2}{10}$	Now look for the outcomes in the heads column that have an even number. There are two of them out of the 10 possible outcomes, so the probability is $\dfrac{2}{10}$

Example 2

A fair spinner is split into four equal sections numbered 1 to 4

The spinner is spun twice, and the outcomes are multiplied to give a resulting score.

a Construct a sample space to show all the possible scores.

b What is the probability that the score is greater than 10?

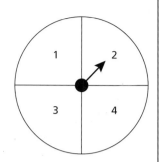

Method

Solution	Commentary
a	This time the score is the product of the two single outcomes.

		First spin			
	×	**1**	**2**	**3**	**4**
Second spin	**1**	1	2	3	4
	2	2	4	6	8
	3	3	6	9	12
	4	4	8	12	16

So if the first spinner lands on 3 and the second lands on 2, the score is 6 because $3 \times 2 = 6$

b

		First spin			
	×	**1**	**2**	**3**	**4**
Second spin	**1**	1	2	3	4
	2	2	4	6	8
	3	3	6	9	12
	4	4	8	12	16

3 of the 16 possible scores are greater than 10

$\dfrac{3}{16}$

Practice

1 A fair spinner has four equal sections labelled A, B, C, and D.

The spinner is spun twice.

		First spin			
		A	**B**	**C**	**D**
Second spin	**A**	AA	BA	CA	
	B				
	C				
	D				

a Copy and complete the sample space diagram to show all the possible outcomes.

b What is the probability that the spinner lands on the same letter twice?

2 A bag contains three red balls labelled R1, R2 and R3

Another bag contains two blue balls labelled B1 and B2

A ball is removed from each bag at random.

	R1	R2	R3
B1			
B2			

   a Copy and complete the sample space diagram to represent all possible outcomes.

   b What is the probability that the balls removed are R2 and B1?

3 A fair, six-sided dice numbered 1 to 6 is rolled twice and the outcomes are added together.

+	1	2	3	4	5	6
1	2	3	4			
2						
3						
4						
5						
6						

   a Copy and complete the sample space diagram to show all the possible totals.

   b Find the probability that the total is:

     i 5   **ii** 10   **iii** 12   **iv** 1

   c Find the probability that the total is:

     i greater than 5   **ii** less than or equal to 5

4 A fair, six-sided dice numbered 1 to 6 is rolled twice and the outcomes are multiplied.

×	1	2	3			
	1		3			
4						
6						

   a Copy and complete the sample space diagram to show all the possible outcomes.

   b Which outcomes are the most likely?

   c Which outcomes are the least likely?

   d Find the probabilities.

     i P(3)   **ii** P(20)   **iii** P(12)   **iv** P(greater than 10)   **v** P(odd)

5 Two bags each contain some counters.

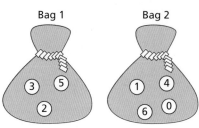

A counter is removed from each bag at random and the numbers are added together.

a Construct a sample space diagram to show all the possible outcomes.

b Find the probabilities.

   i P(even)   **ii** P(odd)   **iii** P(greater than 7)

  iv P(less than 10)   **v** P(1)   **vi** P(less than 20)

6 Here are two fair spinners:

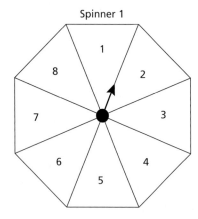

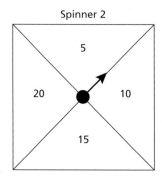

Each spinner is spun, and the score is the positive difference between the numbers.

a Construct a sample space diagram to show all the possible outcomes.

b Find the probabilities.

   i P(odd)   **ii** P(0)   **iii** P(prime)

  iv P(greater than 10)   **v** P(less than 18)   **vi** P(even or prime)

Consolidate – do you need more?

1 A spinner has four equal sections labelled A, B, B, and C. The spinner is spun twice.

		First spin			
		A	B	B	C
Second spin	A	AA	BA	BA	
	B				
	B				
	C				

   a Copy and complete the sample space diagrams to show all the possible combined outcomes.

   b What is the probability that the spinner lands on the same letter twice?

2 A bag contains three counters labelled 1, 2 and 3

A box contains two counters labelled A and B.

A counter is removed at random from each.

	1	2	3
A			
B			

   a Copy and complete the sample space diagram to represent all possible outcomes.

   b What is P(3A)?

3 Two bags each contain some counters.

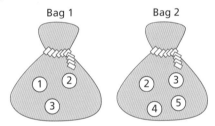

A counter is removed at random from each bag and the numbers are added together.

   a Construct a sample space diagram to show all the possible outcomes.

   b Find the probabilities.

     i P(even)   **ii** P(odd)   **iii** P(greater than 7)

     iv P(less than 4)   **v** P(3)   **vi** P(less than 10)

4 Here are two fair spinners:

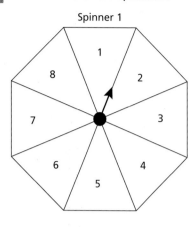

Spinner 1

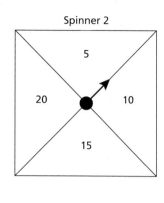

Spinner 2

Each spinner is spun, and the score is the sum of the numbers.

a Construct a sample space diagram to show all the possible outcomes.

b Find the probabilities.

   i P(odd)   ii P(0)   iii P(prime)

   iv P(greater than 10)   v P(less than 18)   vi P(even or prime)

Stretch – can you deepen your learning?

1 Ron flips a coin and rolls a dice.

If the coin lands on heads, he doubles the score on his dice.

If the coin lands on tails, he subtracts 1 from the score on his dice.

a Construct a sample space diagram to show the possible outcomes.

b Find the probabilities.

   i P(greater than 6)   ii P(less than 3)   iii P(0)

2 A bag contains one red counter, one yellow counter and two blue counters.

A second bag contains five counters numbered 2, 4, 6, 8 and 10

A counter is taken from each bag at random.

If a red counter is removed, the number on the other counter is doubled.

If a yellow counter is removed, the number on the other counter is halved.

If a blue counter is removed, the number on the other counter is subtracted from 10

a Construct a sample space diagram to show the possible outcomes.

b What is the most likely outcome?

c Find the probabilities.

   i P(square number)   ii P(multiple of 4)   iii P(factor of 30)   iv P(prime)

11.4 Venn diagrams

Are you ready? (A)

1 A fair, six-sided dice numbered 1 to 6 is rolled twice.

The two numbers obtained are multiplied.

Draw a sample space diagram to show all the possible outcomes.

2 A fair coin is flipped twice.

What is the probability that it lands on heads twice?

3 A group of students are asked if they like maths, and if they like science.

86 students in total like maths.

28 of them also like science.

How many students only like maths?

A **Venn diagram** is a way of representing data from two or more sets. In this Venn diagram, A and B are two different sets of data each represented by a circle, and the overlap represents data that fits into both sets.

Note the symbol ξ, which is used to represent the **universal set**. This is the set of all the data in the situation.

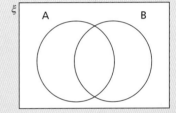

Here are two examples of situations that can be represented using a Venn diagram:

100 people are asked if they like pizza and if they like pasta.
42 people like pasta only.
28 people like both.
9 people like neither.

ξ = {Numbers from 1–10}   1, 2, 3, 4, 5, 6, 7, 8, 9, 10
A = {Even numbers}   2, 4, 6, 8, 10
B = {Prime numbers}   2, 3, 5, 7

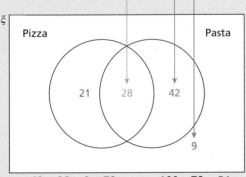

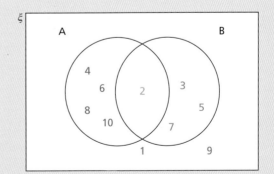

$42 + 28 + 9 = 79$ $100 - 79 = 21$

By drawing a Venn diagram, you can find probabilities. In the left-hand example,

P(pizza and pasta) = $\frac{28}{100}$ because 28 of the 100 people like both. In the right-hand example,

P(neither A nor B) = $\frac{2}{10}$ because two of the 10 numbers are not in either set A or set B.

Example

200 students in Year 10 can choose to study French or Spanish.

18 students study neither.

123 students study Spanish only.

41 students study both.

a Draw a Venn diagram to represent this.

b How many students study French only?

c A student is chosen at random. What is the probability they study French?

d A student who studies Spanish is chosen at random. What is the probability that they also study French?

Method

Solution	Commentary
a ξ F ⟨ 18 ⟩ 41 ⟨ 123 ⟩ S 18 $\begin{array}{r} 1\;2\;3 \\ 4\;1 \\ 1^{1}8\;+ \\ \hline 1\;8\;2 \end{array}$ $\qquad$ $\begin{array}{r} 2\;0\;0 \\ 1\;8\;2\;- \\ \hline 1\;8 \end{array}$	The two sets are French and Spanish. 18 study neither, so 18 goes outside the circles but within the rectangle. 123 students study only Spanish so this goes in the Spanish circle. 41 study both so this goes in the overlap. Then for French only, use the fact that the numbers need to total 200. Therefore, French only is 18
b 18	
c $18 + 41 = 59$ $\dfrac{59}{200}$	18 study French only and 41 study both.
d $123 + 41 = 164$ $\dfrac{41}{164}$	164 people study Spanish in total, so it is out of 164 not 200

Practice (A)

1 The Venn diagram shows the number of people who said they like rugby and football.

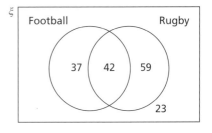

   a How many people only like rugby?

   b How many people only like football?

   c How many people like both?

   d How many people like neither?

   e How many people like football in total?

   f How many people were asked in total?

2 140 students are in Year 8

   The Venn diagram shows the number of students who attend a drama club and a music club after school.

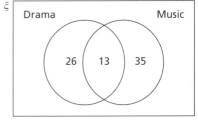

   a How many children attend both drama and music clubs?

   b How many children just attend the drama club?

   c There is a number missing from the Venn diagram. What is this number? What does this number represent?

3 110 people attend the gym.

   56 people only attend the spin class.

   18 people attend the spin class and the circuit class.

   22 people do not attend either class.

   a Draw a Venn diagram to represent this information.

   b How many people attend the circuit class only?

   c A person is selected at random. What is the probability they attend the circuit class?

   d A person who attends the spin class is selected at random. What is the probability that they also attend the circuit class?

4 In a group of 32 people, 8 have just a dog, 11 have just a cat and 4 have both.

   a Draw a Venn diagram to represent this information.

   b A person is selected at random. What is the probability they have a cat?

Are you ready? (B)

1 Write down the first five multiples of: **a** 2   **b** 3   **c** 4

2 Write down the factors of 50

3 Write down the first five prime numbers.

Example

ξ = {numbers from 1–10}

A = {multiples of 3}

B = {factors of 100}

a Draw a Venn diagram to represent this.

b A number is selected at random. What is the probability that it is a multiple of 3?

Method

Solution	Commentary
a ξ = {1, 2, 3, 4, 5, 6, 7, 8, 9, 10} A = {multiples of 3} B = {factors of 100} 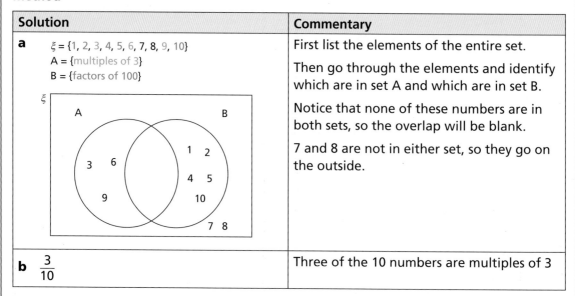	First list the elements of the entire set. Then go through the elements and identify which are in set A and which are in set B. Notice that none of these numbers are in both sets, so the overlap will be blank. 7 and 8 are not in either set, so they go on the outside.
b $\dfrac{3}{10}$	Three of the 10 numbers are multiples of 3

Practice (B)

1 Some children are asked if they study History or Geography.

The results are organised in the Venn diagram.

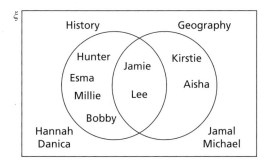

a Write down the names of the children who study History and Geography.

b Write down the name of a student who studies just History.

c Does Kirstie study History? Explain how you know.

2 ξ = {1, 2, 3, 4, 5, 6, 7, 8, 9, 10, 11, 12, 13, 14, 15}

A = {multiples of 2}

B = {multiples of 3}

a List the elements of set A.

b List the elements of set B.

c List the elements that are in both sets A and B.

d Copy and complete the Venn diagram to represent this information.

3 ξ = {numbers 1 to 20}

A = {multiples of 4}

B = {factors of 50}

a List the elements of set A.

b List the elements of set B.

c List the elements that are in both sets A and B.

d Copy and complete the Venn diagram to represent this information.

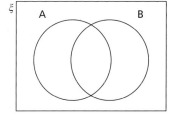

4 ξ = {numbers 1 to 20}

A = {even numbers}

B = {prime numbers}

a Draw and complete a Venn diagram to show this.

b One of the numbers is selected at random. What is the probability it is not in set A or set B?

Consolidate – do you need more?

1 Some people take part in a survey about music and dancing.

The Venn diagram shows the number of people who like either activity.

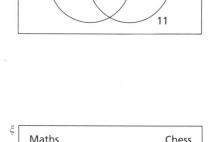

a How many people only like dancing?

b How many people only like music?

c How many people like both?

d How many people like neither?

e How many people like music in total?

f How many people are asked in total?

2 180 children are in Year 9

The Venn diagram shows the number of students who attend a maths club and a chess club after school.

a How many children attend both the maths club and the chess club?

b How many children just attend the chess club?

c There is a number missing from the Venn diagram. What is this number? What does this number represent?

3 200 people visit a café.

52 of the people get a drink only.

81 people get both food and drink.

7 people do **not** get food or drink.

a Draw a Venn diagram to represent this information.

b How many people get food only?

c A person is selected at random. What is the probability they get a drink?

4 ξ = {1, 2, 3, 4, 5, 6, 7, 8, 9, 10, 11, 12, 13, 14, 15}

A = {multiples of 5}

B = {factors of 30}

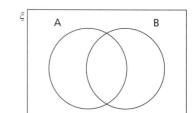

a List the elements of set A.

b List the elements of set B.

c List the elements that are in both sets A and B.

d Copy and complete the Venn diagram to represent this information.

5 ξ = {numbers from 1 to 20}

A = {even numbers}

B = {factors of 50}

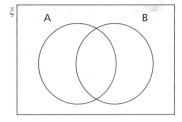

a List the elements of set A.

b List the elements of set B.

c List the elements that are in both sets A and B.

d Copy and complete the Venn diagram to represent this information.

Stretch – can you deepen your learning?

1 ξ = {Letters in the word UNCOPYRIGHTABLE}

A = {vowels}

B = {consonants}

a Explain why the intersection will be blank.

b Explain why there will be no letters on the outside of the circles.

c Draw and complete a Venn diagram to show this.

2 200 people were surveyed about their phone activity in the last hour:

- 176 sent a text message

- 138 made a phone call

- 17 people did not make a phone call or send a text message.

A person who sent a text message is selected at random. What is the probability they did not make a phone call?

3 What could be represented in the Venn diagram? Explain your answer.

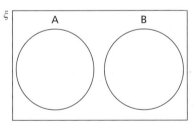

1-3

1 Amir spins a fair, five-sided spinner.

He then throws a fair coin.

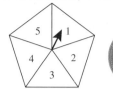

a) List all the possible outcomes he could get.

The first one has been done for you.

(1, tails) **(2)**

b) Amir spins the spinner once and throws the coin once.

Work out the probability that he will get a 4 and a tail. **(1)**

2 100 students in Year 11 can choose to study French or German.

The Venn diagram shows how many students study French, German, or both.

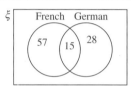

a) How many students study French only? **(1)**

b) A student is chosen at random. What is the probability they study French? **(2)**

c) A student who studies German is chosen at random. Find the probability that they also study French. **(2)**

3-5

3 The frequency tree shows some information about food at a party.

a) Complete a copy of the frequency tree. **(2)**

b) Sophie picks a curry at random.

Find the probability that she chooses rice with her curry. **(2)**

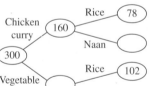

4 Two fair, six-sided dice are rolled.

The score is the positive difference between the numbers on each dice.

a) Complete a copy of the table to show all possible scores. **(1)**

b) Find the probability of scoring greater than 4 **(2)**

		Dice 1					
		1	2	3	4	5	6
	1	0	1	2			
	2	1	0				
Dice 2	3	2	1				
	4	3					
	5						
	6						

White Rose
M▲THS

In this block, we will cover...

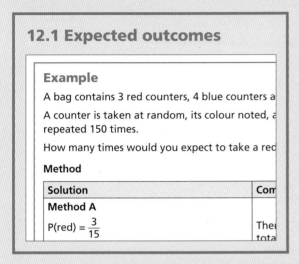

12.1 Expected outcomes

Example

A bag contains 3 red counters, 4 blue counters a

A counter is taken at random, its colour noted, a
repeated 150 times.

How many times would you expect to take a red

Method

Solution	Com
Method A	
P(red) = $\frac{3}{15}$	Ther total

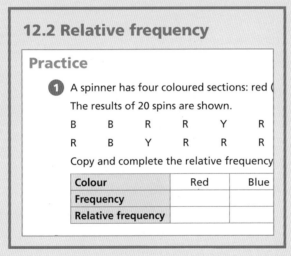

12.2 Relative frequency

Practice

1. A spinner has four coloured sections: red (

   The results of 20 spins are shown.

   | B | B | R | R | Y | R |
   | R | B | Y | R | R | R |

   Copy and complete the relative frequency

Colour	Red	Blue
Frequency		
Relative frequency		

Are you ready?

1 A fair, six-sided dice numbered 1 to 6 is rolled.

What is the probability that it lands on 3?

2 A fair coin is tossed.

What is the probability that it lands on heads?

3 A fair spinner is spun. It is split into five equal sections numbered 1 to 5

What is the probability that it lands on an even number?

4 A bag contains 6 red counters, 9 blue counters and 5 yellow counters.

A counter is picked at random.

What is the probability that it is **not** yellow?

In probability, the **expected outcome** is what we predict will happen when we perform an experiment.

Imagine rolling a fair, six-sided dice numbered 1 to 6. We know that each number from 1 to 6 has an equal chance of showing up because the dice is fair. If we rolled it, say, 600 times, we would expect each number (1, 2, 3, 4, 5, 6) to appear around 100 times each because there are six sides on the dice and they are all equally likely. So the **expected frequency** of rolling, say, the number 3 is 100 when the experiment is performed 600 times.

Example

A bag contains 3 red counters, 4 blue counters and 8 yellow counters.

A counter is taken at random, its colour noted, and it is then replaced in the bag. This is repeated 150 times.

How many times would you expect to take a red counter?

Method

Solution	Commentary
Method A	
$P(\text{red}) = \frac{3}{15}$ $\frac{3}{15} = \frac{30}{150}$ So you would expect to get a red counter 30 times.	There are 3 red counters and 15 counters in total. This means that 3 in every 15 times you would expect to pick a red counter. You can use equivalent fractions to work out how many times you would expect to pick a red counter out of 150 attempts.
Method B $\frac{3}{15} \times 150 = 30$	If using equivalent fractions doesn't help then you can also multiply the probability by the number of trials.

Practice

1. If you flip a fair coin 10 times, how many times would you expect it to land on heads?

2. A bag contains 6 red balls, 4 blue balls and 5 green balls.

   If you pick a ball randomly 15 times, how many times would you expect to get a blue ball?

3. A fair, six-sided dice numbered 1 to 6 is rolled 30 times.

   How many times would you expect it to land on 5?

4. A card is selected at random from a pack of 100 picture cards and then replaced.
   25 of the picture cards have hearts on them.
   This is repeated 400 times.

   How many times would you expect to select a card that shows a heart?

5. A spinner is divided into five equal sections labelled 1 to 5

   If you spin it 45 times, how many times would you expect to land on an odd number?

6. A box contains 3 yellow sweets, 7 blue sweets and 5 green sweets.

   If you randomly pick a sweet from the box 20 times and replace it, how many times would you expect to get a yellow sweet?

7. There are 20 marbles in a bag: 9 red, 6 blue and 5 green.

   If you randomly pick a marble from the bag 16 times, how many times would you expect to get a green marble?

8. A fair, eight-sided dice numbered 1 to 8 is rolled 24 times.

   How many times would you expect an even number to be rolled?

9. A box contains 4 white balls, 3 black balls and 5 red balls.

   If you pick a ball randomly 24 times, how many times would you expect to get a red ball?

10. If you flip a fair coin 14 times, how many times would you expect it to land on heads?

11. There are 30 sweets in a jar. 10 are orange-flavoured, 12 are lemon-flavoured and 8 are strawberry-flavoured.

    A sweet is picked at random and put back in the jar. This is done 120 times.

    How many times would you expect a lemon-flavoured sweet to be picked?

12 If you flip a fair coin 22 times, how many times would you expect it to land on heads?

13 There are 25 marbles in a box. 10 marbles are white, 8 marbles are black and 7 marbles are blue.

A marble is taken at random from the box and replaced. This is done 100 times.

How many times would you expect a white marble to be taken?

14 A spinner is divided into eight equal sections labelled 1 to 8

If you spin it 20 times, how many times would you expect to land on an odd number?

15 The probability of Sam winning a game is 0.6
He plays the game 70 times.

How many times should he expect to win?

16 The probability of passing a test is 0.85
200 people sit the test.

How many people would be expected to pass?

Consolidate – do you need more?

1 If you flip a fair coin 18 times, how many times would you expect it to land on tails?

2 A fair, six-sided dice numbered 1 to 6 is rolled 48 times.

How many times would you expect it to land on 4?

3 A fair, six-sided dice numbered 1 to 6 is rolled 72 times.

How many times would you expect it to land on an even number?

4 A spinner is divided into six equal sections labelled A to F.

If you spin it 18 times, how many times would you expect to land on the letter B?

5 A fair, 10-sided dice numbered 1 to 10 is rolled 20 times.

How many times would you expect a number greater than 7 to be rolled?

6 A bag contains 12 red balls, 8 blue balls and 10 green balls.

A ball is picked randomly and put back in the bag. This is done 60 times.

How many times would you expect to pick a green ball?

Stretch – can you deepen your learning?

1 A fair, six-sided dice numbered 1 to 6 is rolled 60 times.

How many more times would you expect to roll a number between 2 and 5 inclusive than not?

2 On average, a footballer scores 40% of the penalties she takes.

She takes 100 penalties in training.

She scores 32 penalties.

How many more penalties would she have been expected to score in training than she actually did?

3 A spinner has five equal sections.

John spins the spinner 20 times. He records the scores.

What is the mean expected score that John gets?

The mean is covered in Chapter 14.1

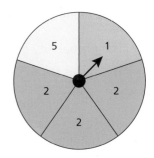

4 In a game, you roll a fair, six-sided dice.

If the dice shows a 1 or 2, you win £10

If the dice shows a 3 or 4, you win £20

If the dice shows a 5 or 6, you win £30

What is the expected amount of money you will win per roll?

Are you ready?

1 A fair, six-sided dice numbered 1 to 6 is rolled 300 times.

How many times would you expect it to land on 3?

2 A fair coin is flipped 40 times.

How many times would you expect it to land on heads?

3 The probability of winning a game is 0.6
The game is played by 900 people.

How many people would you expect to win?

4 The probability of passing a test is 68%
The test is taken by 300 people.

How many people would you expect to pass?

The probability you have looked at so far is called **theoretical probability**, which is based on assumptions. You can work out theoretical probabilities without actually performing an experiment.

Imagine that a dice is rolled 600 times. Using theoretical probability, you would expect the dice to land on each outcome an equal number of times (100 times each), based on the assumption that the dice is fair. You can work this out without rolling the dice at all.

However, to find **relative frequency**, you actually carry out the **experiment** (rolling the dice in this case). If you repeat this 600 times, you perform 600 **trials**. You then record the outcomes.

Here is a possible result of this experiment:

Number	Expected frequency	Theoretical probability	Actual frequency	Relative frequency
1	100	$\frac{1}{6}$	149	$\frac{149}{600}$
2	100	$\frac{1}{6}$	231	$\frac{231}{600}$
3	100	$\frac{1}{6}$	19	$\frac{19}{600}$
4	100	$\frac{1}{6}$	101	$\frac{101}{600}$
5	100	$\frac{1}{6}$	46	$\frac{46}{600}$
6	100	$\frac{1}{6}$	54	$\frac{54}{600}$

In the table, you can see that theoretical probability is **not** the same as the relative frequency. This is because the experiment is random, and in a single trial anything can happen.

If the dice is fair, you might expect the relative frequency to come closer to the theoretical probability the more times you roll the dice. If it doesn't, then the initial theoretical assumptions may be incorrect or the dice may be biased. Therefore, the greater the number of trials, the closer the relative frequency is to the actual probability of an outcome occurring.

Example 1

A spinner has four equal sections numbered 1 to 4

It is spun 10 times. Here are the results:

1   1   1   2   4   1   4   3   1   2

Complete the relative frequency table for these results.

Number	1	2	3	4
Frequency				
Relative frequency				

Method

Solution					Commentary
Number	1	2	3	4	Divide the frequency by the number of trials to work out the relative frequency.
Frequency	5	2	1	2	
Relative frequency	0.5	0.2	0.1	0.2	

Example 2

A fair coin is flipped 100 times. It lands on heads 72 times.

a What is the relative frequency of heads?

b Do you think the coin is fair? Why?

Method

Solution	Commentary
a $72 \div 100 = 0.72$	Remember, probability is the number of favourable outcomes divided by the total number of outcomes.
b It doesn't seem to be fair because it has landed on heads significantly more than half the time.	

Practice

1 A spinner has four coloured sections: red (R), blue (B), yellow (Y) and green (G).

The results of 20 spins are shown.

B	B	R	R	Y	R	G	Y	B	B
R	B	Y	R	R	R	Y	B	R	B

Copy and complete the relative frequency table for these results.

Colour	Red	Blue	Yellow	Green
Frequency				
Relative frequency				

2 A dice numbered 1 to 6, which is believed to be fair, is rolled 30 times.

a How many times do you expect each number to appear?

In fact, the dice is biased. The actual results of 30 throws are shown below.

> Remember that 'biased' means that each outcome does **not** have an equal chance of occurring.

2	2	3	3	5	3	3	6	1	3
5	3	3	3	3	2	4	1	5	4
6	2	3	3	2	3	1	4	3	3

b Copy and complete the relative frequency table for these results.

Score	1	2	3	4	5	6
Frequency						
Relative frequency						

3 Mo rolls a dice 30 times and gets a 4 on six occasions.

What is the relative frequency of rolling a 4?

4 A bag contains 20 red marbles, 15 blue marbles and 5 green marbles.

a What is the theoretical probability of randomly selecting a blue marble?

b Sam takes a marble at random, writes down the colour, and replaces it. He repeats this 30 times.

He takes 11 red marbles, 9 blue marbles and 10 green marbles.

What is the relative frequency of picking a green marble?

5 Out of 50 throws, a basketball player makes 15 successful shots.

What is the relative frequency of successful shots?

6 A spinner has eight equal sections, numbered 1 to 8

If it lands on the number 3 five times out of 40 spins, what is the relative frequency of landing on 3?

7 If you flip a coin 25 times and get heads 10 times, what is the relative frequency of getting tails?

8 The relative frequency of a biased coin landing on heads is 0.35

The coin was thrown 80 times.

a How many times did it land on heads?

b How many times did it land on tails?

9 A biased dice numbered 1 to 6 is rolled 20 times. The results are shown in the table.

Score	1	2	3	4	5	6
Frequency	7	2	1	3	5	2

a Write down the relative frequency of getting a 4

b Write down the relative frequency of getting more than 3

c Use the results to estimate how many times you would expect the dice to land on 2 if you rolled it 100 times.

10 A fair coin is flipped and the outcome recorded.

a When the coin is flipped 20 times, it lands on heads 5 times.

What is the relative frequency of heads?

b When the coin is flipped 50 times, it lands on heads 17 times.

What is the relative frequency of heads?

c When the coin is flipped 100 times, it lands on heads 48 times.

What is the relative frequency of heads?

d When the coin is flipped 1000 times, it lands on heads 493 times.

What is the relative frequency of heads?

e What do you notice about your answers to parts **a** to **d**? Why does this happen?

Consolidate – do you need more?

1 A spinner has four coloured sections: red (R), blue (B), yellow (Y) and green (G).

The results of 10 spins are:

B   G   R   R   Y   Y   G   Y   B   B

Copy and complete the relative frequency table for these results.

Colour	Red	Blue	Yellow	Green
Frequency				
Relative frequency				

2 A dice numbered 1 to 6 is rolled 18 times. It is believed to be fair.

a How many times would you expect each number to appear?

The actual results of 18 throws are:

2   2   3   3   5   3   3   6   1

5   3   3   3   3   2   4   1   5

b Copy and complete the relative frequency table for these results.

Score	1	2	3	4	5	6
Frequency						
Relative frequency						

3 During tests of a new medicine, 18 out of 25 trials resulted in a successful outcome.

What is the relative frequency of a successful outcome?

4 Over one month, a train was on time for 24 out of 30 journeys.

Write down the relative frequency of a train being on time.

5 The probability that a biased dice will land on 2 is 0.3

Zak is going to roll the dice 400 times.

Work out an estimate for the number of times the dice will land on 2

Stretch – can you deepen your learning?

1 A coin is flipped 10 times.

The results are shown in the table.

Heads	Tails
2	8

a What is the relative frequency of getting a head?

b What is the relative frequency of getting a tail?

c Is there enough evidence to suggest that the coin is biased?

The same coin is then flipped another 90 times.

The results of all 100 trials are shown in the table.

Heads	Tails
17	83

d Do you think the coin is biased? Explain your answer.

2 Ali is doing an experiment. He butters one side of a slice of bread and then throws it into the air 10 times.

Ali records the number of times that it lands buttered side down and buttered side up. The results are shown in the table.

Buttered side down	Buttered side up
7	3

a What is the relative frequency of the bread landing buttered side down?

Jack also does the experiment. He does it 100 times and his results are shown in this table.

Buttered side down	Buttered side up
55	45

b Based on Jack's results, what is the relative frequency of the bread landing buttered side down?

c Which relative frequency gives the best estimate of the probability of a slice of bread landing buttered side down? Explain your answer.

3 A TV talent show final involves four acts.

120 people are asked to choose their favourite act. The results are shown in the table.

Act	Act 1	Act 2	Act 3	Act 4
Votes	12	54	38	16

On Saturday night, the four acts perform and 20 000 people vote for their favourite.

Assuming the results in the table are representative, how many people would you expect to vote for Act 3?

Theory and experiment: exam practice

White R**o**se
M**▲**THS

1 Chloe rolls a six-sided dice 60 times. The table gives information about her scores.

Score on dice	Frequency
1	9
2	13
3	6
4	20
5	10
6	2

Do you think Chloe's dice is fair? Give a reason for your answer. **(1)**

2 Ron sows 200 wildflower seeds.

The probability of a seed flowering is 0.6

Work out an estimate for the number of seeds that will flower. **(2)**

3 A box contains coloured pencils that are blue, red, green or yellow.

Amir takes a pencil at random from the box.

The table shows the probability that he takes a blue, a red or a yellow pencil.

Colour	Blue	Red	Green	Yellow
Probability	0.2	0.3		0.1

a) Work out the probability that Amir takes a green pencil. **(2)**

Amir puts the pencil back into the box.

Sophie takes a pencil at random from the box. She looks at its colour then puts the pencil back into the box. She does this 50 times.

b) Work out an estimate for the number of times Sophie takes a red pencil. **(2)**

4 A counter has a red side and a yellow side.

The table shows the relative frequency of the counter landing on red after it is flipped 100, 200, 300, 400 and 500 times.

Number of flips	Relative frequency of red	Relative frequency of yellow
100	0.43	
200	0.51	0.49
300	0.48	
400	0.53	0.47
500	0.55	

a) Complete a copy of the table. **(1)**

b) How many times does the counter land on red after 300 flips? **(2)**

1–3

3–5

302

13 Combined events

In this block, we will cover...

13.1 The multiplication rule

Example 1

A fair coin is flipped and a fair, six-sided dice nur

What is the probability of the coin landing on ta

landing on 3?

Method

Solution
P(T **AND** 3) = P(T) × P(3)
P(T) = $\frac{1}{\_}$ P(3) = $\frac{1}{\_}$

13.2 Tree diagrams

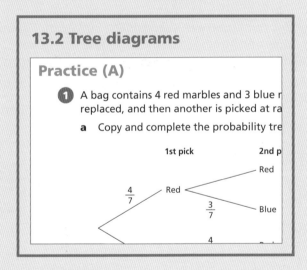

Practice (A)

① A bag contains 4 red marbles and 3 blue r
replaced, and then another is picked at ra

a Copy and complete the probability tre

Are you ready?

1 A fair, six-sided dice numbered 1 to 6 is rolled.

What is the probability that the dice lands on 1?

2 A bag contains 3 red counters, 4 blue counters and 2 yellow counters. Jack picks a counter at random.

What is the probability that the counter is **not** red?

3 A spinner is split into five equal sections numbered 1 to 5. The spinner is spun.

What is the probability that the spinner lands on an even number?

Combined events in probability occur together in an experiment as two or more separate events. These events are often **independent**, meaning that one event does not rely on or affect the other.

As an example of an independent combined event, consider a survey of 100 cars. Event A is 'The car is red' and event B is 'The car contains passengers'. These events are combined because there will be some red cars containing passengers; they are also independent because the colour of the car does not affect the number of passengers.

You can work out the probability of a combined event by using the **multiplication rule**.

This rule states that the probability of event A happening **AND** event B happening is equal to the product of their two probabilities, as long as they are independent.

So for independent events, P(A **AND** B) = P(A) × P(B)

The multiplication rule of probability is often called the 'And Rule'.

Example 1

A fair coin is flipped and a fair, six-sided dice numbered 1 to 6 is rolled.

What is the probability of the coin landing on tails and the dice landing on 3?

These two events are independent.

Method

Solution	Commentary
P(T **AND** 3) = P(T) × P(3)	You are looking for the probability of one thing happening AND another, so you use the multiplication rule.
$P(T) = \frac{1}{2}$ $P(3) = \frac{1}{6}$ So P(T **AND** 3) $= \frac{1}{2} \times \frac{1}{6} = \frac{1}{12}$	First consider the probability of each event separately. Then multiply them together to find the probability of both things happening.
<table><tr><td></td><td>1</td><td>2</td><td>3</td><td>4</td><td>5</td><td>6</td></tr><tr><td>H</td><td>H1</td><td>H2</td><td>H3</td><td>H4</td><td>H5</td><td>H6</td></tr><tr><td>T</td><td>T1</td><td>T2</td><td>T3</td><td>T4</td><td>T5</td><td>T6</td></tr></table>	You could also draw a **sample space diagram**. There are 12 possible outcomes and only one of them is T3 so this confirms that the probability is $\frac{1}{12}$

Example 2

A pack contains 100 picture cards:

- 25 have stars
- 25 have hearts
- 40 have dots
- 10 have stripes.

Seb chooses a card at random, looks at it and puts it back. He then chooses another card at random.

What is the probability that he chooses a star and a stripe?

Method

Solution	Commentary
P(Star AND Stripe) = P(Star) × P(Stripe) $P(\text{Star}) = \frac{25}{100}$ $P(\text{Stripe}) = \frac{10}{100}$ P(Star AND Stripe) $= \frac{25}{100} \times \frac{10}{100} = \frac{250}{10000}$	There are 25 cards out of 100 with stars on them so the probability of choosing a star is $\frac{25}{100}$ Then there are 10 cards with stripes out of 100 so the probability of choosing a stripe is $\frac{10}{100}$
Solution using simplified fractions: $\frac{1}{4} \times \frac{1}{10} = \frac{1}{40}$	You don't need to simply your answers but you could.

Practice

1 A fair coin is flipped twice.

    a What is the probability that the coin lands on heads and then tails?

    b What is the probability that the coin lands on tails twice?

2 A fair, six-sided dice numbered 1 to 6 is rolled twice.

    a What is the probability that the dice lands on 3 and then 5?

    b What is the probability that the dice lands on 1 and then 6?

    c What is the probability that the dice lands on an even number and then an odd number?

3 A bag contains 4 red marbles and 3 blue marbles. A marble is taken at random, put back in the bag, and another marble is taken at random.

    What is the probability of getting two red marbles?

4 A bag contains 6 red sweets and 5 blue sweets. A sweet is taken at random, put back in the bag, and another sweet taken at random.

    What is the probability of getting a red sweet followed by a blue sweet?

5 A box contains 5 green balls and 4 yellow balls. Jack picks a ball at random, replaces it, and then picks another ball at random.

    a What is the probability that he picks a green ball and then a yellow ball?

    b What is the probability that he picks a yellow ball and then a green ball?

    c What do you notice? Why does this happen?

6 A box contains 3 black pens, 4 blue pens and 2 yellow pens. Kim randomly takes a pen, puts it back, and then randomly takes another pen.

    a What is the probability that she takes a blue pen and then a yellow pen?

    b What is the probability that she takes a blue pen then another blue pen?

    c Next, Kim randomly takes three pens, replacing each pen after the first and second picks.

       What is the probability that she takes a black pen, then a blue pen, then a yellow pen?

7 A spinner is divided into five equal sections numbered 1 to 5. It is spun twice.

    What is the probability of getting a 3 on the first spin and a 5 on the second spin?

8 A fair, six-sided dice numbered 1 to 6 is rolled three times.

    What is the probability of it landing on 6 each time?

Consolidate – do you need more?

1 A bowl contains 3 green balls and 4 red balls. One ball is taken at random, put back in the bowl, and then another ball is picked at random.

    What is the probability of getting a red ball and then a green ball?

2   A bag contains 5 blue marbles and 6 white marbles. One marble is taken at random, put back in the bag, and then another marble is taken at random.

What is the probability of getting two white marbles?

3   A box contains 2 black socks and 5 white socks. One sock is taken at random, put back in the box, and then another sock is taken at random.

What is the probability of getting two black socks?

4   A spinner has five equal sections numbered 1 to 5. It is spun twice.

What is the probability of getting 3 on the first spin and 5 on the second spin?

5   A jar contains 8 sweets: 3 are chocolate and 5 are caramel. A sweet is taken at random, returned to the jar, and then another sweet is selected at random.

What is the probability of getting a chocolate followed by a caramel?

6   There are 4 green apples and 6 red apples in a basket. An apple is taken at random, put back in the basket, and then another apple is picked at random.

What is the probability of getting a red apple followed by a green apple?

Stretch – can you deepen your learning?

1   An experiment involves rolling a fair, six-sided dice four times.

What is the probability of rolling a 5 on the first and third rolls, and a 2 on the second and fourth rolls?

2   A bag contains 8 yellow sweets, 6 orange sweets and 4 purple sweets. Sweets are picked and replaced repeatedly.

What is the probability of getting an orange sweet, then two yellow sweets, then a purple sweet?

3   In a box, there are 7 white balls, 5 black balls and 4 red balls. Four balls are picked one after the other with replacement.

What is the probability of getting a red ball, then two black balls in a row, and finally a white ball?

4   A spinner, with eight equal sections labelled 1 to 8, is spun five times.

What is the probability of getting a 4 on the first spin and the second spin, a 7 on the third, a 2 on the fourth, and finally a 5 on the fifth spin?

5   There are 10 cards in a pack labelled from 1 to 10. A card is picked at random and put back in the pack. This is performed three times.

What is the probability of getting a card less than 5 on the first pick, a card greater than 7 on the second pick, and a card that is a multiple of 3 on the third pick?

13.2 Tree diagrams

Are you ready? (A)

1 A fair, six-sided dice numbered 1 to 6 is rolled twice.

What is the probability that it lands on 4 both times?

2 A box contains 5 blue and 3 black pens. A pen is selected at random.

What is the probability that it is **not** blue?

3 A jar contains 20 biscuits. 10 are chocolate, 6 are oaty and the rest are plain.

Eva picks a biscuit at random.

What is the probability that the biscuit is oaty or plain?

4 A fair spinner is split into five equal sections numbered 1 to 5

Mo rolls a fair, six-sided dice numbered 1 to 6 and spins the spinner.

What is the probability that he gets an even number on both the dice and the spinner?

A probability **tree diagram** shows different events in a scenario, along with their probabilities. The diagram can be used to work out the probability of combined events.

Imagine you are flipping a coin twice.

On the first flip, you can either get heads or tails.

On the second flip, you can either get heads or tails.

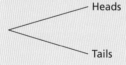

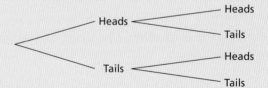

There are two pairs of 'branches' on the second flip because you could have got either heads or tails first.

If you follow each of the different paths, you can see all the possible events. The probability of each event is written on the branches. If the coin is fair, this will be $\frac{1}{2}$ in each case.

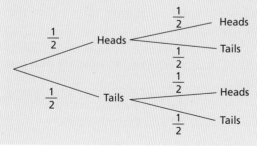

You find the probability of a sequence of events, or a **combined event**, by multiplying the probabilities along the branches that make up that sequence.

The multiplication rule was covered in Chapter 13.1

Example

A box contains 5 blue pens and 2 yellow pens. Max picks a pen at random, replaces it, and then picks another pen at random.

a   Draw and label a probability tree diagram to represent this information.

b   What is the probability that Max picks a blue pen and then a yellow pen?

c   What is the probability that he picks a blue and a yellow pen in any order?

d   What is the probability that he picks two pens that are the same colour?

Method

Solution	Commentary
a 1st pick $\frac{5}{7}$ Blue $\frac{2}{7}$ Yellow	On the first pick, Max can choose blue or yellow, and these choices go at the ends of the branches. Then the probabilities are labelled on the branches.
1st pick 2nd pick $\frac{5}{7}$ Blue $\frac{5}{7}$ Blue $\frac{2}{7}$ Yellow $\frac{2}{7}$ Yellow $\frac{5}{7}$ Blue $\frac{2}{7}$ Yellow	Then on the second pick, Max can also choose either blue or yellow. The probabilities don't change because the pens are replaced.

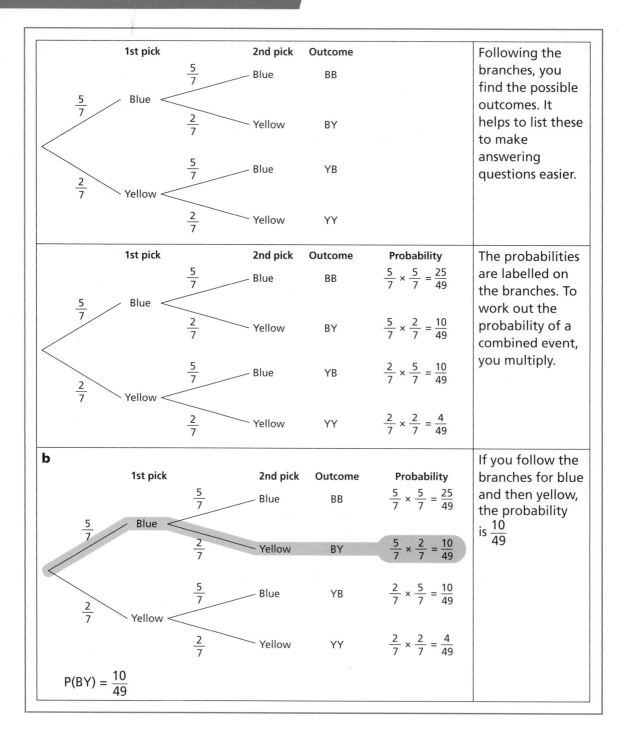

Following the branches, you find the possible outcomes. It helps to list these to make answering questions easier.

The probabilities are labelled on the branches. To work out the probability of a combined event, you multiply.

If you follow the branches for blue and then yellow, the probability is $\frac{10}{49}$

$P(BY) = \frac{10}{49}$

c

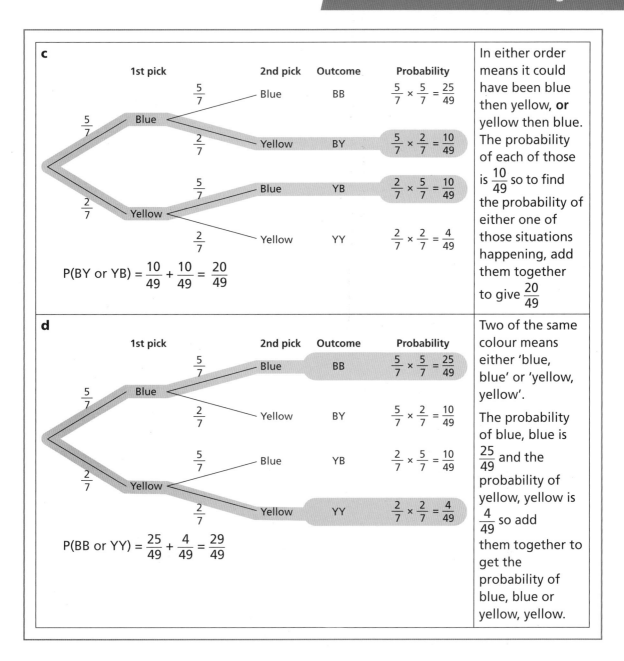

1st pick	2nd pick	Outcome	Probability

$\frac{5}{7}$ Blue

$\frac{5}{7}$ — Blue — BB — $\frac{5}{7} \times \frac{5}{7} = \frac{25}{49}$

$\frac{2}{7}$ — Yellow — BY — $\frac{5}{7} \times \frac{2}{7} = \frac{10}{49}$

$\frac{2}{7}$ Yellow

$\frac{5}{7}$ — Blue — YB — $\frac{2}{7} \times \frac{5}{7} = \frac{10}{49}$

$\frac{2}{7}$ — Yellow — YY — $\frac{2}{7} \times \frac{2}{7} = \frac{4}{49}$

$$P(\text{BY or YB}) = \frac{10}{49} + \frac{10}{49} = \frac{20}{49}$$

In either order means it could have been blue then yellow, **or** yellow then blue. The probability of each of those is $\frac{10}{49}$ so to find the probability of either one of those situations happening, add them together to give $\frac{20}{49}$

d

1st pick	2nd pick	Outcome	Probability

$\frac{5}{7}$ Blue

$\frac{5}{7}$ — Blue — BB — $\frac{5}{7} \times \frac{5}{7} = \frac{25}{49}$

$\frac{2}{7}$ — Yellow — BY — $\frac{5}{7} \times \frac{2}{7} = \frac{10}{49}$

$\frac{2}{7}$ Yellow

$\frac{5}{7}$ — Blue — YB — $\frac{2}{7} \times \frac{5}{7} = \frac{10}{49}$

$\frac{2}{7}$ — Yellow — YY — $\frac{2}{7} \times \frac{2}{7} = \frac{4}{49}$

$$P(\text{BB or YY}) = \frac{25}{49} + \frac{4}{49} = \frac{29}{49}$$

Two of the same colour means either 'blue, blue' or 'yellow, yellow'.

The probability of blue, blue is $\frac{25}{49}$ and the probability of yellow, yellow is $\frac{4}{49}$ so add them together to get the probability of blue, blue or yellow, yellow.

Practice (A)

1 A bag contains 4 red marbles and 3 blue marbles. A marble is picked at random, replaced, and then another is picked at random.

a Copy and complete the probability tree diagram to show this information.

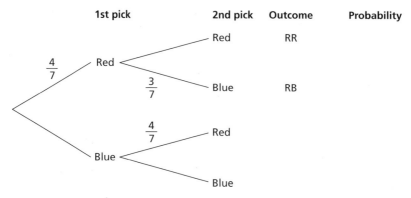

b What is the probability that both marbles are red?

c What is the probability that a red and blue marble are picked in any order?

2 In a pack of cards, half of the cards have a black side and half of the cards have a red side. A card is taken at random, its colour noted, and then replaced. Then a second card is taken at random.

a Copy and complete the probability tree diagram to show this information.

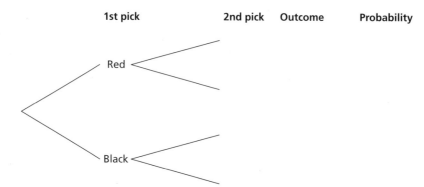

b What is the probability that both cards are different colours?

3 A box contains 5 green marbles and 4 yellow marbles. A marble is taken at random, replaced in the box, and then another marble is taken at random.

a Draw a probability tree diagram to represent this information.

b What is the probability that both marbles are the same colour?

4 A bag contains 6 red sweets and 4 blue sweets. A sweet is taken at random, its colour noted and put back in the bag. Then another sweet is taken at random.

  a Draw a probability tree diagram to represent this information.

  b What is the probability that neither of the sweets are blue?

5 A box contains 3 black pens and 4 blue pens. A pen is taken at random, replaced in the box, and then another pen is taken at random.

  What is the probability that at least one of the pens is black?

6 A bag contains 2 white balls and 3 black balls. A ball is taken, replaced in the bag, and then another ball is taken.

  What is the probability that both balls are the same colour?

7 A box contains 4 red socks and 3 blue socks. A sock is taken at random, put back in the box, and then another sock is taken at random.

  What is the probability that both socks are the same colour?

Are you ready? (B)

1 Work out:

  a $\frac{2}{3} \times \frac{1}{5}$ **b** $\frac{1}{6} \times \frac{3}{7}$ **c** $\frac{3}{20} \times \frac{5}{20}$

2 Work out:

  a $\frac{1}{5} + \frac{2}{5}$ **b** $\frac{2}{9} + \frac{4}{9}$ **c** $\frac{6}{150} + \frac{18}{150}$

Example

A box contains 5 blue pens and 2 yellow pens. Flo picks a pen at random, does not replace it, and then picks another pen at random.

a Draw and label a probability tree diagram to represent this information.

b What is the probability that Flo picks a blue pen and then a yellow pen?

c What is the probability that she picks a blue and a yellow pen in any order?

d What is the probability that she picks two pens that are the same colour?

Method

Solution	Commentary

a
 	
 1st pick   2nd pick   Outcome   Probability
 	
 $\frac{5}{7}$ Blue $\frac{4}{6}$ Blue   BB $\frac{5}{7} \times \frac{4}{6} = \frac{20}{42}$
 	
     $\frac{2}{6}$ Yellow   BY $\frac{5}{7} \times \frac{2}{6} = \frac{10}{42}$
 	
 $\frac{2}{7}$ Yellow $\frac{5}{6}$ Blue   YB $\frac{2}{7} \times \frac{5}{6} = \frac{10}{42}$
 	
     $\frac{1}{6}$ Yellow   YY $\frac{2}{7} \times \frac{1}{6} = \frac{2}{42}$
	This time, the first pen is **not** being replaced in the box, so the probabilities on the second pairs of branches change.
	
	 When a blue pen is taken first, there is one fewer blue pen as well as one fewer pen in total for the second pick. This means that the denominator changes. This also applies for the yellow pen.
	
	 Once you have labelled your tree diagram, you still multiply along the branches.

b
 	
 1st pick   2nd pick   Outcome   Probability
 	
 $\frac{5}{7}$ Blue $\frac{4}{6}$ Blue   BB $\frac{5}{7} \times \frac{4}{6} = \frac{20}{42}$
 	
     $\frac{2}{6}$ Yellow   BY $\frac{5}{7} \times \frac{2}{6} = \frac{10}{42}$
 	
 $\frac{2}{7}$ Yellow $\frac{5}{6}$ Blue   YB $\frac{2}{7} \times \frac{5}{6} = \frac{10}{42}$
 	
     $\frac{1}{6}$ Yellow   YY $\frac{2}{7} \times \frac{1}{6} = \frac{2}{42}$
 	
 $P(BY) = \frac{10}{42}$	

c

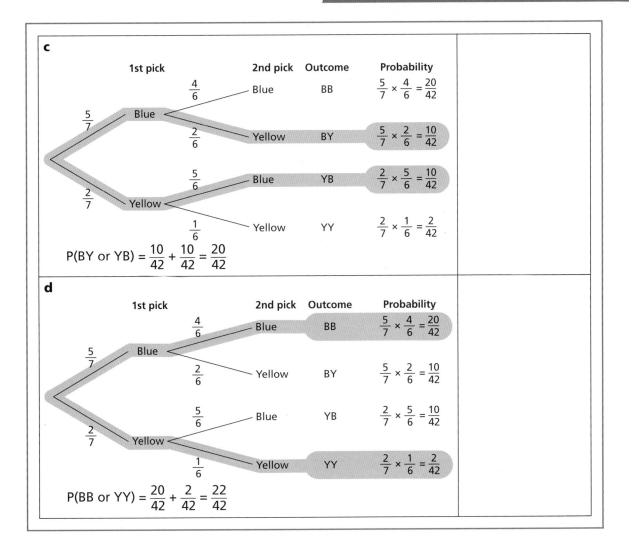

$$P(BY \text{ or } YB) = \frac{10}{42} + \frac{10}{42} = \frac{20}{42}$$

d

$$P(BB \text{ or } YY) = \frac{20}{42} + \frac{2}{42} = \frac{22}{42}$$

Practice (B)

1 A bag contains 4 red marbles and 3 blue marbles. A marble is picked at random, not replaced, and then another marble is picked at random.

a Copy and complete the probability tree diagram to show this information.

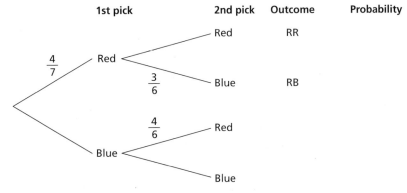

b What is the probability that both marbles are red?

c What is the probability that a red marble and a blue marble are picked in any order?

2 A pack contains 26 red cards and 26 black cards. A card is taken at random, its colour noted, and not replaced. Then a second card is taken at random.

a Copy and complete the probability tree diagram to show this information.

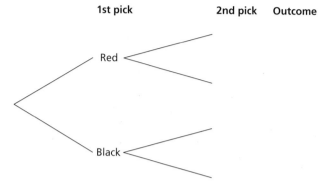

1st pick **2nd pick** **Outcome** **Probability**

Red

Black

b What is the probability that both cards are different colours?

3 A box contains 5 green counters and 4 yellow counters. A counter is taken at random, its colour recorded, and it is not replaced in the box. A second counter is then taken at random.

a Draw a probability tree diagram to represent this information.

b What is the probability that both counters are the same colour?

4 A bag contains 6 red sweets and 4 blue sweets. A sweet is taken at random, its colour noted and it is eaten. A second sweet is then taken at random from the bag.

a Draw a probability tree diagram to represent this information.

b What is the probability that neither of the sweets are blue?

5 A box contains 3 black pens and 4 blue pens. A pen is chosen at random, not replaced in the box, and then another pen is chosen at random.

What is the probability that at least one of the pens taken is black?

6 A bag contains 2 white balls and 3 black balls. Two balls are taken randomly one after the other, without being replaced in the bag.

What is the probability that both balls are the same colour?

7 A drawer contains 4 red socks and 3 blue socks. Two socks are taken randomly one after the other, without being replaced in the drawer.

What is the probability that both socks are the same colour?

8 In a pack of cards, each card shows one of four different symbols: circle, square, triangle, and wave. There are 13 cards with each symbol.

Two cards are selected at random one after the other, without being replaced in the pack.

What is the probability that the two cards selected have the same symbol?

Consolidate – do you need more?

1 A bag contains 12 red counters and 8 yellow counters.

The probability tree diagram shows the outcomes and probabilities of selecting two counters at random, with replacement.

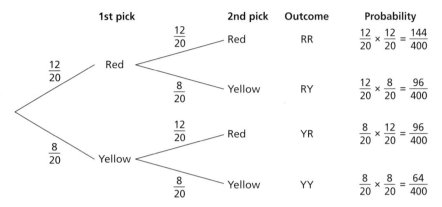

What is the probability of selecting two counters that are the same colour?

2 A box contains 6 green counters and 4 yellow counters. One counter is taken at random, replaced in the box, and then another counter is taken at random.

   a Draw a probability tree diagram to represent this information.

   b What is the probability that both counters are the same colour?

3 Max flips a fair coin twice.

   a Draw a probability tree diagram to represent this information.

   b What is the probability that it lands on heads at least once?

4 A bag contains 12 red counters and 8 yellow counters. The probability tree diagram shows the outcomes and probabilities of selecting two counters at random, without replacement.

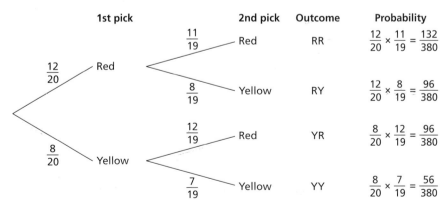

What is the probability of selecting two counters that are the same colour?

5 A box contains 6 green counters and 4 yellow counters. Two counters are taken randomly one after the other, without being replaced in the box.

    a Draw a probability tree diagram to represent this information.

    b What is the probability that both counters taken are the same colour?

6 A drawer contains 8 identical white socks and 7 identical green socks. Two socks are taken at random one after the other, without being replaced in the drawer.

    What is the probability that the socks are a matching pair?

Stretch – can you deepen your learning?

1 A spinner is divided into five equal sections numbered 1 to 5. It is spun twice.

    What is the probability that it lands on an even number at least once?

2 A fair, six-sided dice numbered 1 to 6 is rolled twice.

    What is the probability of rolling an odd number on the first roll and a prime number on the second roll?

3 Cards numbered from 1 to 10 are placed face down in a pile. A card is selected at random, put back in the pile, and then another card is taken at random.

    a What is the probability that at least one of the cards is greater than 6?

    b What is the probability that both cards have values less than 3?

Combined events: exam practice

1 Aisha is going to play one squash match and one tennis match.

The probability that she will win the squash match is $\frac{7}{10}$

The probability that she will win the tennis match is $\frac{3}{5}$

a) Complete a copy of the probability tree diagram. (2)

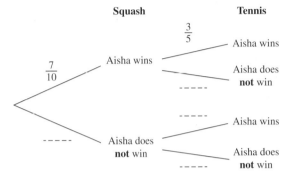

Squash	Tennis

$\frac{3}{5}$ — Aisha wins

$\frac{7}{10}$ — Aisha wins — Aisha does **not** win

Aisha wins

Aisha does **not** win — Aisha does **not** win

b) Work out the probability that Aisha will win both matches. (2)

2 Ron goes to an activity centre. He has one game of archery and one fencing match.

The probability that he wins at archery is 0.6

The probability that he wins at fencing is 0.2

a) Complete copy of the probability tree diagram. (2)

Archery	Fencing

0.2 — Ron wins

0.6 — Ron wins — Ron does **not** win

Ron wins

Ron does **not** win — Ron does **not** win

b) Work out the probability that Ron wins at least one game. (2)

3 A box contains 5 blue pens, 3 black pens and 2 red pens.

Alex takes a pen at random from the box and then puts it back.

He then takes another pen from the box at random.

Work out the probability that both pens are the same colour. (4)

4 A box contains 5 blue pens, 3 black pens and 2 red pens.

Chloe takes a pen at random from the box and gives it to her friend.

Chloe then takes another pen at random from the box.

Work out the probability that both pens are the same colour. (4)

3–5

1 A bag contains nine marbles.

Four marbles are blue, two marbles are red and three marbles are green.

Mo takes a marble at random from the bag.

Mark the probabilities for each question on a copy of the scale below.

a) Mark with the letter B the probability that Mo will take a blue marble. **(1)**

b) Mark with the letter R the probability that Mo will take a red marble. **(1)**

c) Mark with the letter P the probability that Mo will take a purple marble. **(1)**

2 Iqra rolls a fair, six-sided dice numbered 1 to 6

a) Write down the probability that she rolls a 4 **(1)**

b) Write down the probability that she rolls an even number. **(1)**

c) Write down the probability that she rolls a number less than 7 **(1)**

3 Alex has the following hats and scarfs.

Hats	Scarfs
Red	Pink
Black	Green
Yellow	Teal

Alex chooses one hat and one scarf.

List all the possible combinations he could choose. **(2)**

4 Two bags contain number cards.

Bag 1 contains these cards: **1**   **2**   **3**   **4**

Bag 2 contains these cards: **5**   **6**   **7**

A card is chosen from bag 1 and a card is chosen from bag 2. The numbers on the two cards are multiplied together to give a score.

a) Draw a sample space diagram to show all the possible scores. (2)

b) What is the probability that the score is greater than 20? (2)

---

5 A dance studio runs two classes, tap and jazz.

On Saturday, 100 people visited the dance studio.

    28 people attended only the tap class.

    25 people attended both classes.

    10 people did not attend either class.

a) Represent this information on a Venn diagram. (3)

b) A person who attended the dance studio is selected at random.

Find the probability that this person attended only the jazz class. (2)

---

6 Charlie has a four-sided spinner.

The sides of the spinner are numbered 1, 2, 3 and 4

The spinner is biased.

The probability that the spinner lands on 1, 2 or 3 is 0.9

Charlie spins the spinner 400 times.

Estimate the number of times the spinner will land on 4 (3)

---

7 Aisha has 20 pieces of fruit in a bowl.

She has: 12 apples

            5 oranges

            3 kiwis

Aisha takes two pieces of fruit from the bowl at random.

Work out the probability that the two pieces of fruit are **not** the same type. (4)

In this block, we will cover...

14.1 The averages

Example 1

The ages of six infants at a playgroup are 19 mon
16 months and 21 months.

Find the mean, median and mode of the ages of

Method

Solution	Commentary
Mean = $\dfrac{\text{total}}{\text{number of items}} = \dfrac{107}{6}$	
$\quad\quad = 17.8$ months (to 1 d.p.)	

14.2 The range

Practice

1. Here are the ages, in months, of five infan
   Work out the range of the ages.

2. Work out the range of each set of lengths.
   a   130 cm, 103 cm, 127 cm, 92 cm, 112 cm
   b   76 cm, 84 cm, 105 cm, 100 cm, 91 cm, 71

3. Here are the number of cakes made by a b
   51   86   25   35   98
   a   Samira says, "The range of the cakes is

14.3 Grouped data

Consolidate – do you need more

1. The table shows how many hours of home
   40 students did last week.

   Calculate an estimate for the mean numbe
   of hours of homework done. Give your ans
   1 decimal place.

2. The table shows the masses of some dogs.

   a   Estimate the mean mass of the dogs.
       Give your answer to 2 decimal places.

14.4 Talking about data

Stretch – can you deepen your le

1. The maximum daily temperature (in °C) is
   5   6   3   –4   4   5   2
   a   Find the mean, median, mode and ran
   b   Faith thinks that one of the temperatu
       Do you agree? Can you be sure?
   c   How would the mean and range chang
       i   the temperature of –4°C was exclude
       ii the temperature of –4°C was replace

Are you ready?

1 Here are some numbers: 4 5 6 3 7

    a Find the total of the numbers.

    b Divide the total by 5

2 Put each set of numbers in order from smallest to largest.

    a 10, 15, 12, 8, 7, 4, 3, 9

    b 20, 25, 17, 27, 19, 26, 19

    c 8, −3, 0, −8, 6, −5, −2

There are three types of **average** used to represent a set of data:

- The **mean** is found by dividing the total of the data set by the number of items.
- The **median** is the middle item of an ordered set of data. If there is an even number of values in the data set, you need to find the mean of the two values that are in the middle.
- The **mode** is the value in a set of data that appears the most often.

Sometimes a data set can have more than one mode.
For example, in the set 2, 2, 2, 3, 3, 4, 4, 4, 5, 5, 6, 7 the modes are 2 and 4

Example 1

The ages of six infants at a playgroup are 19 months, 20 months, 17 months, 14 months, 16 months and 21 months.

Find the mean, median and mode of the ages of the infants.

Method

Solution	Commentary
Mean $= \dfrac{\text{total}}{\text{number of items}} = \dfrac{107}{6}$ $= 17.8$ months (to 1 d.p.)	
14 16 ⟨17 19⟩ 20 21 Median $= \dfrac{17 + 19}{2} = 18$	There is an even number of items in the data set, so find the median by working out the mean of the middle pair of numbers. The numbers must be ordered.
There is no mode.	No item occurs more often than any of the others, so there is no mode.

Example 2 ▣

In a class of 30 students, 12 students have one pet, 7 have two pets, 5 have three pets and the rest have no pets.

a Show this information in a frequency table.

b Find the total number of pets owned by the class.

c Find the mean number of pets owned by the students.

Method

Solution	Commentary
a $30 - (12 + 7 + 5) = 6$	Work out how many students have no pets.

a

Number of pets	Frequency
0	6
1	12
2	7
3	5
Total	30

Put the information in a table.

Include a row for the total.

b

Number of pets	Frequency	Subtotals
0	6	$0 \times 6 = 0$
1	12	$1 \times 12 = 12$
2	7	$2 \times 7 = 14$
3	5	$3 \times 5 = 15$
Total	30	41

Total number of pets = 41

Add a third column and fill it in with the total number of pets owned by the students with 3, 2, 1 and no pets.

Multiply each number of pets by the corresponding frequency.

You find the total number of pets by adding up the subtotals in your table.

c

Number of pets	Frequency	Subtotals
0	6	$0 \times 6 = 0$
1	12	$1 \times 12 = 12$
2	7	$2 \times 7 = 14$
3	5	$3 \times 5 = 15$
Total	30	41

This is a much better way of finding the total than by adding up each number individually:
$0 + 0 + 0 + 0 + 0 + 0 + 1 + 1 + ...$ etc.
would take a long time and be prone to error.

$$\text{Mean} = \frac{\text{total}}{\text{number of items}} = \frac{41}{30}$$

$$= 1.37 \text{ (to 3 s.f.)}$$

The mean is the total number of pets divided by the total number of students in the class.

Practice ▦

1 Find the mean, median and mode of this set of numbers.

    5   7   11   11   16

2 Here are the heights of five sunflowers:

    72 cm   91 cm   86 cm   102 cm   89 cm

  a Find the mean height of the sunflowers.

  b Find the median height.

3 **a** What is the same and what is different about finding the median of these sets of data?

    i 2, 3, 4, 5, 6   **ii** 2, 3, 4, 4, 5, 6   **iii** 2, 3, 4, 5

  b Find the median of each set of data in part **a**.

  c Find the mean of each set of data in part **a**.

4 The table shows the number of goals scored by a football team in 20 matches.

Number of goals	Frequency	Subtotals
0	4	
1	3	
2	7	
3	5	
4	0	
5	1	
Total		

  a Copy and complete the table.

  b Write down the modal number of goals scored.

  c Find the mean number of goals scored.

> The modal number just means 'the mode'.

5 The masses, in kilograms, of the players in a rugby team are:

    120.4   102.8   99.7   116.1   127.6   105.9

  a Explain why the data has no mode.

  b Find the mean mass of the rugby players. Give your answer to 1 decimal place.

  c Find the median mass.

  d Which, if any, of the averages will change if the heaviest player is replaced by a player of mass 130 kg?

6 The table shows the shoe sizes of a group of people in a running club.

Shoe size	4	5	6	7	8	9
Number of people	5	11	16	7	2	1

  a Write down the modal shoe size.

  b Find the mean shoe size.

Consolidate – do you need more? 🖩

1   Find the mean, median and mode of each set of numbers.

   a   9   11   11   17   17   25   b   8   10   10   14

   c   8   8   10   14   d   9   3   7   6   10   8   5

2   Here are the ages, in years, of 10 people:

   18   23   17   25   26   31   16   18   25   30

   a   Find the mode.   b   Find the median.   c   Calculate the mean.

3   The table shows the number of cups of coffee that a sample of people drank in a single day.

Number of cups of coffee	Frequency
1	5
2	9
3	6
4	8
5	2

   a   Write down the modal number of cups of coffee that the people drank.

   b   Find the mean number of cups of coffee that the people drank.

4   Here are Tiff's scores in a series of maths tests:

   20   18   9   17   16   19   15   14

   a   What can be said about the mode?

   b   Find the other two averages of the scores.

Stretch – can you deepen your learning?

1   The mean of four integers is 9

   A fifth number is added to the list and the mean is now 8

   What is the fifth number?

2   The mean weight of seven students is 50 kg.

   The mean weight of another three students is 45 kg.

   Find the mean weight of all 10 students.

3   Here are seven number cards. Two of the numbers are hidden.

   (5)   (8)   (1)   (3)   (4)   (?)   (?)

   The mode of the seven numbers is 4

   The mean of the seven numbers is 5

   Work out the two hidden numbers.

Are you ready?

1 Write down the greatest number in each list.

    a 25, 63, 52   **b** 205, 150, 502, 200   **c** –5, 5, –9, –1, 9

2 Write down the smallest number in each of the lists in question 1.

3 Order each of the numbers in the lists in question 1 from smallest to largest.

4 Work out:

    a 85 – 56   **b** 150 – 93   **c** 395 – 379   **d** 2000 – 860

The **range** is a measure of spread. It tells us how spread out a set of data is.

To find the range of a set of data, subtract the smallest value from the largest value.

Example 1

Here are the shoe sizes of six people: 6   10   10   5   11   7

What is the range of the shoe sizes?

Method

Solution	Commentary
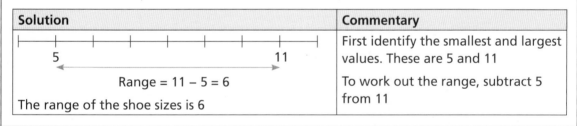 Range = 11 – 5 = 6 The range of the shoe sizes is 6	First identify the smallest and largest values. These are 5 and 11 To work out the range, subtract 5 from 11

Example 2

Rob goes shopping to buy some clothes. The range of the cost of his items is £16. The cheapest item he bought was £23.

How much did the most expensive item cost?

Method

Solution	Commentary
Least expensive Most expensive £23 £23 + £16 = £39 Range = £16 The most expensive item cost £39	Sketch a number line.

Practice

1 Here are the ages, in months, of five infants:　　9　　7　　2　　5　　10

Work out the range of the ages.

2 Work out the range of each set of lengths.

a 130 cm, 103 cm, 127 cm, 92 cm, 112 cm

b 76 cm, 84 cm, 105 cm, 100 cm, 91 cm, 71 cm

3 Here are the number of cakes made by a bakery each day in a week:

　　51　　　86　　　25　　　35　　　98　　　171　　　140

a Samira says, "The range of the cakes is 25 to 171"

Explain the mistake Samira has made.

b Find the range of the number of cakes made in a week.

4 Here are the number of miles Ali walks each day in a week:

　　5　　　2　　　1.5　　　7　　　0.5　　　8　　　11

Find the range of the number of miles he walks in a week.

5 The table shows the number of visitors to a zoo each month.

Month	Number of visitors
April	3201
May	4910
June	6029
July	10 298
August	15 824
September	9382

Work out the range of the number of visitors.

6 The range of a set of numbers is 15

The largest number is 72

What is the smallest number?

7 The bar chart shows the number of students in each year group who are members of a running club.

a Which year group has:

　i the smallest number of students in the running club

　ii the largest number of students in the running club?

b Find the range of the number of students who are in the running club.

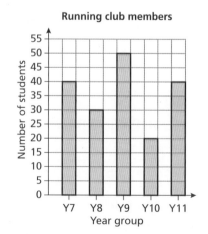

Running club members

8 Here are the masses of seven parcels:

3 kg 500 g 2 kg 200 g 350 g 1 kg 950 g

Benji is finding the range of this data.

He says, "To work out the range, I need to subtract 1 from 500"

a Explain a mistake Benji has made.

b Find the range of the masses of the parcels.

Consolidate – do you need more?

1 Work out the range of each set of data.

a 13, 16, 15, 18

b 60, 90, 30, 45, 80, 65, 70

c £300, £350, £180, £210, £182, £280

d 73 g, 27 g, 19 g, 92 g, 55 g

2 The table shows the number of cups of coffee sold in a café each day.

Day	Number of cups of coffee sold
Monday	128
Tuesday	132
Wednesday	254
Thursday	119
Friday	219
Saturday	368

Work out the range of the number of cups of coffee sold.

3 The range of some numbers is 20

The smallest number is 8

What is the largest number?

4 The range of some numbers is 17

The largest number is 250

What is the smallest number?

Stretch – can you deepen your learning?

1 The range of the times taken to complete a puzzle is 36 seconds.

The fastest time was 1 minute and 50 seconds.

What was the slowest time?

2 The table shows the temperatures in six cities.

City	Temperature
London	6°C
Cambridge	5°C
Leeds	3°C
Edinburgh	–1°C
Belfast	5°C

Work out the range of temperatures.

3 Work out the range of each set of data.

a 5, 9, –3, –8, 10

b –20, 19, 30, –17, 41, 29, –18

4 Here are the heights of 10 sunflowers:

92 cm, 107 cm, 121 cm, 98 cm, 86 cm, 112 cm, 104 cm, 99 cm, 117 cm, 91 cm

a Another sunflower is measured. The range of the heights of the sunflowers remains the same.

What could the height of the sunflower be?

b Another sunflower is measured. The range of the heights of the sunflowers increases by 4 cm.

What could the height of the sunflower be?

Are you ready?

1   Find the mean of each set of data.

    a 10   11   18   21   36

    b 6   9   9   9   9   13   10

2   Kath counts the number of paper clips in 10 boxes of paper clips.

    There are 600 paper clips altogether.

    Find the mean number of paper clips in a box.

3   Find the number halfway between:

    a 0 and 20   **b** 30 and 39   **c** 40 and 45   **d** 10 000 and 15 000

4   Round 36.7218 to:

    a the nearest integer   **b** 1 decimal place   **c** 1 significant figure.

Here is a **grouped frequency table** showing the heights of a random sample of 100 people.

Height, h (cm)	Frequency
$150 < h \leqslant 160$	10
$160 < h \leqslant 170$	27
$170 < h \leqslant 180$	29
$180 < h \leqslant 190$	22
$190 < h \leqslant 200$	12
Total	100

$150 < h \leqslant 160$ means the height is greater than 150 cm but less than or equal to 160 cm. Putting data into groups like this makes it easier to organise and to understand than just showing the raw data.

However, if the data has been put into groups, you do not know the values of all the data items and so you cannot find the exact mean of the data. You can use the **midpoint** of each group to give an **estimate** of each subtotal and then use these to work out an estimate of the mean.

In the grouped frequency table above, the class intervals are the same size. This is not always the case so care must be taken when finding the midpoint.

The midpoint is the value in the middle of each class interval.

Example 🖩

The table shows the time taken for students to complete a puzzle.

a Work out an estimate for the mean time taken.

b Identify the class containing the median value.

c Identify the modal class.

Time, t (seconds)	Frequency
$0 < t \leqslant 5$	1
$5 < t \leqslant 10$	7
$10 < t \leqslant 15$	15
$15 < t \leqslant 20$	11
$20 < t \leqslant 25$	5

Method

Solution	Commentary
a	For each row, work out the midpoint of the group.

Time, t (seconds)	Frequency	Midpoint	Midpoint × frequency
$0 < t \leqslant 5$	1	2.5	2.5
$5 < t \leqslant 10$	7	7.5	52.5
$10 < t \leqslant 15$	15	12.5	187.5
$15 < t \leqslant 20$	11	17.5	192.5
$20 < t \leqslant 25$	5	22.5	112.5
Total	39		547.5

Multiply the midpoint by the frequency to find an estimate for the total time for each group.

Work out the total frequency and the total time.

$$\text{Mean} \approx \frac{547.5}{39} = 14.0 \text{ s (to 1 d.p.)}$$

Divide the total time by the total frequency.

b The class containing the median value is $10 < t \leqslant 15$

There are 39 pieces of data so the median will be the $\frac{39 + 1}{2} = 20$th piece of data. This is the middle peice of data.

c The modal class is $10 < t \leqslant 15$

Identify the row with the greatest frequency.

Practice 🖩

1 The table shows the heights of 100 students.

Height, h (cm)	Frequency	Midpoint	Midpoint × Frequency
$140 < h \leqslant 150$	17		
$150 < h \leqslant 160$	21		
$160 < h \leqslant 170$	33		
$170 < h \leqslant 180$	29		
Total	100		

a Copy and complete the table to find an estimate of the mean height of the students. Give your answer to 1 decimal place.

b Why is there no space for the total of the 'Midpoint' column?

2 The table shows information about the ages of visitors to a museum on one day.

  a Estimate the mean age of the visitors to the museum. Give your answer to the nearest integer.

  b Explain why your answer to part **a** is an estimate.

  c State the modal class.

Age, a (years)	Frequency
$0 < a \leqslant 10$	9
$10 < a \leqslant 20$	45
$20 < a \leqslant 30$	62
$30 < a \leqslant 40$	53
$40 < a \leqslant 50$	35

3 The table shows information about the times taken for 50 people to run a 10 km race.

  a Work out an estimate for the mean time.

  b State the modal class.

  c Find the class interval that contains the median.

Time, t (minutes)	Frequency
$30 < t \leqslant 35$	3
$35 < t \leqslant 40$	8
$40 < t \leqslant 45$	11
$45 < t \leqslant 50$	17
$50 < t \leqslant 55$	9
$55 < t \leqslant 60$	2

4 The table shows information about the salaries of some people.

  a State the modal class.

  b Work out an estimate for the mean salary.

  c Find the class interval that contains the median.

Salary, x (£)	Frequency
$10\,000 < x \leqslant 15\,000$	7
$15\,000 < x \leqslant 20\,000$	14
$20\,000 < x \leqslant 25\,000$	23
$25\,000 < x \leqslant 30\,000$	27
$30\,000 < x \leqslant 35\,000$	9

5 Kath recorded the amount of rainfall every day in April. The table shows information about her results.

Amount of rainfall, r (mm)	$2 < r \leqslant 18$	$18 < r \leqslant 30$	$30 < r \leqslant 65$	$65 < r \leqslant 100$
Frequency	4	8	8	10

Calculate an estimate for the mean rainfall in April.

Consolidate – do you need more? 🖩

1 The table shows how many hours of homework 40 students did last week.

Calculate an estimate for the mean number of hours of homework done. Give your answer to 1 decimal place.

Time, t (hours)	Frequency
$0 < t \leqslant 2$	7
$2 < t \leqslant 4$	15
$4 < t \leqslant 6$	13
$6 < t \leqslant 8$	5

2 The table shows the masses of some dogs.

  a Estimate the mean mass of the dogs. Give your answer to 2 decimal places.

  b State the modal class.

Mass, m (kg)	Frequency
$0 < m \leqslant 10$	23
$10 < m \leqslant 30$	37
$30 < m \leqslant 50$	29
$50 < m \leqslant 70$	9
$70 < m \leqslant 100$	2

3 The table shows the times that 60 patients waited at the doctors before their appointment.

a Find an estimate for the mean time that these patients waited. Give your answer to the nearest minute.

b State the modal class.

c Find the class interval that contains the median.

Time, t (minutes)	Frequency
$0 < t \leqslant 5$	4
$5 < t \leqslant 10$	9
$10 < t \leqslant 15$	25
$15 < t \leqslant 20$	16
$20 < t \leqslant 25$	5
$25 < t \leqslant 30$	1

Stretch – can you deepen your learning? ▣

1 Rob measured the heights of some sunflowers. His results are shown in the table.

a Find the percentage of sunflowers that are taller than 125 cm. Give your answer to 1 decimal place.

b Find the class interval that contains the median.

c Find an estimate for the mean height of the sunflowers. Give your answer to 2 significant figures.

Height, h (cm)	Frequency
$90 < h \leqslant 120$	39
$120 < h \leqslant 125$	26
$125 < h \leqslant 170$	47
$170 < h \leqslant 195$	38

2 The diagram shows the times taken for 50 people to travel to work.

Calculate an estimate for the mean time taken for people to travel to work.

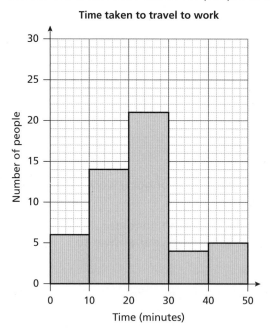

Time taken to travel to work

Are you ready?

1 Here are the heights of seven children:

  92 cm   87 cm   104 cm   98 cm   101 cm   95 cm   101 cm

   a Work out the range of the heights.

   b Write down the modal height.

   c Find the median height.

   d Calculate the mean height. Give your answer to 1 decimal place.

2 The tallest student in a class is 174 cm. The range of the heights of the students is 47 cm.

  Work out the height of the shortest student in the class.

Data sometimes contains values that do not seem to fit with the rest of the data. These are called **outliers** as they lie outside the expected range of the data.

You can compare two different sets of data using a measure of average (mean, median or mode) and a measure of spread (usually the range).

Example 1 ▦

Here are the scores obtained by a group of students in a test:

  56%   71%   63%   81%   4%   59%   70%   68%   61%   90%   82%   66%

a Find the mean and the range of the scores.

b Which data value might be regarded as an outlier?

c How do the mean and range of the scores change if the outlier is excluded?

Method

Solution	Commentary
a Mean = $\dfrac{\text{total}}{\text{number of items}} = \dfrac{771}{12}$ = 64.3% (to 1 d.p.) Range = 90% − 4% = 86%	To find the range, subtract the smallest value from the largest value.
b The 4% score is the outlier.	4% is very different from the rest of the scores.
c New mean = $\dfrac{\text{total}}{\text{number of items}} = \dfrac{767}{11}$ = 69.7% (to 1 d.p.) The mean has gone up by more than 5% Range = 90% − 56% = 34% The range is less than half the size it was before.	One outlier can have a big effect on the mean and the range.

335

Example 2

The table shows some information about the masses of apples grown on two farms.

	Mean (g)	Range (g)
Farm A	171	22
Farm B	178	59

Compare the masses of the apples grown on the two farms.

Method

Solution	Commentary
On average, the apples from farm B are heavier than the apples from farm A, because the mean mass of the apples is greater.	You can compare the masses using an average; this is usually the mean or the median.
The range of the masses of the apples from farm A is smaller, so they are more similar in size.	The range tells you how spread out the data is. The smaller the range, the closer together the masses are.

Practice

1   The times taken, in seconds, for eight students to complete a question were recorded.

35   39   8   52   44   35   29   46

   a   Which measurement is an outlier?

   b   Find the mean, median and mode of the data after the outlier is removed.

2   Here is a set of data:

3   7   37   8   7   5

   a   Find the mean, median and mode of the data.

   b   Which data item is an outlier?

   c   Find the mean, median and mode of the data after the outlier is removed.
        What effect does removing the outlier have on these averages?

3   Students in class A and class B both take a maths test.

   The table shows the mean and the range of the scores from the test.

   Compare the performances in the tests, explaining your reasoning.

	Mean	Range
Class A	68	27
Class B	72	58

4 The Internet speed in megabits per second (Mbps) is recorded for 10 households.

50   65   58   57   68   18   54   63   61   52

a Find the mean, median and range of the data.

b Which data item is an outlier?

c Find the mean, median and range of the data after the outlier is removed.

What effect does removing the outlier have on the mean, median and range?

5 The masses of eight parcels are recorded as follows:

3.2 kg   5.1 kg   4.9 kg   4.1 kg   17.9 kg   3.8 kg   5.2 kg   4.5 kg

If the outlier is excluded:

a by how much does the range change

b by how much does the mean change?

6 The table shows the daily profits from a shop over two weeks.

Week 1	£254	£189	£350	£287	£192	£401	£372
Week 2	£178	£291	£284	£382	£173	£268	£405

a Use the median and range to compare the profits of the two weeks.

b Would your conclusion be different if you used the mean instead of the median?

Consolidate – do you need more?

1 Write down the outliers in this data.

75   21   81   79   83   72   69   16   89   73   192

2 Ten students estimated the size of an angle. Here are the results:

37°   44°   39°   85°   42°   36°   39°   42°   49°   41°

a Find the mean, median, mode and range of the data.

b Which item of the data is an outlier?

c Find the mean, median, mode and range of the data when the outlier is removed.

d What effect does removing the outlier have on the averages and range?

e The outlier was recorded incorrectly and its digits should be reversed. Which measures will change when this is corrected?

3 Which average is most affected by outliers: the mean, the median or the mode?

4 The table shows the mean and the range of the points scored for two basketball teams over a season.

	Mean points	Range of points
Team A	82	34
Team B	79	56

Compare the performance of the teams, explaining your reasoning.

Stretch – can you deepen your learning? 🖩

1 The maximum daily temperature (in °C) is recorded each day for a week:

     5   6   3   −4   4   5   2

   a Find the mean, median, mode and range of the temperatures.

   b Faith thinks that one of the temperatures was recorded incorrectly.

      Do you agree? Can you be sure?

   c How would the mean and range change if:

     i the temperature of −4°C was excluded

     ii the temperature of −4°C was replaced with 4°C?

2 The times, in seconds, for some people to solve a puzzle were recorded.
The table shows the results.

Age (years)	Mean (seconds)	Range (seconds)
11–16	41	21
17–35	33	17
36–50	52	14
Over 50	65	23

   a Sven thinks that the 17–35 year olds did the worst because they have the smallest mean.

     Explain why Sven is incorrect.

   b Use the mean and range to compare the results of the different age groups.

There are 10 people in each age group.

The slowest time for the over 50s was 128 seconds. This is treated as an outlier and replaced with the next slowest time of 76 seconds.

   c Calculate the new mean time for the over 50s. Does this affect your conclusion in part **b**?

3 A class of 25 students complete a test.

The mean score is 67

One student scored 5 on the test.

If this outlier is removed:

   a find the new mean of the scores

   b work out the percentage change in the mean.

Statistical measures: exam practice

1 Here are the ages of six people:

6   17   9   15   21   13

   a) Work out the range of these ages. **(1)**

   b) Find the median age. **(2)**

   c) Work out the mean age. **(2)**

2 A rugby team played seven games.

Here are the points they scored in each game:

4   8   8   8   12   12   15

   a) What is the modal score? **(1)**

   b) What is the median score? **(1)**

The rugby team played another game. They scored 10 points.

   c) Find the median number of points scored in the eight games. **(2)**

3 Five numbers have:

   ● a mode of 3   ● a median of 3   ● a mean of 5

What could the five numbers be? **(2)**

4 The mean of eight numbers is 39

The mean of two of the numbers is 15

What is the mean of the other six numbers? **(3)**

5 Here are some number cards:

The mean of the cards is 9

What is the value of the card labelled with a question mark? **(3)**

6 Nick carried out a survey on the number of bottles of water some students drank in one day. The frequency table shows his results.

Number of bottles of water	Frequency
1	8
2	13
3	7
4	2

   a) Work out the number of students that Nick asked. **(1)**

   b) Work out the mean number of bottles of water drunk. **(3)**

1–3

3–5

15 Charts and diagrams

In this block, we will cover...

15.1 Bar and line charts

Example 1

A group of people were asked to name their favo

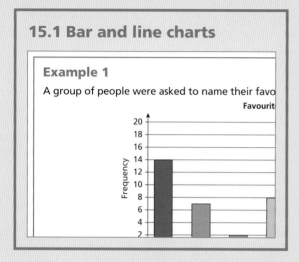

15.2 Other charts

Practice

1. A company uses email, telephone or letter
The customers are grouped by age as 'und

The two-way table shows information abo
for 260 customers.

	Email	Telephone	L
Under 40			
40 and over		47	
Total	107	103	

Copy and complete the two-way table.

15.3 Time series

Consolidate – do you need more

1. The time students spent on their smartpho
shows the average daily time per student

Year	2017	2018	2019
Time (minutes)	135	155	140

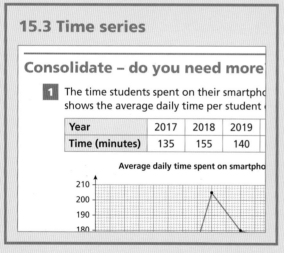

15.4 Pie charts

Stretch – can you deepen your le

1. The pie chart shows information about the
of some students.

165 students said that rugby is their favou

a How many students were surveyed in t

b A student is chosen at random.

Write down the probability that this st
sport is hockey.

15.5 Grouped frequency diagrams

Example

The times taken (in minutes) by a group of stude

Here are the results:

32	24	40	35	28	31	25
31	23	39	35	27	26	39

a Draw a grouped frequency table to represent

b Draw a frequency diagram to represent the

Method

Solution		C

Are you ready?

1 What number is each arrow pointing to?

a

b

2 Huda has 15 red counters and 26 blue counters.

How many more blue counters does she have than red counters?

3 There are 295 students in Year 11. There are 342 students in Year 10.

How many fewer students are in Year 11 than Year 10?

Categorical data is in the form of words rather than numbers and it can usually be represented using a statistical diagram. Two common types of diagram are **bar charts** and **line charts**.

Bar charts and line charts

Make sure your axes are labelled and your chart has a title.

There should be a gap between each bar in a bar chart.

Both bar charts and line charts can be drawn vertically or horizontally.

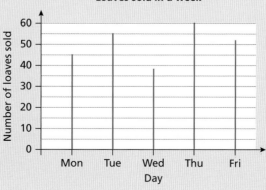

A line chart is like a bar chart but it uses lines rather than bars.

This **dual bar chart** shows the number of shoes and trainers sold in a shop in each of four months. The height of each bar shows how many shoes or trainers were sold.

Bar charts must have bars of equal width.

Charts with bars showing multiple pieces of information must also include a key.

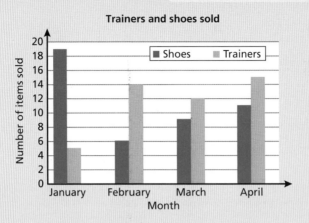

Trainers and shoes sold

Frequency scales must be consistent and the axes should be labelled.

Example 1

A group of people were asked to name their favourite colour. The bar chart shows the results.

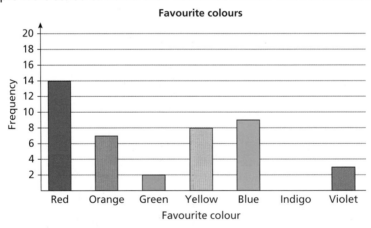

Favourite colours

a How many more people chose red than yellow?

b How many people were asked altogether?

Method

Solution	Commentary
a $14 - 8 = 6$	The bar chart shows that 14 people chose red and 8 chose yellow. To find how many more chose red than yellow, subtract to find the difference.
b $14 + 7 + 2 + 8 + 9 + 0 + 3 = 43$	Read off the heights of the bars to see how many people chose each colour. Then add to find the total.

Example 2

The bar chart shows the numbers of students in Years 7, 8 and 9 who play football and rugby.

a How many students in Year 8 play football?

b In which year do the same number of students play football and rugby?

c How many students in Year 7 play rugby?

d What is the difference between the total number of students who play football and the total number of students who play rugby?

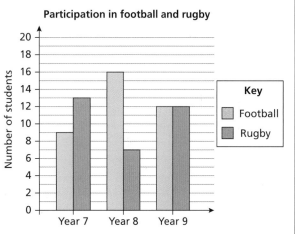

Participation in football and rugby

Method

Solution	Commentary
a 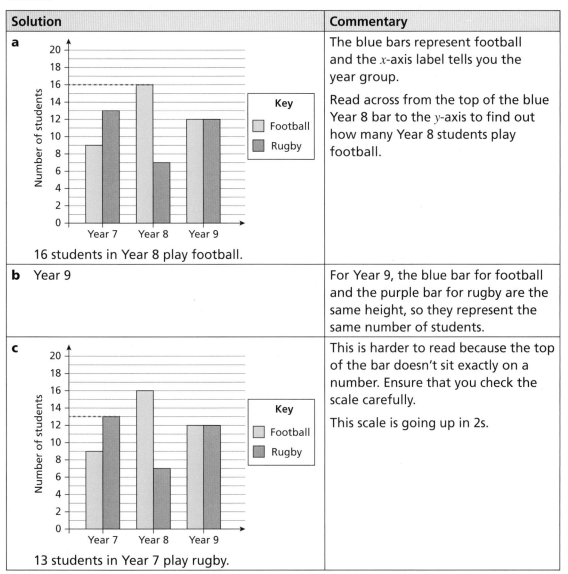 16 students in Year 8 play football.	The blue bars represent football and the *x*-axis label tells you the year group. Read across from the top of the blue Year 8 bar to the *y*-axis to find out how many Year 8 students play football.
b Year 9	For Year 9, the blue bar for football and the purple bar for rugby are the same height, so they represent the same number of students.
c 13 students in Year 7 play rugby.	This is harder to read because the top of the bar doesn't sit exactly on a number. Ensure that you check the scale carefully. This scale is going up in 2s.

343

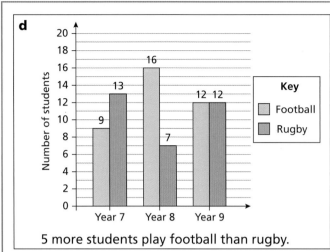

d

Find the number of students represented by each bar.

Add up the total for the bars representing football.

9 + 16 + 12 = 37

Add up the total for the bars representing rugby.

13 + 7 + 12 = 32

Find the difference by subtracting one from the other.

37 – 32 = 5

5 more students play football than rugby.

Practice

1 The bar chart shows the number of students absent in a week.

   a How many students were absent on:

      i Tuesday   **ii** Friday?

   b How many more students were absent on Monday than Tuesday?

   c Work out the total number of absences over the week.

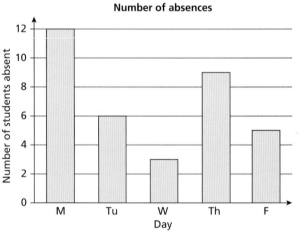

2 The bar chart shows the choices of sport that some students made for the summer term.

   a How many students chose football?

   b How many more students chose athletics than tennis?

   c Find the difference between the numbers playing the most popular and least popular sport.

   d Find the total number of students.

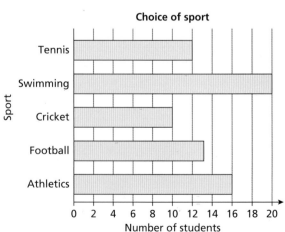

3 Some students were asked their favourite colours. The line chart shows the results.

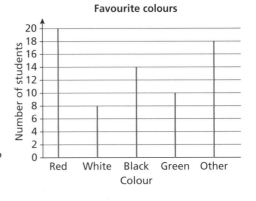

Favourite colours

a How many students chose green as their favourite colour?

b Which was the most popular colour?

c How many more students chose black than white?

d How many students were asked altogether?

4 The bar chart shows the number of people who went on holiday to different countries.

Holiday destinations

a How many more people visited the UK than France?

b How many fewer people visited USA than Spain?

c Seventeen people visited Italy. Copy and complete the bar chart to include this information.

d How many people were asked in total?

5 The bar chart shows information about the languages studied by students in each year group.

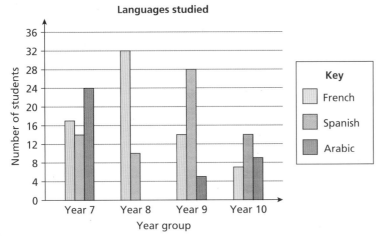

Languages studied

a How many students study Arabic in Year 9?

b In which year groups do more students study French than Spanish?

c How many students in total study language subjects in Year 10?

d Without counting, is it possible to tell from the bar chart which language was studied the most overall?

Consolidate – do you need more?

1 The bar chart shows the favourite fruit of each student in Year 11.

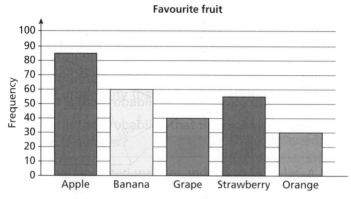

Favourite fruit

a Which was the least popular fruit?

b How many students said their favourite fruit was strawberry?

c How many more students chose apples than grapes?

d How many students were asked in total?

2 The line chart shows how many text messages Emily received in one week.

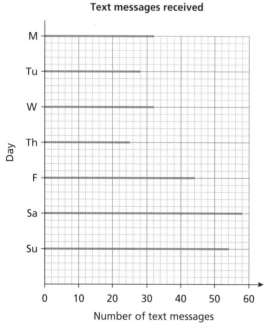

Text messages received

a How many text messages did Emily receive on Friday?

b How many more text messages did Emily receive on Saturday than on Monday?

c Find the difference between the total number of text messages Emily received from Monday to Friday compared to the total of Saturday and Sunday.

3 The bar chart shows sales of ice creams and cakes at a café on five different days.

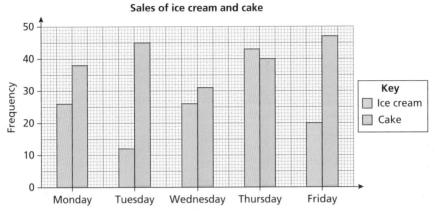

Sales of ice cream and cake

a How many ice creams were sold on Thursday?

b How many cakes were sold on Tuesday?

c On which day did the café sell the most ice creams?

d On which days were more cakes sold than ice creams?

e Did the café sell more ice creams or more cakes over the week? How do you know?

Stretch – can you deepen your learning?

Ages of students in art club

1 The bar chart shows the ages of students in an art club.

a What is the modal age?

b Work out the range of the ages.

c What fraction of the students in the art club are 15 years old?

d What percentage of the students in the art club are less than 12 years old? Give your answer to 1 decimal place.

2 Make three criticisms of this bar chart.

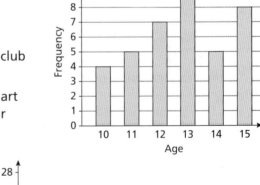

3 Benji asks some students in Year 10 and Year 11 which subject they prefer. The table shows the results.

Draw a suitable chart to display Benji's results. Make sure you label your chart.

Favourite subject	Year 10	Year 11
Maths	12	15
English	8	9
Science	17	8
Art	10	4
History	3	10

347

Are you ready?

1 Here are some numbers:

31, 24, 42, 39, 18, 20, 35, 28, 25

a Put the numbers in order, starting with the smallest.

b Work out the range of the numbers.

c Work out the median of the numbers.

d What fraction of the numbers are greater than 30?

2 Work out:

a $\frac{1}{2}$ of 10   **b** $\frac{1}{4}$ of 8   **c** $\frac{3}{4}$ of 20

3 Convert each fraction to a percentage.

a $\frac{2}{5}$ **b** $\frac{3}{4}$ **c** $\frac{5}{8}$

Bar charts and line charts are not the only statistical diagrams used for representing categorical data. Here are three other types of diagram that are commonly used.

Two-way tables

A two-way table displays two sets of data in rows and columns.

	Under 15	15 or over	Total
Male	25	29	54
Female	19	27	46
Total	44	56	100

Pictograms

Pictograms always need a key to show what value each picture represents.

Name	Goals
Flo	🏀🏀
Benji	🏀🏀🏀◖
Jakub	🏀🏀🏀🏀🏀

Key

🏀 = 2 goals

Stem-and-leaf diagrams

A stem-and-leaf diagram is usually ordered, with the data presented from smallest to greatest.

A key should be included to explain what the numbers mean.

```
1  5 | 2  3
1  6 | 1  7  9
1  7 | 0  2          ← This means 186
1  8 | 3  4  6  8
```

Stem   Leaf

Key: 16 | 7 means 167

Example 1

The two-way table shows the number of students in Years 7, 8 and 9 who have hot lunches or packed lunches.

Complete the two-way table.

	Year 7	Year 8	Year 9	Total
Hot lunch	12			58
Packed lunch		8		
Total	30	32		90

Method

Solution	Commentary
<table><tr><td></td><td>**Year 7**</td><td>**Year 8**</td><td>**Year 9**</td><td>**Total**</td></tr><tr><td>**Hot lunch**</td><td>12</td><td>24</td><td></td><td>58</td></tr><tr><td>**Packed lunch**</td><td></td><td>8</td><td></td><td></td></tr><tr><td>**Total**</td><td>30</td><td>32</td><td></td><td>90</td></tr></table>	There are usually several places to start with questions like this. To work out the number of Year 8 students who have a hot lunch, subtract the number who have a packed lunch from the total number of Year 8 students: $32 - 8 = 24$
<table><tr><td></td><td>**Year 7**</td><td>**Year 8**</td><td>**Year 9**</td><td>**Total**</td></tr><tr><td>**Hot lunch**</td><td>12</td><td>24</td><td></td><td>58</td></tr><tr><td>**Packed lunch**</td><td>18</td><td>8</td><td></td><td></td></tr><tr><td>**Total**</td><td>30</td><td>32</td><td></td><td>90</td></tr></table>	To work out the number of Year 7 students who have a packed lunch calculate $30 - 12 = 18$
<table><tr><td></td><td>**Year 7**</td><td>**Year 8**</td><td>**Year 9**</td><td>**Total**</td></tr><tr><td>**Hot lunch**</td><td>12</td><td>24</td><td></td><td>58</td></tr><tr><td>**Packed lunch**</td><td>18</td><td>8</td><td></td><td></td></tr><tr><td>**Total**</td><td>30</td><td>32</td><td>28</td><td>90</td></tr></table>	You can work out the Year 9 total by adding together the Year 7 and Year 8 totals and subtracting the answer from the total number of students in all three year groups. $30 + 32 = 62$ $90 - 62 = 28$
<table><tr><td></td><td>**Year 7**</td><td>**Year 8**</td><td>**Year 9**</td><td>**Total**</td></tr><tr><td>**Hot lunch**</td><td>12</td><td>24</td><td>22</td><td>58</td></tr><tr><td>**Packed lunch**</td><td>18</td><td>8</td><td>6</td><td>32</td></tr><tr><td>**Total**</td><td>30</td><td>32</td><td>28</td><td>90</td></tr></table>	Once you have completed the table, check that all the rows and columns add up to the corresponding totals.

Example 2

The ages, in years, of 10 people are shown.

8   19   9   21   17   32   16   10   8   34

Show the ages in a stem-and-leaf diagram.

Method

Solution	Commentary
8, 8, 9, 10, 16, 17, 19, 21, 32, 34	Write the numbers in order from smallest to largest.
People's ages 0 | 8 8 9 1 | 0 6 7 9 2 | 1 3 | 2 4 Key: 1 | 6 means 16 years	Next choose the stem, then write the leaves. The smallest number is 8 and the greatest number is 34, so the 'stem' (representing 10s) needs to go from 0 to 3 Don't forget to include a key to explain the values in the stem-and-leaf diagram. It doesn't matter which value you choose for the key.

Practice

1 A company uses email, telephone or letters to communicate with customers. The customers are grouped by age as 'under 40' or '40 and over'.

The two-way table shows information about the preferred method of communication for 260 customers.

	Email	Telephone	Letter	Total
Under 40			18	152
40 and over		47		
Total	107	103		260

Copy and complete the two-way table.

2 The pictogram shows the number of pizzas sold over five days.

Pizzas sold

Monday	⬤⬤⬤⬤
Tuesday	⬤⬤⬤
Wednesday	⬤⬤⬤⬤⬤⬤
Thursday	
Friday	⬤⬤⬤⬤⬤⬤⬤⬤⬤⬤⬤

Key: ⬤ represents 2 pizzas

Half as many pizzas were sold on Thursday than Friday.

a   Copy and complete the pictogram.

b   How many pizzas were sold on Thursday?

c   On which day were 12 pizzas sold?

d   How many pizzas were sold in total over the five days?

3 Some students do the long jump event. Information about the distances achieved are shown in the stem-and-leaf diagram.

Long jump distances

```
3 | 9
4 | 1  2
5 | 3  6  6
6 | 4  7  8  8
7 | 1  3  6  7  8
8 | 4  7
```

Key: 4 | 2 means 4.2 metres

  a What was the shortest distance jumped?

  b What was the longest distance jumped?

  c Calculate the range of the distances jumped.

  d How many students jumped exactly 5.6 metres?

  e Work out the median distance jumped.

4 The two-way table shows information about the effects of two types of medication on 500 patients.

	Medication A	Medication B	Total
Improved	179		362
No change		56	
Worse	38	19	
Total	242		500

  a Copy and complete the two-way table.

  b What fraction of the patients had an improved effect?

  c What percentage of the patients taking medication A had no change?

5 Some students were asked to choose their favourite animal. The results are shown in the table.

Animal	Number of students
Lion	12
Giraffe	16
Elephant	6
Rhino	5

Kath is going to draw a pictogram to represent the data. She decides to use ■ to represent 4 students.

Benji says, "5 ÷ 4 = 1.25, so Kath won't be able to represent the number of students who picked 'rhino' in the pictogram."

  a Explain why Benji is incorrect.

  b Use the table and Kath's key to copy and complete the pictogram.

Animal	Number of students
Lion	
Giraffe	
Elephant	
Rhino	

Key: ■ = 4 students

6 The masses, in grams, of some parcels are shown below.

137, 168, 136, 195, 163, 159, 146, 142, 172, 125,

159, 138, 197, 169, 140, 165, 129, 158, 145, 167

Emily is going to draw a stem-and-leaf diagram to show this information.

She says, "The smallest value is 125 and the greatest value is 197 so there will only be one row with 1 in the stem."

a Explain why Emily is incorrect.

b Draw a stem-and-leaf diagram to show the masses of the parcels.

Consolidate – do you need more?

1 The two-way table shows the number of drinks sold on Saturday and Sunday.

	Tea	Coffee	Hot chocolate	Total
Saturday		17		61
Sunday		42	25	
Total			66	

150 drinks were sold in total.

a Copy and complete the two-way table.

b What fraction of the drinks were hot chocolate?

c What percentage of the drinks sold on a Sunday were coffee?

2 The times taken, in seconds, for 15 students to complete a maths question are shown below.

2.9, 4.3, 0.8, 2.7, 1.5, 4.2, 3.5, 0.9, 2.3, 3.8, 1.3, 4.8, 3.1, 4.5, 2.7

a Draw a stem-and-leaf diagram to show this information.

b Work out the median time taken.

3 The pictogram shows the number of mobile phones sold in a shop on specific days.

Mobile phones sold

Wednesday	●●◖
Thursday	●●●●
Friday	●●●●●●●
Saturday	
Sunday	●●●●●●◖

Key: ● represents 4 mobile phones

a How many mobile phones were sold on Wednesday?

b How many more mobile phones were sold on Sunday than Thursday?

c Twenty-one mobile phones were sold on Saturday.

How many circles would be used in this pictogram to represent the 21 phones?

d How many mobile phones were sold in total?

Stretch – can you deepen your learning?

1 The pictogram shows how many students play particular sports at a school. 450 students were surveyed in total.

Student participation in sport

Rugby	◯◯◯
Football	◯◯◯◯◯◯◖
Tennis	◯◯
Netball	◯◯◯◖

How many students play football?

2 85 people were asked if they went to the cinema at the weekend.

35 of the people were adults.

20 children went to the cinema.

45 people did not go to the cinema.

One of these people is to be chosen at random.

Use a two-way table to work out the probability that the person chosen will be an adult who went to the cinema at the weekend. Give your answer as a fraction in its simplest form.

Are you ready?

1 The graph shows the number of drinks sold in a café each day.

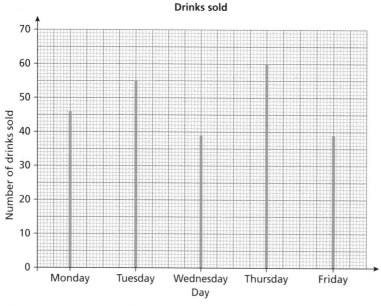

a How many drinks were sold on Tuesday?

b On which day were the greatest number of drinks sold?

c On which two days were the same number of drinks sold?

2 Calculate the mean of these numbers.

1300   1150   1200   900   600   400

A **time series** graph is a line graph that shows how data changes over time.

This time series graph shows information about the amount of profit made in a shop each day during a particular working week.

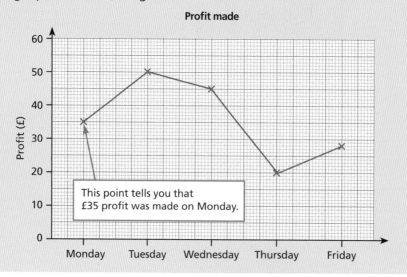

Example

The time series graph shows the number of items sold in a shop from Monday to Friday.

a On which day was the fewest number of items sold?

b How many items were sold in total on Tuesday and Wednesday?

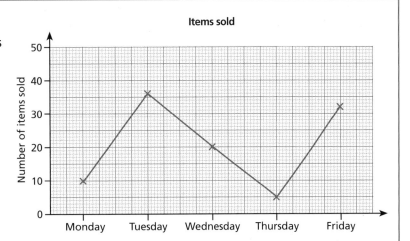

Items sold

Method

Solution	Commentary
a Thursday	This is the lowest point of the graph.
b 36 + 20 = 56	Add the sales for the two days.

Practice

1. The time series graph shows the number of customers who visited a shop in a week.

Shop customers

a How many customers visited the shop on Tuesday?

b On which day did the greatest number of customers visit the shop?

c Which two days had the same number of customers?

2. The time series graph shows the quarterly sales of a company for 2022 and 2023.

> Quarterly means every three months.

a In 2023, which quarter had the highest number of sales?

b How many sales were there in quarter 2 in 2023?

c In which year and quarter did the company record its highest number of sales?

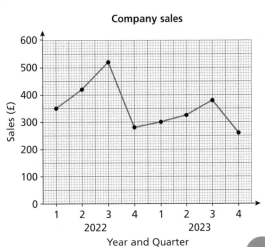

Company sales

Year and Quarter

3 Copy the axes and use the table to plot a time series graph.

Day	Monday	Tuesday	Wednesday	Thursday	Friday
Profit (£)	45	50	30	55	40

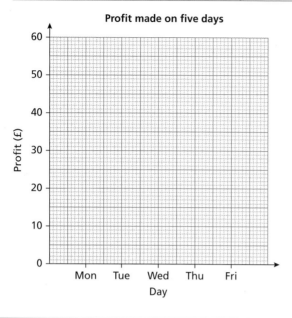

Profit made on five days

Consolidate – do you need more?

1 The time students spent on their smartphone was recorded. The time series graph shows the average daily time per student each year from 2017 to 2023.

Year	2017	2018	2019	2020	2021	2022	2023
Time (minutes)	135	155	140	205	180	175	170

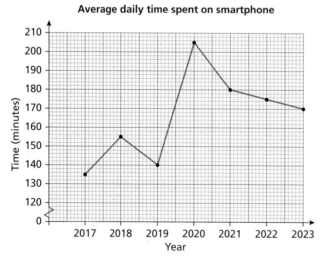

Average daily time spent on smartphone

> Notice that the vertical axis has a broken scale. See page 372 for more on broken scales.

a What was the average daily time per student in 2018?

b In which year was the greatest average daily time spent on a smartphone?

c In which year was the least average daily time spent on a smartphone?

d On average, how many more daily minutes were spent on smartphones in 2022 compared to 2019?

2 Copy the axes and use the table to plot a time series graph.

Month	Jun	Jul	Aug	Sep	Oct	Nov
Average amount of rainfall (mm)	48	42	36	50	42	54

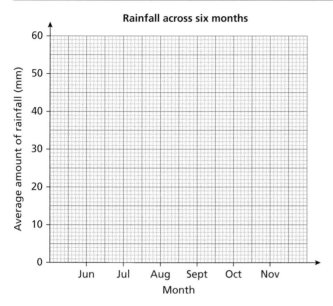

Stretch – can you deepen your learning?

1 Energy is measured in kWh (kilowatt hours). The graph shows the amount of energy being used each month in one household.

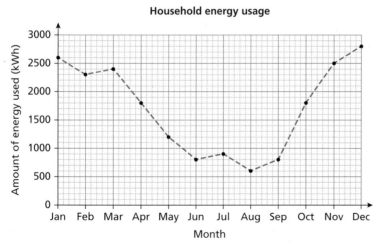

a In which month did the household use the least amount of energy?

b What is the difference in energy consumption used in July compared to the energy consumption used in November?

c Zach says, "The average energy consumption for the first six months of the year is greater than the second six months of the year."

Show that Zach is correct.

Are you ready?

1 State the number of degrees in a full turn.

2 Use a protractor to draw the following angles.

    a 30°   **b** 150°   **c** 28°   **d** 243°

3 Work out:

    a $\frac{90}{360} \times 500$ **b** $\frac{240}{360} \times 690$ **c** $\frac{20}{360} \times 720$ **d** $\frac{15}{360} \times 300$

Another type of statistical diagram used for categorical data is the **pie chart**. Pie charts are particularly useful in showing and comparing proportions.

You can work out the size of each sector in a pie chart using the fact that the angles in a circle add to 360°. So if you know the total number of all the data items, you can work out the angle that a single data item represents.

Favourite colours of a group of people

This represents the smallest frequency as it has the smallest area.

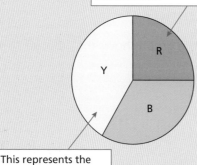

In a pie chart, frequency is represented by the area of the sectors. The larger the area of the sector, the greater the frequency.

This represents the greatest frequency as it is the largest sector.

Example 1

The table shows information about sandwiches sold at a shop one day.

Draw a pie chart to represent the information.

Sandwich	Frequency
Cheese	55
Tuna	27
Egg	38

Method

Solution	Commentary
360° ÷ 120 = 3° for each sandwich	There are 120 sandwiches in total, so divide 360 by 120 to work out the angle per sandwich.

Sandwich	Frequency	Working	Angle
Cheese	55	55 × 3	165
Tuna	27	27 × 3	81
Egg	38	38 × 3	114
	120		360

Add columns to the table to work out the angle to represent each type of sandwich.

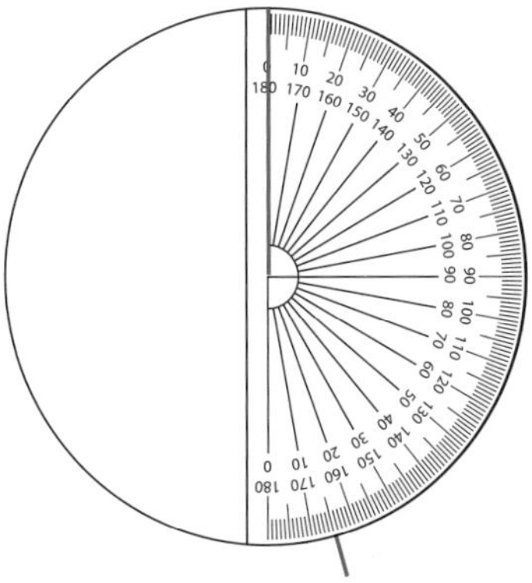

Measure and mark the first angle.

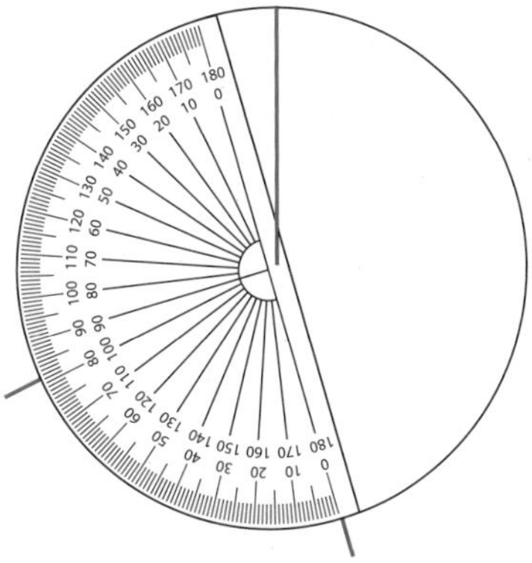

Complete the first sector and mark the next angle.

Line up the 0° on the protractor with the end of the first sector.

Sandwiches sold

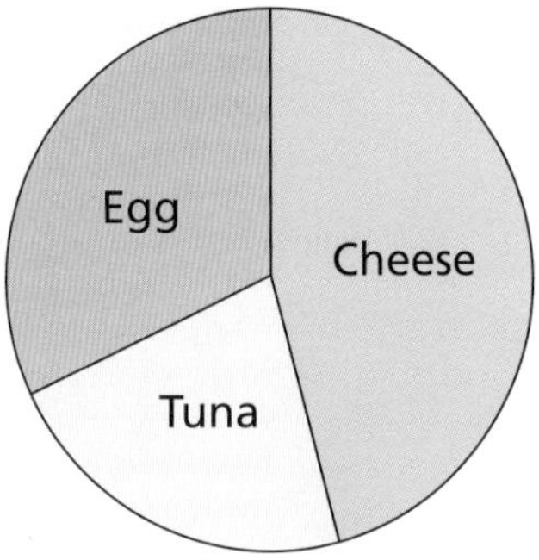

Finish drawing the pie chart.

Remember to label each sector or include a key.

Example 2

The pie chart shows the favourite fruit of 720 people.

a Which fruit was the most popular?

b How many people chose pear?

c How many people chose banana?

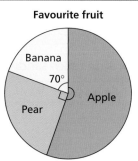

Favourite fruit

Method

Solution	Commentary
a Apple	The largest sector is apple, therefore this represents the highest frequency.
b $\frac{90}{360} \times 720 = \frac{1}{4} \times 720 = 180$	The angle of the pear sector is 90° so use this as a fraction of 360°.
c $\frac{70}{360} \times 720 = 140$	The angle of the banana sector is 70° so use this as a fraction of 360°.

Practice

1 A café sells 72 sandwiches in one day. The type of sandwich is recorded in the frequency table below.

Sandwich	Number sold	Angle
Beef salad	12	12 × 5 = 60°
Cheese and pickle	15	
Egg mayonnaise	24	
Chicken tikka	21	
Total	72	72 × 5 = 360°

a Copy and complete the table.

b Draw a pie chart to show the information. Make sure you label your pie chart.

2 The pie chart shows the survey results of the favourite colours of some people.

a Which colour is the most popular?

b What fraction of the pie chart represents:

   i red   **ii** blue   **iii** yellow?

c 300 people were surveyed in total.

   Calculate the number of people who said:

   i red   **ii** blue   **iii** yellow.

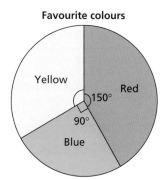

Favourite colours

3 The table gives information about the numbers of flowers in a garden.

Flower	Frequency
Daisy	20
Sunflower	78
Tulip	46

Draw an accurate pie chart to show this information.

4 The pie chart shows the number of phones sold in one week on four different network providers.

a Which was the most popular network provider?

b What fraction of the phones sold were on the C2 network?

c 240 phones were sold in the week.

How many phones were sold on the 'Modophone' network?

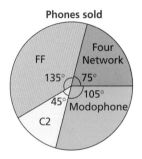
Phones sold

Consolidate – do you need more?

1 Some students were asked to choose their favourite pet.

a Which pet is least popular?

b What fraction of the pie chart represents:

   i cat   **ii** dog   **iii** guinea pig?

c 1800 students were asked in total.

Calculate the number of people who said:

   i cat   **ii** dog   **iii** guinea pig.

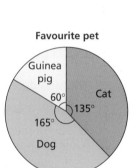
Favourite pet

2 The table shows the colour of pencils found in a desk drawer.

Colour	Number	Angle
Green	18	
Red	6	
Black	21	
Blue	15	
Total	60	

a Copy and complete the table.

b Draw a pie chart to show the information.

Stretch – can you deepen your learning?

1 The pie chart shows information about the favourite sports of some students.

165 students said that rugby is their favourite sport.

a How many students were surveyed in total?

b A student is chosen at random.

Write down the probability that this student's favourite sport is hockey.

Favourite sports

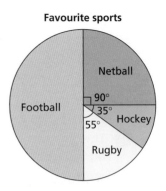

2 The pie charts show information about the results for two football teams last year.

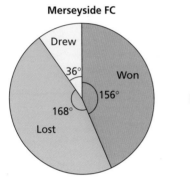

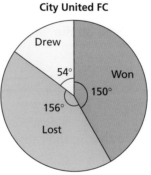

Merseyside FC lost 14 matches.

a How many matches did Merseyside FC win?

b Benji says, "The pie charts show that Merseyside FC drew fewer matches than City United FC."

Is Benji correct? Explain your answer.

Are you ready?

1 The table shows the favourite flavour of crisps of some students.

Crisp flavour	Ready salted	Cheese and onion	Salt and vinegar	Prawn cocktail	Beef
Frequency	10	13	12	9	7

Copy and complete the bar chart to represent the information in the table.

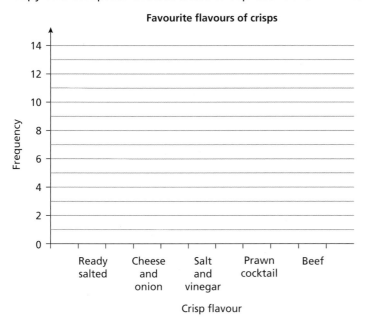

2 Here are the ages, in months, of some babies:

7   9   10   15   18   6   8   11   12   15

5   7   8   15   2   8   17   19   16   15

Copy and complete the table to show the ages of the babies.

Age, m (months)	Tally	Frequency
$0 < m \leqslant 5$		
$5 < m \leqslant 10$		
$10 < m \leqslant 15$		
$15 < m \leqslant 20$		

A **frequency diagram** can be used to display continuous data. Unlike a bar chart, the bars should touch.

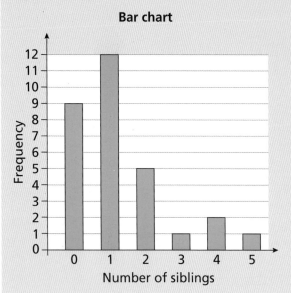

Bar chart

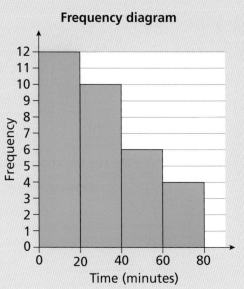

Frequency diagram

Example

The times taken (in minutes) by a group of students to complete a maths test were recorded.

Here are the results:

32	24	40	35	28	31	25	27	40	22	37	30
31	23	39	35	27	26	39	28	35	29	29	31

a Draw a grouped frequency table to represent the data.

b Draw a frequency diagram to represent the data.

Method

Solution	Commentary
a <table><tr><th>Time taken, m (minutes)</th><th>Frequency</th></tr><tr><td>$20 < m \leqslant 25$</td><td>3</td></tr><tr><td>$25 < m \leqslant 30$</td><td>9</td></tr><tr><td>$30 < m \leqslant 35$</td><td>7</td></tr><tr><td>$35 < m \leqslant 40$</td><td>5</td></tr></table>	The quickest time was 23 minutes and the slowest time was 40 minutes, so it makes sense to have four equal groups of 5 minutes for the class intervals. The four class intervals here are: $20 < m \leqslant 25$ $25 < m \leqslant 30$ $30 < m \leqslant 35$ $35 < m \leqslant 40$

b

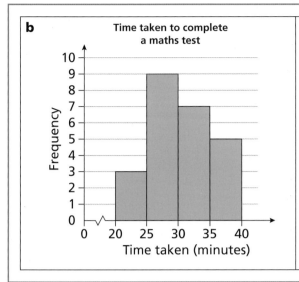

Time is continuous data, so the bars in the frequency diagram should touch.

The groups and bars should always be equal in width when drawing frequency diagrams.

Practice

1 A vet recorded the mass of each animal that came to a surgery one day. The results are shown in the table.

Mass, m (kg)	Frequency
$0 < m \leqslant 5$	5
$5 < m \leqslant 10$	8
$10 < m \leqslant 15$	24
$15 < m \leqslant 20$	15
$20 < m \leqslant 25$	10

On a copy of the grid, draw a frequency diagram to represent the data in the table.

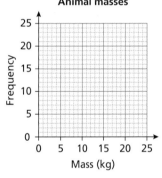

2 The table shows the ages of some members of a running club.

Age, a (years)	Frequency
$15 < a \leqslant 25$	19
$25 < a \leqslant 35$	26
$35 < a \leqslant 45$	31
$45 < a \leqslant 55$	28
$55 < a \leqslant 65$	34
$65 < a \leqslant 75$	17

On a copy of the grid, draw a frequency diagram to represent the data in the table.

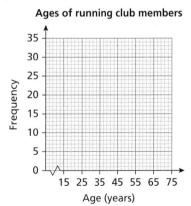

3 The frequency diagram shows the time spent studying for an exam by some students.

a State the number of students who studied:

   i between 3 and 6 hours

   ii between 9 and 12 hours.

b In which class interval did the greatest number of students study?

c How many students studied for the exam altogether?

d A student is chosen at random.

   What is the probability that the student studied for 15 to 18 hours?

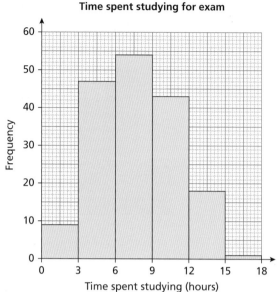

Time spent studying for exam

4 The frequency diagram shows the distances travelled to school by the students in Year 11.

a Use the frequency diagram to copy and complete the frequency table.

Distance, d (miles)	Frequency
$0 < d \leqslant 2$	
$2 < d \leqslant 4$	
$4 < d \leqslant 6$	
$6 < d \leqslant 8$	

b How many students are in Year 11?

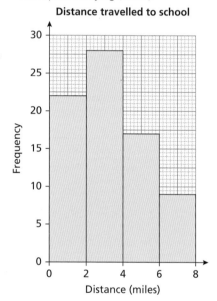

Distance travelled to school

Consolidate – do you need more?

1 Some students completed a test. Their scores are recorded in the table.

Score, s	Frequency
$0 < s \leqslant 10$	3
$10 < s \leqslant 20$	9
$20 < s \leqslant 30$	7
$30 < s \leqslant 40$	5
$40 < s \leqslant 50$	4

On a copy of the grid, draw a frequency diagram to represent the data in the table.

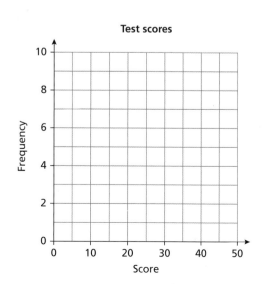

Test scores

2 The frequency diagram shows the number of daily sales that a shop had in a month.

a Use the frequency diagram to complete the frequency table.

Number of sales, s	Frequency
$60 < s \leqslant 80$	
$80 < s \leqslant 100$	
$100 < s \leqslant 120$	
$120 < s \leqslant 140$	

b How many days are in the month?

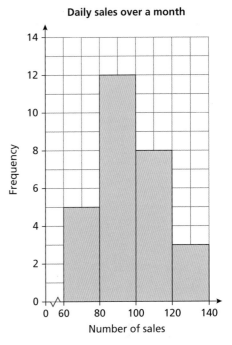

Daily sales over a month

3 The table and frequency diagram show some information about the battery life, in hours, of 41 mobile phones.

Time, h (hours)	Frequency
$5 < h \leqslant 10$	5
$10 < h \leqslant 15$	17
$15 < h \leqslant 20$	14
$20 < h \leqslant 25$	

a Copy and complete the table and the frequency diagram.

b Huda claims, "Over 80% of the phones have a battery life of more than 10 hours."

Is she correct?

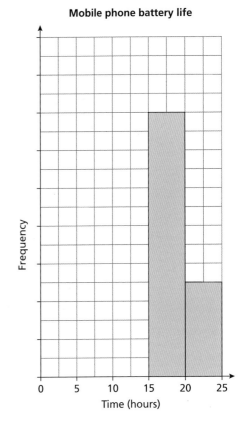

Mobile phone battery life

Stretch – can you deepen your learning?

1 The frequency diagram represents the amount of time that 100 students spent doing their homework over the course of one week.

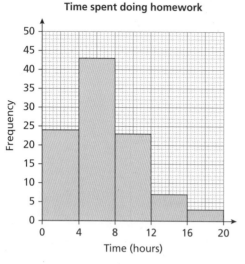

Time spent doing homework

Draw a grouped frequency table for the information shown in the diagram.

2 Flo surveyed 50 students to find out how much money they spent at the weekend.

The frequency table and the frequency diagram show information from her survey.

Money spent, m (£)	Frequency
$0 < m \leqslant 10$	y
$10 < m \leqslant 20$	16
$20 < m \leqslant 30$	$3y$
$30 < m \leqslant 40$	
$40 < m \leqslant 50$	

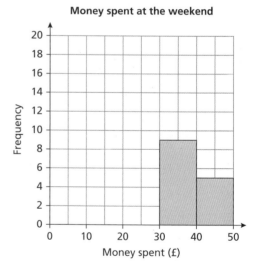

Money spent at the weekend

a Find the value of y.

b Copy and complete the frequency table and the frequency diagram.

1 Sophie surveyed her friends to find their favourite vegetable.

The results are shown in the tally chart but some information is missing.

Vegetable	Tally	Frequency
Broccoli	卌	5
Carrots	||||	
Sweetcorn		7
Sprouts	|||	3
Other	||	2

a) Complete a copy of the tally chart. (1)

b) Complete a copy of the bar chart below to show her results. (2)

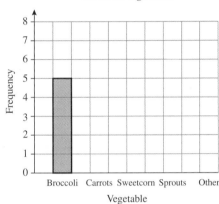

Favourite vegetables

2 Rhys has a fever. The graph shows his body temperature between 6 am and 6 pm.

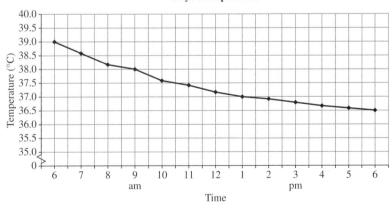

Rhys's temperature

a) What was Rhys's temperature at 6 am? (1)

Normal body temperature is approximately 37°C.

b) At what time did Rhys's temperature start returning to normal? (1)

3 Here are the speeds, in miles per hour, of 14 cars:

| 31 | 52 | 43 | 49 | 36 | 35 | 33 |
| 54 | 43 | 44 | 46 | 42 | 39 | 55 |

   a) Draw an ordered stem-and-leaf diagram for the speeds.   (4)

   b) What is the mode of the speeds?   (1)

4 The pie chart shows how Amir spent his money during a visit to a supermarket.

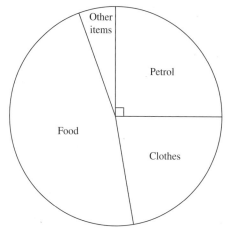

Amir's supermarket spending

Other items

Petrol

Food

Clothes

   a) What did Amir spend the least amount of money on?   (1)

Amir spent £210 in total.

   b) How much did Amir spend on petrol?   (2)

3–5

16 Applying statistics

In this block, we will cover...

16.1 Scatter graphs

Example

Here is a scatter graph comparing temperature and the number of ice creams sold in a park.

a Use the table below to add two additional points to the graph.

Temperature (°C)	22	25
Ice creams sold	78	77

b Describe the relationship between the temperature and the number of ice creams sold.

16.2 Making predictions

Practice

1 Sven, Beca and Flo have all drawn a line o

Which lines of best fit are correctly drawn

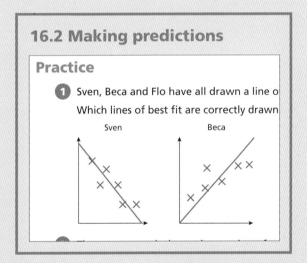

16.3 Samples and populations

Consolidate – do you need more

1 Jakub is carrying out a survey to find out i the number of after-school clubs offered.

He selects seven of his friends to take part

a What is the population Jakub is studyi

b Give a reason why his sample may be b

c Suggest a way that Jakub's sample cou

2 Decide if the following statements are **tru** your answers.

Are you ready?

1 Write the coordinates of each point marked on the grid.

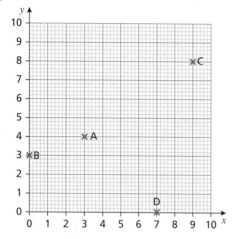

2 Draw a grid with x and y values from 0 to 10

Plot the following points on your grid.

A (4, 6)   B (0, 7)   C (6, 0)   D (4.5, 7.5)

Scatter graphs

Scatter graphs are a good way of displaying two sets of data to see if there is a correlation or connection.

A

B

C

| This graph compares the height of a person and their IQ. It shows there is **no correlation** between the height of a person and their IQ. | This graph compares the number of ice creams sold and the temperature outside. It shows a **positive correlation**. The warmer it is, the more ice creams are sold. | This graph compares the number of scarves sold and the temperature outside. It shows a **negative correlation**. The warmer it is, the fewer scarves are sold. |

Sometimes scatter graphs don't start at the **origin** so the graph is drawn using a **broken scale**.

A **broken scale** is used when values close to 0 are not required. In this case, you can start the x-axis at 8 and the y-axis at 15

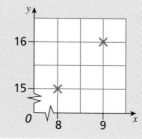

Example

Here is a scatter graph comparing temperature and the number of ice creams sold in a park.

a Use the table below to add two additional points to the graph.

Temperature (°C)	22	25
Ice creams sold	78	77

b Describe the relationship between the temperature and the number of ice creams sold.

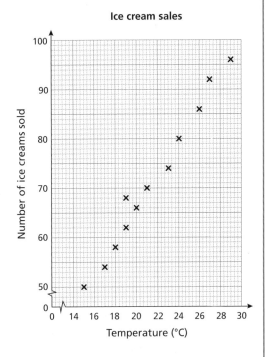

Ice cream sales

Method

Solution	Commentary
a 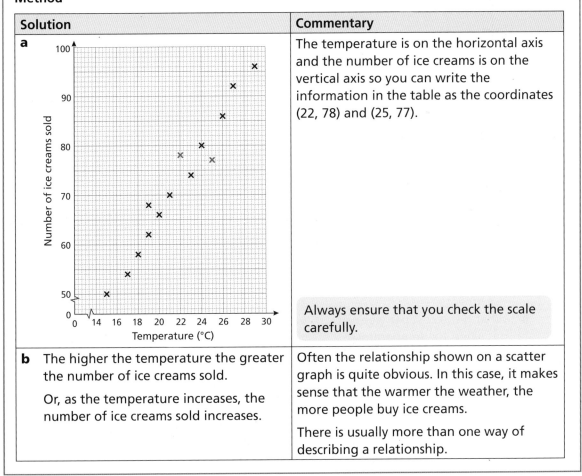	The temperature is on the horizontal axis and the number of ice creams is on the vertical axis so you can write the information in the table as the coordinates (22, 78) and (25, 77). Always ensure that you check the scale carefully.
b The higher the temperature the greater the number of ice creams sold. Or, as the temperature increases, the number of ice creams sold increases.	Often the relationship shown on a scatter graph is quite obvious. In this case, it makes sense that the warmer the weather, the more people buy ice creams. There is usually more than one way of describing a relationship.

Practice

1 Match the graph to the correct description.

A   **B**   **C**

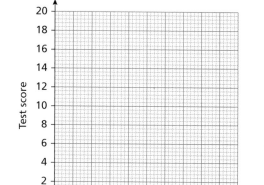

Positive correlation

Negative correlation

No correlation

2 The table shows information about the number of hours of study and the test scores of a group of students.

Hours of study	16	15	10	11	18	12	10	13	14	15
Test score	18	19	15	14	20	12	11	15	16	17

a On a copy of the grid, plot the information from the table.

b Describe the relationship between the test score and the number of hours of study.

Time spent studying and test scores

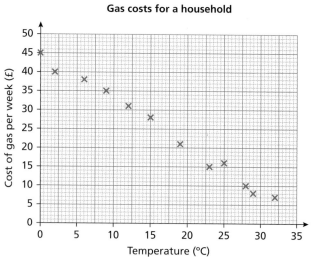

3 The scatter graph shows information about the temperature and the cost of gas for a household.

a What is the cost per week of gas when the temperature is 0°C?

b What is the cost per week of gas when the temperature is 25°C?

c What is the temperature when the cost of gas is £28 per week?

d Describe the relationship between the temperature and the cost of gas per week.

Gas costs for a household

④ The scatter graph shows information about the height and the weight of 11 students.

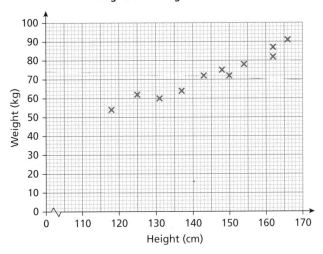

Heights and weights of students

a What is the weight of the student who has a height of 125 cm?

b What is the weight of the student who has a height of 148 cm?

c Two students have a weight of 72 kg. What are their heights?

The table shows the height and the weight for four more students.

Height (cm)	126	157	169	170
Weight (kg)	58	80	88	95

d On a copy of the scatter graph, plot the information from the table.

e What type of correlation does this scatter graph show?

⑤ **a** Draw a scatter graph for each set of data.

i

Number of siblings	2	1	3	4	1	2	3	5	2	0
Favourite number	10	4	8	3	2	5	1	6	8	3

ii

Customer wait time (minutes)	3	10	15	2	5	9	7	12
Customer satisfaction (%)	90	60	20	95	75	65	70	55

iii

Age (years)	25	70	35	60	45	40	55	50	30	65
Blood pressure (mm Hg)	110	145	118	135	122	120	130	125	115	140

b Describe the relationship shown by each scatter graph.

Consolidate – do you need more?

1 The scatter graph shows information about the age and the number of hours of exercise per week for some people.

a How many hours of exercise does the 25-year-old person do per week?

b How old is the person who exercises 1.5 hours per week?

c Describe the relationship between the age and the number of hours of exercise each week.

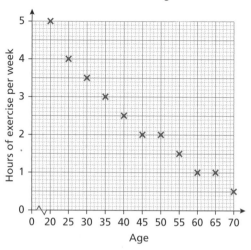

Amount of exercise for people of different ages

2 The scatter graph shows the distances some students live from school and their test results.

a What was the test score of the student who lives 2 miles from school?

b How far from school does the student live who got a test score of 52%?

c Describe the relationship between the distance a student lives from school and their test result.

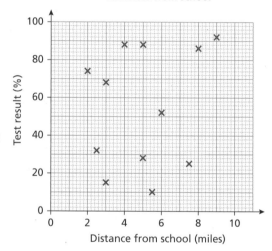

Test scores for students living different distances from school

3 **a** Draw a scatter graph for each set of data.

i

Commuting time per week (hours)	20	24	10	6	36	16	30	2	40	10	14	5
Job satisfaction (1–10)	5	4	7	8	2	6	3	9	1	8	6	8

ii

Test 1	13	15	19	19	18	14	11	18	20	10
Test 2	12	13	18	20	19	13	12	17	19	10

b Describe the relationship shown by each scatter graph in part **a**.

Stretch – can you deepen your learning?

1 Here are some graphs:

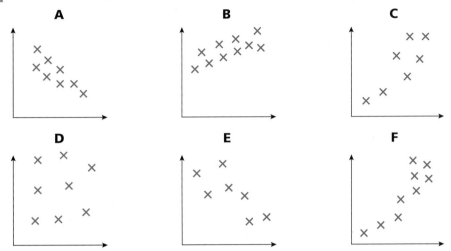

a Identify the graphs that show:

    i a positive correlation   **ii** a negative correlation   **iii** no correlation.

b Which graph shows the strongest positive correlation?

c Which graph shows the strongest negative correlation?

d Suggest a context for each graph.

2 The table shows some information about 12 petrol cars.

For each car, the table shows the engine size in litres and the distance in miles that the car travels on 1 litre of petrol.

Engine size (litres)	1	1.4	2	1.8	3	1.5	3	3.5	4	1.6	2.8	3.2
Distance (miles)	15	14.2	11.8	13.6	10.2	13.8	9.8	8.6	7.8	13.6	16.1	9.2

a Plot these points on a scatter graph.

b Which car do you think is an outlier? Explain your reason.

c Another car has an engine size of 2.5 litres.

Estimate the distance, in miles, that this car can travel on 1 litre of petrol.

16.2 Making predictions

Are you ready?

1 Draw a grid with x and y values from 0 to 10

Plot the following points on your grid.

A (6, 4)   B (8, 0)   C (0, 3.5)   D (2.5, 0.5)

2 For each scatter diagram, write whether it shows a **positive** correlation, a **negative** correlation or **no** correlation.

a   b   c   d

Scatter diagrams can be used to represent **bivariate data** to identify whether there is a correlation.

   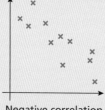   

Positive correlation   Negative correlation   No correlation

Lines of best fit can be added to scatter diagrams. These can then be used to make estimates from the data.

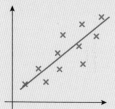

Here is an example of a line of best fit on a scatter diagram showing a positive correlation. It does not necessarily need to pass through the origin. Nor does it need to pass through any of the data points.

Example

The scatter graph shows the relationship between the outside temperature in degrees Celsius and the number of people in a park.

a What type of correlation does the scatter graph show?

b Estimate the outside temperature when the number of people in the park is 45

c Peter estimates that when the outside temperature is 0°C, there will be 26 people in the park.

Explain why Peter's estimate may not be accurate.

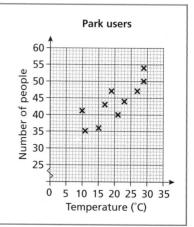

Park users

Method

Solution	Commentary
a Positive correlation	As the value of one variable increases, so does the other.
b 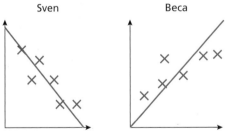 22°C	Draw a line of best fit that follows the trend and has roughly the same number of points on each side. Use a ruler and a pencil to draw a line horizontally from 45 people until you meet the line of best fit. Then draw a line vertically down to find the corresponding temperature. Your line of best fit may be in a slightly different position. This is fine, as long as it is roughly in the middle of the crosses. A range of answers in the follow-up questions is allowed.
c Peter is using a value outside of the points that have been plotted.	You can't assume that the trend will continue beyond the given data.

Practice

1. Sven, Beca and Flo have all drawn a line of best fit.

   Which lines of best fit are correctly drawn and which are not? Explain your answers.

   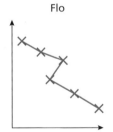

2. The scatter graph shows the number of ice creams sold and the maximum temperature for 10 days.

   a Describe the relationship between the sales of ice creams and the maximum temperature.

   b **i** On a copy of the graph, draw a line of best fit.

   ii Use your line of best fit to estimate the maximum temperature on a day that 160 ice creams were sold.

   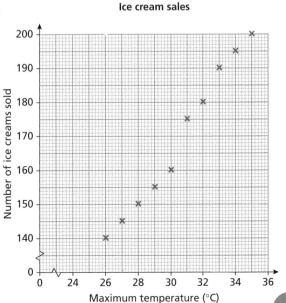

   Ice cream sales

379

3 The table shows the amount of rainfall, in millimetres, and the number of visitors to an outdoor event.

Rainfall (mm)	5	8	20	25	30	10	15	18	22	28
Number of visitors	200	150	100	60	30	180	120	80	50	20

a Plot this information on a scatter graph.

b Draw a line of best fit and use it to estimate the number of visitors that would attend the event if there were 12 mm of rainfall.

4 The scatter graph shows information about the value of 10 used cars.

a Another car is 6 years old and worth £8000
On a copy of the scatter graph, show this information.

b Using the graph, describe the correlation between the age of a car and its value.

c A different car is 4 years old.
Use the graph to estimate its value.

d If the graph was extended to include cars up to 50 years old, do you think the trend shown by the line of best fit would continue? Explain your answer.

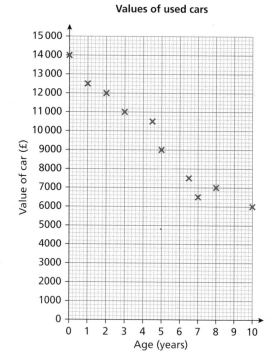

Values of used cars

Consolidate – do you need more?

1 Filipo records the ages and the reaction times, in seconds, of 10 people.

Person	1	2	3	4	5	6	7	8	9	10
Age (years)	18	30	40	50	60	25	35	45	55	65
Reaction time (s)	3	2.5	2.1	1.7	1.3	2.7	2.3	1.9	1.5	1.1

The points for the first eight people have been plotted on the scatter graph.

a On a copy of the graph, plot the points for the remaining two people.

b A 20-year-old person claims their reaction time is 2.9 seconds.
Does the scatter graph support his statement? Explain your answer.

c Use the graph to estimate the age of a person who has a reaction time of 2 seconds.

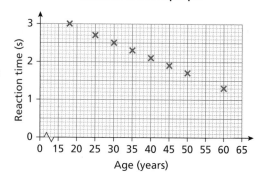

Reaction times of people

2 The table shows the number of hours worked by nine electricians and the cost charged.

Number of hours worked	5	10	15	20	8	12	18	22	25
Cost (£)	150	300	400	500	250	350	450	550	600

a Plot this information on a scatter graph.

b Draw a line of best fit and use it to estimate the cost of a 6-hour job.

c Explain why it may **not** be appropriate to use your line of best fit to estimate the charge for a job lasting 30 hours.

Stretch – can you deepen your learning?

1 The scatter graph shows the relationship between the number of people wearing sunglasses and the number of cups of coffee sold per day in a town.

Ali says, "The more sunglasses worn per day, the less coffee is sold. This means that people who wear sunglasses buy less coffee."

Explain why Ali's statement may be **incorrect**.

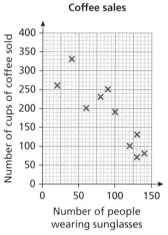

Coffee sales

2 The scatter graph shows information about the number of people at a cinema and the temperature on 10 different days.

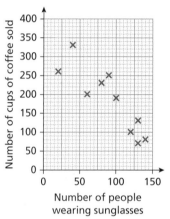

Visitors to a cinema

a Use the graph to estimate the number of people in the cinema when the temperature is 15°C.

b Marta draws a line of best fit on the graph and says, "On a day with a temperature of 35°C, there will be approximately 95 people at the cinema."

Explain why this estimate may be unreliable.

c On the day when the temperature was 22°C, three-fifths of the people who went to the cinema were adults.

How many adults were at the cinema that day?

d On the day when the temperature was 21°C, the ratio of the number of adults to the number of children was 9 : 5

How many adults were at the cinema that day?

Are you ready?

1 Work out 30% of 1500

2 Kath scores 24 out of 50 on a test.

Write her score as a percentage.

3 Work out:

a $\frac{1}{15} \times 75$ b $\frac{7}{29} \times 145$

When collecting statistical data, the **population** is the whole group being studied. As it might be impractical or expensive to study every member of a population, it is more common to select a **sample**. A sample is a smaller group from the population.

A sample is **random** if every member of the population has an equal chance of being selected.

A **biased** sample does not represent the population fairly; for example, leaving out or having too many people from certain groups, such as gender or age. A sample that is too small may also be biased.

Example 1

Darius is investigating whether people in his town would support the construction of a new sports centre. He selects 10 of his friends to take part in his investigation.

a What is the population that Darius is studying?

b Give a reason why his sample may be biased.

c Suggest how Darius's sample could be improved.

Method

Solution	Commentary
a The people who live in his town	The population is the whole group being studied.
b Darius's friends might all be his age and the sample might not represent the town as a whole.	You could also say that 10 is a very small sample size.
c He could take a random sample of all the people in the town.	You could also suggest a larger sample size.

Example 2

A survey was carried out to see how many investors own cryptocurrency.

22 investors said they own cryptocurrency and 8 said they did not.

Estimate the number of the 9000 investors in the population who own cryptocurrency.

Method

Solution	Commentary
$8 + 22 = 30$	Find the total sample size.
$\dfrac{22}{30}$ said they own cryptocurrency.	Find the fraction of the sample who said they own cryptocurrency.
$\dfrac{22}{30} \times 9000 = 6600$ people	Work out this fraction of the whole population.

Practice

1. Ed wants to know if students at his school are interested in joining a debating club. He asks 80 people.

    a What is the population?

    b What is the sample?

2. A sports club has 530 members.

    The owner of the club wants to know if the members are happy with the facilities.

    The owner asks 10 members who go to the sports club on a Monday morning.

    Give two reasons why this may not be a good sample to use.

3. Abdullah is doing a survey to find out how often people go to the theatre and how much they spend. He stands outside a theatre and asks people as they go in.

    Explain why the sample is biased.

4. Eight people are given a number from 1 to 8

    A fair spinner has eight sections and is spun to choose a person.

    Explain why this method selects one of the people at random.

5. A supermarket has 200 employees. The manager takes a sample of 76 employees.

    What percentage of the supermarket employees does this sample represent?

Consolidate – do you need more?

1   Jakub is carrying out a survey to find out if the students in his school are happy with the number of after-school clubs offered.

He selects seven of his friends to take part in his survey.

   a   What is the population Jakub is studying?

   b   Give a reason why his sample may be biased.

   c   Suggest a way that Jakub's sample could be improved.

2   Decide if the following statements are **true** or if they are **false**. Give reasons for your answers.

   a   A sample uses all the population.

   b   A larger sample gives better results than a smaller sample.

   c   Every member of the population has an equal chance of being selected if a sample is random.

   d   A biased sample represents the population fairly.

3   Ten people are given a number from 1 to 10

A fair, 10-sided dice is then rolled to choose a person.

Explain why this method selects one of the people at random.

4   There are 1500 students in a school.

A survey is carried out to find out how many students like pizza.

Six students say they do not like pizza and 39 students say they do like pizza.

Estimate the number of students in the population who like pizza.

Stretch – can you deepen your learning?

1   A sample of 60 is taken from a population.

The sample represents 15% of the population.

What is the size of the population?

2   A sample of 20 students from Year 11 are asked which flavour of crisps they prefer.

The results are shown in the table.

Flavour	Frequency
Ready salted	8
Salt and vinegar	5
Prawn cocktail	3
Cheese and onion	4

There are 240 students in Year 11.

Estimate how many students in Year 11 prefer each flavour of crisp.

Applying statistics: exam practice

White Rose
MATHS

1 Point P is marked on the grid.

    a) Write down the coordinates of point P.   **(1)**

    b) Plot the point (−2, −1) on the grid and label it Q.   **(1)**

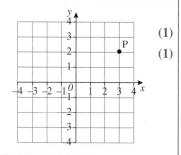

1–3

2 The scatter graph shows the height and mass of 10 horses.

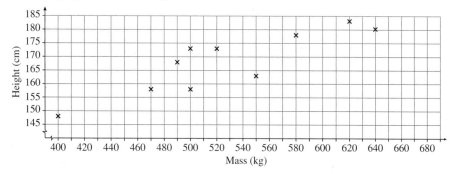

3–5

    a) Another horse is 168 cm tall and has a mass of 550 kg.

       Show this information on the scatter graph.   **(1)**

    b) Draw a line of best fit on the scatter graph.   **(1)**

    c) What type of correlation does the scatter graph show?   **(1)**

    d) Estimate the height of a horse with a mass of 600 kg.   **(2)**

3 Rav draws a scatter graph showing information about the heights and arm lengths of 8 people.

    Which graph, A, B or C, is most likely to represent his information?

    Explain your answer.   **(2)**

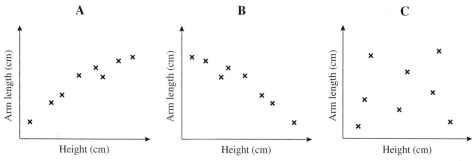

4 A library has 500 members.

    A librarian is investigating the number of books that members take out of the library.

    The librarian checks the records of 80 readers. On average, these members take out 6 books a year.

    Identify the population and the sample in this case.   **(2)**

Statistics: exam practice

1 The pictogram shows the number of meals sold in a café on Monday, Tuesday, Wednesday and Thursday of one week.

a) How many meals were sold on Wednesday? **(1)**

b) How many meals were sold on Tuesday? **(1)**

c) On Friday, 25 meals were sold.

   On Saturday, 40 meals were sold.

   Show this information on the pictogram. **(2)**

d) How many meals in total were sold from Monday to Saturday inclusive? **(2)**

Meals sold

Monday	◯ ◯ ◯
Tuesday	◯ ◖
Wednesday	◯ ◯ ◯
Thursday	◯ ◯
Friday	
Saturday	

Key: ◯ represents 10 meals

---

2 Chloe recorded the shoe sizes of five of her friends.

Here are her results:

   5   4   2   6   7

a) Work out the median shoe size. **(2)**

Chloe's shoe size is 4

b) Work out the median shoe size of Chloe and her five friends. **(2)**

---

3 Six students each sat a maths test and science test.

Each test was out of 40 marks.

The marks of five of the six students have been drawn on this bar chart.

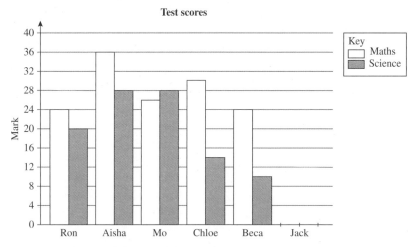

a) How many marks did Ron get on the maths test? **(1)**

b) How many marks did Beca get on the science test? **(1)**

c) Who scored the highest on the maths test? **(1)**

d) Jack scored 30 marks on the maths test and got full marks on the science test.

   Show this information on the bar chart. **(2)**

4 Speed checks were performed on cars at a police checkpoint on a particular day.

The stem-and-leaf diagram shows the speeds of the cars that passed the checkpoint.

Car speeds

```
2 | 0 4 9
3 | 4 5 5 6 6 6 7 7 9
4 | 0 1 4 4 5 6 7
5 | 2
```

Key: 2 | 0 represents 20 mph

  a) How many cars passed the police checkpoint? **(1)**

  b) The speed limit on the road is 40 mph.

    How many cars were breaking the speed limit? **(1)**

  c) Motorists travelling over 45 mph were stopped and fined.

    How many motorists were stopped and fined? **(1)**

  d) What was the median speed? **(2)**

5 The frequency diagram shows the number of goals scored by a football team over 23 games.

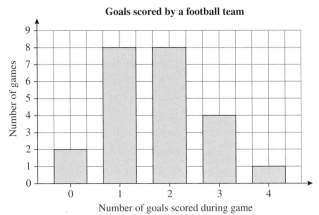

Goals scored by a football team

  a) Find the total number of goals scored in the 23 games. **(2)**

  b) Find the mean number of goals scored per game. Give your answer to 1 decimal place. **(3)**

6 The heights of 35 trees are shown in the table.

Height of tree (m)	$5 < h \leqslant 10$	$10 < h \leqslant 15$	$15 < h \leqslant 20$	$20 < h \leqslant 25$
Number of trees	4	16	9	6

  a) How many trees are taller than 20 m? **(1)**

  b) Draw a grouped frequency diagram to represent the information, using a copy of these axes. **(4)**

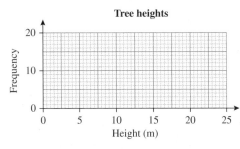

Tree heights

2D shape – a flat shape with two dimensions such as length and width

3D shape – a shape with three dimensions: length, width and height

Acute angle – an angle less than 90°

Adjacent – next to each other

Alternate angles – a pair of angles between a pair of lines on opposite sides of a transversal

Angle – a measure of turn between two lines around their common point

Anticlockwise – in the opposite direction to the way the hands of an analogue clock move

Arc – a part of the circumference of a circle

Area – the space inside a 2D shape

Ascending – increasing in size

Associative law for addition – when you add numbers it does not matter how they are grouped

Average – a number representing the typical value of a set of data

Average speed – the total distance travelled divided by the total time taken

Axis – a line on a graph that you can read values from

Bar chart – a chart that uses horizontal or vertical rectangles to show frequencies

Base – a side of a shape that is used as the foundation of the shape

Bearing – the angle measured clockwise from a North line at a fixed point

Biased – all possible outcomes are not equally likely

Bisect – cut in half

Bisector – a line that divides something into two equal parts

Capacity – how much space a container holds

Centre – the point at the middle of a shape

Centre of enlargement – the point from which the enlargement is made

Centre of rotation – the point around which a shape can rotate

Chord – a line joining two points on the circumference of a circle

Circumference – the distance around the edge of a circle

Class interval – the range of data in a group

Clockwise – in the same direction as the hands of an analogue clock move

Co-interior angles – a pair of angles between a pair of lines on the same side of a transversal

Collinear – passing through, or lying on, the same straight line

Column vector – a description of a vector showing its horizontal and vertical components

Complement – the elements of the universal set that do not belong to a set

Compound shape – also known as a composite shape, this is a shape made up of two or more other shapes

Common factor – a factor that is shared by two or more numbers

Conditional probability – the probability that an event will occur given that another event has already occurred

Cone – a 3D shape with a plane circular face, a curved surface and one vertex

Congruent – exactly the same size and shape, but possibly in a different orientation

Construct – draw accurately using a ruler and compasses

Continuous data – data that is measured and so does not take exact values

Correlation – the relationship between the values of two variables

Corresponding angles – a pair of angles in matching positions compared with a transversal

Cosine – the cosine of an angle is the ratio of the length of the adjacent side to the length of the hypotenuse in a right-angled triangle

Cross-section – the shape of a slice through a solid

Cube – a 3D shape with six square faces

Cuboid – a 3D shape with six rectangular faces

Cylinder – a 3D shape with a constant circular cross-section

Data – a collection of numbers or information

Degree – a unit of measurement of temperature; a degree is also a unit of measurement of angles

Derive – find or discover something from existing knowledge

Describe – say what you see, or what is happening

Diagonal – a line segment that joins two opposite vertices of a polygon

Diagram – a simplified drawing showing the appearance, structure, or workings of something

Diameter – a straight line across a circle, from circumference to circumference and passing through the centre

Dimensions – measurements such as the length, width and height of an object

Discrete data – data that can only take certain values

Edge – a line segment joining two vertices of a 3D shape; it is where two faces of a 3D shape meet

Element – a member of a set

Enlargement – a transformation of a shape that makes it bigger or smaller

Equally likely – having the same probability of happening

Equidistant – at the same distance from

Equilateral – all sides of equal length

Event – a set of one or more outcomes of an experiment

Expected outcome – an estimate of how many times a possible outcome will occur based on relative frequency (experimental probability) or theoretical probability

Experiment – a test or a trial

Exterior angle – an angle between the side of a shape and a line extended from the adjacent side

Face – the flat surface or side of a 3D shape

Fair – an item or event that isn't biased

Frequency – the number of times something happens

Frequency density – the frequency per unit for the data in each class, found by diving the frequency of class interval by the width of class interval

Frequency tree – a diagram showing a number of people/objects grouped into categories

Front elevation – the 2D view of a 3D shape or object as seen from the front

Give a reason – state the mathematical rule(s) you have used, not just the calculations you have done

Gradient – the measure of the steepness of a line or a curve

Grouped data – data that is organised into groups

Hemisphere – half of a sphere

Hypothesis – an idea to investigate that might be true or false

Image – the result of a transformation of an object

Independent events – two events are independent if the outcome of one event isn't affected by the outcome of the other event

Interior angle – an angle on the inside of a shape

Intersection of sets A and B – the set containing all the elements of A that also belong to B

Irregular – not regular; a shape where sides and/or angles are not all equal

Isosceles – having two sides the same length

Key – used to identify the categories present in a graph or chart

Kite – a quadrilateral with two pairs of adjacent sides that are equal in length

Line graph – this has connected points and shows how a value changes over time

Line of symmetry – a line that cuts a shape exactly in half

Line segment – a part of a line that connects two points

Locus (plural: **loci**) – a set of points that describe a property

Mean – the result of sharing the total of a set of data equally between them

Measure of spread – shows how similar or different a set of values are

Median – the middle number in an ordered list

Misleading graph – a graph that suggests an incorrect conclusion or assumption

Modal class – the class in a grouped frequency distribution that has the greatest frequency

Mode – the item which appears most often in a set of data

Multiple bar chart – a way to represent several, related sets of data

Mutually exclusive events – two or more events that cannot happen at the same time

Net – a 2D shape that can be folded to make a 3D shape

Obtuse angle – an angle more than 90° but less than 180°

Opposite sides/angles – sides or angles that are not next to each other in a quadrilateral

Order of rotational symmetry – the number of positions where the shape looks the same when rotated through 360°

Orientation – the position of an object based on the direction it is facing

Outcome – the possible result of an experiment

Outlier – a value that differs significantly from the others in a data set

Parallel – always the same distance apart and never meeting

Parallelogram – a quadrilateral with two pairs of parallel sides

Perimeter – the total distance around a two-dimensional shape

Perpendicular – at right angles to

Perpendicular bisector – a line that is drawn at right angles to the midpoint of a line segment

Perpendicular height – the height of a shape measured at a right angle to the base

Pi – pronounced 'pie' and written using the symbol π. It is the ratio of the circumference of a circle to its diameter

Pie chart – a graph in which a circle is divided into sectors that each represent a proportion of the whole

Plan view – the 2D view of a 3D shape or object as seen from above

Polygon – a closed 2D shape with straight sides

Population – the whole group that is being investigated

Predict – make a statement as to what will happen based on information you already know

Primary data – data you collect yourself

Prime factor decomposition – writing numbers as a product of their prime factors

Prism – a 3D shape with a constant cross-section

Probability – how likely an event is to occur

Proof – an argument that shows that a statement is true

Properties – features of something that are always true

Pyramid – a 3D shape with triangular faces meeting at a vertex

Qualitative – data that describes characteristics

Quantitative – numerical data

Questionnaire – a list of questions to gather information

Radius – the distance from the centre of a circle to a point on the circle

Random – each outcome is equally likely to occur

Random sample – each item of the population has an equal probability of being chosen

Range – the difference between the greatest value and the smallest value in a set of data

Reflection – a type of geometrical transformation, where an object is flipped to create a mirror image

Reflex angle – an angle more than 180° but less than 360°

Regular – a shape that has all equal sides and all equal angles

Regular polygon – a polygon whose sides are all equal in length and whose angles are all equal in size

Relative frequency – the number of times an event occurs divided by the number of trials

Replacement – putting back – when an item is replaced, the probabilities do not change; when an item is not replaced, the probabilities do change

Represent – draw or show

Right angle – an angle of exactly 90°

Rotation – a geometrical transformation in which every point on a shape is turned through the same angle about a given point

Sample – a selection taken from a population

Sample space – the set of all possible outcomes or results of an experiment

Scale – the ratio of the length in a drawing or a model to the length on the actual object

Scale drawing – a diagram that represents a real object with accurate sizes reduced or enlarged by a ratio

Scale factor – how much a shape has been enlarged by

Scatter diagram – a statistical graph that compares two variables

Secondary data – data already collected by someone else

Sector – a part of a circle formed by two radii and a fraction of the circumference

Segment – a chord splits a circle into two segments

Set – a collection of objects or numbers

Side – a line segment that joins two vertices in a 2D shape

Side elevation – the 2D view of a 3D shape or object as seen from the side

Similar – two shapes are similar if their corresponding sides are in the same ratio, so one shape is an exact enlargement of the other shape

Sine – the sine of an angle is the ratio of the length of the opposite side to the length of the hypotenuse in a right-angled triangle

Sketch – a rough drawing

Sphere – a 3D shape in which all points of its surface are equidistant from its centre.

Surface area – the sum of the areas of all the faces of a 3D shape

Tabular – organised into a table

Tangent (to a circle) – a straight line that touches the circumference of a circle at one point only

Tangent (trigonometry) – the tangent of an angle is the ratio of the length of the opposite side to the length of the adjacent side in a right-angled triangle

Timetable – a table showing times

Translation – a type of geometrical transformation, where an object is moved left or right and/or up or down

Transversal – a line that crosses at least two other lines

Trapezium – a quadrilateral with one pair of parallel sides

Tree diagram – a way of recording possible outcomes that can be used to find probabilities

Trigonometry – the study of lengths and angles in triangles

Two-step – when a calculation involves two processes rather than one

Two-way table – a table that displays two sets of data in rows and columns

Union of sets A and B – the set containing all the elements of A or B or both A and B

Universal set – the set containing all relevant elements

Vector – a quantity with both magnitude and direction, e.g. velocity, force, displacement

Venn diagram – a diagram used for sorting data

Vertex (plural: **vertices**) – a point where two line segments meet; a corner of a shape

Vertically opposite angles – angles opposite each other when two lines cross

Volume – the amount of solid space in a 3D shape

Block 1 Constructions (1)

Chapter 1.1

Are you ready?

1 ———————————————————
7.4 cm

2
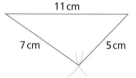
85°

3 AB = 6 cm   Angle BCD = 110°

Practice

1 a
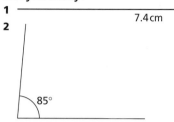
11 cm
7 cm   5 cm

b
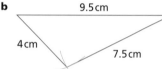
9.5 cm
4 cm
7.5 cm

c

120 mm
6 cm   8 cm

2
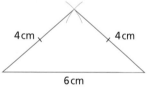
4 cm   4 cm
6 cm

3
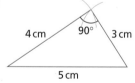
4 cm   90°   3 cm
5 cm

4 The two shorter sides add up to less than 10 cm.

5 a
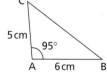
C
5 cm
95°
A   6 cm   B

b
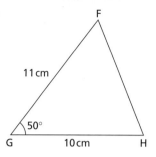
F
11 cm
50°
G   10 cm   H

6 a Triangle accurately constructed to the given side lengths and angle size.
b Triangle accurately constructed to the given side lengths and angle size.
c Triangle accurately constructed to the given side lengths and angle size.

7 a
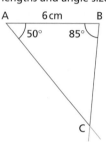
A   6 cm   B
50°   85°
C

b
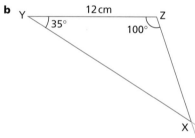
Y   12 cm   Z
35°   100°
X

8 a
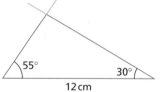
55°   30°
12 cm

b
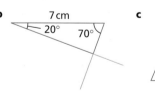
7 cm
20°   70°

c
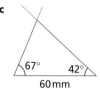
67°   42°
60 mm

9 C – a triangle can have no more than one obtuse angle
10 A has the greater perimeter.

What do you think?
1 SSS, SAS and ASA

Consolidate

1 a

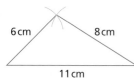

b

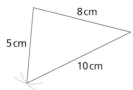

2

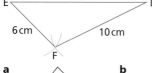

3 a **b**

4

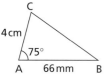

5 a

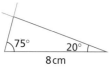

b

6

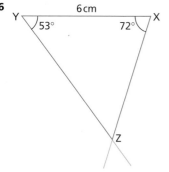

Stretch

1 Seb is correct. There is only one way to construct a triangle with two angles of 70° and two sides of 7 cm.

Chapter 1.2

Are you ready? (A)
1 100
2 a 2 m   **b** 3.5 m   **c** 4.72 m
3 a 400 cm   **b** 560 cm   **c** 123.6 cm

Practice (A)
1 Length 7; width 3
2 Length 6.5; width 5
3 a  **b**

4 a 11.9 m
   b 7 m length = 10 cm; 4.9 m length = 7 cm
5 a 4.05 m   **b** 30 cm

What do you think? (A)
1 Same. 1 : 300 is 1 cm : 300 cm
   300 cm = 3 m

Are you ready? (B)
1 km
2 1000
3 100

Practice (B)
1

Map distance (cm)	Real distance (cm)	Real distance (m)	Real distance (km)
1	**40 000**	400	0.4
5	200 000	**2000**	2
7.5	**300 000**	3000	3
25	1 000 000	**10 000**	10

2 825 000 cm = 8250 m = 8.25 km
3 a A to B = 8 cm
     Real life = 400 000 cm = 4000 m = 4 km
   b B to C = 5.5 cm
     Real life = 275 000 cm = 2750 m = 2.75 km

What do you think? (B)
1 The drive is not likely to be the same distance because it is unlikely to be a straight-line journey.

Consolidate
1 a 16 m and 26 m   **b** 208 m²
2 a

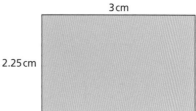

   b 10.5 cm   **c** 6.75 cm²
3 7 m
4 3.75 km

Stretch

1 3.75 cm

2 Real-life distance = 75 km
Time = 75 ÷ 60 = 1.25 hours
The journey will take Marta 1 hour 15 minutes.

Chapter 1.3

Are you ready? (A)

1 Clockwise from North: East; South; West

2 223°

3 a

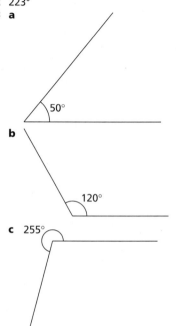

4 a 45°   **b** 165°   **c** 320°

Practice (A)

1 a   **b**

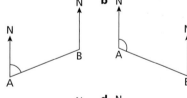

c   **d**

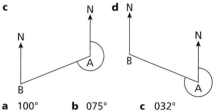

2 a 100°   **b** 075°   **c** 032°
3 a 280°   **b** 255°   **c** 212°
4 a 060°   **b** 110°   **c** 150°   **d** 230°
5 a   **b**

 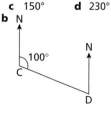

c   **d**

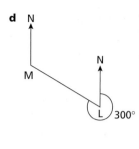

6 a 070°   **b** 100°   **c** 170°   **d** 280°

What do you think? (A)

1 A and B

Are you ready? (B)

1 *Lines drawn accurately to the following lengths.*

2 a   **b**

c

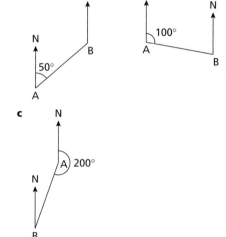

3 10 km

Practice (B)

Note: all lengths should be measured accurately to those indicated.

1 a   **b**

c

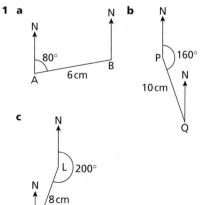

2 a 065° **b** 245° **c** 40 metres

3

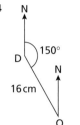

4

5

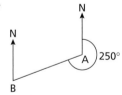

c

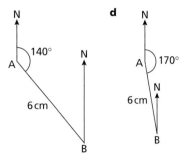

d

e

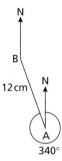

Consolidate

1 a

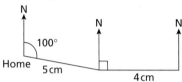

b

c

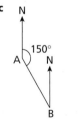

d

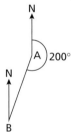

e

2 *Note: all lengths should be measured accurately to those indicated.*

a

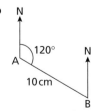

b

Stretch

1

2 a *Note: all lengths should be measured accurately to those indicated.*

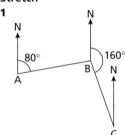

b 254°
3 250°

Constructions (1): exam practice

1 Accurate construction of triangle with side AB 7 cm, side AC 6 cm and angle A = 48°.
2 20 miles
3 Accurate construction of equilateral triangle with sides 6 cm.
4 218°
5 a 10 miles
b

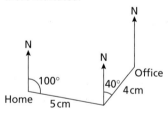

Block 2 Constructions (2)

Chapter 2.1

Are you ready? (A)

1 a 40° **b** 130°

2 a Check that the triangle has been constructed accurately (SAS)

  b Check that the triangle has been constructed accurately (ASA)

  c Check that the triangle has been constructed accurately (SSS)

Practice (A)

1 a Check the two angles produced are both 30°

  b Check the two angles produced are both 60°

  c Check the two angles produced are both 73°

2 a Check the two angles produced are both 45°

  b Check the two angles produced are both 80°

  c Check the two angles produced are both 105°

3

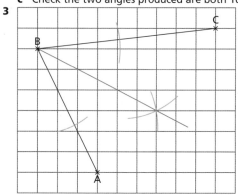

4 No, the angles are not equal.

5 a & b

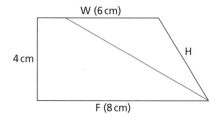

What do you think? (A)

1 No

Are you ready? (B)

1 A and B

2

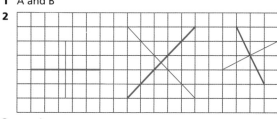

3

Practice (B)

1 a

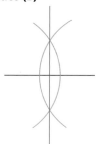

  b

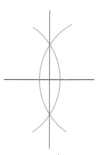

  c

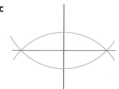

  d

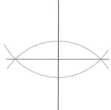

2 a

  b

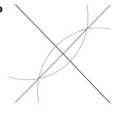

  c

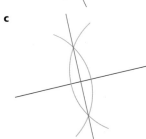

  d

3

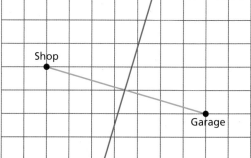

4

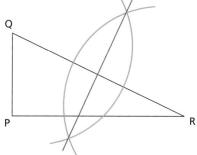

5

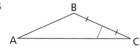

6 The pair of compasses needed to be set to a longer length (bigger radius) in order for the arcs to intersect above and below the line segment.

What do you think? (B)

1 Yes

Consolidate

1 a   **b**

c 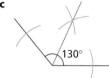 **d**

2 a 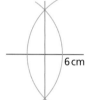 **b**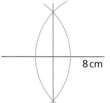

c 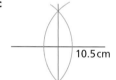 **d**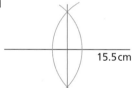

Stretch

1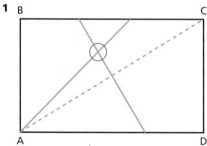

2 Possible answers: 90°; 45°; 135°
3 Possible answers: 30°; 15°

Chapter 2.2

Are you ready?

1

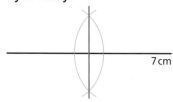

2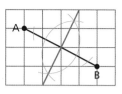

Practice

1 a   **b**

c   **d**

2 a 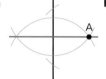 **b**

c 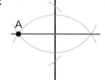 **d**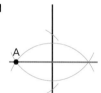

3 a   **b**

c

4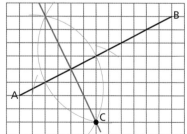

5

6 a

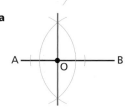

b

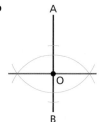

c

7

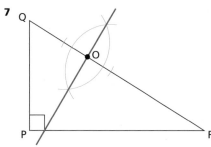

8 Any two points on the red perpendicular line are acceptable.

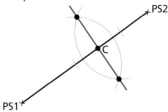

9 a & b

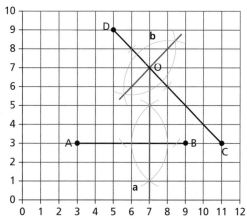

c The two lines intersect at O (7, 7)

10

What do you think?

1 Yes. Extending AB makes it possible.

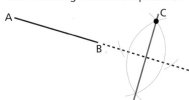

Consolidate

1 a

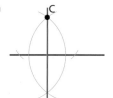

b

c

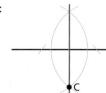

d

e

f

2 a

b

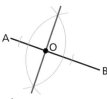

c

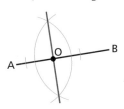

d

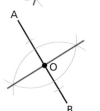

e

f

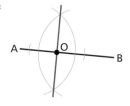

Stretch

1

The gradients are $-\frac{2}{5}$ and $\frac{5}{2}$

They are negative reciprocals.

This will always happen with two perpendicular lines.

Chapter 2.3

Are you ready? (A)

1

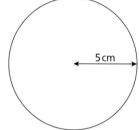

2

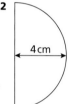

3

Practice (A)

1

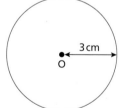

2 a

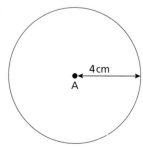

b

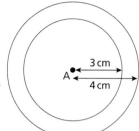

c

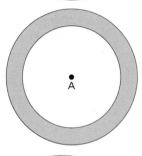

3 a

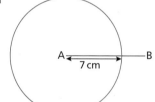

b

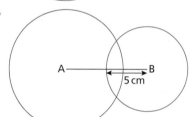

c

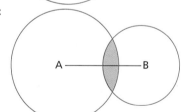

4

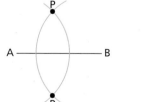

5 a

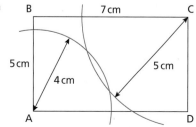

Answers

b

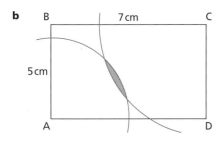

What do you think? (A)

1 No. The loci of points will not intersect.

Are you ready? (B)

1

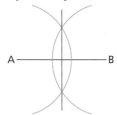

2

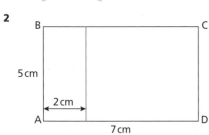

Practice (B)

1

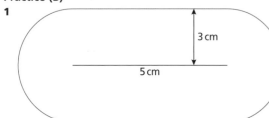

2

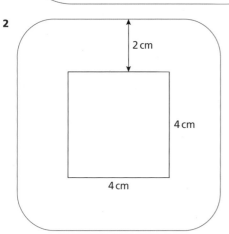

3

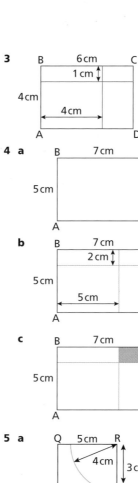

4 a

b

c

5 a

b

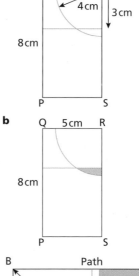

6

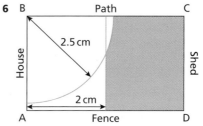

7 More than 2 cm from AB and less than 4 cm from A

8

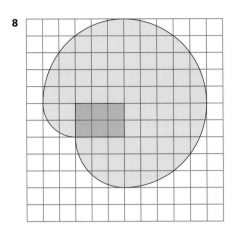

What do you think? (B)

1 The corners are more than 2 cm from the red line.

Consolidate

1 a

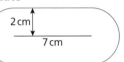

2 cm

7 cm

b

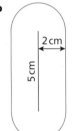

2 cm

5 cm

c

2 cm 6 cm

2 a

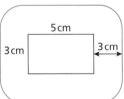

5 cm

3 cm 3 cm

b

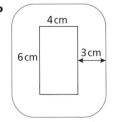

4 cm

6 cm 3 cm

c

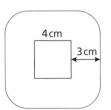

4 cm

3 cm

3 a

B 10 cm C

4 cm

8 cm

5 cm

A D

b

B 10 cm C

4 cm

8 cm

5 cm

A D

c

B 10 cm C

4 cm

8 cm

4 cm

A D

d

B 10 cm C

4 cm

8 cm

A D

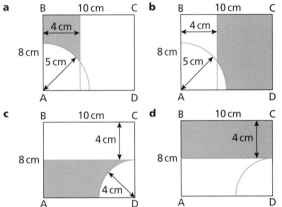

4

Q 8 cm R

2 cm

12 cm

P S

Stretch

1 30 cm
2 52.6 cm²

Constructions (2): exam practice

1 A
2

A ——————— B

3

R

S T

4

3 cm

A ——————— B

5

B

P

A

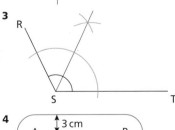

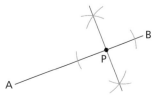

Block 3 Shapes and angles

Chapter 3.1

Are you ready? (A)

1 a Acute   **b** Obtuse
   c Reflex   **d** Right angle
2 90°

Practice (A)

1 a 281°   **b** 61°   **c** 58°   **d** 134°
2 a $a = 45°$ **b** $b = 68°$
3 A, C, E
4 a 68°   **b** 123°   **c** 80°   **d** 67°
5 No, the angles sum to 178°
6 a $a = 45°$ **b** $a = 60°$, $2a = 120°$
7 A, C, E
8 a 92°   **b** 165°   **c** 100°   **d** 137°
9 a $a = 22°$ **b** $b = 26°$, $2b = 52°$
   c $c = 118°$, $d = 62°$, $e = 118°$

What do you think? (A)

1 $a = 88°$. You can use vertically opposite angles are equal, angles on a straight line sum to 180° or angles at a point sum to 360°.

Are you ready? (B)

1 a Equilateral **b** Isosceles   **c** Scalene
2 Isosceles triangle; Scalene triangle; Right-angled triangle

Practice (B)

1 a 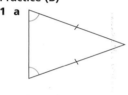   **b**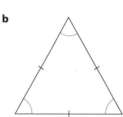

   c

2 a $d = 51°$ **b** $e = 35°$ **c** $f = 38°$ **d** $g = 70.5°$
3 a a, b and $c = 60°$ **b** d and $e = 70°$
   c $f = 75°$, $g = 30°$ **d** h and $i = 45°$
4 The angle could be the equal angle or the unequal angle in the isosceles triangle.
   $50° + 50° + 80° = 180°$ $50° + 65° + 65° = 180°$
5 a $a = 25°$, $4a = 100°$ **b** $b = 127.5°$
   c $c = 62°$, $d = 69°$ **d** $e = 60°$

What do you think? (B)

1 It could be an equilateral triangle or a scalene triangle. It cannot be an isosceles triangle.
   Equilateral: $60° + 60° + 60° = 180°$
   Scalene, for example: $60° + 40° + 80° = 180°$

Consolidate

1 a $d = 145°$ **b** $g = 202°$
2 a $f = 109°$ **b** $a = 50°$
3 a $h = 64°$ **b** $p = 145°$, $q = 35°$, $r = 145°$
4 a $x = 81°$ **b** $y = 49°$ **c** $z = 74°$

Stretch

1 $a = 123°$, $b = 57°$
2 Yes; angle ABC = angle ACB = 80°; angle ACD = 100° so angle CAD = angle ADC = 40°
3 $x = 20°$, $y = 25°$, $z = 50°$

Chapter 3.2

Are you ready?

1 A, C
2 a $w = 50°$ **b** $x = 52°$ **c** $y = 108°$ **d** $z = 88°$

Practice

1 a g
   b c and h d and e
2 a h
   b b and e c and f a and h d and g
3 a a
   b c and e d and h
4 a $a = 81°$, alternate angles are equal.
   b $b = 115°$, co-interior angles add up to 180°.
   c $c = 72°$, corresponding angles are equal.
   d $d = 101°$, corresponding angles are equal.
5 Multiple angle facts can be used.
   a $a = 56°$ **b** $b = 98°$, $c = 82°$
   c $d = 50°$, $e = 50°$ **d** $f = 87°$, $g = 93°$, $h = 93°$
6 79°, corresponding angles are equal.
7 No, they are not alternate angles as both angles must be between the parallel lines. $x = 70°$.
8 Multiple angle facts can be used.
   $a = 140°$, $b = 37°$, $c = 140°$, $d = 37°$
9 Multiple angle facts can be used.
   a $a = 72°$, $b = 52°$ **b** $c = 128°$, $d = 47°$ **c** $e = 81°$

What do you think?

1 a Yes, alternate angles are equal.
   b No, corresponding angles must be equal.
   c Yes, co-interior angles add up to 180°.

Consolidate

1 a EFD or EFB **b** FBA or HBA   **c** BFG or DFG
2 a $x = 140°$, co-interior angles add up to 180°.
   b $y = 134°$, alternate angles are equal.
   c $z = 77°$, corresponding angles are equal.
3 Multiple angle facts can be used.
   a $a = 151°$, $b = 29°$ **b** $c = 30°$, $d = 30°$
   c $e = 76°$, $f = 76°$, $g = 104°$

Stretch

1 a 85°   **b** 33°   **c** 33°   **d** 62°
2 $x = 15$
3 $x = 32$

Chapter 3.3

Are you ready?

1 8
2 A pair of lines drawn that remain the same distance apart and never meet.
3 A pair of lines drawn that meet at a right angle.
4 a Parallelogram   **b** Trapezium
   c Kite   **d** Rectangle

Practice

1 a 3   **b** 6   **c** 5   **d** 4   **e** 8
2 a Hexagon   **b** Quadrilateral
   c Triangle   **d** Octagon
3 No, a parallelogram has two pairs of parallel sides. The shape is a trapezium.
4 A, C, D
   A pentagon is a five-sided shape, with sides that are straight and enclosed.
5 a $a = 66°$ **b** $b = 122°$
6 a $a = 138°$, $b = 42°$, $c = 138°$
   b $x = 130°$, $y = 50°$, $z = 130°$
7 a $f = 110°$, $g = 47°$ **b** $j = 132.5°$, $k = 132.5°$
8 a $c = 85°$, $d = 120°$ **b** $l = 116°$, $m = 64°$, $n = 64°$
9 a $a = 60°$ **b** $b = 25°$ **c** $c = 35°$ **d** $d = 42°$
10 The eight angles at vertices ABCD are equal.
   The other two angles at point E are equal.

What do you think?

1 Yes, a square is a type of rectangle.

Consolidate

1 **a** Any six-sided shape where all the sides are straight and enclosed.
  b Any five-sided shape where all the sides are straight and enclosed.

2 **a** Example answer: **b** Example answer:

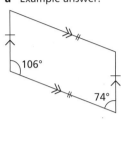 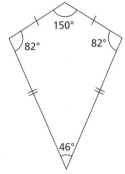

3 **a** $x = 44°$ **b** $a = 118°$ **c** $b = 27°$ **d** $y = 90.5°$

Stretch

1 $a = 28$
2 **a** $y = 17$ **b** PQR $= 50°$

Chapter 3.4

Are you ready? (A)

1 180°
2 360°
3 **a** 5   **b** 8   **c** 9

Practice (A)

1

Polygon	No. of triangles	Sum of the interior angles
Triangle	1	1 × 180 = 180°
Quadrilateral	2	2 × 180 = 360°
Pentagon	3	3 × 180 = 540°
Hexagon	4	**720°**
Heptagon	5	**900°**
Octagon	6	**1080°**
Nonagon	7	**1260°**
Decagon	8	**1440°**
Hendecagon	9	**1620°**
Dodecagon	10	**1800°**
n-sided polygon	$n-2$	$(n-2) \times 180°$

2 Method A
3 **a** $p = 77°$ **b** $q = 279°$ **c** $r = 58°$ **d** $s = 98°$
4 **a** 120°   **b** 128.57°   **c** 135°   **d** 144°
5 Kath. Jakub didn't do $(n - 2) \times 180°$
6 15
7 102°
8 45°
9 36°

What do you think? (A)

1 No. A regular quadrilateral has an interior angle of 90° and a regular pentagon has an interior angle of 108°, so there isn't a polygon with a number of sides in-between.

Are you ready? (B)

1 180°
2 360°
3 117°
4 122°

Practice (B)

1

Polygon	One exterior angle
Triangle	360° ÷ 3 = 120°
Quadrilateral	**90°**
Pentagon	**72°**
Hexagon	**60°**
Heptagon	**51.43°**
Octagon	**45°**
Nonagon	**40°**
Decagon	**36°**
Hendecagon	**32.73°**
Dodecagon	**30°**
n-sided polygon	**360° ÷ n**

2 **a** 72°   **b** 60°
3 **a** $a = 88°$, $b = 101°$ **b** $c = 78°$, $d = 90°$
4

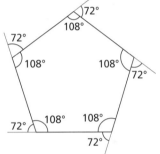

72° + 72° + 72° + 72° + 72° = 360°
5 41° each
6 100°, 115° and 145°
7 16

What do you think? (B)

1 No. 360° ÷ 85° = 4.235...
The answer needs to be an integer as it represents the number of sides.

Consolidate

1 **a** 720°   **b** 1260°   **c** 1440°
2 **a** 90°   **b** 135°   **c** 150°
3 **a** 120°   **b** 90°   **c** 72°
4 **a** $a = 134°$, $b = 46°$ **b** $c = 76°$, $d = 93°$

Stretch

1 10 sides

Shapes and angles: exam practice

1 **a** Obtuse   **b** Reflex
  c Right angle   **d** Acute
2 37°
  Vertically opposite angles are equal.
3 65°
  Alternate angles are equal, and angles on a straight line sum to 180°.
  Or Corresponding angles are equal, and angles on a straight line sum to 180°.
4 **a** A reflex angle   **b** 275°
5 144°

Block 4 Congruence and similarity

Chapter 4.1

Are you ready?

1 Same: they are identical square shapes.
   B has a different orientation
   C has side length in different units (50 mm = 5 cm)
2 Same rectangle but different orientation
3 Yes, all interior angles of a triangle will sum to 180°.

Practice

1 **a** Yes   **b** Yes   **c** No
2 C and D
3 Example answer:

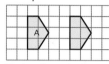

4 Zach – there isn't any information about whether the sides are the same lengths.
5 **a** Yes   **b** No   **c** Yes
6 **a** 65°   **b** 6 cm   **c** 50°

What do you think?

1 The rectangles are congruent if the single and double hatch marks represent the same values in both diagrams. The rectangles could be non-congruent if the hatch marks in one diagram represent different values to those in the other.

Consolidate

1 **a** No   **b** Yes   **c** Yes
2 A, E, F and H are congruent.
   B, C and G are congruent.
3 **a** Yes
   b Not enough information (about the side lengths)
   c Yes

Stretch

1 1 : 1
2

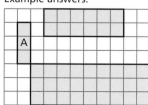

Chapter 4.2

Are you ready?

1 **a** 5   **b** 5
2 **a** 2 : 1   **b** 3 : 2
3 WX or YZ

Practice

1 Example answers:

2 B, C and E
3 **a i** 7 : 21 (or 1 : 3)   **ii** 3
   b i 20 : 8 (or 5 : 2)   **ii** 2.5
4 Example answers: 12 cm and 8 cm; 18 cm and 12 cm;
   9 cm and 6 cm
5 **a** Similar   **i** 1 : 3   **ii** 3
   b Not similar
   c Not similar
   d Similar   **i** 1 : 2   **ii** 2
6 B and E
7 No. Shapes can be rotated and still be similar. The rotation doesn't change the shape's dimensions or angles.
8 **a i** 1.5   **ii** $a = 8, b = 6$ **iii** $x = 105°$
   b i 3   **ii** $p = 5$ **iii** $x = 90°$
   c i 2   **ii** $y = 18, z = 10.4$ **iii** $x = 55°$
   d i 2.5   **ii** $r = 30$

What do you think?

1 To ensure the picture remains in the same proportion

Consolidate

1 Example answers:
   Scale factor 4 gives a 12 cm by 20 cm rectangle
   Scale factor 2.5 gives a 7.5 cm by 12.5 cm rectangle
   Scale factor 3 gives a 9 cm by 15 cm rectangle
2 B, D and E
3 **a i** 2   **ii** $a = 5$ **iii** $x = 85°$
   b i 3   **ii** $b = 15$
   c i 2   **ii** $y = 18$ **iii** $z = 5$

Stretch

1 No. The perimeter will be doubled, but the area will be quadrupled.
2 16 cm

Chapter 4.3

Are you ready?

1 **a** Isosceles   **b** Isosceles   **c** Scalene
   d Isosceles   **e** Equilateral
2 **a** Congruent   **b** Neither   **c** Similar
3 **a** DE   **b** Angle ABC
4 Side, Side, Side (SSS), or
   Angle, Side, Angle (ASA), or
   Side, Angle, Side (SAS)

Practice

1 **a** SAS   **b** ASA   **c** RHS   **d** SSS
2 **a** Congruent, SSS   **b** Congruent, SAS
   c Not congruent   **d** Congruent, RHS
   e Congruent, SAS   **f** Congruent, SSS
3 A and C, SAS
4 Yes, ASA
5 Yes, ASA
6 Yes

What do you think?

1 SAS or ASA

Consolidate

1 **a** SSS   **b** SAS   **c** ASA
   d RHS   **e** ASA   **f** SAS
   g SSS   **h** SAS   **i** ASA
2 **a** Congruent, RHS
   b Congruent, SAS
   c Congruent, ASA (or AAS)

Stretch

1 $x = 3$, $y = 5$
2 $\angle BCD = \angle AEB$ because alternate angles are equal.
$\angle ABE = \angle CBD$ because vertically opposite angles are equal.
BC = BE
The triangles are congruent using the condition ASA.

3

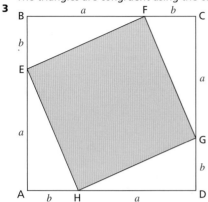

If AE = a and AH = b, it follows that the side length of ABCD is $a + b$.
The triangles are all congruent using the conditions SSS or RHS.

4 A and B

Chapter 4.4

Are you ready?

1 No
2 $a = 16$, $b = 2.25$
3 a FG   **b** FGH   **c** $\frac{1}{2}$

Practice

1

Side/angle in ABC	Corresponding side/angle in DEF
AB	EF
BC	DE
AC	DF
$\angle ABC$	$\angle DEF$
$\angle ACB$	$\angle EDF$
$\angle BAC$	$\angle EFD$

2 AC = 18 cm, QR = 55 cm
3 $a = 4.5$, $b = 36$
4 Amir. Emily multiplied by the scale factor when she should have divided.
5 $y = 3$
6 AE = 13.5 cm
7 CD
8 DE = 36 cm

What do you think?

1 A is true. B and C are not true.

Consolidate

1 ED = 3 cm, YZ = 14 cm
2 AC = 27 cm, DE = 14 cm
3 PR = 3 cm

Stretch

1 a EC = 20 cm   **b** BD = 3 cm
2

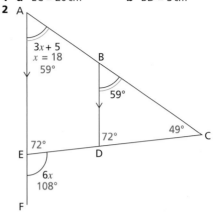

Congruence and similarity: exam practice

1 Example answer:

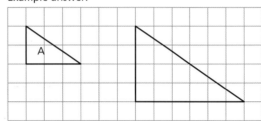

2 A and C
3 a 7.5 cm   **b** 8 cm
4 40°

Block 5 Transformations

Chapter 5.1

Are you ready? (A)

1 B and C
2 Shape A

Practice (A)

1 a

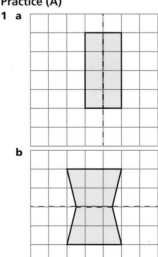

b

c

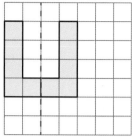

2 a

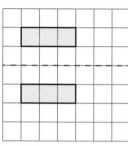

b

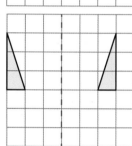

c

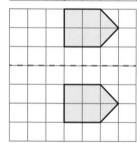

3 a C
b A and B: the shapes have been translated rather than reflected.
D: the shapes are not equidistant from the mirror line.

4 a

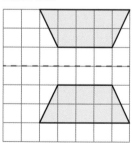

b

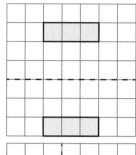

c

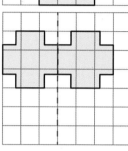

d

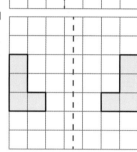

Are you ready? (B)
1 A = (2, 3)   B = (0, 4)   C = (–2, 1)   D = (3, –2)
2 a A and D   **b** B   **c** A   **d** $x = -4$

Practice (B)
1 a

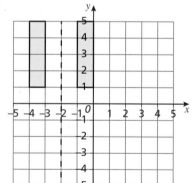

b

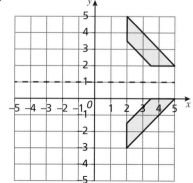

c

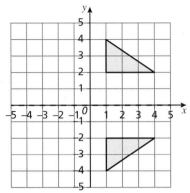

2 Reflection A is correct.
3 Reflection B: mirror line is $x = 1$ and the shape has been translated
Reflection C: mirror line is $y = 0$
4 a $x = 1$ **b** $x = 0$ (or y-axis)   **c** $y = 0.5$

What do you think? (B)

1 The mirror line goes through the shape/object and the image will overlap.

Are you ready? (C)

1 Table completed from the left: 1, 2, 3, 4, 5
2 (3, 3)   (–6, –6)   (1.5, 1.5)
3 (7, –7)   (1, –1)   (4.5, –4.5)

Practice (C)

1 a

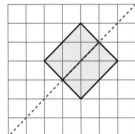

b

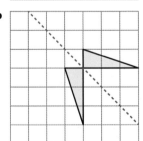

c

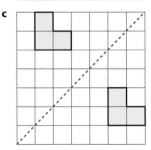

2 a

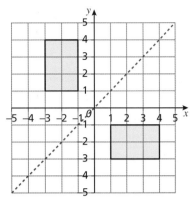

b

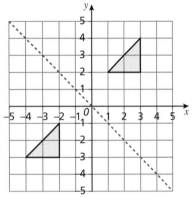

3 a The orientation should have changed. The points are not equidistant from the mirror line.

b

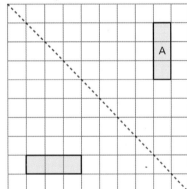

What do you think? (C)

1 Yes, the points will end up at the same coordinates.

Consolidate

1 a

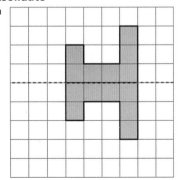

b

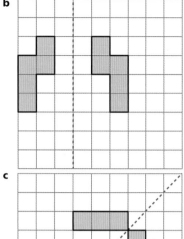

c

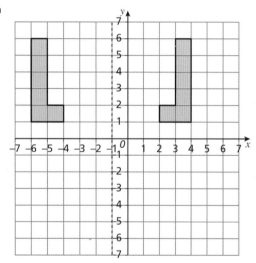

2 a

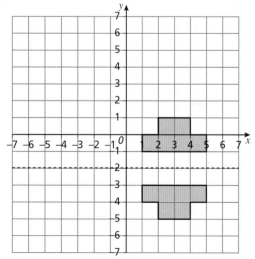

b

c

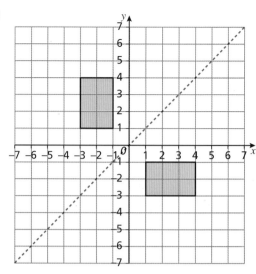

3 a $y = -1$ **b** $x = 0$ (or y-axis)   **c** $y = -x$

Stretch

1 a (3, 6)   **b** (3, 2) (4, −2) (8, 2) (7, −2)

Chapter 5.2

Are you ready?

1 A = (3, 5)   B = (0, 4)   C = (−2, −1)   D = (3, −2)
2 The rectangle has to be exactly the same.
3 a clockwise   **b** anticlockwise
4 a 90°   **b** 180°   **c** 360°

Practice

1 a

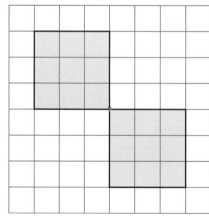

b

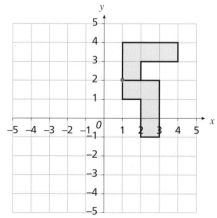

c

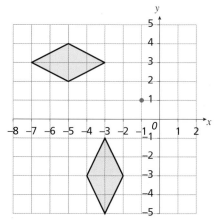

2 a

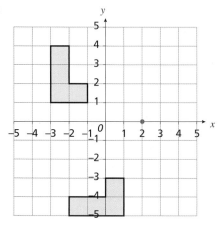

b

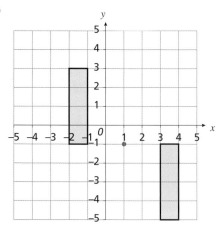

c

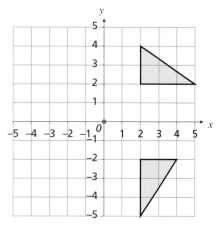

3 B

4 a Rotation, 90° anticlockwise or 270° clockwise, centre of rotation (0, –2)

b Rotation, 180°, centre of rotation (–6, –4)

What do you think?

1 270° anticlockwise

Consolidate

1

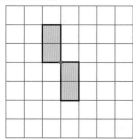

2

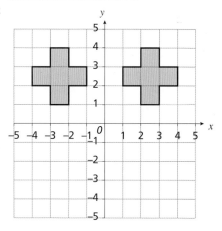

3

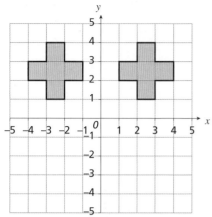

4 The rotations end up in the same position on the axes. 90° clockwise is the same rotation as 270° anticlockwise – only the direction is different.

5 Rotated trapezium should have vertices at (–3, 9), (–2, 7), (2, 9), (1, 7)

6 a Rotation, 90° clockwise or 270° anticlockwise, centre of rotation (0, 0)

b Rotation, 90° anticlockwise or 270° clockwise, centre of rotation (–5, –2)

Stretch

1 a & b

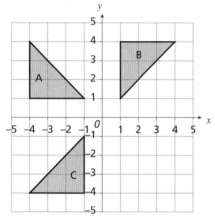

c Rotation, 90° anticlockwise or 270° clockwise, centre of rotation (0, 0)

2 a (–7, 2), (–7, 4), (–3, 2), (–3, 4)

b Rotation, 90° anticlockwise or 270° clockwise, centre of rotation (–2, –2)

Chapter 5.3

Are you ready?

1 A = (2, 2)   B = (–4, 4)   C = (–2, –2)   D = (0, –4)

2 (2, –5)

3 a 6 squares left, 2 squares up

b 6 squares right, 2 squares down

c 2 squares right, 2 squares down

Practice

1 B

2 a

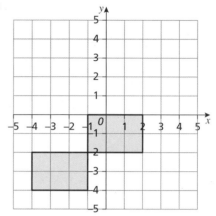

b

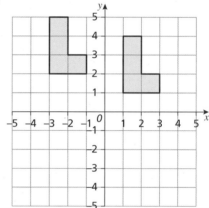

c

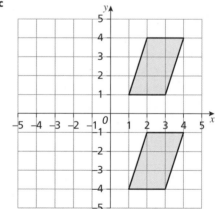

3 a Translation by $\begin{pmatrix} 5 \\ 3 \end{pmatrix}$ **b** Translation by $\begin{pmatrix} 6 \\ 0 \end{pmatrix}$

c Translation by $\begin{pmatrix} -5 \\ 3 \end{pmatrix}$

4 Translation by $\begin{pmatrix} 2 \\ -2 \end{pmatrix}$

5 Junaid: the bottom number should be –5
Tiff: has translated shape B to A
6 B and F; A, G, and E
Examples of other transformations:
A and F – reflection; G and D – enlargement

What do you think?

1 It could be any. Translation $\begin{pmatrix} 9 \\ 0 \end{pmatrix}$ or reflection in the
mirror line $x = 1$ or 90° clockwise rotation about (1, –1).

Consolidate

1 a

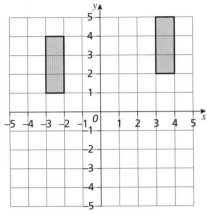

b

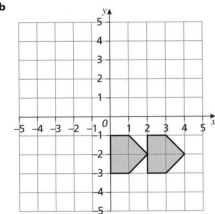

c

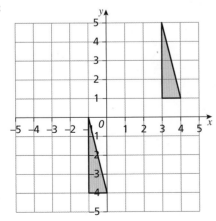

2 a Translation by $\begin{pmatrix} -6 \\ 1 \end{pmatrix}$ **b** Translation by $\begin{pmatrix} 6 \\ 6 \end{pmatrix}$

c Translation by $\begin{pmatrix} 0 \\ -6 \end{pmatrix}$

Stretch

1 (19, 3) (8, –2) (30, –2)
2 A to B: disagree; it could be a reflection, but in the
line $y = 1$
C to D: disagree; the corresponding vertices of the
shapes are not equidistant from the mirror line.

Chapter 5.4

Are you ready? (A)

1 a 3   **b** 12   **c** 4
2 Yes

Practice (A)

1 *Enlargements can be placed anywhere on the grid.*

a

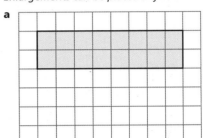

b

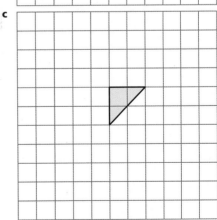

c

2 a 2   **b** $\frac{1}{2}$ **c** 1.5
3 a The horizontal edge should be 6 squares and the
vertical edge should be 12 squares.

b The shape has been enlarged by $\frac{1}{4}$

c The vertical edge should be 24 squares.

What do you think? (A)

1 Yes, but it would stay the same size.

Are you ready? (B)

1 a (2, −2)   **b** (−4, 2)

c

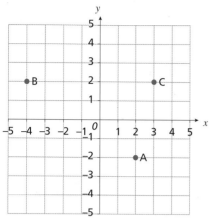

d (0, 0)

Practice (B)

1 a i

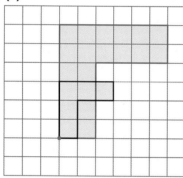

ii

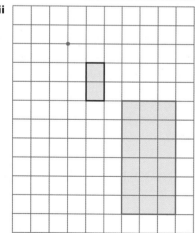

iii

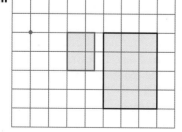

b Enlargements **i** and **ii** made the shape larger.
Enlargement **iii** made it smaller.

2 a

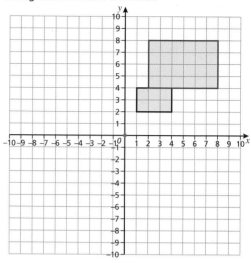

b

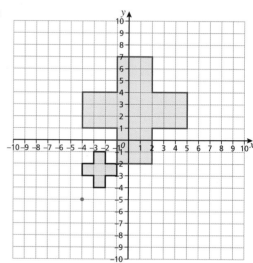

c

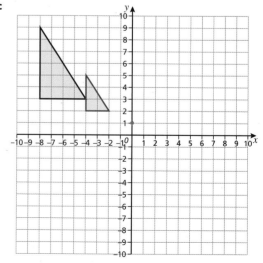

3 a Enlargement, scale factor 2, centre of enlargement (0, 0)
 b Enlargement, scale factor $\frac{1}{3}$, centre of enlargement (–4, 4)
 c Enlargement, scale factor 2, centre of enlargement (–5, –5)

What do you think? (B)

1 Yes, student's own example.

Consolidate

1 *Enlargements can be placed anywhere on the grid.*

a

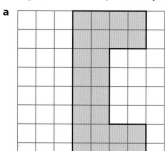

b

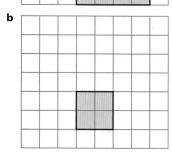

2 a 2   **b** $\frac{1}{2}$

3 a

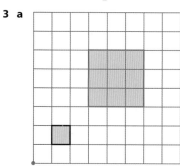

b

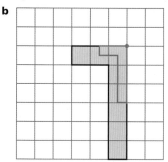

4 a

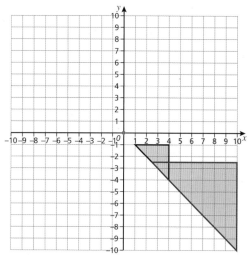

b

5 a Enlargement, scale factor 1.5, centre of enlargement (–4, –4)
 b Enlargement, scale factor 2, centre of enlargement (3, –4)

Stretch

1 a

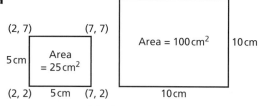

(2, 7)   (7, 7)

5 cm   Area = 25 cm²

(2, 2)   5 cm   (7, 2)

Area = 100 cm²   10 cm

10 cm

25 × 2 ≠ 100

b 25 : 100 = 1 : 4

2 (–7, –5) (5, –5), (–7, 7)
 The centre of enlargement is the vertex of the triangle where the horizontal and vertical sides meet. Use the coordinates to work out that these sides are both 4 units long. So the coordinates of the enlargement are (–7, –5), (–7 + 12, –5) and (–7, –5 + 12).

Transformations: exam practice

1

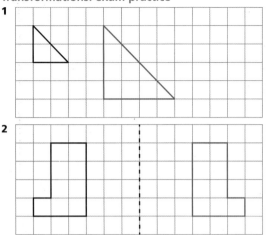

2

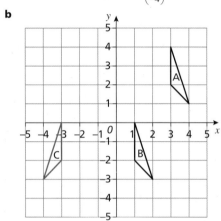

3 a A translation by 2 squares left and 4 squares down

Or a translation by vector $\begin{pmatrix} -2 \\ -4 \end{pmatrix}$

b

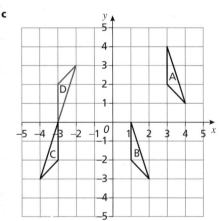

c

Block 6 Area and perimeter

Chapter 6.1

Are you ready? (A)

1 a square   **b** parallelogram   **c** rectangle
   d triangle   **e** trapezium

2 a 8   **b** 9   **c** 17.5

3 C

Practice (A)

1 a 15 cm²   **b** 20 cm²   **c** 14 m²
   d 81 m²   **e** 200 cm² or 0.02 m²

2 a 12 m   **b** 6 cm

3 a 8 cm²   **b** 24 m²   **c** 24 m²
   d 55 cm²   **e** 400 mm² or 4 cm²

4 a 6 m   **b** 6 cm

5 a 7.5 cm²   **b** 8 cm²   **c** 21 cm²   **d** 36 mm²
   e 10 m²   **f** 6 cm²   **g** 60 ft²   **h** $\frac{1}{15}$ cm²
   i 15 cm² or 0.0015 m²

6 a 6 cm   **b** 10 m

7 a 12 cm²   **b** 35 cm²   **c** 148.5 mm²
   d 28 m²   **e** 1.5 m² or 15 000 cm²

8 a 5 m   **b** 24 cm

9 a All the sides have been multiplied.
   b The units haven't been converted.
   c The area hasn't been divided by 2.

10 No, he hasn't used the perpendicular height.

11 £35.96

12 8 cows

What do you think? (A)

1 Area is the space inside a 2D shape.
Perimeter is the total distance around.

Are you ready? (B)

1 a 19   **b** 4.76

2 Shapes A and C; all sides and angles are equal.

3 Equilateral, isosceles, scalene and right-angled (can be isosceles or scalene)

Practice (B)

1 a 20 m   **b** 17 cm   **c** 13.37 ft

2 a 15 cm   **b** 32 ft   **c** 24 m

3 a 40 cm   **b** 7.5 m   **c** 18 m

4 B
A: the numerical value of the area has been calculated
C: only two of the sides have been added

5 No, he doesn't have enough money; it will cost £593.73

What do you think? (B)

1 Area – the question will use vocabulary to indicate it is referring to the inside of the shape (e.g. 'lay', 'cover') and the units will have the power of 2.
Perimeter – the question will use vocabulary to indicate it is referring to the outer edge of the shape (e.g. 'distance', 'around') and the units will have power 1.

Consolidate

1 a 25 cm²   **b** 15 cm²   **c** 10 cm²   **d** 12 cm²

2 a 15 m²   **b** 6.25 ft²   **c** 33 m²   **d** 45 cm²
   e 52.5 cm²   **f** 52 cm²   **g** 20 ft²   **h** 19.5 m²

3 a 16 cm   **b** 31 cm   **c** 18 m
   d 32 mm   **e** 26 cm

Stretch

1 200 tiles

2 $x = 5$

Chapter 6.2

Are you ready? (A)

1 a

circumference | diameter | radius | centre

b

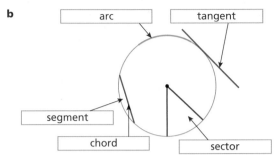

arc   tangent

segment

chord   sector

Practice (A)

1 a Radius   **b** Diameter   **c** Chord
   d Tangent   **e** Sector
2 The line doesn't touch the circumference twice.
3 Only when they are formed using a diameter

What do you think?

1 Yes, a diameter is a chord that runs through the centre of a circle. It is the longest possible chord of any circle.

Are you ready? (B)

1 A. The line goes from the centre to the circumference.
2 B. The line goes from one part of the circumference to the other, passing through the centre.
3 a 3.14   **b** 3

Practice (B)

1 a $9\pi\,cm^2$ **b** $16\pi\,m^2$ **c** $6.25\pi\,ft^2$
2 a $50.27\,m^2$ **b** $63.62\,cm^2$ **c** $38.48\,cm^2$
3 a $3\pi\,mm$ **b** $8\pi\,ft$ **c** $9\pi\,cm$
4 a $15.71\,m$ **b** $17.28\,cm$ **c** $75.40\,cm$
5 a Radius = 7 cm   Diameter = 14 cm
   b Radius = 10 cm   Diameter = 20 cm
6 a Radius = 6.91 m   **b** Radius = 43.8 cm
7 She hasn't used the radius.
8 30.70 cm

Consolidate

1 a Area = $64\pi\,m^2$ Circumference = $16\pi\,m$
   b Area = $100\pi\,cm^2$ Circumference = $20\pi\,cm$
2 a Area = $86.6\,cm^2$ Circumference = 33.0 cm
   b Area = $1.77\,mm^2$ Circumference = 4.71 mm
3 a Radius = 8 cm   Diameter = 16 cm
   b Radius = 18.5 cm   Diameter = 37 cm
4 a Radius = 4.41 ft   Diameter = 8.81 ft
   b Radius = 19.42 m   Diameter = 38.83 m

Stretch

1 10.6 cm
2 79%
3 318

Chapter 6.3

Are you ready? (A)

1 Clockwise from top left: chord; radius; sector; segment
2 a $\frac{1}{2}$ **b** $\frac{1}{4}$ **c** $\frac{3}{4}$ **d** $\frac{120}{360} = \frac{1}{3}$
3 Area = πr^2

Practice (A)

1 a $4\pi\,m^2$ **b** $12.5\pi\,cm^2$ **c** $\frac{3}{16}\pi\,m^2$
2 a $8.0\,ft^2$ **b** $11.9\,cm^2$ **c** $6.9\,m^2$
3 a $10.5\,cm^2$ **b** $139\,mm^2$ **c** $157\,ft^2$
4 10 cm
5 5.4 cm
6 137.5°

Are you ready? (B)

1 Clockwise from top left: circumference; diameter; sector
2 a $\frac{1}{2}$ **b** $\frac{300}{360} = \frac{5}{6}$ **c** $\frac{45}{360} = \frac{1}{8}$
3 $C = \pi d$

Practice (B)

1 a $2\pi\,m$ **b** $5\pi\,cm$ **c** $0.75\pi\,m$
2 a 5.0 ft   **b** 10.6 cm   **c** 6.6 m
3 a 10.5 cm   **b** 13.2 mm   **c** 33.9 ft
4 40 cm
5 74.5 cm
6 267.4°

Consolidate

1 a Area = $\frac{121}{4}\pi\,m^2$ Arc = $\frac{11}{2}\pi\,m$
   b Area = $\frac{289}{8}\pi\,m^2$ Arc = $\frac{17}{2}\pi\,m$
2 a Area = $129.03\,mm^2$ Arc = 34.87 mm
   b Area = $192.68\,cm^2$ Arc = 48.17 cm
3 a Radius = 16 cm   Diameter = 32 cm
   b Radius = 32.7 cm   Diameter = 65.5 cm
4 a 169.5°   **b** 112.1°

Stretch

1 27.44 cm
2 $\frac{81}{8}\pi\,cm^2$
3 44.9 cm

Chapter 6.4

Are you ready? (A)

1 a $24\,cm^2$ **b** $40\,m^2$ **c** $27\,cm^2$
2 a 14 cm   **b** 29 mm
3 11 m

Practice (A)

1 a $62\,cm^2$ **b** $100\,m^2$ **c** $112\,mm^2$ **d** $72\,cm^2$
2 a 38 cm   **b** 46 m   **c** 46 mm   **d** 46 cm
3 a $92\,cm^2$ **b** $84\,cm^2$
4 a $75\,m^2$ **b** $40\,cm^2$
5 46
6 He hasn't changed the length of the sides when the shapes have been split up.

What do you think? (A)

1 Yes – same perpendicular height and base
   $12 \times 4 = 48\,cm^2$
   $2(6 \times 4) = 48\,cm^2$

Are you ready? (B)

1 a $25\,cm^2$ **b** $49\pi\,cm^2$ **c** $12.5\pi\,cm^2$
2 a 20.2 cm   **b** $14\pi\,cm$ **c** 25.7 cm

Practice (B)

1 a $99.5\,cm^2$ **b** $72\,m^2$ **c** $140\,mm^2$
2 a $96.24\,m^2$ **b** $146.55\,cm^2$
3 $85.8\,cm^2$
4 Lida's method is more efficient
5 £62.93

What do you think? (B)

1 rectangle + triangle   trapezium + triangle
   rectangle + rectangle + triangle
   full rectangle – trapezium
   full rectangle – (rectangle + triangle)

Consolidate

1 a $93\,m^2$ **b** $75\,ft^2$ **c** $120\,cm^2$
   d $160\,cm^2$ **e** $96\,mm^2$ **f** $120.75\,cm^2$
   g $261.37\,m^2$ **h** $144.62\,cm^2$

2 a 46 m   **b** 42 ft   **c** 51 cm
  d Not enough information   **e** 49.9 m
  f 50.9 cm   **g** 63.4 m   **h** 46.3 cm

Stretch

1 37.5%
2 Various possible answers, e.g. an 'L' shape with sides of 10 cm, 8 cm, 15 cm, 7 cm, 25 cm and 15 cm
3 a $(14y + 14)$ cm   **b** $y = 3$

Area and perimeter: exam practice

1 a 20 cm^2 **b** 20 cm
2 12 cm^2
3 44 mm
4 a 21.99 ft   **b** 38.48 ft^2
5 £99 000
6 83.78 cm^2

Block 7 3D shapes

Chapter 7.1

Are you ready?

1 a 21 cm^2 **b** 40 mm^2
2 a Cube   **b** Cuboid   **c** Triangular prism
3 A, C and D

Practice

1 a 60 cm^3 **b** 27 cm^3 **c** 56 cm^3
2 a 192 cm^3 **b** 198 mm^3
  c 125 cm^3 **d** 12 m^3 or 12 000 000 cm^3
3 a 168 ft^3 **b** 75 mm^3 **c** 96 cm^3
4 a 520 cm^3 **b** 8 m^3 **c** 140 cm^3
5 a 520 mm^3 **b** 2640 cm^3
6 a 5   **b** 9   **c** 10   **d** 2
7 320
8 10 minutes

What do you think?

1 All options will give the correct answer because multiplication is commutative.

Consolidate

1 a 702 cm^3 **b** 512 cm^3
  c 144 ft^3 **d** 210 mm^3
2 a 245 ft^3 **b** 1138.5 mm^3 **c** 720 cm^3
3 130 ft^3
4 a 4   **b** 9

Stretch

1 14
2 16 000
3 3 hours 45 minutes
4 2.5 cm

Chapter 7.2

Are you ready?

1 a 78.5 mm^2 **b** 50.3 cm^2 **c** 56.5 cm^2
2 a $a = 3$ cm   **b** $b = 3.75$ cm
3 a 12   **b** 16   **c** 80   **d** 4

Practice

1

Radius (cm)	Diameter (cm)	Height (cm)	Volume (cm^3)
3	6	12	**339.3**
5	10	18	**1413.7**
7	**14**	2.3	360
2.5	**5.0**	20	400
8.5	17	**3.3**	750
3.6	**7.1**	25	1000

2 a i 48π cm^3 **ii** 150.80 cm^3
  b i 900π m^3 **ii** 2827.43 m^3
  c i 270π cm^3 **ii** 848.23 cm^3
  d i 245π cm^3 **ii** 769.69 cm^3
  e i 288π cm^3 **ii** 904.78 cm^3
  f i 4500π mm^3 **ii** 14 137.17 mm^3
3 a $h = 10$ cm   **b** $x = 5$ cm
  c $x = 24$ cm   **d** $x = 5$ cm
  e $x = 6$ m   **f** $y = 4$ m
4 a 288.6 m^3 **b** 261.8 mm^3
5 a 386 cm^3 **b** 3050 m^3
6 The diameter has been used in the calculations instead of the radius.
7 A football, because the radius would be around 23 cm.

What do you think?

1 Because its cross-section has curved sides.

Consolidate

1 a 90π m^3 **b** 480 000π cm^3, 0.48π m^3
  c 84π cm^3 **d** $\frac{3179}{3}\pi$ mm^3
  e 36π cm^3 **f** 972π mm^3
2 a 160 cm^3 **b** 390 000 cm^3, 0.39 m^3
  c 150 cm^3 **d** 1200 mm^3
  e 1400 cm^3 **f** 270 m^3

Stretch

1 163.5 cm^3
2 4.96 cm
3 48 cm
4 12 862.8 cm^3

Chapter 7.3

Are you ready?

1 Cuboid: faces = 6, edges = 12, vertices = 8
  Triangular prism: faces = 5, edges = 9, vertices = 6
2 a Cuboid
  b Triangular prism
  c Triangular-based pyramid, or tetrahedron
  d Square-based pyramid
3 a 20 cm^2 **b** 30 cm^2 **c** 25 cm^2
  d 30 cm^2 **e** 153.94 cm^2 **f** 39.27 cm^2

Practice

1 a 132 cm^2
  b 38 m^2, 380 000 cm^2
2 a 1240 cm^2 **b** 1831.2 cm^2
3 a 402.1 cm^2 **b** 747.7 cm^2
4 a 203 cm^2 **b** 376 m^2
5 615.75 cm^2
6 339.7 cm^2
7 9 m
8 216 cm^2
9 £2.40

What do you think?

1 You can make 11 different nets.

Consolidate

1 a 100 cm^2 **b** 100 cm^2 **c** 200 ft^2
2 Cube
3 $a = 2$

Stretch

1 31%
2 $6y^2 + 32y$

Chapter 7.4

Are you ready?

1 a 6 faces, 12 edges, 8 vertices
  b 7 faces, 15 edges, 10 vertices
  c 2 faces, 1 edge, 1 vertex
  d 5 faces, 9 edges, 6 vertices

2 a Four triangles, one square
 b Two triangles, three rectangles
 c Two compound shapes (rectangles), six rectangles
 d Six rectangles

Practice

1 a

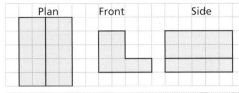

 b

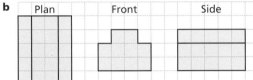

 c

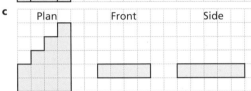

2 a

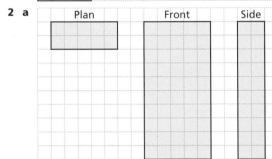

 b

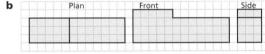

 c

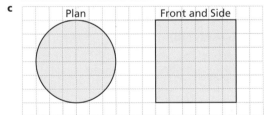

3 a Cuboid   **b** Cylinder   **c** Square-based pyramid

4

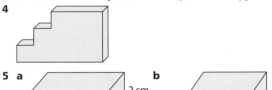

5 a **b**

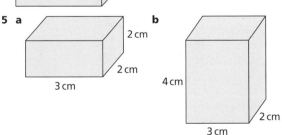

6 a Sketch of a cylinder
 b Sketch of a square-based pyramid

What do you think?

1 No – the shape could be another 3D shape. A cylinder has rectangles for its front elevation and side elevation and a circle for its plan view.

Consolidate

1

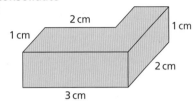

2 Sketch of a triangular prism

3

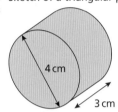

4 a

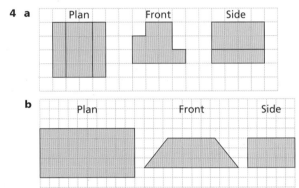

 b

Stretch

1

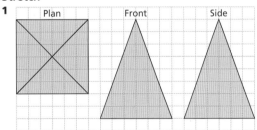

3D shapes: exam practice

1 a Cuboid   **b** Cylinder
2 a 6   **b** 12   **c** 8
3

4 8000 m²
5 a 216 cm³   **b** 264 cm²

Block 8 Right-angled triangles

Chapter 8.1

Are you ready? (A)

1 B
2 41
3 12
4 15

Practice (A)

1 a 5 cm   **b** 14.42 mm   **c** 9.49 m   **d** 10.05 cm
2 a AB   **b** XZ   **c** IJ   **d** PR
3 In all parts, the hypotenuse should be labelled on the side opposite the right angle.
4 a Right angle marked between the 4 m and 7 m sides.
   b Right angle marked between the 12 cm and 5 cm sides.
   c Right angle marked between the 15 mm and 4 mm sides.

What do you think?

1 B: 90 cm because it is greater than the other two sides, and the hypotenuse is the longest side.

Are you ready? (B)

1 64
2 85
3 11
4 13

Practice (B)

1 a 13 cm   **b** 5 mm   **c** 25 m
   d 37 cm   **e** 45 mm   **f** 85 cm
2 a 3.9 cm   **b** 5.5 mm   **c** 6.9 m
   d 8.6 cm   **e** 10.6 cm   **f** 12.1 m
3 3.75 m
4 8 cm
5 a 49 + 64 is not equal to 81, so no
   b $400 + 441 = 841 = 29^2$, so yes
   c $0.25 + 1.44 = 1.69 = 1.3^2$, so yes

Are you ready? (C)

1 9.43 cm
2 12.5 cm
3 24

Practice (C)

1 a 23.3 cm   **b** 2.75 m   **c** 11.9 mm
2 a 8.53 cm   **b** 8 mm   **c** 50 m
   d 0.82 m   **e** 5.06 m   **f** 12.7 cm
   g 600 mm   **h** 0.779 m   **i** 10.5 cm
3 6 cm
4 245 km

Consolidate

1 a 4.9 cm   **b** 4.7 mm   **c** 9 m   **d** 10.7 cm
2 a $7^2 + 24^2 = 25^2$ **b** $9^2 + 40^2 = 41^2$ **c** $11^2 + 60^2 = 61^2$
3 a 37 cm   **b** 85 mm   **c** 65 m
4 a 21 cm   **b** 28 mm   **c** 56 m

Stretch

1 28 cm
2 22.67 cm or 22.7 cm (to 1 d.p.)
3 $24^2 + 32^2 = 40^2$

Chapter 8.2

Are you ready? (A)

1 AC
2 40°
3 8

Practice (A)

1 a

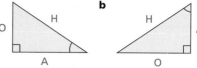

   b

c

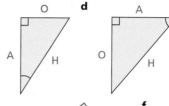

   d

e

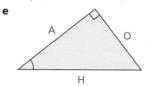

   f

2 a adj XZ   **b** adj PQ   **c** adj JK
3 a opp YZ   **b** opp PR   **c** opp KL
4 a

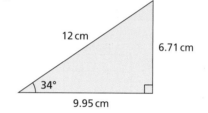

b

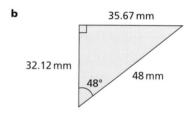

What do you think?

1 Adjacent side (between the right angle and the 60° angle) labelled as 100 m.

Are you ready? (B)

1 a

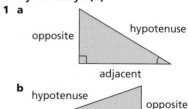

b

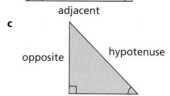

c

Practice (B)

1 a sin   **b** tan   **c** sin
  d cos   **e** tan   **f** cos
2 a cos   **b** sin   **c** tan
  d tan   **e** sin   **f** tan
3 Any three right-angled triangles with correct labels on the hypotenuse and the side opposite the angle.
4 Any three right-angled triangles with correct labels on the hypotenuse and the side adjacent the angle.
5 Any three right-angled triangles with correct labels on the sides adjacent and opposite the angle.

Are you ready? (C)

1 a tan   **b** sin   **c** cos
2 a cos   **b** tan   **c** sin

Practice (C)

1 a 8.6 cm   **b** 13.4 mm   **c** 7.8 m
2 a 10.1 cm   **b** 1.6 m   **c** 44.0 mm
3 a 8.3 cm   **b** 6.2 m   **c** 11.0 mm
4 a 25.4°   **b** 16.1°   **c** 53.1°
5 a 62.2°   **b** 72.5°   **c** 48.2°
6 a 43.2°   **b** 71.6°   **c** 20.6°
7 a 17.0 cm   **b** 5.4 cm   **c** 17.2 cm
  d 15.3 mm   **e** 0.3 m   **f** 5.2 mm
8 a 65.4°   **b** 39.5°   **c** 77.5°
  d 32.0°   **e** 6.4°   **f** 71.6°

Consolidate

1 a 6.9 cm   **b** 13.9 m   **c** 11.5 cm
  d 10.6 m   **e** 8.5 units   **f** 9 km
  g 10 cm   **h** 12.5 mm   **i** 6 cm
2 a 53.1°   **b** 28.7°   **c** 53.1°
  d 30.0°   **e** 35.0°   **f** 58.6°
  g 50.2°   **h** 36.9°   **i** 50.2°

Stretch

1 Unknown angles 53.13° and 36.87°
2 Unknown angles 36.87° and 53.13°
3 Hypotenuse is 11.31 cm. Both methods give the same result and students will have their own preferences for method.

Chapter 8.3

Are you ready? (A)

1 24 mm
2 20 mm

3 a $1\frac{1}{3}$ **b** $\frac{1}{3}$

Practice (A)

1 $\sin 30° = \frac{1}{2}$, $\cos 30° = \frac{\sqrt{3}}{2}$, $\tan 30° = \frac{\sqrt{3}}{3}$

2 $\sin 60° = \frac{\sqrt{3}}{2}$, $\cos 60° = \frac{1}{2}$, $\tan 60° = \sqrt{3}$

3

	0°	30°	45°	60°	90°
sin	0	$\frac{1}{2}$	$\frac{\sqrt{2}}{2}$	$\frac{\sqrt{3}}{2}$	1
cos	1	$\frac{\sqrt{3}}{2}$	$\frac{\sqrt{2}}{2}$	$\frac{1}{2}$	0
tan	0	$\frac{\sqrt{3}}{3}$	1	$\sqrt{3}$	Undefined

4 a 1   **b** 1   **c** 0   **d** $\frac{\sqrt{2}}{2}$
  e $\frac{1}{2}$ **f** 0   **g** $3\frac{1}{2}$ **h** 3

Are you ready? (B)

1 Table completed as in Practice (A), question 3.

Practice (B)

1 a 8 mm   **b** 4 m   **c** 10 cm
  d 7 cm   **e** 8 m   **f** $\frac{\sqrt{3}}{3}$ m
2 a 60°   **b** 60°   **c** 30°
  d 45°   **e** 30°   **f** 60°

Consolidate

1 a 6 cm   **b** 10 mm   **c** 8 m
  d 12 cm   **e** 10 m   **f** $\frac{\sqrt{3}}{6}$ cm
2 a 60°   **b** 30°   **c** 30°
  d 45°   **e** 60°   **f** 60°

Stretch

1

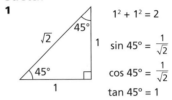

$1^2 + 1^2 = 2$

$\sin 45° = \frac{1}{\sqrt{2}}$

$\cos 45° = \frac{1}{\sqrt{2}}$

$\tan 45° = 1$

Right-angled triangles: exam practice

1 Example answer:

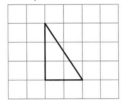

2 89 km
3 5 fence panels
4 $\frac{1}{2}$
5 7.05 cm

Block 9 Vectors

Chapter 9.1

Are you ready? (A)

1 a 5 right and 3 up   **b** 5 up   **c** 7 right

Practice (A)

1 a 6 right and 2 up   **b** 6 right and 2 down
  c 6 left and 2 up   **d** 6 left and 2 down
  The numbers are the same but the direction changes.

2 a $\begin{pmatrix} -9 \\ 5 \end{pmatrix}$ **b** $\begin{pmatrix} 9 \\ 5 \end{pmatrix}$ **c** $\begin{pmatrix} 9 \\ -5 \end{pmatrix}$ **d** $\begin{pmatrix} -9 \\ -5 \end{pmatrix}$
  The numbers are the same but the signs are different.

3 a 7 right and 3 up   **b** 12 right and 5 down
  c 16 left and 1 up   **d** 19 right and 19 down
  e 6 left and 3 down   **f** 1 right and 2 up
  g 8 left and 4 up   **h** 15 left and 19 down
  i 5 right   **j** 3 left
  k 12 up   **l** 1 down

4 a $\begin{pmatrix} 5 \\ -1 \end{pmatrix}$ **b** $\begin{pmatrix} -6 \\ -3 \end{pmatrix}$ **c** $\begin{pmatrix} 12 \\ 14 \end{pmatrix}$

  d $\begin{pmatrix} -16 \\ 4 \end{pmatrix}$ **e** $\begin{pmatrix} -1 \\ 5 \end{pmatrix}$ **f** $\begin{pmatrix} 9 \\ -11 \end{pmatrix}$

  g $\begin{pmatrix} 12 \\ 0 \end{pmatrix}$ **h** $\begin{pmatrix} -8 \\ 0 \end{pmatrix}$ **i** $\begin{pmatrix} 0 \\ -3 \end{pmatrix}$

5 a 7 right and 2 down   **b** $\begin{pmatrix} 7 \\ -2 \end{pmatrix}$

6 a i 3 right and 5 down   **ii** $\begin{pmatrix} 3 \\ -5 \end{pmatrix}$

   b i 3 left and 5 up   **ii** $\begin{pmatrix} -3 \\ 5 \end{pmatrix}$
The signs are reversed.

7 a i 5 right   **ii** $\begin{pmatrix} 5 \\ 0 \end{pmatrix}$

   b i 5 left   **ii** $\begin{pmatrix} -5 \\ 0 \end{pmatrix}$
The signs are reversed.

Are you ready? (B)

1 a

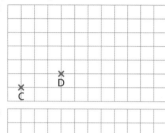

   b

Practice (B)

1 a $\begin{pmatrix} 3 \\ 4 \end{pmatrix}$ **b** $\begin{pmatrix} 5 \\ -1 \end{pmatrix}$ **c** $\begin{pmatrix} -5 \\ 2 \end{pmatrix}$

  d $\begin{pmatrix} -3 \\ -4 \end{pmatrix}$ **e** $\begin{pmatrix} 1 \\ 6 \end{pmatrix}$ **f** $\begin{pmatrix} 6 \\ 0 \end{pmatrix}$

  g $\begin{pmatrix} 0 \\ -3 \end{pmatrix}$ **h** $\begin{pmatrix} -2 \\ 0 \end{pmatrix}$ **i** $\begin{pmatrix} 0 \\ 7 \end{pmatrix}$

2

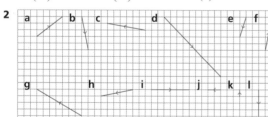

Consolidate

1 a 1 right and 8 up   **b** 2 right and 4 down
  c 10 left and 10 up   **d** 11 right and 9 down
  e 1 left and 6 down   **f** 3 right and 12 up
  g 15 left and 7 up   **h** 5 left and 9 down
  i 8 right   **j** 16 left
  k 14 up   **l** 10 down

2 a $\begin{pmatrix} 8 \\ -4 \end{pmatrix}$ **b** $\begin{pmatrix} -9 \\ -1 \end{pmatrix}$ **c** $\begin{pmatrix} 2 \\ 5 \end{pmatrix}$

  d $\begin{pmatrix} -6 \\ 1 \end{pmatrix}$ **e** $\begin{pmatrix} -5 \\ 9 \end{pmatrix}$ **f** $\begin{pmatrix} 2 \\ -1 \end{pmatrix}$

  g $\begin{pmatrix} 5 \\ 0 \end{pmatrix}$ **h** $\begin{pmatrix} -7 \\ 0 \end{pmatrix}$ **i** $\begin{pmatrix} 0 \\ 6 \end{pmatrix}$

3 a $\begin{pmatrix} -2 \\ -5 \end{pmatrix}$ **b** $\begin{pmatrix} 5 \\ 1 \end{pmatrix}$ **c** $\begin{pmatrix} 0 \\ -6 \end{pmatrix}$

  d $\begin{pmatrix} -6 \\ -4 \end{pmatrix}$ **e** $\begin{pmatrix} -5 \\ 0 \end{pmatrix}$ **f** $\begin{pmatrix} 7 \\ 5 \end{pmatrix}$

4

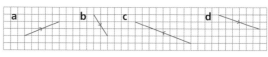

Stretch

1 2 right and 1 down, $\begin{pmatrix} 2 \\ -1 \end{pmatrix}$

2 a $\begin{pmatrix} 2 \\ 4 \end{pmatrix}$ **b** Triangle

3 a A has been translated by the vector $\begin{pmatrix} 5 \\ 5 \end{pmatrix}$ to give B.

   b B has been translated by the vector $\begin{pmatrix} -5 \\ -5 \end{pmatrix}$ to give A.

Chapter 9.2

Are you ready? (A)

1 a   **b**

   c 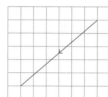   **d**

2 a $\begin{pmatrix} 4 \\ 6 \end{pmatrix}$ **b** $\begin{pmatrix} 4 \\ 0 \end{pmatrix}$ **c** $\begin{pmatrix} 2 \\ -7 \end{pmatrix}$ **d** $\begin{pmatrix} -5 \\ -2 \end{pmatrix}$

Practice (A)

1 a $\begin{pmatrix} 7 \\ 7 \end{pmatrix}$ **b** $\begin{pmatrix} 5 \\ 11 \end{pmatrix}$ **c** $\begin{pmatrix} 5 \\ 7 \end{pmatrix}$

  d $\begin{pmatrix} 6 \\ 3 \end{pmatrix}$ **e** $\begin{pmatrix} -6 \\ 10 \end{pmatrix}$ **f** $\begin{pmatrix} -6 \\ 7 \end{pmatrix}$

  g $\begin{pmatrix} -4 \\ 10 \end{pmatrix}$ **h** $\begin{pmatrix} 9 \\ -3 \end{pmatrix}$ **i** $\begin{pmatrix} 215 \\ 185 \end{pmatrix}$

2 a $\begin{pmatrix} 4 \\ 2 \end{pmatrix}$ **b** $\begin{pmatrix} 8 \\ -5 \end{pmatrix}$ **c** $\begin{pmatrix} 8 \\ -5 \end{pmatrix}$

  d $\begin{pmatrix} 3 \\ 0 \end{pmatrix}$ **e** $\begin{pmatrix} -9 \\ -8 \end{pmatrix}$ **f** $\begin{pmatrix} 11 \\ -5 \end{pmatrix}$

  g $\begin{pmatrix} 50 \\ -50 \end{pmatrix}$ **h** $\begin{pmatrix} 3 \\ 41 \end{pmatrix}$ **i** $\begin{pmatrix} 300 \\ -45 \end{pmatrix}$

3 a $\begin{pmatrix} 2 \\ 2 \end{pmatrix}$ **b** $\begin{pmatrix} -5 \\ 8 \end{pmatrix}$ **c** $\begin{pmatrix} 10 \\ 5 \end{pmatrix}$ **d** $\begin{pmatrix} 3 \\ -5 \end{pmatrix}$

  e $\begin{pmatrix} 5 \\ 8 \end{pmatrix}$ **f** $\begin{pmatrix} -15 \\ 3 \end{pmatrix}$ **g** $\begin{pmatrix} 12 \\ 7 \end{pmatrix}$ **h** $\begin{pmatrix} -15 \\ 11 \end{pmatrix}$

Are you ready? (B)

1 a 1   **b** −11   **c** 12
2 D

Practice (B)

1 a $\begin{pmatrix} 10 \\ -2 \end{pmatrix}$ **b** $\begin{pmatrix} 25 \\ -5 \end{pmatrix}$ **c** $\begin{pmatrix} 35 \\ -7 \end{pmatrix}$ **d** $\begin{pmatrix} 50 \\ -10 \end{pmatrix}$

2 Correct diagrams drawn to show the following:

   a $\begin{pmatrix} 8 \\ -4 \end{pmatrix}$ **b** $\begin{pmatrix} 12 \\ -6 \end{pmatrix}$ **c** $\begin{pmatrix} 20 \\ -10 \end{pmatrix}$ **d** $\begin{pmatrix} 40 \\ -20 \end{pmatrix}$

3 a $\begin{pmatrix} 9 \\ 4 \end{pmatrix}$ **b** $\begin{pmatrix} -5 \\ 24 \end{pmatrix}$ **c** $\begin{pmatrix} 10 \\ 37 \end{pmatrix}$ **d** $\begin{pmatrix} 53 \\ -20 \end{pmatrix}$

e $\begin{pmatrix} 10 \\ 8 \end{pmatrix}$ **f** $\begin{pmatrix} -25 \\ 3 \end{pmatrix}$ **g** $\begin{pmatrix} 26 \\ 11 \end{pmatrix}$ **h** $\begin{pmatrix} -25 \\ 14 \end{pmatrix}$

4 a $\begin{pmatrix} -6 \\ -1 \end{pmatrix}$ **b** $\begin{pmatrix} -8 \\ 42 \end{pmatrix}$ **c** $\begin{pmatrix} -6 \\ 28 \end{pmatrix}$ **d** $\begin{pmatrix} 38 \\ -22 \end{pmatrix}$

e $\begin{pmatrix} -14 \\ 25 \end{pmatrix}$ **f** $\begin{pmatrix} 24 \\ 0 \end{pmatrix}$ **g** $\begin{pmatrix} -12 \\ -13 \end{pmatrix}$ **h** $\begin{pmatrix} -34 \\ -34 \end{pmatrix}$

Consolidate

1 a $\begin{pmatrix} 11 \\ 16 \end{pmatrix}$ **b** $\begin{pmatrix} 17 \\ 2 \end{pmatrix}$ **c** $\begin{pmatrix} 5 \\ 0 \end{pmatrix}$ **d** $\begin{pmatrix} -13 \\ 8 \end{pmatrix}$

2 a $\begin{pmatrix} 5 \\ 2 \end{pmatrix}$ **b** $\begin{pmatrix} -6 \\ 6 \end{pmatrix}$ **c** $\begin{pmatrix} -6 \\ -1 \end{pmatrix}$ **d** $\begin{pmatrix} -1 \\ -5 \end{pmatrix}$

3 a $\begin{pmatrix} 3 \\ 1 \end{pmatrix}$ **b** $\begin{pmatrix} 8 \\ 4 \end{pmatrix}$ **c** $\begin{pmatrix} 5 \\ 5 \end{pmatrix}$

d $\begin{pmatrix} 3 \\ -1 \end{pmatrix}$ **e** $\begin{pmatrix} 5 \\ 3 \end{pmatrix}$ **f** $\begin{pmatrix} -2 \\ -3 \end{pmatrix}$

4 a $\begin{pmatrix} 8 \\ 2 \end{pmatrix}$ **b** $\begin{pmatrix} 9 \\ 0 \end{pmatrix}$ **c** $\begin{pmatrix} 15 \\ 0 \end{pmatrix}$ **d** $\begin{pmatrix} 24 \\ 6 \end{pmatrix}$

e $\begin{pmatrix} 40 \\ 10 \end{pmatrix}$ **f** $\begin{pmatrix} 36 \\ 0 \end{pmatrix}$ **g** $\begin{pmatrix} 11 \\ 2 \end{pmatrix}$ **h** $\begin{pmatrix} 5 \\ -1 \end{pmatrix}$

i $\begin{pmatrix} 17 \\ 5 \end{pmatrix}$ **j** $\begin{pmatrix} 17 \\ 2 \end{pmatrix}$ **k** $\begin{pmatrix} 39 \\ 6 \end{pmatrix}$ **l** $\begin{pmatrix} 25 \\ 10 \end{pmatrix}$

Stretch

1 7
2 $p = 9$, $q = -2$
3 $r = 7$, $s = -2$
4 $\begin{pmatrix} -3 \\ 7 \end{pmatrix}$

Vectors: exam practice

1 a $\begin{pmatrix} 4 \\ 3 \end{pmatrix}$ **b** $\begin{pmatrix} -1 \\ 4 \end{pmatrix}$

2
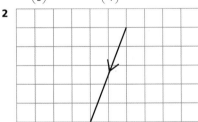

3
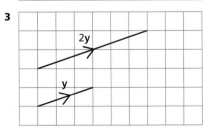

4 a $\begin{pmatrix} -4 \\ -4 \end{pmatrix}$ **b** $\begin{pmatrix} 5 \\ -10 \end{pmatrix}$

Geometry and measures: exam practice

1 40 cm²
2 Correct circle drawn.

3
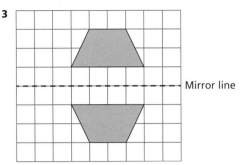
Mirror line

4 $y = 72°$
5 It is an acute angle so it should be less than 90°
6 $\begin{pmatrix} -5 \\ -4 \end{pmatrix}$

7 a $a = 33°$ **b** $b = 114°$
8 19.24 cm
9 4.5 cm²
10 a (10, 15) **b** 9.43 units

Block 10 Single event probability

Chapter 10.1

Are you ready?

1 a Even chance **b** Unlikely
 c Impossible **d** Likely
2 a yellow and blue **b** green
3 a
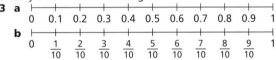
 b

Practice

1 a D **b** A **c** C **d** B **e** E
2 a

 b

 c

3 All three are correct as the values given are equivalent.

4 Kim is correct as $\frac{3}{5} = 0.6$

5 a

 b

 c

6
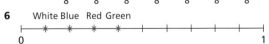
White Blue Red Green

7 a

Black square

b

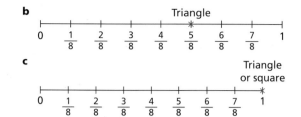

Triangle

0    $\frac{1}{8}$ $\frac{2}{8}$ $\frac{3}{8}$ $\frac{4}{8}$ $\frac{5}{8}$ $\frac{6}{8}$ $\frac{7}{8}$ 1

c

Triangle or square

0    $\frac{1}{8}$ $\frac{2}{8}$ $\frac{3}{8}$ $\frac{4}{8}$ $\frac{5}{8}$ $\frac{6}{8}$ $\frac{7}{8}$ 1

What do you think?

1   **a** $\frac{2}{12}$ or $\frac{1}{6}$ **b** $\frac{6}{12}$ or $\frac{1}{2}$ **c** 4

Consolidate

1   **a** D   **b** A   **c** E   **d** B   **e** C
2   **a** Z   **b** V   **c** W   **d** Y   **e** X
3   **a**   **i** 4 out of **7** counters are red
        ii 3 out of **7** counters are blue

   b   **i** $\frac{4}{7}$ **ii** $\frac{3}{7}$

   c

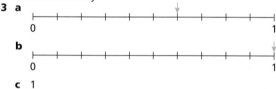

Blue   Red

0   1

Stretch

1 No. Although there are only two colours as options, the yellow section is bigger so there is more chance of landing on yellow than blue.
2 Statement A because 0.1 is closer to 0 than 1, which makes it unlikely.
3   **a**

0   1

   b

0   1

   c 1

Chapter 10.2

Are you ready?

1   **a** $\frac{4}{5}$ **b** 0.5   **c** 0.77
2   **a** $\frac{7}{10}$ **b** 0.4   **c** 0.16
3 $\frac{1}{2}$
4 $\frac{1}{6}$

Practice

1   **a** $\frac{5}{9}$ **b i** $\frac{4}{9}$ **ii** $\frac{7}{9}$ **iii** $\frac{6}{9}$ or $\frac{2}{3}$

   c i $\frac{1}{10}$ **ii** $\frac{5}{10}$ or $\frac{1}{2}$ **iii** $\frac{7}{10}$

2   **a** 0.7   **b** 0.1   **c** 0.7
3   0.45
4 $\frac{3}{5}$
5   **a** 0.22   **b** 0.62   **c** 0.71
6   **a** 0.81   **b** 0.19
7   **a i** 0.2   **ii** 0.78   **iii** 0.63

   b $\frac{5}{10}$ or $\frac{1}{2}$

8   0.15
9   **a** 0.32   **b** 0.5   **c** 0.92

Consolidate

1   **a** $\frac{1}{6}$ **b** 0   **c** $\frac{3}{6}$ or $\frac{1}{2}$ **d** $\frac{5}{6}$

   e $\frac{3}{6}$ or $\frac{1}{2}$ **f** $\frac{2}{6}$ or $\frac{1}{3}$ **g** $\frac{5}{6}$ **h** $\frac{6}{6}$ or 1

2   **a** $\frac{8}{14}$ or $\frac{4}{7}$ **b** $\frac{6}{14}$ or $\frac{3}{7}$

3   **a** $\frac{15}{90}$ or $\frac{1}{6}$ **b** $\frac{65}{90}$ or $\frac{13}{18}$

4   0.73
5 $\frac{4}{11}$
6   **a** 0.2   **b** 0.44   **c** 0.7

Stretch

1   **a** $\frac{120}{730}$ **b** $\frac{285}{730}$ **c** $\frac{580}{730}$

2 $\frac{23}{24}$

3   **a** $\frac{170}{420}$ **b** $\frac{2}{420}$ **c** $\frac{1}{420}$

Single event probability: exam practice

1   **a** certain   **b** likely
2   **a** Cross marked at 1
   b Cross marked at 0
   c Cross marked at $\frac{1}{2}$
3 $\frac{1}{8}$
4   **a** $\frac{7}{20}$ **b** $\frac{9}{20}$
5   **a** 0.3   **b** 4

Block 11 Probability diagrams

Chapter 11.1

Are you ready?

1 1, 2, 3, 4, 5, 6
2 Heads, Tails
3 Red counter, blue counter, yellow counter
4 1

Practice

1 (Long-sleeved, Shorts), (Long-sleeved, Joggers), (Long-sleeved, Jeans), (Long-sleeved, Cargos), (Plain, Shorts), (Plain, Joggers), (Plain, Jeans), (Plain, Cargos), (Striped, Shorts), (Striped, Joggers), (Striped, Jeans), (Striped, Cargos)
2 (1, 1), (1, 2), (1, 3), (1, 4), (1, 5), (1, 6), (2, 1), (2, 2), (2, 3), (2, 4), (2, 5), (2, 6), (3, 1), (3, 2), (3, 3), (3, 4), (3, 5), (3, 6), (4, 1), (4, 2), (4, 3), (4, 4), (4, 5), (4, 6), (5, 1), (5, 2), (5, 3), (5, 4), (5, 5), (5, 6), (6, 1), (6, 2), (6, 3), (6, 4), (6, 5), (6, 6)
3 (1, H), (1, T), (2, H), (2, T), (3, H), (3, T), (4, H), (4, T), (5, H), (5, T), (6, H), (6, T)
4 HHH, HHT, HTH, HTT, THH, THT, TTH, TTT
5 CCW, CCJ, CCF, CBW, CBJ, CBF, CFW, CFJ, CFF, TCW, TCJ, TCF, TBW, TBJ, TBF, TFW, TFJ, TFF, BCW, BCJ, BCF, BBW, BBJ, BBF, BFW, BFJ, BFF
6 123, 132, 213, 231, 312, 321
7 ABC, ACB, BAC, BCA, CAB, CBA
8 RR, RB, RG, BR, BB, BG, GR, GB, GG
9 45, 46, 54, 56, 64, 65
10 RB, RG, RY, BG, BY, GY
11 XYZW, XYWZ, XZYW, XZWY, XWYZ, XWZY, YXZW, YXWZ, YZXW, YZWX, YWZX, YWXZ, ZYXW, ZYWX, ZXYW, ZXWY, ZWXY, ZWYX, WXYZ, WXZY, WYXZ, WYZX, WZXY, WZYX
12 12, 13, 14, 21, 23, 24, 31, 32, 34, 41, 42, 43

Consolidate

1 A1, A2, A3, A4, B1, B2, B3, B4, C1, C2, C3, C4, D1, D2, D3, D4, E1, E2, E3, E4

2 11, 12, 13, 14, 15, 21, 22, 23, 24, 25, 31, 32, 33, 34, 35, 41, 42, 43, 44, 45, 51, 52, 53, 54, 55

3 BB, BY, BG, YB, YY, YG, GB, GY, GG

4 SSC, SSI, SCC, SCI, SLC, SLI, PSC, PSI, PCC, PCI, PLC, PLI

5 591, 519, 159, 195, 915, 951

6 PST, PSW, PTS, PTW, PWS, PWT, SPW, SPT, STW, STP, SWT, SWP, TPS, TPW, TSP, TSW, TWP, TWS, WPS, WPT, WSP, WST, WTP, WTS

Stretch

1 (Tomato, Onion), (Tomato, Chicken), (Tomato, Chilli), (Tomato, Peppers), (Onion, Chicken), (Onion, Chilli), (Onion, Peppers), (Chicken, Chilli), (Chicken, Peppers), (Chilli, Peppers)

2 a A1, A2, A3, A4, A5, B1, B2, B3, B4, B5, C1, C2, C3, C4, C5, D1, D2, D3, D4, D5

b $\frac{1}{20}$

c $\frac{2}{20}$ or $\frac{1}{10}$

3 370, 307, 730, 703

4 a 248, 249, 428, 429, 824, 829, 842, 849, 924, 928, 942, 948

b $\frac{8}{12}$ or $\frac{2}{3}$

Chapter 11.2

Are you ready?

1 46

2 25

3 72

4 105

Practice

1 a

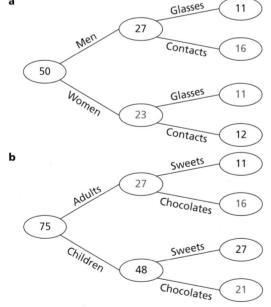

b

c

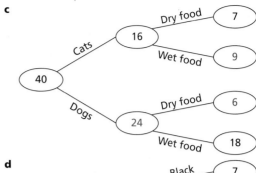

d

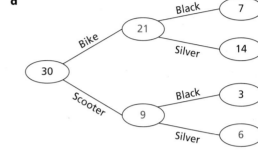

2 a

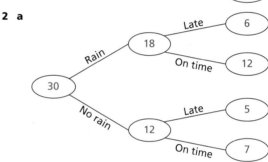

b 19

3 a

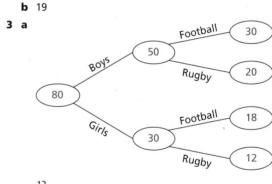

b $\frac{12}{80}$

4 a

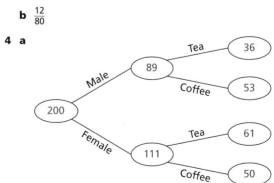

b $\frac{89}{200}$

c $\frac{36}{89}$

5 a

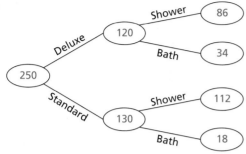

b $\frac{34}{250}$

c $\frac{112}{130}$

6 a

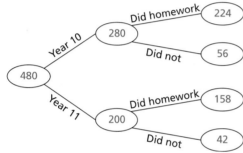

b $\frac{158}{200}$

Consolidate

1 a

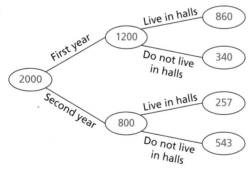

b $\frac{257}{2000}$

2 a

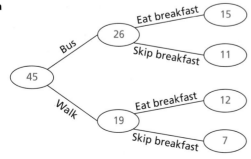

b $\frac{12}{19}$

3 a

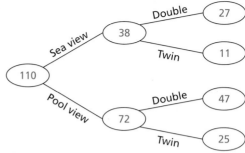

b $\frac{47}{72}$

Stretch

1 a

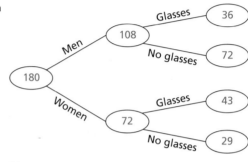

b $\frac{36}{79}$

2 a

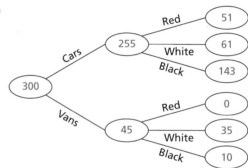

b $\frac{10}{45}$

3 a

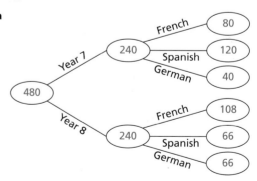

b $\frac{66}{106}$

Chapter 11.3

Are you ready?

1 (1, 1), (1, 2), (1, 3), (1, 4), (1, 5), (2, 1), (2, 2), (2, 3), (2, 4), (2, 5), (3, 1), (3, 2), (3, 3), (3, 4), (3, 5), (4, 1), (4, 2), (4, 3), (4, 4), (4, 5), (5, 1), (5, 2), (5, 3), (5, 4), (5, 5)

Practice

1 a

		First spin			
		A	B	C	D
Second spin	A	AA	BA	CA	DA
	B	AB	BB	CB	DB
	C	AC	BC	CC	DC
	D	AD	BD	CD	DD

b $\frac{4}{16}$

2 a

	R1	R2	R3
B1	R1, B1	R2, B1	R3, B1
B2	R1, B2	R2, B2	R3, B2

b $\frac{1}{6}$

3 a

+	1	2	3	4	5	6
1	2	3	4	5	6	7
2	3	4	5	6	7	8
3	4	5	6	7	8	9
4	5	6	7	8	9	10
5	6	7	8	9	10	11
6	7	8	9	10	11	12

b i $\frac{4}{36}$ **ii** $\frac{3}{36}$ **iii** $\frac{1}{36}$ **iv** 0

c i $\frac{26}{36}$ **ii** $\frac{10}{36}$

4 a

×	1	2	3	4	5	6
1	1	2	3	4	5	6
2	2	4	6	8	10	12
3	3	6	9	12	15	18
4	4	8	12	16	20	24
5	5	10	15	20	25	30
6	6	12	18	24	30	36

b 6 and 12
c 1, 9, 16, 25 and 36
d i $\frac{2}{36}$ **ii** $\frac{2}{36}$ **iii** $\frac{4}{36}$ **iv** $\frac{17}{36}$ **v** $\frac{9}{36}$

5 a

	2	3	5
0	2	3	5
1	3	4	6
4	6	7	9
6	8	9	11

b i $\frac{5}{12}$ **ii** $\frac{7}{12}$ **iii** $\frac{4}{12}$ **iv** $\frac{11}{12}$ **v** 0   **vi** 1

6 a

	1	2	3	4	5	6	7	8
5	4	3	2	1	0	1	2	3
10	9	8	7	6	5	4	3	2
15	14	13	12	11	10	9	8	7
20	19	18	17	16	15	14	13	12

b i $\frac{16}{32}$ **ii** $\frac{1}{32}$ **iii** $\frac{14}{32}$ **iv** $\frac{12}{32}$ **v** $\frac{30}{32}$ **vi** $\frac{26}{32}$

Consolidate

1 a

		First spin			
		A	B	B	C
Second spin	A	AA	BA	BA	CA
	B	AB	BB	BB	CB
	B	AB	BB	BB	CB
	C	AC	BC	BC	CC

b $\frac{6}{16}$

2 a

	1	2	3
A	1A	2A	3A
B	1B	2B	3B

b $\frac{1}{6}$

3 a

	1	2	3
2	3	4	5
3	4	5	6
4	5	6	7
5	6	7	8

b i $\frac{6}{12}$ **ii** $\frac{6}{12}$ **iii** $\frac{1}{12}$
iv $\frac{1}{12}$ **v** $\frac{1}{12}$ **vi** 1

4 a

	1	2	3	4	5	6	7	8
5	6	7	8	9	10	11	12	13
10	11	12	13	14	15	16	17	18
15	16	17	18	19	20	21	22	23
20	21	22	23	24	25	26	27	28

b i $\frac{16}{32}$ **ii** 0   **iii** $\frac{10}{32}$ **iv** $\frac{27}{32}$ **v** $\frac{17}{32}$ **vi** $\frac{26}{32}$

Stretch

1 a

	1	2	3	4	5	6
H	2	4	6	8	10	12
T	0	1	2	3	4	5

b i $\frac{3}{12}$ **ii** $\frac{4}{12}$ **iii** $\frac{1}{12}$

2 a

	2	4	6	8	10
Red	4	8	12	16	20
Yellow	1	2	3	4	5
Blue	8	6	4	2	0
Blue	8	6	4	2	0

b 4

c i $\frac{6}{20}$ **ii** $\frac{10}{20}$ **iii** $\frac{8}{20}$ **iv** $\frac{5}{20}$

Chapter 11.4

Are you ready? (A)

1

		First dice					
		1	2	3	4	5	6
Second dice	1	1	2	3	4	5	6
	2	2	4	6	8	10	12
	3	3	6	9	12	15	18
	4	4	8	12	16	20	24
	5	5	10	15	20	25	30
	6	6	12	18	24	30	36

2 0.25
3 58

Practice (A)

1 a 59 **b** 37 **c** 42 **d** 23 **e** 79 **f** 161
2 a 13 **b** 26 **c** 66, students who go to neither
3 a

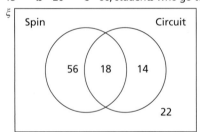

b 14 **c** $\frac{32}{110}$ **d** $\frac{18}{74}$

4 a

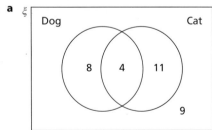

b $\frac{15}{32}$

Are you ready? (B)

1 a 2, 4, 6, 8, 10 **b** 3, 6, 9, 12, 15 **c** 4, 8, 12, 16, 20
2 1, 2, 5, 10, 25, 50
3 2, 3, 5, 7, 11

Practice (B)

1 a Jamie and Lee
b Hunter, Esma, Millie or Bobby
c No, she isn't in the History-only portion or in the overlap
2 a 2, 4, 6, 8, 10, 12, 14 **b** 3, 6, 9, 12, 15 **c** 6, 12

d

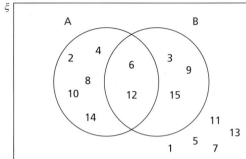

3 a 4, 8, 12, 16, 20
b 1, 2, 5, 10
c None
d

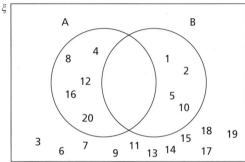

4 a

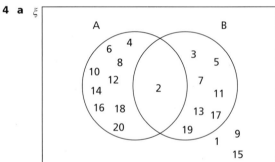

b $\frac{3}{20}$

Consolidate

1 a 31 **b** 56 **c** 29
d 11 **e** 85 **f** 127
2 a 17 **b** 19
c 113, people who go to neither
3 a

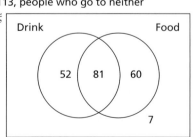

b 60 **c** $\frac{133}{200}$

4 a 5, 10, 15
b 1, 2, 3, 5, 6, 10, 15
c 5, 10, 15

d ξ

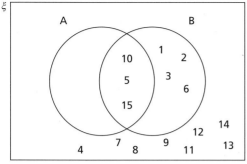

5 a 2, 4, 6, 8, 10, 12, 14, 16, 18, 20
b 1, 2, 5, 10
c 2, 10
d ξ

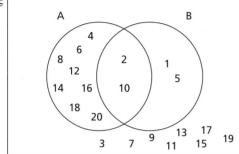

Stretch

1 a A letter can't be a vowel and a consonant.
b Every letter is a vowel or a consonant.
c ξ

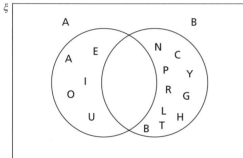

2 $\frac{45}{176}$

3 Example answer: odd and even numbers, or vowels and consonants; the sets would not have any elements in common.

Probability diagrams: exam practice

1 a (1, tails) (1, heads) (2, tails) (2, heads) (3, tails) (3, heads) (4, tails) (4, heads) (5, tails) (5, heads)

b $\frac{1}{10}$

2 a 57 **b** $\frac{72}{100}$ **c** $\frac{15}{43}$

3 a

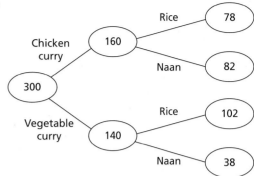

b $\frac{180}{300}$

4 a

		Dice 1					
		1	**2**	**3**	**4**	**5**	**6**
	1	0	1	2	3	4	5
	2	1	0	1	2	3	4
Dice 2	**3**	2	1	0	1	2	3
	4	3	2	1	0	1	2
	5	4	3	2	1	0	1
	6	5	4	3	2	1	0

b $\frac{2}{36}$

Block 12 Theory and experiment

Chapter 12.1

Are you ready?

1 $\frac{1}{6}$

2 $\frac{1}{2}$

3 $\frac{2}{5}$

4 $\frac{15}{20} = \frac{3}{4}$

Practice

1 5 times
2 4 times
3 5 times
4 100 times
5 27 times
6 4 times
7 4 times
8 12 times
9 10 times
10 7 times
11 48 times
12 11 times
13 40 times
14 10 times
15 0.6 × 70 = 42, so 42 times
16 0.85 × 200 = 170, so 170 people

Consolidate

1 9 times
2 8 times
3 36 times

4 3 times
5 6 times
6 20 times

Stretch
1 20 more times
2 8
3 2.4 per spin
4 £20

Chapter 12.2

Are you ready?
1 50 times
2 20 times
3 540 people
4 204 people

Practice

1

Colour	Red	Blue	Yellow	Green
Frequency	8	7	4	1
Relative frequency	0.4	0.35	0.2	0.05

2 a 5
b

Score	1	2	3	4	5	6
Frequency	3	5	14	3	3	2
Relative frequency	0.1	0.17	0.47	0.1	0.1	0.07

3 0.2
4 a 0.375　　**b** 0.333
5 0.3
6 0.125
7 0.6
8 a 28 times　　**b** 52 times
9 a 0.15　　**b** 0.5　　**c** 10
10 a 0.25　　**b** 0.34　　**c** 0.48　　**d** 0.493
　　e The relative frequency gets closer and closer to the theoretical probability of 0.5. This is because more and more trials are performed.

Consolidate

1

Colour	Red	Blue	Yellow	Green
Frequency	2	3	3	2
Relative frequency	0.2	0.3	0.3	0.2

2 a 3
b

Score	1	2	3	4	5	6
Frequency	2	3	8	1	3	1
Relative frequency	$\frac{2}{18}$	$\frac{3}{18}$	$\frac{8}{18}$	$\frac{1}{18}$	$\frac{3}{18}$	$\frac{1}{18}$

3 0.72
4 0.8
5 120

Stretch
1 a 0.2　　**b** 0.8　　**c** No
　　d Yes, it landed on tails far more than heads.
2 a 0.7　　**b** 0.55
　　c The second one (Jack's) as there are more trials.
3 6333

Theory and experiment: exam practice
1 No, if it was fair the results would be more evenly spread.
2 120
3 a 0.4　　**b** 15

4 a

Number of flips	Relative frequency of red	Relative frequency of yellow
100	0.43	**0.57**
200	0.51	0.49
300	0.48	**0.52**
400	0.53	0.47
500	0.55	**0.45**

b 144

Block 13 Combined events

Chapter 13.1

Are you ready?
1 $\frac{1}{6}$

2 $\frac{6}{9}$ or $\frac{2}{3}$

3 $\frac{2}{5}$

Practice

1 a $\frac{1}{4}$　　**b** $\frac{1}{4}$

2 a $\frac{1}{36}$　　**b** $\frac{1}{36}$　　**c** $\frac{1}{4}$

3 $\frac{16}{49}$

4 $\frac{30}{121}$

5 a $\frac{20}{81}$　　**b** $\frac{20}{81}$

　　c Probabilities are the same because the multiplications can be done in either order to give the same answer.

6 a $\frac{8}{81}$　　**b** $\frac{16}{81}$　　**c** $\frac{24}{729}$

7 $\frac{1}{25}$

8 $\frac{1}{216}$

Consolidate

1 $\frac{12}{49}$

2 $\frac{36}{121}$

3 $\frac{4}{49}$

4 $\frac{1}{25}$

5 $\frac{15}{64}$

6 $\frac{24}{100}$

Stretch

1 $\frac{1}{1296}$

2 $\frac{1536}{104\,976} = \frac{32}{2187}$

3 $\frac{700}{65\,536} = \frac{175}{16\,384}$

4 $\frac{1}{32\,768}$

5 $\frac{36}{1000}$

Chapter 13.2

Are you ready? (A)

1 $\frac{1}{36}$

2 $\frac{3}{8}$

3 $\frac{10}{20}$ or $\frac{1}{2}$

4 $\frac{6}{30}$ or $\frac{1}{5}$

Practice (A)

1 a Missing information completed as follows:

1st pick: Blue $\frac{3}{7}$; 2nd pick: Red $\frac{4}{7}$, Blue $\frac{3}{7}$; outcome RR has probability $\frac{16}{49}$, outcome RB has probability $\frac{12}{49}$, outcome BR has probability $\frac{12}{49}$, outcome BB has probability $\frac{9}{49}$

b $\frac{16}{49}$ **c** $\frac{24}{49}$

2 a Missing information completed as follows:

1st pick: Red $\frac{1}{2}$, Black $\frac{1}{2}$; 2nd pick: Red $\frac{1}{2}$, Black $\frac{1}{2}$, Red $\frac{1}{2}$, Black $\frac{1}{2}$; Outcome RR has probability $\frac{1}{4}$, outcome RB has probability $\frac{1}{4}$, outcome BR has probability $\frac{1}{4}$, outcome BB has probability $\frac{1}{4}$

b $\frac{2}{4}$ or $\frac{1}{2}$

3 a

b $\frac{41}{81}$

4 a

b $\frac{36}{100}$ or $\frac{9}{25}$

5 $\frac{33}{49}$

6 $\frac{13}{25}$

7 $\frac{25}{49}$

Are you ready? (B)

1 a $\frac{2}{15}$ **b** $\frac{3}{42}$ or $\frac{1}{14}$ **c** $\frac{15}{400}$ or $\frac{3}{80}$

2 a $\frac{3}{5}$ **b** $\frac{6}{9}$ or $\frac{2}{3}$ **c** $\frac{24}{150}$ or $\frac{4}{25}$

Practice (B)

1 a Missing information completed as follows:

1st pick: Blue $\frac{3}{7}$; 2nd pick: Red $\frac{3}{6}$, Blue $\frac{2}{6}$; outcome RR has probability $\frac{12}{42}$, outcome RB has probability $\frac{12}{42}$, outcome BR has probability $\frac{12}{42}$, outcome BB has probability $\frac{6}{42}$

b $\frac{12}{42}$ **c** $\frac{24}{42}$ or $\frac{4}{7}$

2 a Missing information completed as follows:

1st pick: Red $\frac{26}{52}$, Black $\frac{26}{52}$; 2nd pick: Red $\frac{25}{51}$, Black $\frac{26}{51}$, Red $\frac{26}{51}$, Black $\frac{25}{51}$; Outcome RR has probability $\frac{650}{2652}$, outcome RB has probability $\frac{676}{2652}$, outcome BR has probability $\frac{676}{2652}$, outcome BB has probability $\frac{650}{2652}$

b $\frac{1352}{2652}$ or $\frac{26}{51}$

3 a

b $\frac{32}{72}$ or $\frac{4}{9}$

4 a

b $\frac{30}{90}$ or $\frac{1}{3}$

5 $\frac{30}{42}$

6 $\frac{8}{20}$

7 $\frac{18}{42}$

8 $\frac{12}{51}$

Consolidate

1 $\frac{208}{400}$ or $\frac{13}{25}$

2 a

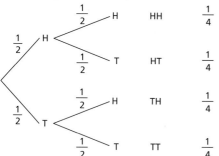

b $\frac{52}{100}$ or $\frac{13}{25}$

3 a

1st flip 2nd flip Outcome Probability

$\frac{1}{2}$ H — $\frac{1}{2}$ H — HH — $\frac{1}{4}$

$\frac{1}{2}$ T — HT — $\frac{1}{4}$

$\frac{1}{2}$ T — $\frac{1}{2}$ H — TH — $\frac{1}{4}$

$\frac{1}{2}$ T — TT — $\frac{1}{4}$

b $\frac{3}{4}$

4 $\frac{188}{380}$ or $\frac{47}{95}$

5 a

1st pick 2nd pick Outcome Probability

$\frac{6}{10}$ Green — $\frac{5}{9}$ Green — GG — $\frac{30}{90}$

$\frac{4}{9}$ Yellow — GY — $\frac{24}{90}$

$\frac{4}{10}$ Yellow — $\frac{6}{9}$ Green — YG — $\frac{24}{90}$

$\frac{3}{9}$ Yellow — YY — $\frac{12}{90}$

b $\frac{42}{90}$ or $\frac{7}{15}$

6 $\frac{98}{210}$ or $\frac{7}{15}$

Stretch

1 $\frac{16}{25}$

2 $\frac{1}{4}$

3 a $\frac{16}{25}$ **b** $\frac{1}{25}$

Combined events: exam practice

1 a

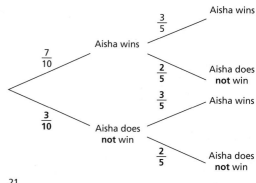

Squash Tennis

$\frac{7}{10}$ Aisha wins — $\frac{3}{5}$ Aisha wins

$\frac{2}{5}$ Aisha does **not** win

$\frac{3}{10}$ Aisha does **not** win — $\frac{3}{5}$ Aisha wins

$\frac{2}{5}$ Aisha does **not** win

b $\frac{21}{50}$

2 a

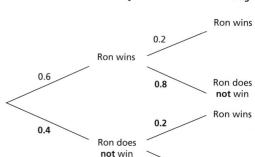

Archery Fencing

0.6 Ron wins — 0.2 Ron wins

0.8 Ron does **not** win

0.4 Ron does **not** win — 0.2 Ron wins

0.8 Ron does **not** win

b 0.68

3 $\frac{38}{100}$

4 $\frac{28}{90}$

Probability: exam practice

1 a

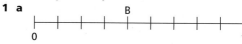

b

R

c P

2 a $\frac{1}{6}$ **b** $\frac{3}{6}$ or $\frac{1}{2}$ **c** $\frac{6}{6}$ or 1

3 (Red, Pink), (Red, Green), (Red, Teal), (Black, Pink), (Black, Green), (Black, Teal), (Yellow, Pink), (Yellow, Green), (Yellow, Teal)

4 a

	1	2	3	4
5	5	10	15	20
6	6	12	18	24
7	7	14	21	28

b $\frac{3}{12}$ or $\frac{1}{4}$

5 a

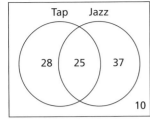

Tap   Jazz

28   25   37

10

b $\frac{37}{100}$

6 40 times

7 $\frac{222}{380}$

Block 14 Statistical measures

Chapter 14.1

Are you ready?

1 a 25   **b** 5
2 a 3, 4, 7, 8, 9, 10, 12, 15
   b 17, 19, 19, 20, 25, 26, 27
   c −8, −5, −3, −2, 0, 6, 8

Practice

1 Mean = 10   Median = 11   Mode = 11
2 a 88 cm   **b** 89 cm
3 a Various possible answers, e.g. the first one has a number in the middle whereas the last two do not.
   b i 4   **ii** 4   **iii** 3.5
   c i 4   **ii** 4   **iii** 3.5
4 a

Number of goals	Frequency	Subtotals
0	4	0
1	3	3
2	7	14
3	5	15
4	0	0
5	1	5
Total	20	37

   b 2
   c 1.85 ≈ 2 goals
5 a There is no number that appears more often than the other numbers.
   b 112.1 kg   **c** 111 kg   **d** The mean
6 a 6   **b** 5.83 ≈ 6

Consolidate

1 a Mean = 15   Median = 14   Mode = 11 and 17
   b Mean = 10.5   Median = 10   Mode = 10
   c Mean = 10   Median = 9   Mode = 8
   d Mean = 6.86   Median = 7   Mode = no mode
2 a 18 and 25   **b** 24   **c** 22.9
3 a 2   **b** 2.77 ≈ 3
4 a There is no mode.
   b Mean = 16   Median = 16.5

Stretch

1 4
2 48.5 kg
3 4 and 10

Chapter 14.2

Are you ready?

1 a 63   **b** 502   **c** 9
2 a 25   **b** 150   **c** −9

3 a 25, 52, 63
   b 150, 200, 205, 502
   c −9, −5, −1, 5, 9
4 a 29   **b** 57   **c** 16   **d** 1140

Practice

1 8 months
2 a 38 cm   **b** 34 cm
3 a She has identified the smallest and largest number but has not found the difference.
   b 146
4 10.5 miles
5 12 623
6 57
7 a i Y10   **ii** Y9   **b** 30
8 a He has not taken the units into account.
   b 2800 g

Consolidate

1 a 5   **b** 60   **c** £170   **d** 73 g
2 249
3 28
4 233

Stretch

1 2 minutes and 26 seconds
2 7 °C
3 a 18   **b** 61
4 a Any height between 86 cm and 121 cm inclusive
   b 125 cm or 82 cm

Chapter 14.3

Are you ready?

1 a 19.2   **b** 9.29
2 60
3 a 10   **b** 34.5   **c** 42.5   **d** 12 500
4 a 37   **b** 36.7   **c** 40

Practice

1 a 162.4 cm
   b The total of the midpoints is not needed to work out the mean.
2 a 28 years
   b The data is grouped so we cannot be sure of the exact ages of the people in each group.
   c $20 < a \leqslant 30$
3 a 45.2 minutes   **b** $45 < t \leqslant 50$ **c** $45 < t \leqslant 50$
4 a $25\,000 < x \leqslant 30\,000$
   b £23 562.50
   c $20\,000 < x \leqslant 25\,000$
5 47.9 mm

Consolidate

1 3.8 hours
2 a 27.25 kg   **b** $10 < m \leqslant 30$
3 a 14 minutes   **b** $10 < t \leqslant 15$ **c** $10 < t \leqslant 15$

Stretch

1 a 56.7%   **b** $125 < h \leqslant 170$ **c** 140 cm
2 22.6 minutes

Chapter 14.4

Are you ready?

1 a 17 cm   **b** 101 cm   **c** 98 cm   **d** 96.9 cm
2 127 cm

Practice

1 a The outlier is 8
   b Mean = 40   Median = 39   Mode = 35
2 a Mean = 11.17   Median = 7   Mode = 7
   b 37

c Mean = 6   Median = 7   Mode = 7
The median and mode have stayed the same but the mean has decreased.

3 Class B has a higher mean and a larger range, indicating that, on average, Class B performed better but also had a greater variability in scores.

4 a Mean = 54.6   Median = 57.5   Range = 50
b The outlier is 18
c Mean = 58.7   Median = 58   Range = 18
The median and mean have increased. The range has decreased.

5 a The range decreases by 12.7 kg.
b The mean decreases by approximately 1.69 kg.

6 a Week 1: Median = £287   Range = £212
Week 2: Median = £284   Range = £232
Both weeks have similar medians, but Week 2 has a larger range, indicating more spread or variability (the amount of difference between the numbers in the data) in profits.
b If the mean were used instead of the median, the extreme values (like £401 and £405) would have a stronger impact, potentially skewing (distorting) the comparisons.

Consolidate

1 21, 16 and 192
2 a Mean = 45.4°   Median = 41.5°
Mode = 39° and 42°   Range = 49°
b 85°
c Mean = 41°   Median = 41°
Mode = 39° and 42°   Range = 13°
d The mode stays the same. The mean and median decrease slightly and the range decreases significantly.
e Mean and range
3 Mean
4 Team A scored more points on average as the mean is higher. Team A were more consistent as the range is smaller.

Stretch

1 a Mean = 3°C   Median = 4°C
Mode = 5°C   Range = 10°C
b −4°C could have been recorded incorrectly as it is significantly lower than the other temperatures in the data set and it is not often that temperatures fluctuate (change) like that over a week.
c i The mean would increase to 4.2°C and the range would decrease to 4°C.
ii The mean would increase to 4.1°C and the range would decrease to 4°C.

2 a When dealing with time, the smallest mean indicates less time to complete the puzzle and so the 17–35 year olds did it quicker than the other age groups.
b The 17–35 year olds completed the puzzle fastest on average, as their mean time is the smallest.
The 36–50 year olds had the most consistent times as they have the smallest range.
The over 50s completed the puzzle in the slowest amount of time on average as their mean is the greatest. They were also the most inconsistent group as their range is the greatest.
c Mean = 59.8 seconds. This does not affect the conclusion as the over 50s still have the slowest time.

3 a 69.6   **b** 3.86% increase

Statistical measures: exam practice

1 a 15   **b** 14   **c** 13.5
2 a 8   **b** 8   **c** 9
3 Example answer: 1, 3, 3, 3, 15
4 47
5 10
6 a 30   **b** 2.1

Block 15 Charts and diagrams

Chapter 15.1

Are you ready?

1 a 7   **b** 14
2 11
3 47

Practice

1 a i 6   **ii** 5   **b** 6   **c** 35
2 a 13   **b** 4   **c** 10   **d** 71
3 a 10   **b** Red   **c** 6   **d** 70
4 a 12   **b** 18
c

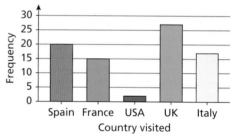

Holiday destinations

d 81
5 a 5
b Year 7 and Year 8
c 30
d Answers will vary.

Consolidate

1 a Orange   **b** 55   **c** 45   **d** 270
2 a 44   **b** 26   **c** 49
3 a 43   **b** 45   **c** Thursday
d Monday, Tuesday, Wednesday and Friday
e The café sold more cakes as the proportion of bars for cake is higher than the proportion of bars for ice cream.

Stretch

1 a 13   **b** 5   **c** $\frac{8}{38} = \frac{4}{19}$ **d** 23.7%

2 Various possible answers, e.g. uneven scale on the y-axis; no labels or title; the bars are different widths; the gaps between bars are uneven.

3 Possible answer:

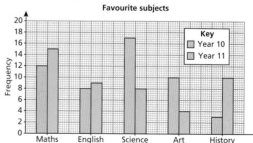

Favourite subjects

Chapter 15.2

Are you ready?

1 a 18, 20, 24, 25, 28, 31, 35, 39, 42

   b 24   **c** 28   **d** $\frac{4}{9}$

2 a 5   **b** 2   **c** 15

3 a 40%   **b** 75%   **c** 62.5%

Practice

1

	Email	Telephone	Letter	Total
Under 40	**78**	**56**	18	152
40 and over	**29**	47	**32**	**108**
Total	107	103	50	260

2 a

Pizzas sold

Monday	●●●●
Tuesday	●●●
Wednesday	●●●●●
Thursday	●●●●◖
Friday	●●●●●●●●●●●

   b 11   **c** Wednesday   **d** 59

3 a 3.9 m   **b** 8.7 m   **c** 4.8 m

   d 2   **e** 6.8 m

4 a

	Medication A	Medication B	Total
Improved	179	**183**	362
No change	**25**	56	**81**
Worse	38	19	**57**
Total	242	**258**	500

   b $\frac{362}{500}$ **c** 10%

5 a 1.25 can be drawn by drawing one full square and one-quarter of a square.

   b   Key: ■ = 4 students

Animal	Number of students
Lion	■ ■ ■
Giraffe	■ ■ ■ ■
Elephant	■ ▮
Rhino	■ ▮

6 a The stem will contain two digits from 12 to 19

   b   **Parcel masses**

```
12 | 5  9
13 | 6  7  8
14 | 0  2  5  6
15 | 8  9  9
16 | 3  5  7  8  9
17 | 2
19 | 5  7
```

   Key: 15 | 8 means 158 grams

Consolidate

1 a

	Tea	Coffee	Hot chocolate	Total
Saturday	3	17	**41**	61
Sunday	22	42	25	**89**
Total	25	**59**	66	150

   b $\frac{66}{150}$ **c** 47%

2 a Completion times

```
0 | 8  9
1 | 3  5
2 | 3  7  7  9
3 | 1  5  8
4 | 2  3  5  8
```

   Key: 3 | 8 means 3.8 seconds

   b 2.9 seconds

3 a 10   **b** 11

   c $5\frac{1}{4}$ circles

   d 102

Stretch

1 195

2 $\frac{4}{17}$

Chapter 15.3

Are you ready?

1 a 55   **b** Thursday   **c** Wednesday and Friday

2 925

Practice

1 a 17   **b** Sunday   **c** Thursday and Friday

2 a Quarter 3   **b** 325   **c** In year 2022 in quarter 3

3

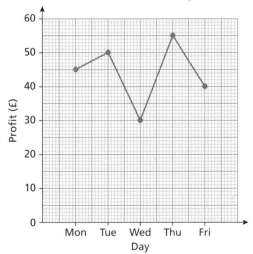

Profit made on five days

Consolidate

1 a 155 minutes   **b** 2020
   c 2017   **d** 35 minutes

2

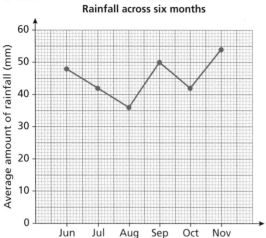

Rainfall across six months

Stretch

1 a August   **b** 1600 kWh
   c Mean energy consumption for the first six months
of the year = $\frac{2600 + 2300 + 2400 + 1800 + 1200 + 800}{6}$ =
1850 kWh
Mean energy consumption for the second six months
of the year = $\frac{900 + 600 + 800 + 1800 + 2500 + 2800}{6}$ =
1566.7 kWh
1850 > 1566.7 so Zach is correct.

Chapter 15.4

Are you ready?

1 360
2 Check accuracy with a protractor.
3 a 125   **b** 460   **c** 40   **d** 12.5

Practice

1 a

Sandwich	Number sold	Angle
Beef salad	12	12 × 5 = 60°
Cheese and pickle	15	**15 × 5 = 75°**
Egg mayonnaise	24	**24 × 5 = 120°**
Chicken tikka	21	**21 × 5 = 105°**
Total	72	72 × 5 = 360°

b Sandwiches sold

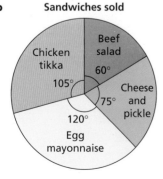

2 a Red
   b i $\frac{150}{360}$ **ii** $\frac{90}{360}$ **iii** $\frac{120}{360}$
   c i 125   **ii** 75   **iii** 100

3 Flowers in a garden

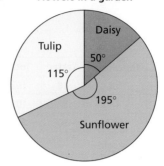

4 a FF   **b** $\frac{45}{360}$ **c** 70

Consolidate

1 a Guinea pig
   b i $\frac{135}{360}$ **ii** $\frac{165}{360}$ **iii** $\frac{60}{360}$
   c i 675   **ii** 825   **iii** 300

2 a

Colour	Number	Angle
Green	18	18 × 6 = **108°**
Red	6	6 × 6 = **36°**
Black	21	21 × 6 = **126°**
Blue	15	15 × 6 = **90°**
Total	60	60 × 6 = **360°**

b Pencil colours

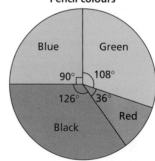

Stretch

1 a 1080   **b** $\frac{35}{360}$
2 a 13
   b It is impossible to say as we do not know the
number of matches played by City United FC and so
we don't know how many matches they drew.

Chapter 15.5

Are you ready?

1

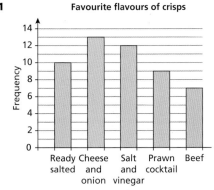

Favourite flavours of crisps

2

Age, m (months)	Tally	Frequency
$0 < m \leqslant 5$	II	2
$5 < m \leqslant 10$	TTTT III	8
$10 < m \leqslant 15$	TTTT I	6
$15 < m \leqslant 20$	IIII	4

Practice

1

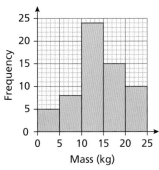

Animal masses

2

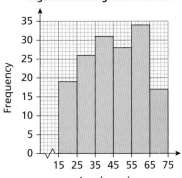

Ages of running club members

3 a i 47 **ii** 43
b 6 to 9 hours **c** 172 **d** $\frac{1}{172}$

4 a

Distance, d (miles)	Frequency
$0 < d \leqslant 2$	22
$2 < d \leqslant 4$	28
$4 < d \leqslant 6$	17
$6 < d \leqslant 8$	9

b 76

Consolidate

1

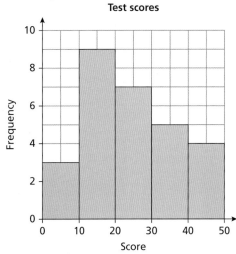

Test scores

2 a

Number of sales, s	Frequency
$60 < s \leqslant 80$	5
$80 < s \leqslant 100$	12
$100 < s \leqslant 120$	8
$120 < s \leqslant 140$	3

b 28

3 a

Time, h (hours)	Frequency
$5 < h \leqslant 10$	5
$10 < h \leqslant 15$	17
$15 < h \leqslant 20$	14
$20 < h \leqslant 25$	5

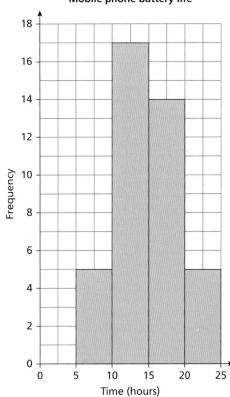

Mobile phone battery life

b Yes, she is correct as 36 out of 41 phones have a battery life of more than 10 hours. 36 out of 41 is 87.8%, which is greater than 80%.

Stretch

1

Time, t (hours)	Frequency
$0 < t \leqslant 4$	24
$4 < t \leqslant 8$	43
$8 < t \leqslant 12$	23
$12 < t \leqslant 16$	7
$16 < t \leqslant 20$	3

2 a $y = 5$

b

Money spent, m (£)	Frequency
$0 < m \leqslant 10$	5
$10 < m \leqslant 20$	16
$20 < m \leqslant 30$	15
$30 < m \leqslant 40$	9
$40 < m \leqslant 50$	5

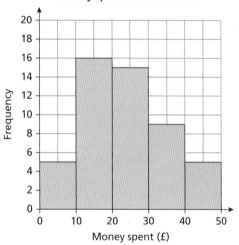

Money spent at the weekend

Charts and diagrams: exam practice

1 a

Vegetable	Tally	Frequency
Broccoli	𝗡𝗡	5
Carrots	||||	4
Sweetcorn	𝗡𝗡 ||	7
Sprouts	|||	3
Other	||	2

b

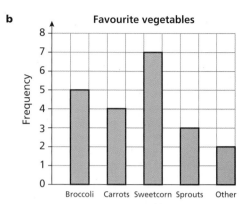

Favourite vegetables

2 a 39°C   **b** 1pm

3 a

Car speeds

3	1 3 5 6 9
4	2 3 3 4 6 9
5	2 4 5

Key: 3 | 1 = 31 mph

b 43 mph

4 a Other items   **b** £52.50

Block 16 Applying statistics

Chapter 16.1

Are you ready?

1 A (3, 4)   B (0, 3)   C (9, 8)   D (7, 0)

2

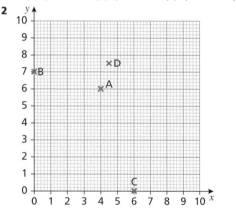

Practice

1 Graph A: No correlation
Graph B: Positive correlation
Graph C: Negative correlation

2 a   Time spent studying and test scores

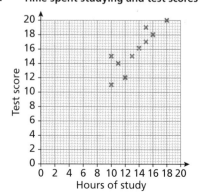

b There is a positive correlation, i.e. as the number of hours of study increases, the test score increases.

3 a £45 **b** £16 **c** 15°C

d There is a negative correlation, i.e. as the temperature increases, the cost of gas per week decreases.

4 a 62 kg **b** 75 kg **c** 143 cm and 150 cm

d Heights and weights of students

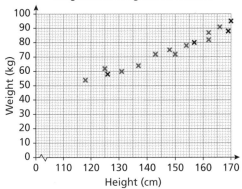

e Positive correlation

5 a i Number of siblings and favourite number

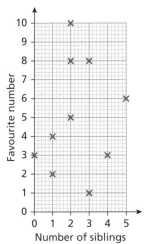

ii Customer experiences

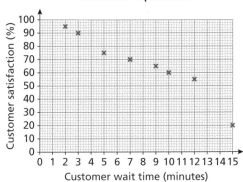

iii Blood pressure readings

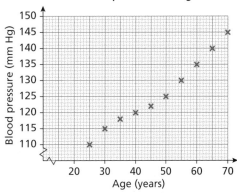

b i There is no correlation between the number of siblings and favourite number, i.e. the number of siblings has no impact on that person's favourite number.

ii There is a negative correlation between customer wait time and customer satisfaction, i.e. as the customer wait time increases, customer satisfaction decreases.

iii There is a positive correlation between age and blood pressure, i.e. as age increases, blood pressure also tends to increase.

Consolidate

1 a 4 hours **b** 55 years

c There is a negative correlation between age and the number of hours of exercise per week, i.e as the age increases, the number of hours of exercise each week decreases.

2 a 74% **b** 6 miles

c There is no correlation between the distance a student lives from school and their test result, i.e. the distance a student lives from school has no impact on their test result.

3 a i Job satisfaction for different employees

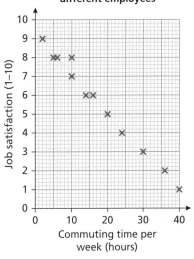

ii

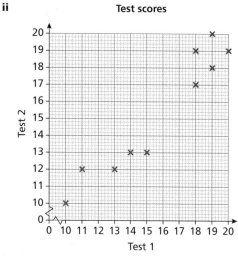

Test scores

b i There is a negative correlation between the number of hours spent commuting and the job satisfaction, i.e. as the commuting time increases, the job satisfaction decreases.

ii There is a positive correlation between test 1 and test 2, i.e. the higher the score in test 1, the higher the score in test 2.

Stretch

1 a i B, C and F   **ii** A and E   **iii** D

   b B   **c** A

   d Various possible answers, e.g. positive correlation could be height and arm span. Negative correlation could be maths test result and art test result. No correlation could be house number and shoe size.

2 a

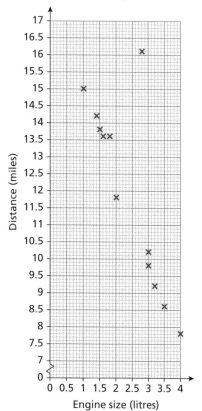

Distances travelled on 1 litre of petrol

b 2.8 litres and 16.1 miles, as these values do not fit with the rest of the data.

c Various possible answers between 10 and 12 miles.

Chapter 16.2

Are you ready?

1

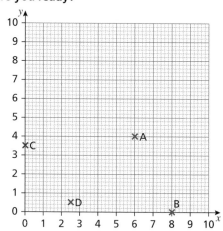

2 a Negative correlation   **b** No correlation

   c Negative correlation   **d** Positive correlation

Practice

1 Sven's line of best fit is drawn correctly, as his line shows the general trend of the data. Beca's line of best fit does not go with the trend of the data and does not need to start at the origin. Flo's line of best fit isn't a straight line; it is a collection of lines joining the points like a dot-to-dot picture.

2 a The graph shows a positive correlation, i.e. as the temperature increases, the number of ice creams sold increases.

b i

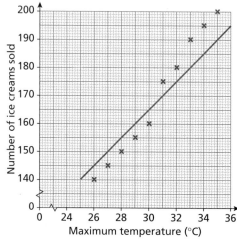

Ice cream sales

ii 29°C (estimate can be between 27°C and 31°C)

3 a

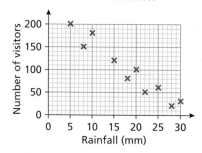

Event attendance

b A suitable line of best fit should be drawn on the graph above, giving an estimate of between 140 and 145 visitors.

4 a Values of used cars

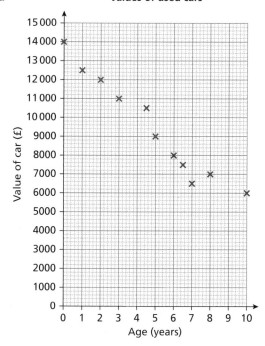

b Negative correlation: as a car gets older, its value decreases.

c £10 700 (estimate can be between £10 600 and £10 800)

d No, an age of 50 years old on the extended graph would suggest that the value of the car would be negative.

Consolidate

1 a Reaction times of people

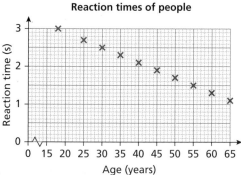

b Yes, as it follows the trend of the data.

c 43 years old (estimate can be between 41 and 45 years old)

2 a Electrician charges

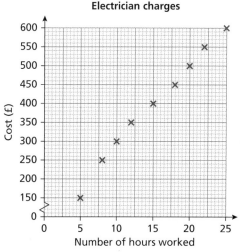

b A suitable line of best fit should be drawn on the graph above, giving an estimate of between £195 and £205.

c 30 hours is outside the data range and you cannot assume that the trend will continue beyond the given data.

Stretch

1 There is a correlation between the variables but this does not mean that one directly affects the other. The correlation is likely to be caused by both variables being affected by the temperature.

2 a 350 (estimate can be between 345 and 355)

b 35°C is outside the data range and you cannot assume that the trend will continue beyond the given data.

c 130

d 180

Chapter 16.3

Are you ready?

1 450

2 48%

3 a 5   **b** 35

Practice

1 a Students in Ed's school   **b** 80 people

2 Example answers: The sample size is too small. It only takes the views of people who attend the club on a Monday morning.

3 If someone is not at the theatre then they can't be included in the sample and the sample is not representative of the whole population.

4 The number obtained when spinning the spinner is random, therefore the choice of person with the corresponding number is also random.

5 38%

Consolidate

1 a The people who attend his school
  b Example answers: His friends may not represent the school as a whole. The sample size is too small.
  c Example answers: He could take a random sample of students in his school. He could use a larger sample.
2 a False. A sample is a part of the population, not the entire population.
  b True. A larger sample size provides more accurate estimates of the population.
  c True. Random sampling helps to ensure that the sample is representative of the entire population and each member of the population has an equal opportunity of being included in the sample.
  d False. A biased sample is one that does not represent the population fairly.
3 The number obtained when rolling a dice is random, therefore the choice of person with the corresponding number is also random.
4 1300

Stretch

1 400
2 96 ready salted; 60 salt and vinegar; 36 prawn cocktail; 48 cheese and onion

Applying statistics: exam practice

1 a (3, 2)
  b

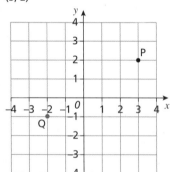

2 a Point correctly plotted at (550, 168)
  b

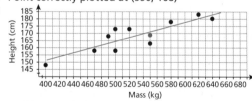

  c Positive correlation
  d Any answer in range 175–180 cm

3 Graph A because it is most likely that the taller someone is, the longer their arms are.

4 Population = 500 members
  Sample = 80 readers checked

Statistics: exam practice

1 a 30   **b** 15
  c

Meals sold

Monday	○ ○ ○
Tuesday	○ ◖
Wednesday	○ ○ ○
Thursday	○ ○
Friday	○ ○ ◖
Saturday	○ ○ ○ ○

  d 160
2 a 5   **b** 4.5
3 a 24   **b** 10   **c** Aisha
  d

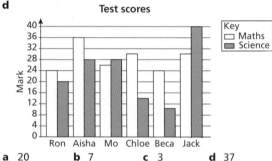

4 a 20   **b** 7   **c** 3   **d** 37
5 a 40   **b** 1.7
6 a 6
  b

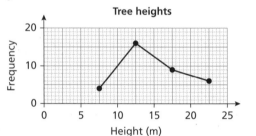